A LUCID DREAMER

BY THE SAME AUTHOR

NON-FICTION

George Eliot: Her Beliefs and Her Art

Ted Hughes: A Critical Study (with Terry Gifford)

The Lover, The Dreamer and the World: the Poetry of Peter Redgrove

Meredith and the Novel

Narrative and Voice in Post-War Poetry

D.H. Lawrence, Travel and Cultural Difference

Ted Hughes: A Literary Life

EBOOKS

D.H. Lawrence: Women in Love

Ted Hughes: New Selected Poems

AS EDITOR

A Companion to Twentieth-Century Poetry

Peter Redgrove: The Colour of Radio

A LUCID DREAMER

The Life of Peter Redgrove

NEIL ROBERTS

JONATHAN CAPE
LONDON

Published by Jonathan Cape 2012

2 4 6 8 10 9 7 5 3 1

First published in Great Britain in 2012 by
Jonathan Cape
Random House, 20 Vauxhall Bridge Road,
London SW1V 2SA

www.randomhouse.co.uk

Addresses for companies within The Random House Group Limited can be found at:
www.randomhouse.co.uk/offices.htm

The Random House Group Limited Reg. No. 954009

ISBN 9780224090292

A CIP catalogue record for this book is available from the British Library

The Random House Group Limited supports The Forest Stewardship Council (FSC®),
the leading international forest certification organisation. Our books carrying the FSC label are
printed on FSC® certified paper. FSC is the only forest certification scheme endorsed by the leading
environmental organisations, including Greenpeace. Our paper procurement
policy can be found at www.randomhouse.co.uk/environment

Typeset in Sabon LT Std by Palimpsest Book Production Limited,
Falkirk, Stirlingshire

Printed and bound by
CPI Group (UK) Ltd, Croydon, CR0 4YY

To Bill, Kate, Zoe
and the Memory of Pete

Contents

List of Illustrations

Preface

In the early 1990s Peter Redgrove sold a large archive of drafts, correspondence, working papers and journals to the University of Sheffield. The archive has been the single most important resource in writing this book. At the time Redgrove expressed a hope that the archive would provide material for the study not just of his work but of the psychology of poetic creation. This biography doesn't claim to be such a study, but I have benefited enormously from being able to read the often startlingly naked records of the author's psychological struggles, alongside the drafts of his poems.

Negotiation over the sale of the archive was prolonged because Redgrove was anxious about some of the personal revelations in his journals. He was worried that, if read unsympathetically, they could be 'occasions for vilification'. He wrote a letter telling me the nature of these revelations, and this information has been deeply important to my understanding of his life and poetry. But he did not send the letter. It is disconcerting to read a letter to oneself that the writer decided not to send: it can't help feeling like a silent judgement. Our correspondence had begun in the late 1970s, as a result of my writing about his work. Since then we had met a number of times, and the relationship of poet and critic had developed into a friendship. This didn't compare in importance with his friendships with people such as Philip Hobsbaum, Ted Hughes, Martin Bell and Peter Porter, but I believe that he was fortified by what I wrote about his work, and he always treated me with great warmth and consideration.

But when after his death I read this unsent letter in his archive (where he had put it, along with many other letters, knowing I would read it one day), I felt that I had failed him in some way. I looked back through my correspondence with him and discovered that the secret was in fact an open secret: he had been telling me all the time, but I hadn't wanted to know. As a critic of his poetry I didn't want to get too close to his intimate secrets. This, no doubt, was why he didn't send the letter. By the time I read it, however, I had become his biographer. Now I wanted to know all his secrets. Perhaps he knew all this, and spared me the awkwardness of being privy to his intimate life while trying to be a literary critic, but wrote to me from beyond the grave as it were, in the hope that I would then take on the challenge that the archive presents. If so, I am profoundly grateful to him, for this consideration as well as for the magnificent body of work that made writing his biography such a rewarding task.

I am equally grateful to Penelope Shuttle. I could not have asked for a more helpful combination of cooperation and lack of interference. I could not have written the book without her generosity with permission to quote, and with her own memories, but I have never felt inhibited by the thought of her looking over my shoulder. She is a wonderful example to all people who control literary estates.

I am also very grateful to other members of Peter Redgrove's family, especially his surviving children Bill, Kate and Zoe. They too have been very generous with their memories and feelings about their father.

My wife Christine, as always, has supported and encouraged me, kept me company on my travels to meet people and consult archives, and given me invaluable advice about the drafts.

Any biography of a near-contemporary is a work of collaboration, and I want to thank all my other collaborators, who have contributed by talking to me, writing for me, providing me with material or reading what I have written: Cliff Ashcroft, June Banister, Martin Bax, Michael Bayley, Bruce Berlind, David Brighton, Alan Brownjohn, Caroline Carver, Dorothy Coventon, Dennis Creffield, Marguerite Feitlowitz, Victoria Field, Claire Fox, Norman Franklin, Philip Fried, Roger Garfitt, Zulfikar Ghose, Terry Gifford, Elaine Glover, Jon Glover, Renée Gregorio, Harry Guest, John Haffenden, Chris Harding, Francis Hewlett, Liz Hewlett, Hannah Hobsbaum-Kelly, Anny Hopley, Ray Hopley, Daniel Huws, Lee Jenkins, Sylvia Kantaris, Kate Kavanagh, P. J. Kavanagh, Jacqueline Korn, Dennis Lowe, Rupert Loydell, Edward Lucie-Smith, Eleanor Maxted, Christine McCausland, Elizabeth McKellar, Brian Miller, Geoffrey Pawling, Phil Penny, the late Peter Porter, Derek Power, Sue Redgrove,

Malcolm Ritchie, Paul Roberts, Robin Robertson, John Ryland, Keith Sagar, John Scotney, Hilary Semmons, John Semmons, Anne Stevenson, D. M. Thomas, Barbara Toyne, Derek Toyne, Jane Tozer, Caroline Trickey, Keith Trickey, Jeffrey Wainwright, David Wevill, Alice Williams, Gerard Woodward.

I have also relied heavily on the support and cooperation of the numerous libraries that hold archive material: the University of Sheffield, the Harry Ransom Center at the University of Texas, the Brotherton Library at the University of Leeds, the University of Glasgow, the University of Reading, the Manuscripts and Rare Books Library at Emory University, the University of California San Diego, the Lilly Library at the University of Indiana, the University of Tulsa, the Surrey History Centre and the BBC Written Archives at Reading. I especially want to thank Jacky Hodgson, Amanda Bernstein and Jane Mason at Sheffield, and Bridget Gayle at the Harry Ransom Center, for their efforts on my behalf. I am also grateful to the Harry Ransom Center for awarding me an Andrew W. Mellon Fellowship to support my research there. Thanks also to the staff at Taunton School, especially David Bridges.

Grateful acknowledgements are also due to the following for permission to quote: Penelope Shuttle for the published and unpublished work of Peter Redgrove; Rosemary Hobsbaum for an extract from Philip Hobsbaum's 'The Group: An Experiment in Criticism'; Christine Porter for extracts from Peter Porter's 'Peter Redgrove: A Brief Memoir'; Edward Lucie-Smith for his unpublished letters; Carol Hughes for Ted Hughes's unpublished letters and Christine McCausland for the unpublished letters of Martin Bell.

I

Oedipus in Kingston 1932–45

A young man is sitting at a table at a *thé dansant*, somewhere in London: a very young man, no more than twenty. Despite his youth he already has the air of a gentleman, with a certain Cary Grant-like suavity and also, perhaps, a certain foxiness. He is physically robust, muscular and confident: even in his eighties his son will call him a 'bull of a man'. It is the mid-1920s. A photo taken the same year shows him genial, handsome and sporting in a striped blazer and white flannels.

His attention has been drawn to two women at another table, a 'massive and distinguished duenna' with a 'pixie green nymph outrageously blonde who peered hauntingly round the duenna's bosom'. He gives the waiter a card to take over to them, which is inscribed 'Baron Redgrove'. The older woman beckons to him graciously, and he hurries over to their table. He is Gordon James Redgrove, known as Jim, the son of a London jeweller, who had to leave Taunton public school after two years because his father could no longer afford the fees. Now Jim makes a living selling space for a newspaper, and supplements this income by boxing in fairground booths. The women are Nancy Lena Cestrilli-Bell (known as Nan) and her mother Mimi, who is working as a midwife. Nan's Italian father deserted them when she was a baby; later she told her son that he had raped Mimi at knifepoint on their wedding night because she was menstruating and reluctant to make love. All her life Nan and her mother have been sheltered by Mimi's mother and stepfather. Her only brother escaped to Australia at the age of sixteen. She and her mother are about to be rescued from indigence by a model of early twentieth-century manhood.

So Peter Redgrove, seventy years later, imagined the meeting of his parents. The card, with its hint of the confidence trickster spicing the gentlemanly demeanour, is too distinctive a detail for him to have invented. The outrageously blonde nymph, however, is his own memory of his mother, who from middle age preserved a Hollywood platinum glamour into her seventies. When she met Jim she was an attractive, brown-haired, sensual-looking young woman with a large nose and strong, not nymph-like, features. This is a natural error; a more revealing one is that Redgrove says his mother was twenty-nine years old which was 'in those days on the shelf'. But Nan was born in 1903: she was only twenty-three years old when she married; twenty-nine was her age in the year Peter was born. She was two years older than her husband, but this is a meeting of two very young people. Redgrove believed that his parents were ill matched, a mismatch that left a deep impression on him, their firstborn. The idea of her being 'on the shelf' seems like an unconscious attempt to explain how his mother came to accept his father.

From a more detached perspective no such explanation seems necessary. Jim was a vigorous, confident, intelligent, good-looking young man who no doubt promised the woman he wooed the materially secure and comfortable future that he in fact delivered. Towards the end of her life she was to write, 'I married the only man I was able to find who would make a good husband and I was certainly wiser than I thought.' He might even be called dashing: they spent their honeymoon cruising in a small boat on the Thames, finding a backwater for the wedding night. We see Nan on honeymoon smiling and relaxed, wearing a headband in twenties style, with a long thick plait of hair (not evident in earlier photos – perhaps Jim had persuaded her to grow it), listening to a gramophone on the boat. At least as far as Jim was concerned, the beginning of the marriage was sexually successful: he records going to bed in the afternoon 'for a wonderful love', and his sensual appreciation of his bride is evident in nude photographs that he took of her in 'artistic' poses.

Jim was an accomplished amateur photographer, and generally enjoyed new technology. In 1926, the year of his marriage and of the foundation of the BBC, he was keen on 'listening in' to the radio and excited about picking up broadcasts from Paris and Barcelona as well as the BBC's new broadcasting station in Daventry. By the time his first son was born he had acquired a movie camera, and was to create a cinematic record of family life over five decades. We see him and Nan enjoying the typical pursuits of the comfortable middle class in the 1930s: holidays on the Sussex and Dorset coasts, Ascot, boating on the Thames, cricket, tennis and motor sports. Jim not only went to motor races at the Brooklands racetrack in Weybridge, Surrey, but drove the track (alone) himself, as well as taking part in off-road time trials in Derbyshire. The impression he projects as director and co-star of his own home movie is of an extrovert young man fond of hearty outdoor pleasures. Later his son felt overwhelmed by his robust manly prowess: 'a sideboard of cups for everything / From golf and tennis to public speaking'. In a restaurant he would call for the chef and ostentatiously give him a ten-shilling note. His character contrasted vividly with that of Nan, who Peter thought was 'imaginative, poetic and very feminine', with a 'desire to run wild in nature'. Even her grandchildren were to describe her as capricious, outrageous, colourful and flamboyant. Jim was a dedicated Freemason who never missed a meeting in fifty years, and Peter records that at a Masons' 'ladies' night' Nan demanded orange ice cream and, when it had been got with great difficulty by sending out, 'proceeded to throw it at the stiff, sheerwhite shirtfronts of the men at the table'. Later in life she complained, 'all my life I have had to live second to Masonic affairs or [Taunton] School affairs'. A marriage of complementary opposites, or a clash of irreconcilables? Peter felt it was the latter, but the marriage lasted more than fifty years, and Jim was to mourn his wife with a red rose in a vase by her picture, every day from her death to his.

When Nan was pregnant with Peter she used to talk to him in the womb, and one time swam in 'tall, fast-breaking waves', shouting to her unborn child, 'You must learn to be brave if you can, and learn to ride the waves.' Film of him aged nineteen months in the sea with his mother shows him laughing exultantly when the waves rise above his head and he goes under.

Peter was not born until six years into Nan and Jim's marriage. Nan went into labour on the evening of New Year's Day 1932, when they were living in a flat on Kingston Hill, beside Richmond Park. It was a long and difficult labour. Peter's 'big head wouldn't slip out', as she later told him. When Nan passed out with the pain Mimi slapped her face to bring her round – the pain was so great she wanted to die. Eventually she had to be cut and Peter was delivered at three in the morning on the kitchen table by Mimi and Dr Young, prophetically pronounced 'Jung'. Dr Young almost immediately circumcised him – a practice common generally at the time for supposedly hygienic reasons. Peter hardly cried during this operation, but it was one of the many aspects of his childhood that later haunted him – at the age of forty he was reading Bruno Bettelheim on circumcision and asking his mother if it had scarred his penis.

The most prolific source of information about Redgrove's childhood is, naturally enough, his own collection of memories, as recorded in his deeply introspective unpublished memoir, *Innocent Street*, his journals and occasional more public statements. His parents' characters, their relationships to each other and to him, marked him deeply and created conflicts that he was still struggling with at the end of his life: his memories are highly processed and interpretive, and should be regarded as insights into his adult consciousness, as much as records of his early life.

His published writings about his childhood often read like parodies of the Oedipal scenario:

> Is this my earliest memory? The complex of soft touch and sweet smells I knew was my mother was steering me into a brightly-lighted room. I paused at the threshold. I did not like the atmosphere, but I was safely enfolded in the aura of my mother's dress. There was a big lumpish armchair on the other side of the room and in the armchair was a man. It was difficult to put the parts of him together: the round head, the smile, the spectacles, the armchair. I pointed. My question was as firm as an adult's speech. 'Who is that man?' 'That's your father, dear.' 'I don't like that, Mummy.' Then from the armchair came over-loud laughter, and I was handed over, before I knew what was happening, transferred to the lap of this amplified presence. He uttered a gargling sound and pointed to me. 'What's that?' 'Your name, Redgrove.' That name of my father was too harsh, it sounded like the tread of a tyre on a red car. I still cannot believe that this is my name.

> Once in bed at ten cuddly with mother:

> He waved a wand in his voice
> And I got out of the silken double-cabinet
> For ever.

The 'earliest memory' is obviously highly processed. The awareness of the mother as a 'complex of soft touch and sweet smells', and the child 'enfolded in the aura' of her dress suggest an almost womb-like intimacy, while the father is distant, alien and unfamiliar. They are even divided by the senses: she is perceived by touch and smell, he by sight and hearing. In Jim's home movies, by contrast, we see him cradling his naked infant son and bathing him. A performance for the camera, maybe, but throughout their lives there is continual evidence that Jim deeply loved his son. As a small boy Peter loved and even hero-worshipped his father in return – he said that he had always loved the radio since hearing his father's voice on it as a child. But as he grew older he was increasingly unable to accept the terms of Jim's love, or respond to it. Jim noted down amusing and precocious doings and sayings of his infant son, one of which, poignantly, was responding to a reprimand from his father with 'I *Mummy's* Peter.' Jim evidently thought this charming and funny, but it was a portent. As late as 1988, the year before Jim's death, Peter wrote in his journal of 'the destructive rejection of my father's love'.

There is nothing unusual about a small boy liking to cuddle with his mother in bed, or about the father deciding that this has to stop at a certain age. The Oedipal scenario of rivalry with the father superseded by identification would not have passed into popular currency if it weren't recognised from common experience. But Peter was never able to identify with his father. The most obvious reasons for conflict between father and son were typical of their class and period, and not inevitably the source of lasting trouble. Jim was materially successful, socially conventional, rigidly masculine, domineering and not given to introspection. 'This triangle is so important,' Peter records him saying, pointing to his collar, tie and the V of his waistcoat. He was also jovial, generous, entertaining and fond of games. His grandchildren were to adore him. Such a character is more difficult for a sensitive and imaginative son to deal with, especially when paired with an 'imaginative, poetic and very feminine' mother. Jim made Peter feel 'small and insecure', whereas Nan 'nurtured his sensitivity'. The contrast between them was exaggerated by their son's highly developed sensory awareness: compared to Nan's 'complex of soft touch and sweet smells' he is repelled by his father's 'rutting smells in the communal bowl'. Even in his fifties, on the occasion of Jim's last visit to him, years after Nan's death, Peter was 'convinced that the smells & electricity off this bull of a man' were the source of his lifelong obsessions and depressions.

But the sexually stereotyped contrast between his parents, even with his heightened sensitivity to it, is unlikely of itself to have created these conflicts and obsessions that were persistently to haunt and inspire him. The home movies of conventional middle-class fun and family fondness conceal a much darker picture, of which Peter is the main witness. He has spoken of his mother taking lovers to 'open her womb' because she and Jim were having difficulty conceiving. She told him of a 'sinister male lover' who 'seemed to be a magician'. He became preoccupied with the idea that she had joined a magic circle, that this lover was the notorious magician Aleister Crowley and (prompted by a physical resemblance) that Crowley might have been his real father. The idea of committing adultery to 'open the womb' is bizarre, and may have been part of Peter's attempt to reconcile himself emotionally to the fact that his mother certainly did have lovers, both before and after he was born. He recalls his mother 'like a whore' with a builder who gave him money, and another man who jumped out of the bedroom window on to the veranda roof as Jim came home unexpectedly. Redgrove believed that one of her lovers was a waterman on the Thames, a prototype of the seductive water-spirit in the prose fantasy 'Mr Waterman', one of his most successful and popular early pieces. Nan was a gifted and enthusiastic ballroom dancer: in the poem 'Joy Gordon' Redgrove says this was her dancing name, signifying that 'When she danced she was my Father's Joy' (FE 24), Gordon being Jim's first name. This is, for Redgrove, an unusual lapse into sentimental wish-fulfilment. In *Innocent Street* by contrast he writes that 'her quest was freedom to relish her dancing partners', and recounts that he and she made up a story about an ideal house 'which had many dancing partners behind locked doors but for access'. He told Peter Porter that even in her later years she used to pick up younger men at Hammersmith Palais.

The idea that Nan's adulteries were motivated by the desire to conceive by Jim is hard to reconcile with the fact that she periodically had abortions which were for Peter a symbol of his parents' 'embattled love life'. His memoir, which he wrote in the late nineties, is prefaced by the question, 'How is a person to decide if they were sexually abused as a child?'. His speculations about this range widely, from excessive physical intimacy with his mother to the possibility that he (and also his younger brother David) was damaged in the womb by attempted abortion. He believed that his aborted siblings were buried in the family garden. There is even a hint in his journal, written many years later in the 1970s, that she made him complicit in termination: 'Talked about it, looked up abortifacients. Eventually the doctor did it, in the bathroom.' At some point Nan told Peter that she had these abortions because she contracted gonorrhoea from Jim, who used to visit prostitutes with friends after rugby matches. Whether it was he or she who brought in this literal poison, one can't help thinking of Blake's 'marriage hearse' blighted with plagues.

Peter experienced his parents as 'an explosive mixture', their relationship marked by vehement rows, in which Nan would taunt Jim with his 'business voice and mannerisms'. In later years he found the film *The War of the Roses*, about a couple going through an acrimonious divorce and culminating in an apocalyptic fight leaving both warring partners dead, cathartic. For him his parents contrasted painfully with a poster on their lounge wall, depicting a loving couple, 'the man with his arms protectively over the woman's shoulders'. During one of his parents' rows he tried to move them together to be like the couple in the picture. They moved to his wishes but he could tell 'by their body tension . . . that as soon as they were able they would be hammering at each other again, stepping out of the silhouette I had made of them'. This atmosphere was noticeable to an outsider. Peter's brother's schoolfriend Chris Harding used to stay at the house and was repelled by the lack of such warmth as he was used to in his own home. He thought Jim was a 'monster' who terrified his sons, and though he then had no knowledge of Nan's adulteries felt uncomfortable in her heavily made-up, sexual presence.

For Peter the house had two conflicting atmospheres emanating from what he thought of as his parents' respective rooms: the 'odorous' kitchen and, 'through a dark hall', the lounge where his father sat, 'his bald head shining, while he worked through his papers . . . I vividly remember changing personalities as I crossed from one room to the other.' Failing to make his parents conform to his ideal of harmony, he felt that he had to choose between them. Inevitably he chose his mother. His reflections on his childhood hover around the troubling question, whether their closeness was incestuous: 'Does the mother abuse her child by dressing him lovingly for school . . . was I sexually abused by the passionate ministrations of parents?' In a letter discussing incest he writes, 'My sin, so far as I'm aware, was only non-genital karezza.' 'Karezza' is another name for 'coitus reservatus', a technique for prolonging intercourse by controlling ejaculation, so the fire blanket of 'non-genital' doesn't entirely douse the suspicion that his 'cuddly' sessions with Nan were more than usually erotic.

However, the most decisive aspect of Peter's relationship with his mother was that when he was ten or twelve years old she made him the confidant of her sexual dissatisfactions and rebellions. She told him that she did not desire Jim, though he was a good and dear man, that she had married him for security. (Photos show that he rapidly lost his muscular attractiveness and was soon stout, balding and prematurely middle-aged.) She also burdened him with the knowledge of her affairs and abortions, and about the menstrual distress that she suffered – he was later to say that, just as Ted Hughes fought his father's war in his writing, so he fought his mother's war against the menstrual taboo. He believed that Jim was 'so virile a man obsessed with manliness that he created by electrical induction the feminine identification in almost anybody he met', but in himself the 'feminine identification' must have been just as strongly encouraged by Nan enlisting him as an ally in the marital war, so that he 'might as a boy learn something of the truth of womanhood' and telling him that he was 'much preferable . . . in so many ways' to his father. A hearty, rigid, outwardly successful and socially conventional man such as Jim would present problems for any sensitive son. But when, as Jim did, the father truly loved his son those problems would eventually be negotiated. Nan's revelations made Jim's masculine assertiveness not just a burden but a sham. Peter's 'feminine identification' went unchallenged and he was never able to accept his father's love.

Nan's menstrual distress was one cause of the tense atmosphere in the house. She 'became transformed just before her period into something wild with staring eyes and startling hair, a virago, swearing bloodily', on one occasion dropping something valuable and shouting, 'Hells Bells and Buckets of Blood.' Peter believed that she 'wanted to smash open Jim's head with the clock'. At such times she would amplify his alienation from his father by (not untypically of the period) delegating punishment to Jim, as one time when he broke a precious vase and she sent him to bed with the words, 'You wait till your father comes home. I'll report you.' When his parents were angry with him they called him by his second name William, 'the naughty name', and when his father returned Peter heard this name called up the stairs. 'I moved to the top of them. My mother passed weeping to show me her weeping from right to left. That black impending gloom turned to deepest shame.' He does not record what, if any, punishment his father dealt him: the enduring memory is the shame at his mother's weeping. He never abandoned his loyalty to his mother but he knew that she played him and his father off against each other, and this episode is an illustration of her manipulativeness.

By the time Peter was five the family had moved to a newly built house, still in Kingston, in a small cul-de-sac near Norbiton railway station. The house was called Orchard End, and was to be the family home until Peter married. It was in a development of individually designed detached villas of the kind that gave the suburbs of English towns their comfortable visual identity in the inter-war years, built of red brick, with a broad, three-room frontage and a red tile facing that swept down from the gable. In his later years this house and its garden increasingly compelled his imagination as the theatre of his childhood and adolescent obsessions and rituals, the knot of troubling family relationships and the awakening of his unorthodox sexuality. In 1997 he named one of his books after it.

He began his formal education at the Misses Williams' kindergarten in Norbiton, a short walk from home. In his published autobiographical essay 'A Poet in Teaching' he portrays this as a place of prissy and oppressive Christianity, where he had to carry the Bible every day and, when he dropped the book on the floor, got on his hands and knees to apologise to it. Jesus Christ was 'somebody whom it was better to keep on the right side of, otherwise one might be stamped on, cruelly', and the Misses Williams' way of pronouncing his name, 'very carefully, in case they did it wrong', left him feeling that these were 'sickly syllables'. He preferred an illustrated book of dinosaurs, which comforted him because it was full of facts discovered by science, giving him more security than 'that curious shifting world of persons, their conflicts and temperaments' which reduced him to 'writhing embarrassment or a blank sheet'. He took the dinosaur book with him on his first day at the school because it made him feel safe.

This opposition of dinosaurs to the Bible is obviously schematic. The young boy will look to science rather than institutional religion to explain the world. At the age of nine he told his father that his favourite books were *Marvels and Mysteries of Science* and *Marvels of Modern Science*. He seems to have the makings of a no-nonsense scientific atheist, but there is also something aesthetic and imaginative in his liking for the dinosaurs, 'with their serpent-heads and swan-bodies and their shiny skins and immense innocent confidence'. He prefers this to 'the piles of foreskins . . . and the sudden bloody deaths, the people struck by fire, and the electrocution if you touched the Ark'. Though he dislikes the Bible he loves the kindergarten's picture of 'All Creatures Great and Small', a simplified and abstracted world with no spiders or worms, which make him feel cruel and want to squash them, revealing the 'unpleasant juices and custards' that they are full of.

But science may also be a refuge from his difficulties with people. As a very young child he was delightfully outgoing, what his father called the 'matey with everyone' period, when strangers would call out, 'Hallo Peter!' in the street and, when his mother asked who they were, he would reply, 'Oh just a friend of mine.' Later by contrast he became a 'chilling kind of child' or 'small Faust' as he calls himself. If, when he was at kindergarten between the ages of five and seven, people made him embarrassed and tongue-tied, he had changed very quickly from a confident little extrovert to a self-conscious child nervous of the human world. By the age of twelve he was plagued by what he called 'robot obsessional automatisms', mainly to do with washing.

The account of the Norbiton kindergarten in 'A Poet in Teaching' is only one part of the story, however. There is another side to his experience of it which emerges shadowily, as if half invented, on the first pages of *Innocent Street*. Here in more searching, introspective prose we glimpse another female teacher – maybe one of the Misses Williams, but if she is, remembered so completely differently as to be another – who like his mother embraces him with an 'aura'. As she sits beside him with pencil and paper her body touches him, or his hand touches her – like his mother in the 'earliest memory' she is recalled by touch and smell, not sight and hearing. She begins to fill the paper with Vs or bird-shaped ticks which have an extraordinary effect on the little boy:

> At the first stroke the paper opened up into a bird-haunted space. My skin opened as my eyes opened . . . assimilating the miracle of the paper turned to air and earth and sky, because the birds were

flying over something, and in something. These are swallows, somebody said. I swallowed, and my neck glowed.

For this little boy (or this recollecting adult) the satisfying approval
shown by the teacher's tick is merged with the implicitly erotic 'aura'
of her presence, which releases his imagination into both the fantasy
of flight and the pun that induces the glowing sensation in his neck.
His writing this at the end of his life is part of a 'search for the
meaning of various compulsive ideas': over and over in his journals
he draws V and Y shapes, which he calls the 'upper yoni' and associates with the throat framed by an open shirt collar.

This eroticism focused on the throat is intimately connected with
memories of his mother who would 'open and close my doors by
dressing me and leaving the neck open – which would be an exquisite
trembling shame' or 'seize the knot she had tied [in his tie] and
shake it a little up and down to make it firm', giving the small boy
an erection: 'What's that, Mummy?' he would ask, pointing to his
'little spike'. Jim was a suit-and-tie man who in Peter's opinion
'dressed for persona and office and not for comfort'. Peter later felt
that if he 'wore anything that did not give a role-message' he would
be 'attacked'. He records an occasion when he was casually dressed
and Jim said, 'You look cool.' This doesn't sound like an attack,
but it made Peter feel that being 'cool' was shameful. Was Jim disap-
proving, or was Peter projecting? It was to be many years before
the adult Peter ceased to be a suit-and-tie man himself, though he
hated the uniform. Beginning his memoir with the memory of the
ticks at kindergarten, Redgrove leaves no doubt that it is more than
a charming childlike fantasy: here begins his difference, that which
will set him apart, which he will struggle with, at times try to
suppress, but more often strive to embrace as his greatest treasure,
the source of his creativity. He was not to write poetry until his late
teens, but here the seed of the poet is sown.

When Peter was six years old his brother David was born. Until
his death four days short of his twentieth birthday in a tragic accident David seems to have adapted more comfortably than Peter to
the models of manliness that were available and approved by Jim:
whereas Peter was to last less than a week in National Service,
David joined the Household Cavalry and throve in it, posing stern-
faced on horseback in dress uniform with tasselled helmet and sword.
Peter was always convinced that he himself was his mother's favourite

and that David was born to compensate his father for this fact, and to be a companion to him. It therefore seems unlikely that David suffered the kinds of conflict that afflicted Peter through his attachment to his mother and alienation from his father, but Peter frequently refers to him as 'poor David', and speculates whether his brother, as well as himself, might have been damaged by attempted abortion. 'Poor David' may, of course, simply reflect sadness at his early death.

David's friend Chris didn't think that he was much attached to his mother, but that he hero-worshipped his father (as Peter did as a young boy), while Jim bullied both his sons. Peter's journals are full of hints that he felt part of a pecking order in the family house, that his compensation for feeling bullied by Jim was bullying David in turn. In his elegy for David, written in 1958, he confessed that he was 'a proper / Bastard to my brother . . . / Until he was able to defend himself'. Elsewhere he recalls gleefully calling David a 'mistake' and persuading him to take the blame for a chip in the playroom fireplace that was in fact his own fault. Such bullying of a younger brother by an elder is commonplace, and it probably wouldn't have haunted Peter if David had not died young, and if he had not felt that they had become estranged before this tragedy. He blamed their growing apart on boarding school. In earlier years he loved his little brother and they seem to have been companions to a surprising degree in view of the six-year age gap. They competed in a game of climbing cupboards without touching the floor, fought with old sabres resulting in a wound to David's nose, and tried to destroy a wasp's nest together. For Peter their most memorable game 'involved taking apart the hooks of [the] Wendy House, and propping the separate walls and ceilings up like theatre scenery, with windows and doors. You could show both interiors and exteriors, and my brother and myself would rehearse our concerns in this small playroom theatre.' Redgrove calls this construction 'Innocent Street', and gives this name to his abortive memoir: a metaphor both for turning the inside outside, and for his determination to claim (and feel) the 'innocence' of troubling obsessions such as the one that had its unlikely beginning in the ticks of his kindergarten teacher.

David shared his low place in the pecking order with Mimi. Nan's mother was an object of pity in the family because of her unhappy past and her lameness but, as often happens, the pity was mixed

with irritation. When Peter was very small she was one of his intim-
ates, sharing the maternal care, but as the precocious boy grew (into
a 'chilling kind of child'?) he became intolerant of her uneducated
speech and physical handicap: 'the sound of her approach' with her
dragging leg 'infuriated' him and he mocked her because he thought
'she used the wrong words all the time'. In his sixties he drafted a
poem in Mimi's voice, recalling her love for the little boy, whom
she bottle-fed, and how by the time he was nine she told him she
hated him.

He does have some more reassuring childhood memories. Kingston
was blessed with one of the country's great independent department
stores, Bentalls, which was a place of magic for children, especially
at Christmas:

> There was an entrance opening by electric eye, a bronze door self-
> opening into the regions of soft music and special offers. There was
> a grand concourse with stairs that were also self-operating, climbing,
> descending. In the theatrical space between these escalators there
> might be a painted galleon heaving its way through a cotton-wool
> sea; or a Father Christmas drawn by reindeers with electrical bulbs
> fastened to their harness, in his sled full of parcels made up exactly
> as the counter-assistant would wrap your purchase, in cubical or
> rhomboidal shapes, very straight-edged with festive paper; or, out of
> season, phalanxes of men's suits worn by moustached wax dummies
> with Brylcreem hair; or a Royal Ball with Cinderella in a dress white
> as the floor-walker's shirt but with flashing sequins all over. To look
> at anything in this shop was to join the multi-media show, to touch,
> taste, smell.

Many years later, in one of his drinking bouts, he dreamed or hallu-
cinated about 'wandering through a store of great rolls of brocade
and draperies' recollected from Bentalls. He learned from one of his
companions that he had passed out while listening to Verdi's
Requiem, and the Bentalls fabric had been his visual and tactile
translation of the music. Thus, as we shall see, the grand old store
was linked to one of Redgrove's greatest poems, 'The Case'.

Jim used to take Peter to magic shows, and in later life Peter
imagined his father as something of a magician himself. He was an
expert at card tricks, but more significantly had the ability to 'disappear' his son, to overwhelm him with his masculine presence. His
mother told him that his father was a genius, and that geniuses are
destructive: a genius would 'project qualities in himself which were

unconscious on another person, and blame them if they did not match up to those qualities in himself he denied unconsciously he possessed'. This process could have the effect of delaying the development of the person receiving these projections. This sounds remarkably psychoanalytically sophisticated, and more Redgrove's interpretation than his mother's. Still he clearly felt that his development had been so affected. Even in his sixties he writes, 'How shall I become the master in my own house, while still surrounded by these influences?'. He had a lasting tendency to project these feelings about his father on to male acquaintances who were literally magicians or men of powerful charisma, resulting in some startling and disturbing obsessions.

Jim worked for thirty-five years in Vernon's advertising agency, rising from office junior to Managing Director and Chairman. During the war he contributed to the campaign directed by Lord Woolton, the Minister for Food, to change the country's eating habits, and if there is a lasting monument to his genius it is probably 'Potato Pete', the character he created as part of the 'Dig for Victory' campaign, to encourage people to grow and eat potatoes. Pete was a cartoon character, with a song recorded by the popular singer, film star, troop entertainer and later star of *Coronation Street*, Betty Driver. Nursery rhymes were adapted to give them a 'Potato Pete' theme, and original rhymes were composed, such as:

> Here's the man who ploughs the fields.
> Here's the girl who lifts up the yield.
> Here's the man who deals with the clamp,
> So that millions of jaws can chew and champ.
> That's the story and here's the star,
> Potato Pete, eat up, ta ta!

This may be an example of Redgrove senior's verse. In 1941 Peter was evacuated with Nan and David for several months to Llandudno, and wrote a number of letters to his father, in one of which he asked, 'Will you be growing me in the garden (meaning "Potato Pete")?'. Peter's son Bill thought it surprising that his father and grandfather could not see what they had in common, being both 'wordsmiths', but, as Peter's attempt to follow his father's profession was to show, the difference in the way they used language intensified the difficulties between them.

Redgrove's most vivid memory of his stay in Llandudno is of

finding a cave in the headland called the Great Orme, which was 'drifted almost full of crystalline sand'. He clambered into the cave and poured the sand from one vessel to another, 'like an alchemist and his dry water'. This sounds like playing at being a scientist, and the comparison with an alchemist is the perspective of the mature Redgrove. But caves, enclosures and secret places occupied a large part of his childhood imagination. A more important one was Kent's Cavern in Devon which he visited when he was about ten. This was a 'special enclosure' which he loved so much he persuaded the custodians to let him crawl about in there in an old boiler suit. He 'crawled and slithered and dislodged a large slab of clay' under which he found hippopotamus teeth, which the custodians allowed him to keep.

In both these anecdotes there are signs of the incipient scientist but also something stranger and more inward, that he calls 'alchemy' in the Great Orme and 'hypnotism' in Kent's Cavern. This hypnotism is akin to what he felt when wrapped in his mother's skirts, and one of the motifs of his memoir is the opposition of his mother's benign feminine hypnotism and his father's oppressive male magic which he thought phoney. The fetishistic sexuality that developed from this, and which lasted his whole adult life, released visions of 'being taken up and pressed to a bosom like a baby'. In Richmond Park he liked to get inside a hollow tree, like 'passing into a secret door', and even in the hall at Orchard End there was wood-veneer panelling which he liked to think could open allowing him to 'go down into magical realms'. As an adult he believed that there was a darker side to his fantasies at the Great Orme, and that they reflected his fears about the war and especially the bombing of London, which his father was exposed to. At the end of the war, like many other children, he was shown films of the concentration camps and 'the piled and mutilated bodies of the Jewish victims'. He called this an end of innocence, which turned him to stone, 'and stone I remained for many years'.

After he left the Misses Williams' school Peter went to Tiffin preparatory school, also in Kingston. His years at Tiffin have left remarkably little trace in his published and unpublished writing, in contrast to all the other educational establishments that he attended. Perhaps this is a sign that he was happy there. His one strong memory of this time is certainly a happy one: walking arm in arm round the playground with another boy who recited to him the stories of Alexandre Dumas and Victor Hugo novels: 'the whole of *Monte Cristo*, the whole of *Les Misérables*'. He remembers this boy as being craggy featured like Ted Hughes, so this is both an anticipation and an idyllic rewriting of one of his most important adult friendships. Walking arm in arm, a sign of innocent homoerotic friendship, contrasts jarringly with his memories of his next school.

The Youthful Scientist 1945–49

In the late 1960s, a time when his life was bursting with impending change, Redgrove wrote a poem titled 'The Youthful Scientist Remembers' (*DF*). The speaker of this poem 'had thought that the stars would only tug at me slightly, / Or sprinkle thin clear visions about me for study', but his female companion reveals to him a world in which the 'black [of the stars] is as full as their white . . . // The mud as full as the sunlight.' As far as Peter's own life was concerned, this was a revelation that had been happening to him continuously since his early adolescence.

At an early age his parents had offered him the choice of a ventriloquist's doll or a microscope for Christmas. He chose the latter, and until his late teens his main ambition was to be a scientist. Even though it was little more than a toy, the microscope revealed to him another world:

It was the world in the water-drop, the drop of dirty water that was crammed with vibrating beings of complex patterned structure. In every drop of water there was the bright green Euglena, the little jumping creature like a twist of lime-peel; the stubbly Paramecium, like slippers of glass, just visible to the naked eye; once seen, the majestically-rolling Volvox; the Desmids, looking like roman quinquiremes, all in green; the Diatoms like the plans of cities. I took my earthworms and insects and woodlice to pieces now not from cruelty, but to investigate their structures in the name of science, though it was really to marvel at what they were in this other world. I cultivated tubes of murky water on my windowsill, assured of marvels and magic therein. I crystallised photographer's hypo, and watched the steely needles shoot across the illuminated field of my microscope; I moved my little microscope about on the table-top and watched the rainbows form within the needles, shifting

like the aurora borealis. I think in doing this I lost my image
of myself: I drew blood from my finger and watched the rouleaux
of incredibly multiplex round corpuscles stream like a population
in the rush hour across the slide, and I was made up of such things
just inside the skin.

As with all Redgrove's writing about his early life there is a lot
of afterthought in this, but there is no reason to doubt either that
the microscope revealed a world of wonderment, or that, now or
soon afterwards, his mind was equally entranced by the methods
of the natural sciences. He once said that people who called him
a surrealist had never looked through a microscope. The hinted
opposition between 'in the name of science' and 'really to marvel'
is not a *necessary* one, but Peter's mind was constructed in such
a way that it became one for him, as it is for the youthful scientist
of his poem.

By the time he was in his early teens the toy microscope had
burgeoned into a whole laboratory: Nan and Jim believed he had
a future as a scientist and gave up a whole room of the house,
in return for his having a smaller bedroom. Jim made a movie of
Peter in his laboratory: hundreds of jars are stacked on shelves
around the walls, along with numerous textbooks. The bench is
decked with flasks, retorts and glass tubes, and Peter stands there,
attended by David, his face a mask of scientific severity, pouring
a fluid from a test tube into a flask clamped to a stand, looking
through the microscope (a full-sized one now), consulting a book
and making notes. His favourite reading at this time was the Fu
Manchu series of books of Sax Rohmer, and he identified with
the sinister, mysterious Chinese scientist.

He loved to walk into town from Orchard End: Bentalls,
Norbiton station near the Misses Williams' school, the hospital
where he was later examined for National Service, the Greek
restaurant where he was to eat moussaka with his first love, and
above all the chemist whose proprietor was fond of him and 'who
got me things I should never have had, such as little white patty-
moulds of crystallised sodium cyanide; a big globe of fuming
bromine like a wonderful reddish-brown vaporous blood; and
mercury which if dropped through the floorboards would poison
a house for ever . . . the wonderful diethyl ether which would
catch fire from twenty feet away if you were careless or malicious

with it'. The ether supplied him with one means of psycho-active experiment: inhaling it gave him 'visions that were streaming past in coloured layers or broad staircases like the mobile inner structure of beach-pebbles become laboratory vessels'. His bible at this time was H. K. Lewis's *Aids to Forensic Medicine and Toxicology*. Another resource was laburnum pods from the garden. To deregulate the senses without ill effect the pods had to be dry and black: 'the green pods make you ill by too much shift of perception and shift you out of this world . . .'. He carried the black seeds about in a pillbox. He invited into his laboratory a friend who offered him another kind of secret enactment. He wanted to rub Peter's penis, but Peter 'drew away, more interested in a different transformation of the world'. In adolescence still a chilling kind of child.

However, the ingestion of substances is not the most important transgression of Peter's teenage years. The real or imagined adventures described at the end of the last chapter, especially crawling in the clay in Kent's Cavern, are closely connected to stranger and more explicitly erotic experiences that preoccupied Redgrove throughout his life. The most vivid of these, to which he returns three times in *Innocent Street*, is what he calls being 'raped by thunder':

> Once, the rain came thundering and clothed me with its electrical silk and made my school-clothes shine with its magic. I rolled on the garden soil among the flowers in my electrocution as the rain turned the earth into high-potency mud, paradise disguised as mud, the mud smelling of stars. Did next-door take any spy-notice? It were best for them not to tell or reveal that they had seen the virgin consummating in his bridebed.

He was presumably not literally struck by lightning, but the electricity in the atmosphere made his skin especially sensitive and this was intensified by the rainwater soaking through his clothes. Whether his rolling in the mud is deliberate or involuntary, it is the most important part of the experience, recollected as 'starlight glittering in the mud' in 'The Youthful Scientist Remembers'. To call this a Wordsworthian 'spot of time' would be to underestimate its centrality in Redgrove's development (though no doubt if there hadn't been a thunderstorm that day another experience would have pointed him in the same direction). In one aspect it represents a literal oneness with the earth, a breaching of the boundaries between the self and the *prima materia* of which it is constituted. But if that were all it was about it would not have been so troubling to Redgrove. The end of the passage from *Innocent Street* makes it clear that it is an erotic experience, and Redgrove associates it with his first wet dream:

> on a motorbike in a leather black jacket driving out of a deep furrow in the wet earth, the door on my neck open, engorged, the upper yoni half-veiled by white cotton – leaping on my machine . . . out of the furrowed earth with a sensation unguessed at, resurrected on my bike.

For many adolescents the motorbike and leather jacket would be the most erotic aspects of this scenario, but for Redgrove the wet earth and the open neck are the two enduring elements of his fetishistic sexuality. The youthful scientist examined his semen under the miscroscope where it looked like 'a field of white wheat that was undulating'. More astonishingly, he rushed into his parents' bedroom with it exclaiming, 'It's immature semen.'

Soon he was intent on repeating the mud-bathing whenever he could. A muddy stream ran across the bottom of the garden, and he would creep out at night, testing each stair as he went, sometimes taking an hour to get to the door, dressed in a clean white shirt, to enjoy the 'vivid sensation' of rolling in the mud and masturbating. As a recollecting adult he wonders how he managed to do this, and wash the clothes to remove the evidence, without arousing his parents' suspicion. He thought what a good murderer he would make, able to wash away all the blood. He also fantasised about wallowing fully clothed, then killing himself with cyanide he had bought from the compliant chemist. The fear of Jim and Nan discovering the dirt 'fed the imagination of his obsessive-cleaning rituals'. He later reflects that the 'penalties for being caught would have been terrible in this middle-class household just post-war, would have included being diagnosed as schizophrenic'.

Although the feeling of connection with the primal earth is essential, this is no naked Adam in a state of nature. Clothes are as important as the mud. Even a drop of water darkening the material of his shirt-breast could be sexually arousing. There is the sensation of 'a skin of clothes wetted and then thrown off exposing a new skin, younger'. But the function of clothes is more than a sensual enhancement. They are also drenched in symbolism. The shirt that he darkened with water was 'sharply ironed' by his mother, part of the symbolism of male self-presentation, but under his mother's influence. These divergent sexual feelings developed into a fetishistic ritual that he called 'the Game', in which he would deliberately soil his clothes with mud, food or even shaving foam, then bathe in them. As an adult he often wanted to play the Game when he was made to feel 'too like a man', adopting a masculine social role. Even studying at Cambridge, or teaching, had this effect on him. Then he would change his clothes, ideally into something unisex, so that he would not feel 'all man'. He acknowledged that the Game was 'incipient' transvestism, but denied that he actually liked wearing women's clothes, and he certainly had no desire to pass as a woman. He liked the feeling of being softly embraced by female clothes, unlike the stiffness of the masculine business suit. Above all the open collar, the free sensation around the throat or 'upper yoni', was a powerful aspect of his 'alternative' sexuality.

There is also a suggestion of coprophilia in his love of mud, but he denied this too (though, typically of his refusal of taboo, he once experimented with tasting his own faeces, and felt sick). Not coprophilia, he insisted, but 'a desire to touch and feel everything'.

By the time he wrote about all of this, even privately, Redgrove had processed it many times. We may guess that the adolescent boy was much more confused about it than his older self makes him appear. Even as an adult Redgrove tried to conform for many years to an orthodox masculine sexual norm, and (apart from the heavily coded 'Lazarus and the Sea') he doesn't start to deal with the Game in his poetry until he has met the Jungian therapist John Layard, with 'The Idea of Entropy at Maenporth Beach'. It would not be an exaggeration to say that he built his whole *Weltanschauung* on this secret aspect of his sexuality. It was an experience both erotic and visionary, in which he subjectively transcended the limits of his ordinary mind and senses, and of his socially inscribed gender; but it was a 'transcendence' that took place entirely in the realm of the natural. Redgrove's preoccupations with the feminisation of the male psyche, with unacknowledged senses, with menstruation, and with a religious dimension of experience within nature, are all rooted in the Game.

However, he never completely escaped self-division in his feelings about the Game. There is both a parallel and a contrast with his attitude to alcohol. He once speculated that men drink 'because they're creating sensation in their bodies', in mimicry of women who are 'connected with their senses by the menstrual cycle'. From time to time he also claimed that alcohol gave access to vision, though he more often deprecated writing under the influence of drink as 'messages from Booze County'. It is not surprising that he brought drink and the Game together in his collection *The Mudlark Poems and Grand Buveur.* He was constantly aspiring to give up drink, sometimes successfully for short periods, until in his last years diabetes forced his hand. His attitude to the Game was, overall, much more positive in the years after his therapy with John Layard and partnership with Penelope Shuttle, but conflict persisted. Fundamentally the Game was autoerotic, and he yearned to bring it into harmony with the other, more orthodox heterosexual, side of his sexuality, and with his most important relationships. In his first marriage this was to prove impossible. Penelope Shuttle was much more sympathetic, but he never finally rid himself of feelings of shame. The Game was the rejected stone on which he built the house of his creative work, and therefore his 'treasure'. But it remained a repetitive compulsion, akin to his youthful OCD, something that he was driven to when he felt overwhelmed by stress or depression. And, despite the manifold clues in works such as 'The Idea of Entropy at Maenporth Beach', 'Dance the Putrefact' and the many poems that fetishise clothing, he was terrified of his private practices being publicly known.

Though the Game seems to have begun with erotic mud-bathing, and this intimacy with the physical earth makes its significance seem easy to grasp, literal mud was not necessary to it. It was the soiling and soaking of clothes, often with food or even shaving foam, and subsequent bathing, that were essential, bringing the feeling of renewal through enhanced senses and freedom from oppressive gender identity. Redgrove even found sexual stimulation in slapstick comedy, as he confessed with the barest fictional disguise in *The Terrors of Dr Treviles.* Laurel and Hardy, dressed as women (each other's wives), start attacking each other with food: 'Mrs Laurel' is 'left sprawling on the floor with her face obliterated by the base-board of the cake, stuck to her by squashed pastry and filling . . . Mrs Laurel, hair and features clotted with

cream, bosom and dress smothered in it, stares at the camera.'
Watching this, Treviles suddenly finds that he has spontaneously
ejaculated: 'What has he done in his nest? His pecker has cacked!'
The uneasy humour betrays how difficult it was for Redgrove to
deal with this material in a direct narrative way.

The unlikely erotic potential, for 'Treviles', of Oliver Hardy
covered in cake must have been enhanced by the fact that he was
dressed as a woman. Redgrove wondered why women were rarely
the victims of custard-pie attacks, and liked to 'imagine a woman
getting it because I desire to be that woman, to induce a transformation'. This accounts for the curious doubleness of perspective
in a poem such as 'The Idea of Entropy at Maenporth Beach': the
woman in it is a sexualised object, and the poem has a voyeuristic
quality, but the speaker and implied observer also strongly identi-
fies with the woman. The same is true of the visual images of
women with wet or mud-stained clothes scattered throughout
Redgrove's journals. Some of these verge on soft-core pornography,
but in the context of the journal they are not merely objects of
the gaze. In the most confessional piece Redgrove ever published,
'Dance the Putrefact', the speaker, dressed all in white, sets out
to 'dance my reflection in the mud'. He begins to draw a human
figure in the mud, but this 'reflection' is a crudely drawn female
figure. His dance culminates in his plunging into the
mud-outline:

> I am down, and within her! I have vaulted into her boundaries and
> I am as black as she is. I am buried deep in her flesh. I pull her
> flesh off her in handfuls and cover my skin in hers. I prance, cool
> and nightladen with exterior cunt. (*FECA*)

The desire to possess a woman and to be a woman are fused, the
fusion made possible by the immersion in mud: this seems to
epitomise the transcendence that Peter sought in the Game.

If these obsessions began with the onset of adolescence, they
coincided with the traumatic experience of going away to boarding
school. They may indeed have magnified the harshness of that
change. Practically, how could he carry on his Game in the tightly
regulated, monitored dormitory life of a mid-century public
school? Emotionally, he was to be separated for the first time
from his mother, the sponsor of the 'feminine identification' that
lay at the root of the Game. Symbolically, Taunton School was

an extension of his father's brand of masculinity, a literal entrapment within the spirit against which he was revolting. Taunton had been Jim's own school: he loved the place and was an active member of the Old Tauntonians, becoming President in 1958. He himself had had to leave after two years because of money difficulties and was determined that his sons should enjoy the privileges that he was denied. In later years he protested to Peter for calling it a 'minor public school' in print.

Before he left for school, in September 1945, Nan treated Peter to a trip to Ham House, a 'wonderful-terrible' experience because of the intensified intimacy and its imminent rupture. He described his departure for school in 'My Father's Trapdoors', a poem unusual for its direct autobiographical narrative:

> Father led me behind some mail-bags
> On Paddington Station, my grief was intense,
> I was a vase of flowing tears with mirror-walls,
>
> He wore a hard white collar and a tight school-tie
> And a bristly moustache which is now ashes
> And he took me behind the newsprint to kiss me hard,
>
> The travelling schoolboy,
> And his kiss was hungry and a total surprise.
> Was it the son? Was it the uniform?
>
> It was not the person, who did not belong
> Not to father, no. (*MFT*)

Redgrove wrote this in the early nineties, after Jim's death, and it shows how the conflicts of his childhood remained active in him to the end of his life. His adult comments on Taunton School are almost without exception vehemently negative. It was a place that 'cut off the natural communications between people', using homosexuality to construct the 'School Spirit – making a powerful spirit by divorcing it from actual homosexual love' and Christianity as 'an instrument of wartime and post-war propaganda'. The school, with its broad, imposing stone facade, steepled tower and tracery windows, has an ecclesiastical appearance reflecting its origins as the West of England Dissenters' Proprietary School. It is close to the station, with a view of the Quantocks rising behind it, and whenever as an adult he passed through Taunton by train, Peter used to look the other way.

In many ways Taunton was a typical English public school, with an ethos and physical regime that a boy such as Peter would have resented at almost any school to which he might have been sent. This was perhaps more true in the years he was there than at any other time. More than 1,500 Old Tauntonians had served in the war. Of these 155 had died, and 161 were decorated. A solemn and coercive reverence for military achievement and sacrifice, and a corresponding ideal of manliness, were the inevitable consequences. Living conditions in those impoverished post-war years were spartan: there was a shortage of hot water, allowing each boy only one hot bath per week, and the mattresses were unsprung and rock hard, though the food was always good. Peter went to Taunton in the immediate aftermath not only of the war but of one of the school's most forceful headmasters, Donald Crichton-Miller, who left in the term Peter arrived, after nine years in the job. He had felt that discipline was lax and set about tightening the regime. He instituted compulsory games, made the boys march to church on Sundays, and increased pressure to join the Officers' Training Corps or Scouts. The school especially gained a reputation for rugby, and during Peter's time there, in 1947–8, won the Public School Sevens competition. Redgrove himself always believed that his formative years, in the shadow of the war, were a time of heightened ideological policing, especially of gender and sexuality. Although Taunton was, in the 1970s, to be a pioneer in developing co-education in an independent boarding school, when Peter was there it was of course single sex. A pupil from the preceding decade described it as 'a complete monastery. One lived in a totally male society and treated that as the norm.' Pupils were forbidden even to speak to girls, a pleasure for which the opportunities were in any case limited, since they were only allowed into town twice a term. (But Peter did manage to escape into the countryside where he bought cider from a farmer and inaugurated his life as a drinker.) There was only one female member of staff, a violin teacher. For the mother's boy who had thrilled to the feminine aura of his kindergarten teacher, this was a severe shock.

However, there were also certain important ways in which Taunton was not typical. It had been founded in the 1840s to provide education for the sons of Congregationalists (or Independents) in the Taunton area. Its development into a national public school in the early twentieth century eroded its sectarian character, but it retained something of its dissenting spirit. Christianity supplied its guiding principles, but religion was not linked so closely to conservative values as it might have been at a school espousing the established Church. The traditions of the Congregationalists were liberal and intellectual, and Taunton was not blighted by an anti-intellectual atmosphere as some public schools were. (Even so, Peter's dislike of sport and reputation for being extremely 'brainy' set him apart from most of his fellows.) Religious tolerance had been especially promoted by perhaps its greatest headmaster, Charles Whitaker, a man 'in the mould of the great idealist headmasters', at the time when Jim was a pupil. Since the late nineteenth century the school had maintained a progressive attitude to the teaching of modern languages and science, and it was especially renowned for the latter: no doubt an additional reason why Jim thought Peter should go there.

Academically, Peter's years at Taunton were an outstanding success. He won school prizes in each of his last three years, and the comments in his reports are a crescendo of praise: '*Very* capable and hardworking'; 'Excellent work'; 'Potential scholar'; 'Open Scholarship standard'. He left school at the end of 1949 with excellent Higher School Certificate results in chemistry, botany and zoology, a State Scholarship and an Open Scholarship to read Natural Sciences at Queens' College, Cambridge. Is it possible to be so successful if one is entirely unhappy at school? He did once publicly acknowledge the high calibre of the science teachers at Taunton, and shortly after he started at the school a teacher arrived who was to be the first important figure in his life outside his family. Ernest Neal was probably the most distinguished man ever to teach at the school. As well as being a gifted and dedicated teacher he was a practising biologist and naturalist who achieved national eminence especially for his work on badgers. He was the first person to film badgers nocturnally, and in 1948 published a book on the subject that was to inspire a generation of young naturalists. An Old Tauntonian himself, he was a lifelong Christian whose motto was 'No man is an island entire of itself'; in the war he had tried unsuccessfully to register as a conscientious objector. When he arrived at the school he found standards rather poor, and energetically set about establishing science at the core of the curriculum. He thought very highly of Peter, and was the first in a line of influential men whom Peter admired and even loved, but in his attitude to whom there was a not entirely explicable instability. Ted Hughes and John Layard were to be notable later examples. Peter's attitude to his science teachers, especially Neal, went beyond admiration – he wanted to become them and to compete with them: 'I loved him so much that I was always contradicting him to make our union solid and unequivocal . . . I wanted both of us to be right, because that would make us the same person.' This made him 'so argumentative in class' that Neal once told him he was 'a very clever boy but a nasty one' – a remark that at the time Peter thought unprofessional, but reflecting on the incident forty years later he acknowledged, 'I must have driven him to distraction.' Characteristically he refers the matter to his family life: 'What was wrong then at home?'

Despite his love of wearing open-necked white shirts and rolling in mud, he was not enthusiastic about the school's most totemic sports, cricket and 'that ritual of fertile mud called Rugby football', much to Jim's disappointment. As he later commented, 'How could I join a pack when I was individuating?' However, the one sport at which he did represent the school, squash, was very much under his father's influence: Jim revived the game at Taunton by organising matches against his own club, Wimbledon, and even played for the school, as an Old Boy, in 1948.

The most surprising aspect of Peter's time at Taunton is that for his last three years he was a member of the Officers' Training Corps. Despite the post-war atmosphere of reverence for the military this was not compulsory: he could have chosen the Scouts, or joined a work gang doing useful tasks around the school. Moreover, he was promoted to the rank of sergeant (some of his contemporaries were still privates when they left school) and acquired qualifications in handling a Bren Gun and a .22 rifle. This evidence of military aptitude is intriguing in view of his later experience in National Service.

More characteristically, Peter was an enthusiastic member of the scientific, naturalist and photography societies, all of which had been revived by Ernest Neal. In his second year at the school the fourteen-year-old future author of the poem 'Picking Mushrooms' gave a talk to the Naturalists' Society on fungi, 'illustrated by specimens recently collected'. Photography was an enthusiasm he shared with Jim, and he listed it as an interest in

Who's Who. He later described his young self as 'a barbarian scientist, and stranger to the refinements and poises of the arts sixth', but we should take this with a pinch of salt. As well as the naturalist and scientific societies he was also a stalwart of the school debating society, known as 'The Burke'. He was a committee member, and the school magazine commended him as one of those on whom the burden of keeping the debates going had fallen heavily. When he was still fifteen he opposed the motion that 'modern clothes need reforming', a debate that was 'remarkable for its wit and humour', and a year later, on the topic 'This house disapproves of all pets', he 'gave us his usual artistically worded views'. If there is a hint of sarcasm in that last comment, it doesn't suggest a 'barbarian scientist' lacking refinement and poise. Clearly, though he had almost certainly not yet started writing poetry, his verbal gifts had made an impression.

Peter went to Taunton at the age of thirteen, which was unusually late, perhaps because of the war. When he had been there for two years his younger brother David arrived, aged only nine: unlike Peter, David was to be at the school for seven years, starting in the preparatory school and leaving after O levels. He was academically far less successful than his elder brother: 'Tries, but is much below average' is a typical report comment. Despite this he may have been happy at school: he was considered a 'good type' who 'pulled his weight in the House', and played for the Second XV. This impression of dull worthiness, however, is contradicted by a reputation for fearlessness bordering on craziness, which earned him the nickname 'Loopy'. His best friend thought he was the kind of youth who in an earlier generation would have led his troops over the top with enthusiasm. Surprisingly, in view of his later career, he only rose to the rank of lance corporal in what was now the Combined Cadet Force, but this may have been because he did not complete the Sixth Form.

As we have seen, when they were younger Peter and David were as close and mutually fond as brothers divided by six years might be. Peter blamed Taunton for separating them, so that in later years they were unable to speak to each other. This was a consequence of what he considered the school's hostility to 'natural communications between people', from fear of homosexuality. He and David addressed each other as 'Brother', presumably because it was not done to use first names. But how close would brothers in the preparatory school and the Sixth Form have been, at any school? According to a Tauntonian of that time, small boys in public schools didn't speak to seniors, even if they were brothers. And would that gap not have been widened by the increasingly obvious difference in their intellectual abilities? Peter hints that the education system in general rather than Taunton in particular might have been to blame when he writes, 'How I loved him and wished that Taunton had not separated us – that Taunton (then U[niversity]) with its qualifications.'

Indeed, Redgrove's later attitude to his academic success suggests that there is no contradiction between it and his hostility to the school. At least until the early 1970s he hated objective, 'scientific' writing (the later success of *The Wise Wound* shows an important change in this respect); he even disliked writing a coherent journal. After winning his Open Scholarship he destroyed all his school science essays: 'He hoped never to have to work like that again, ending in examinations.' The successful schoolboy, the prizewinner, the 'good boy' of his first school report, was the persona that he turned against as he embraced the darker self of the Game. This is vividly and amusingly illustrated in his response to a famous public incident. In 1972 the Prime Minister Edward Heath signed the Treaty of Accession to the European Community, and at the same time was awarded the European Prize for Statesmanship. At the ceremony an anti-European protester threw ink over him. Redgrove pasted photographs of the ink-spattered politician into his journal, together with one of Heath as a schoolboy, and wrote, 'Prize schoolboy. European statesmanship. The sixth-former.' He calls the Game 'a living thing that would not be quenched by prize schoolboyism'. The staining of the public figure in his business suit obviously evoked the Game for Redgrove, and his response has nothing to do with the political substance of the protest. It is as if he sees in Heath a grown-up version of the schoolboy he himself was. It is pertinent that Heath was a bachelor with the persona of a middle-aged virgin: the ink attack represents the revenge of the sexuality of the Game against the virginal prizewinning schoolboy. (Redgrove would have been even more delighted by an earlier incident involving Heath, when a woman wearing a red blouse and black skirt threw red paint over him.)

Redgrove's attitude to Taunton School was overdetermined and captured by a narrative that he needed as he embraced the Game and recognised it as the foundation of his poetic vision. In this narrative his father's kind of masculinity (though not his father personally) is the enemy; Taunton School is the institutionalisation of that enemy; his own success at academic science (though not the 'marvel' of looking through a microscope) is a self-castrating acquiescence to the enemy. He was almost certainly happier at Taunton than he later allowed himself to think, but the revisionary narrative was made unavoidable by what happened to him after leaving school.

III

Lazarus 1950

New Year of 1950 was the peak of the career of the youthful scientist, but this year was also to be the most difficult, and transforming, of Peter's life. New Year brought a flurry of letters from Taunton congratulating him on his Cambridge scholarship and recommending him to aim for a doctorate. The one that showed most insight, and that probably meant most to its recipient, was from Ernest Neal. Neal addressed him as 'Dear Peter', not 'Dear Redgrove' like the other masters, and the former conscientious objector showed a prescient awareness that the impending period of National Service might cause his pupil some temperamental difficulties:

> 'I hope you manage to get everything fitted in satisfactorily & that your period in the army will not be a waste of time. I'm sure that you will see to it that it isn't. There will obviously be much that is annoying, but try not to be too frustrated – it doesn't help!'

Peter became eligible for the call-up when he turned eighteen on 2 January 1950. At that time the period of conscription was eighteen months, which allowed him to go to Cambridge at the beginning of the academic year in October 1951. (Later in 1950, when Britain entered the Korean war, the period was extended to two years.) The armed forces automatically allowed men who had been accepted for university to defer enlistment, preferring the greater maturity and more developed skills of graduates. Oxford and Cambridge, however, preferred their students to do military service before going up. This was one of two challenges that faced the triumphant school-leaver in the New Year. The other was 'Little Go' or more formally the 'Previous Examination' in Latin, which all Cambridge entrants had to pass before they could take up their studies. While he waited for the call-up Peter prepared for the exam with a private tutor, Frank MacNulty, in Pimlico. Soon after his birthday he had to register for conscription at his local branch of the Ministry of Labour and National Service, and two or three weeks later submit himself for a medical examination. The doctor who examined Peter told him he was 'neurotic', but this was no barrier to his enlistment. The medical was followed by a meeting with a military reviewing officer at which he could request to be assigned to a specialised corps. Peter applied for the Royal Army Medical Corps, a natural choice given his scientific background, with perhaps also a hope that this would be one of the more humane corners of the army. The system of assigning men to specialised corps was far from reliable. A qualified electrician was told, 'No, you can't do that. I've got enough electricians for one day.' Peter was fortunate to be accepted for the RAMC.

In March he went to Cambridge to sit the two Latin papers required for the exam, having successfully taken his driving test the same morning. On the 23rd of the same month he travelled to the RAMC depot at Church Crookham in Hampshire, near the garrison town of Aldershot, to begin his basic training. Enlistment was always on a Thursday, and all over the country the trains were full of young men travelling on passes provided by the services.

The eight-week basic training in the army was an organised programme of bullying and humiliation. From the very first day it was designed to shock the young men out of their civilian habits and assumptions, from the brutally short haircut to bundling up and sending home their civilian clothes – a practical measure to deter desertion, but also a powerful emotional symbol of passing out of their previous lives. Many recruits found the army food disgusting, and there were cases of vomiting and diarrhoea, as well as tears, on the first night. They had to do everything 'at the double', orders were invariably shouted, recruits were sworn at and insulted for the slightest infringement, and they had to complete tedious and often pointless tasks to almost impossible standards of perfection, most famously polishing their boots to a glassy surface. One RAMC recruit was put on a charge because a spot of rust developed on his rifle barrel while he was standing in the rain on parade. The reason for all this was not sadism or contempt for unwilling conscripts on the part of professional soldiers, though these might sometimes have been additional factors. The motive was deliberately and systematically to 'break the spirit' of the young men, to suppress their individuality and turn them into a functioning unit that would respond to commands instantly and unquestioningly. In the army's view, a routine that broke spirits in the barrack-room and on the parade-ground would save lives on the battlefield. Most soldiers learned that there was a strong element of role-playing in the NCOs' bullying, insulting demeanour, and not to take it personally – like the round-shouldered man who 'almost died on the spot' when told he looked 'like a vulture about to shit' but later thought it very funny, or the one who reacted similarly to the line, 'If you don't swing that arm, laddie, I'll tear it off, stick it up your arse and have you for a lollipop.'

Within a few days of arriving at Church Crookham, Peter wrote a letter home that reflected these conditions:

> I've got an appetite for tobacco now. Everyone smokes a lot & I find it rather pleasant and soothing. I think it's something to do with being rather jittery, because if you don't respond to an order you get sworn at . . . So many things to do to keep out of the guard room or off a charge . . .
>
> . . . ability tests also today . . . they told us we were not to worry but it's on these that our jobs are determined & I do hope I get a good job . . .
>
> . . . very tired. It's all rather like an exam just before when all the things that you've learnt come crowding into your mind & go round and round. They eventually send you to sleep. I had some very odd dreams during the night. I dreamt last night that I was sowing [*sic*] buttons on my greatcoat with thread that broke as I sowed, a bugle had just gone. At the same time I seemed to be marching. I had the same sort of feeling of swimming along in my sleep when I was learning to ride a bike.
>
> It's the incessant activity which gets you. So many things to do and mostly all at once. People even smoke in bed.

Thousands of letters like this must have been written by National Servicemen during these first weeks of basic training, but in Peter's case it was a serious portent. Almost immediately after joining up he had become confused, beset by feelings of unreality, 'as if suddenly the world was out of focus'. In his own words he 'just stood there, felt quite out of things' and 'lapsed into a strange mode of behaviour'. The letter I have quoted (including the ellipses) is a copy in Jim's hand, with a note: 'Rough writing, scrawling at foot of page, words and phrases repeated.' Much later, in his novel *In the Country of the Skin,* Peter described his autobiographical hero Jonas 'tottering around the tarmac' of the parade-ground 'saying, where am I?' and the 'violent' corporal warning him of the consequences if he was faking. Exactly a week after his enlistment, Jim and Nan received a small, stark card informing them that Private Redgrove P. 22350486 RAMC had been transferred to the military hospital in Aldershot. Presumably Jim copied the letter so that he could give the original to the medical authorities.

Peter wrote to his parents again during that week of basic training or subsequent hospitalisation:

Hello again.

Thank you very much for your very nice letters, etc. I'm sorry I can only dash off these two lines now – I'll write more fully later. Would you keep all mags, etc for me until I come home again, please. I enclose my key. Is my Lewis's Library free? That is, have you got those two books out on my sub., or is it just waiting for me to write to them so I can take 3 books out? You see if so I'll be able to get three books as soon as I can. If you want to look at those Maurice Burton ones, please do, but I'd prefer you to do it one at a time. I would greatly appreciate a postcard on this, if you could manage it, please.

Sorry again I can't write more, in Great hurry

Lots of Love Peter

Maurice Burton is the author of that Natural History you were going to buy for David.

P.S. In case the other is illegible

If you'd like to look at those Maurice Burton books, if you haven't already done so, would you mind doing so one at a time, please? That will leave two books on my sub. for me to send to Lewis's for in my own time, as I shall need a Physiology and a Medical textbook soon, I hope. If you don't want to borrow the Burtons from Lewis's I can recommend them, but it'll be interesting to see whether David's still got the craze.

In any case I shall be sending to Lewis's for my Physiology and Medical books in about a week's time, so if you could leave my subscriptions unoccupied [this word repeated above in capitals] by then, please, I should be very grateful

Love

Peter

The appearance of the first letter, by Jim's description, was probably more disturbing than its content, which is a fairly natural reaction to the shock of basic training. The second one has no superscription and the signature is unnaturally large, again suggesting distraction if not disturbance. Both letters are unusually repetitive, and the second one is obsessive.

A young man's breakdown and consequent discharge from National Service may be viewed in various and conflicting ways. One might judge it as a failure to go through with the foundational experience of young men of Peter's generation – of all the generations of young men born between the late twenties and early forties – equivalent to a young tribesman not being initiated and hence not being accepted as a man by his tribe. Or one might see in it a challenge – however inchoate, inarticulate and even unconscious – to the norms of masculinity that the armed forces prescribed on behalf of society. Our point of view will of course depend on our preconceptions, but also on what the young man goes on to make of his experience, whether he can turn his weakness into strength. When D. H. Lawrence faced conscription in 1916–17 he was eventually rejected because of his poor physical health, but regardless of this he, or his autobiographical character Richard Lovat Somers, resolved to 'act from his soul alone' in opposition to the war. Peter in 1950 had nothing like the maturity or developed consciousness to take such a stand. Very likely he would have had a breakdown even without the provocation of military service. Nevertheless, Redgrove's life's work shows that his refusal of this initiation was not an aberration, but of a piece with a conscious direction that emerged only much later, and to which a challenge to socially prescribed gender definition was central.

Peter had spent four years at a boarding school, and for most of this period had undergone military training in the cadet force. These were both experiences that usually fortified young men facing the ordeal of conscription, but Peter later said that the resemblance to school was what most horrified him. Class may have had something to do with the devastating effect it had on him: he probably did not have much experience of coarse and aggressive working-class humour. But there is little evidence that middle-class boys in general couldn't adapt, and the most unlikely characters throve in the army: the outrageously camp art critic Brian Sewell for example (admittedly probably less camp when he was eighteen) found the whole experience beneficial and became an officer.

In Peter's case the shock of conscription provoked a crisis that had been developing for years. His indulgence in the Game – whether acting it out or as a masturbation fantasy – became obsessive, and so did his feelings of guilt and anxiety about it. He became consumed with fear of blindness and, as confusion weakened his grasp of ideas and of reality, fear too of deteriorating intellectual powers and even of madness. These fears were almost certainly related to current superstitions about the consequences of masturbation, but they became self-fulfilling as he entered a vortex of confusion. He tried to protect himself with 'prayers' or 'magic formulas', and soon his lips were moving constantly as he muttered these to himself.

Within a few days he was transferred from Aldershot to the Royal Victoria Military Hospital at Netley Park, on Southampton Water. This famous hospital was built after the Crimean War, partly at the prompting of Florence Nightingale, and had seen some famous inmates, including the very different soldier-poet Wilfred Owen, who was evacuated there with shell shock in 1917 before being moved to Craiglockhart, and Rudolf Hess after his solo flight to Scotland in 1941. It was a huge hospital with 138 wards and 1,000 beds. Peter was treated in the block which had opened in 1870 as the army's first purpose-built military asylum and through which some 15,000 people had passed during the First World War. Not long after Peter was treated there the hospital fell into disuse and it was eventually demolished, apart from the red-brick chapel with its impressive domed tower.

By the time Peter was moved to Netley, Jim and Nan had received more bad news, via another blunt little card. This was from Queens' College, a standard card announcing the Previous Examination results, with the single word 'Failed'. Jim wrote to G. P. McCullagh, the Senior Tutor, telling him that Peter had suffered 'a minor nervous breakdown, including partial loss of memory' and asking for more details of the exam performance. He hadn't noticed signs of anything more than natural excitement before they heard of the breakdown, but he now wondered if Peter's mental state had already begun to deteriorate when he took the exam, thus accounting for his poor performance. McCullagh replied that Peter had failed badly in one of the two papers, and marginally in the other, but encouraged him to try again when he was fit to do so.

When his parents eventually broke the news of his failure, later in April, Peter seemed to take it philosophically, and Jim believed that his health was improving. On his transfer to Netley he was in the care of Major J. R. Hawkins, whom Jim and Nan found kindly and sympathetic. Hawkins told them that it would take four to six weeks to judge whether Peter should be discharged, adding that if he remained in the army he would still have to complete the full period of basic training. After a couple of weeks Hawkins was transferred, and Lieutenant George Spaul took over responsibility for Peter's treatment.

Spaul was himself a National Service conscript, who had qualified as a doctor only two years earlier. He was only seven years older than Peter. He later became a consultant psychiatrist and, though he confessed that he had no analytic qualifications, he was an enthusiast for psychoanalysis. He became very interested in Peter's case, and felt that he established a good relationship with him. He chose to pursue a course of 'straight psychoanalysis' rather than drug treatment because he thought the latter dangerous.

In later years Peter seems to have regarded Spaul as the main culprit in his diagnosis and treatment. As we shall see, he may have been wrong about this. Certainly at the time he trusted the young doctor, and confided his most troubling secrets to him – probably the first time he had spoken to anybody about the Game. Spaul reported 'a rather unusual perversion consisting of masturbation while clean sports clothes (preferably white) are soiled with mud or water'. Peter was not surprisingly insistent that nothing should be said about this to his parents. The doctors he came in contact with all referred to the Game as a 'perversion'. This of course was normal usage at the time, and there is no evidence that Peter was subjected to any moral judgement about his sexuality. Nevertheless, the medical authorities undoubtedly looked on the Game as a symptom of his illness to be eradicated if possible, and the word 'perversion' highlights the contrast to the approach he was to meet with, much later in life, in therapy with John Layard. Peter also said enough about his family to persuade Spaul that the basis of his troubles was 'a possible Oedipus situation'. Spaul was devoting an hour a day to analytic sessions with Peter. He stressed to Jim that his son's condition was serious, but believed that he could be cured in three months.

Jim's letters to Spaul express his appreciation of the treatment Peter was getting at Netley, but he must have felt some disquiet, because he privately consulted another doctor, T. M. Ling. Ling was the Medical Director of Roffey Park Rehabilitation Centre, which had been established after the war for the treatment of 'sub-health, maladjustment and emotional problems that have become evident in office or factory'. (It still exists but now its mission, in a striking indication of cultural change, is 'delivering results by improving individual and organisational performance'.) Jim's consultation with Ling seems to have been informal: he describes him as a friend with whom he discussed Peter's case over lunch: Ling would be visiting Portsmouth soon and was willing to call at Netley and make Spaul's acquaintance. Although Jim calls him a 'friend' they address each other as 'Dr Ling' and 'Mr Redgrove'. It is tempting to speculate that Ling was in fact a contact of Jim's through the Masons: the help he offered is the kind of thing one Mason would do for another even if they were not on terms of close personal friendship. This is relevant because of the decisive influence Ling was to have on Peter's life, as well as the prominence of Freemasonry in Jim's social position and the kind of masculinity he represented.

On 24 May Spaul wrote to Jim that Peter was progressing well and that he might be sufficiently recovered to take the Latin exam in September and begin his studies at Cambridge in October. It was clear by now that, however rapidly he recovered, Peter's army life was at an end, and he was in fact discharged on 12 July.

Dr Ling visited Netley on 6 June. His report to Jim was deeply disturbing and signalled a dramatic change in Peter's prospects. Ling thought his condition was grave: certainly a case of schizophrenia. He contacted E. Cunningham Dax, the Superintendent of the State Mental Hospital at Netherne, near Croydon in Surrey. Ling thought Dax 'will probably agree that this man requires deep insulin treatment' and asked for him to be put on the waiting list. Ling recommended that Jim should not tell the Cambridge authorities how seriously ill Peter was, but hang on to his place while this treatment was carried out. It may be that, in the two weeks since Spaul wrote to Jim, Peter's condition had seriously worsened, and that Ling was confirming a new and more ominous diagnosis by Spaul. If so, there is no record of correspondence or conversation to this effect. Spaul wrote to Dax expressing the hope and belief that insulin treatment would be effective, but did not say anything to suggest that the treatment was his idea, or that he believed Peter was schizophrenic. He expressed a wish to stay in contact with Peter, but there doesn't seem to have been any further communication between them after Peter left Netley. It seems most likely that Ling made the diagnosis and recommended the treatment on his own responsibility.

In *In the Country of the Skin* 'a medical board . . . insisted [Jonas] have insulin shock treatment before he was discharged from the army'. Fiction this may be, but it is highly likely Peter believed that the army was responsible for his diagnosis and treatment, and that the insulin therapy was a condition of discharge. In all these matters he was almost certainly wrong. All the evidence suggests that Spaul was committed to treating him by psychotherapeutic methods: it seems extraordinary that he forgot this, even if in later years he would have disapproved of Spaul's Freudian approach. Moreover, his discharge was guaranteed by the end of May, contradicting his memory that he submitted to insulin coma therapy in order to get out of the army.

The diagnosis was 'incipient schizophrenia', and his Record of Service states that he was unfit even for 'civil employment' in the army. More than twenty years later he discussed his psychiatric history with his GP, and said that he thought he had not been ill at all, but suffering from exaggerated growing pains of adolescence which he considered normal for people of imaginative temperament. The doctor told him there was no such diagnostic category as 'incipient schizophrenia' and that the infallible signs of schizophrenia in modern practice were hallucinations and lack of insight, neither of which had been observed in his case. This conversation was a great relief to him: he wrote to his father that he felt 'exonerated from what in some minds still counts as a social stigma'. Redgrove was never one who embraced the idea of being, as he put it, an 'accredited madman': on the contrary, the essential sanity of his vision of the world was to him a deeply cherished idea.

However, he was misinformed about the status of the diagnosis. There are numerous papers on 'incipient' or 'pre-psychotic' schizophrenia, both at the time of his breakdown and more recently. Contemporary psychiatrists are confident that they can identify young people with a high risk of developing a psychotic disorder, and that many of the mental health problems associated with the illness occur before the stage of full-blown psychosis. A contemporary psychiatrist would not, therefore, judge that the absence of hallucinations meant Peter was not suffering from – or in danger of developing – schizophrenia. Many centres around the world are engaged in research to identify patients at high risk of developing the illness. The overwhelming majority of these patients are, like Peter, in late adolescence or early adulthood. A lot of the earliest symptoms of pre-psychotic schizophrenia are non-specific. These include sleep disturbance, depressed mood, anxiety and irritability – all of which he suffered from in the spring of 1950. More specific symptoms include 'ideas of reference [i.e. exaggerated belief that contingent events refer to oneself], odd beliefs or magical thinking, perceptual disturbance, paranoid ideation, odd thinking and speech, odd behaviour and appearance'. Apart from paranoia, Peter's doctors record all these symptoms. His condition would have rung alarm bells even for their twenty-first century equivalents.

A contemporary psychiatrist would not, like the doctor Redgrove spoke to in 1973, dismiss the diagnosis of incipient schizophrenia out of hand. The difference between now and 1950 is in how such a patient would be treated. Even of patients considered to be at high risk – in other words 'incipiently' schizophrenic – studies have shown only between 22 per cent and 54 per cent develop full psychotic symptoms within twelve months. Contemporary psychiatrists are much more aware than their predecessors of the ethical dimensions of the subject, including the question of the 'stigma' that Redgrove felt he had carried for more than twenty years. The favoured method of treating such patients is Cognitive Behaviour Therapy, in which therapist and patient cooperate to develop an understanding of the symptoms and ways of coping with and reducing them. Pharmaceutical intervention is sometimes used, but is considered controversial, and when it is used only very low doses are administered.

Netherne Hospital was built in 1905 as a psychiatric hospital or, as it was then called, lunatic asylum. Like Netley it is now demolished, and the site has been developed for luxury apartments. Like many such institutions it was a handsome red-brick building, and one of its last vestiges was a wrought-iron gate, with the remains of its name picked out across the arch. By the standards of its time Netherne was an enlightened place. Its superintendent, E. Cunningham Dax, who told Dr Ling that there was a place for Peter, was an enthusiastic promoter of art in psychiatric practice. In 1946 he had brought to Netherne the art therapy pioneer Edward Adamson, whose large collection of artwork by psychiatric patients is housed in south-west London. It is an irony that such work, which would have enthralled Redgrove in later years, was going on at Netherne while he was there, but there is no evidence that he ever encountered Adamson, and certainly no work by him in the collection.

Despite the art therapy, psychiatric treatment at Netherne was dominated by the favoured physical therapies of the day: Electro-Convulsive Therapy, Leucotomy and Deep Insulin Coma Therapy. This last was regarded as the only specific treatment for schizophrenia from the late 1930s until it was discredited in the late 1950s so that, once the diagnosis had been made, the treatment followed inevitably. One of its pioneers, R. K. Freudenberg, was Dax's deputy superintendent. The theory was that the insulin 'antagonised the neuronal effects of products of the adrenal system' which were the physiological cause of the illness. In deep coma patients entered a state in which they lost their muscle tension and corneal and pupillary reflexes. They were then administered glucose, by a nasal tube or intravenously, to bring them out of the life-threatening hypoglycaemic state. Reactions to this extreme treatment included restlessness, major convulsions, and 'hypoglycaemic aftershocks' which called for continuous nursing supervision and the constant availability of a doctor. It was massively more expensive, in terms of doctors' and nurses' time, than other forms of treatment. About one per cent of patients died from the treatment, and more suffered permanent brain damage. It made most patients grossly obese. It was normal to continue the treatment until fifty to sixty comas had been induced.

Insulin Coma Therapy was challenged by a young doctor, Harold Bourne (who as it happened had practised in the army) in the *Lancet* in 1953. One of Bourne's points is especially relevant to Peter's case: he cited papers to show that early diagnosis was unreliable, but doctors persisted with it because they believed that the therapy was more effective the earlier it was administered. The result in Bourne's view was that treatment was often given 'on a suspicion perhaps bolstered by a Rorschach or other test'. Redgrove claimed that the doctor who diagnosed him said, 'You're schizophrenic. I can tell by the way you're looking at me.' Initially the medical establishment condemned Bourne's paper, but eventually in 1957 a controlled randomised study was published, showing that the recovery rate of the insulin patients was no different from that of the control group: after this the treatment was abandoned.

At Netherne Peter was placed under the care of a woman doctor, Dr E. Dalberg, whom he later rather insensitively described as looking 'as if she had been in the camps.' She was in fact probably a Jewish refugee from Eastern Europe. She was perhaps the prototype of the several 'lady doctors' in his later poetry. Like everyone who was involved in his treatment she was impressed by his intelligence, but noted that he had become 'increasingly obsessional over a number of years'. He came across as an outsider, highbrow and extremely well-read, with remarkable insight into his condition, haughty, reserved and supercilious on first meeting, but eventually opening up to 'excellent contact'. He didn't get on well with other patients, adopting a sarcastic and superior attitude to them, 'throwing his weight about' in what Dalberg considered an infantile way, trying to impress his fellow-patients with his 'Public School Boy role of the omniscient'.

The diagnosis of Peter's condition was now 'schizophrenia in obsessional personality'. His chances of recovery were judged to be no more than fifty-fifty. At times Dalberg considered that his obsessions were of delusional intensity. He was transferred to Netherne in late June, and in early July he was given a range of psychological tests. On the Wechsler IQ test, which he specifically asked for, probably because of his worries about mental deterioration, he scored 148 on verbal IQ, 116 on performance, with a full scale score of 140, which should have reassured him. The Rorschach test examines the form-perception and fantasies of the patient by asking him or her to interpret a series of ink blots. The psychologist who administered the tests was amazed by the number of responses – 126 – that Peter produced for this test, and by his insight, quoting 'insulin helps to coalesce a personality which is beginning to dissociate', his realisation that his 'concepts tend to become vague' and that he 'favours the abstruse, but now tries not to use a long word unless it expresses the exact shade of meaning'. The first of these comments may be no more than astute mimicry of his doctors, since 'dissociate' was one of the terms they used to identify the symptoms of schizophrenia. He had not yet shown any interest in writing poetry, but the preoccupation with language in the last comment clearly foreshadows his artistic development. An even stronger indication of his future path is the fact that he scored a maximum of six on only one of the 'orectic' or affective variables tested for: 'phantastic productivity'! Peter was clearly a rewarding patient. However, the psychologist also reported 'weakened conceptual thinking' and 'disordered judgement', and that he failed to complete one of the tests, which involved placing variously shaped and coloured blocks in order. This was considered to be 'important diagnostic evidence of schizophrenic reactivity.' Surprisingly his score was only moderate

46

for 'sex-preoccupation', since he was still masturbating compulsively, fantasising about the Game and enacting it when he had the opportunity. He was also having sexual fantasies about boys. Homosexuality remained a preoccupation in later life, though there is no evidence, even in his intimate journals, that as an adult he was actually attracted to men. His mature preoccupation was a refraction of his inner struggle with the image of his father, and his juvenile fantasies are natural to someone who had spent his whole adolescence at boarding school.

He was very anxious about his future. He was losing interest in science, and beginning to think that his choice of subjects had been entirely due to his identification with Ernest Neal. He was no longer keen to begin at Cambridge in October, and dreaded retaking the Latin exam. At the same time, he confessed himself hopeless at practical things, and could only envisage a future as a Cambridge don.

His reading at this time shows a strong philosophical inclination: while at Netherne he acquired Pascal's *Pensées*, Berkeley's *The Principles of Human Knowledge* and a volume of essays by William James, as well as the more predictable *Science and the Modern World* by A. N. Whitehead. In this year he also bought Goethe's *Faust* and the *Odyssey*, and at the opposite extreme a selection of Hilaire Belloc. All this is evidence that he was far from the 'barbarous scientist' that he later called himself at this age, but none of it suggests that he was beginning to think of writing poetry himself.

The first of Peter's insulin comas was on 17 July. They continued, nearly every day except Sundays, for nine weeks. His course was of fifty comas, but actually the insulin was administered more than sixty times, because sometimes the coma didn't ensue. Typically he would be injected with insulin at about seven in the morning. Within half an hour he began to feel drowsy, another half-hour and he sweated profusely, then began twitching. He would fall into a coma between two and three hours after the injection, and the coma would last half an hour, until terminated by the injection of glucose. Twenty years later he vividly recreated the experience for Jonas in *In the Country of the Skin*:

> The shock treatment was sensuous. Lay down on a hospital bed in hospital pyjamas no coverings a mattress with a sheet over it. An injection into the veins of the inside crook of his elbow, which

gradually became more and more bruised as the treatment went on. The senior nurse bending over him with the shining needle and his thin clear spectacles. Waking after centuries or no time at all the sheet soaked with sweat and his body aching because he had been in convulsions. He enjoyed all this, and wolfed up the mashed potato they gave each patient after the treatment: insulin snatched all sugar out of the blood and this produced a coma very near to death. The nurses hovered, and when the convulsions ceased and the coma began they gauged the right moment to inject glucose and snatch the patient back from death . . .

Jonas-Silas seemed to thrive, and when they told him this he thought to himself that he loved to please people. The convulsions he was enjoying, the great ejaculations of sweat, became so severe that they changed their procedure slightly, by giving him a draught of luminal before each treatment. The treatments were continuing since he seemed to be enjoying life so much more; naturally, he thought, I have no threat from the army. His rituals continued, and did not abate.

Jonas's 'sensuous' enjoyment of the treatment did not prevent Redgrove, in his own person, describing it as 'a barbarous violence on the body'.

When he was first admitted to Netherne Peter said he came from 'on the whole a happy home', but he may already have aroused Dr Dalberg's suspicions when, after describing his father as a 'powerful, strong personality', he added that his mother 'does not give in'. Dalberg soon realised that he was very strongly attached to his mother and had up to then shown little interest in girls. Much later he recorded in his journal that at some unspecified time, probably during his adolescence, Nan gave him money to go with a prostitute, but he didn't make use of it. This isn't mentioned in Dalberg's notes, and may have been after he left Netherne. When she met Jim Dalberg noted, 'He has no understanding of PWR but tries materially to do his best': an astute observation that remained true throughout Jim's life. She thought it was obvious that David – 'though far from brilliant at school' – was more to Jim's liking; he confessed that Peter made him feel uncomfortable and insecure, at times adopting a sneering attitude to him. But Jim was, as always, trying 'to do his best', and one time took Peter and two of his fellow-patients to the ballet.

After five weeks of the treatment he claimed to be benefiting, informing Dalberg that 'the disintegration appears to be at least arrested'. She noted that he was managing without his magic formulas, was not acting out his 'perversions', and was beginning to show interest in the opposite sex. After 22 September the insulin treatment was concluded, and after a couple more weeks Dalberg thought it had been more effective than she had expected. Nevertheless he was still dreamy, lacking in initiative, unable to concentrate on scientific reading, and she considered the prognosis still doubtful. She told Jim she did not think that Peter would ever make a complete recovery and believed (correctly) that her patient would 'never be suited to ordinary industrial life'. Dalberg recommended Peter to remain at Netherne for another three or four weeks – something he was not keen to do. Jim supported him in his wish, and he was discharged on 7 October. In words that must have confirmed Peter's worst suspicions about the psychiatric profession, when he read them in later years, Dalberg recommended Jim to 'discourage intro-spection' and to encourage social activity. It was, she said, too early to say whether 'normal' life would ever be possible – Peter was 'still only a boy'.

Peter's alter ego Jonas was literally having dreams that spoke to him of the life-changing significance of his experience:

> In one he was dead, truly dead, and dissolved into the soil. Later, when he began to write poetry, he didn't see why anything he had done in his life gave him the right to see things that were true in nature. Then he remembered that death had taken him to pieces, that he was conscious of being the mud and soil, that no mythological personages had greeted or punished him.

Ten years after writing this, Redgrove elaborated in conversation on the feeling of having been 'taken to pieces':

> During these practice 'deaths' (because they were very near death) I had a number of visions and the chief one was rather . . . like the end of *Ivan Ilyich*, Tolstoy's novel, in which one is conscious of the world, of one's self and one's body and then this is taken away, pieces are taken away like a stage-set being dismantled, and gradually this dismantling reaches the part of you that is aware of the dismantling and then that is dismantled and there is nothing . . . I do not know what I expected to see. Did I expect to see Charon with his punt ferrying me across the river? The thing that knew there was nothing was taken away. Then I came across Keats' letters in which he said

the world is a vale of soul-making. And I realised that I did not then have any soul, in other words I had nothing that I could take with me into unconsciousness.

Both these accounts of the experience are refracted by the poem in which Redgrove both drew on and transformed it, 'Lazarus and the Sea' (C). This poem was written several years later, when he was at Cambridge, and was one of his first publications in November 1953. It stands out among his early poems as one that is completely in command of its idiom: personal experience has been completely absorbed into the poem's world. For the work of a twenty-one-year-old it has astonishing authority – an authority that Redgrove was not to achieve consistently for at least another ten years. Its biographical interest is not so much the light it casts on the experience itself, as evidence that, devastating as it was for Peter and his family, it played a significant part in making him a poet. It does not speak with the voice of a callow undergraduate, but with a deeper, more resonant, permanent and impersonal voice that we don't hear again so strongly until poems such as 'The Case' which he wrote in the sixties. Paradoxically, although Peter met no 'mythological personages' in his death-like comas, he had earned the right to speak with the voice of the biblical character whose story he borrowed for the poem. It opens with the couplet:

> The tide of my death came whispering like this
> Soiling my body with its tireless voice.

This is the kind of opening that makes you sit up, and read on in the hope that you are in the presence of an exceptional poet. The rhythm is underpinned by iambic pentameter, but one doesn't think of that, because it is so saturated by the pattern of sounds – internal rhyme, assonance, repeated sibilant, the reversal of the consonant pattern in the first phrase – which obviously evokes the sea, but also fuses it with the death for which it is a simile. (In fact, the sea is never named except in the title: it is dissolved into its attributes.) The word 'soiling' brilliantly (perhaps unconsciously) combines a number of divergent meanings, and in doing so concentrates the way the poem manages its author's 'ritual' obsessions. 'Soil' means to pollute, even 'to roll or wallow in mud', but it is also a variant of 'assoil', to absolve from sin. That which pollutes also purifies: the poem imaginatively redeems the obsessions that were still shameful to the author's everyday consciousness. It is not just the single word that does this:

> I could say nothing of where I had been,
> But I knew the soil in my limbs and the rain-water
> In my mouth, knew the ground as a slow sea unstable
> Like clouds and tolerating no organisation such as mine
> In its throat of my grave.

Compare this from his recollections of the Game in adolescence:

> Sometimes I was a Wild man, shaggy with water and earth and trees
> . . . I remember inching out of the house in the small hours so as
> not to wake my parents or my brother, to lie in the earth in the
> darkness or lightening pearl of the small hours, when the vapours of
> the trees and earth are hallucinatory . . . these were profound erotic
> experiences; my great treasure.

The story of Lazarus gives Redgrove a vehicle for making articulate and public this feeling that what was shameful was also a 'great treasure', even a religious experience. But the story also frustrates that meaning, because its own religious significance is of course not Lazarus's death but his resurrection. Redgrove's Lazarus is haunted by the imagination of where his 'death' might have taken him if another power had not intervened:

> The knotted roots
> Would have entered my nostrils, and held me
> By the armpits, woven a blanket for my cold body
> Dead in the smell of wet earth, and raised me to the sky
> For the sun in the slow dance of the seasons.
> Many gods like me would be laid in the ground
> Dissolve and be formed again in this pure night
> Among the blessing of birds and the sifting water.

Lazarus imagines himself transformed into the Green Man of medieval iconography, like the Wild man of his author's sexual fantasy. In this version of the story Jesus's intervention is an unwelcome judgement that 'tore me to life, uprooted me / Back to my old problems and to the family'. For once, in this line, the twentieth-century subject, steeped in psychoanalysis, shows through the persona. Peter probably did feel torn back to his own problems, to which his family was central. But this complaint also warns us not to take the poem naively as disguised autobiography. There is no sense that the insulin comas were a paradise that he wanted to return to.

In the late fifties Redgrove was to get to know another poetic genius who suffered aggressive psychiatric treatment at the beginning of her adult life. He was always warmly sympathetic to Sylvia Plath, though it is unlikely that they discussed their experiences. It is however hard to believe that Plath did not read 'Lazarus and the Sea', and that it did not influence her own use of the same story in the poem in which she confronted her experience of ECT, 'Lady Lazarus', whose speaker also protests against being brought back to life.

IV

Love and Poetry 1950–54

O n 7 October 1950 Peter was discharged from hospital, but
there was still a lot of anxiety about his long-term prospects.
Dr Dalberg wrote to Jim that the chances of a relapse
depended considerably on his environment. As far as Peter's future
as a scientist was concerned, this anxiety was well founded: his
breakdown, or his treatment, or both had started a process of
increasing and irreversible disillusion with science. But his environment in the next couple of years brought him into contact with two
people who helped to ensure that the death of the scientist was far
from a catastrophe, and heralded the birth of the poet.

There was soon a reinforcement of this anxiety for Jim and Nan.
In early November Jim wrote a sanguine reply to a letter from Dr
Ling congratulating him on Peter's satisfactory progress. But he did
not send this reply: on the day he wrote it Peter had, as Jim put it,
a 'bad turn'. Arrangements were made for him to attend a weekly
therapeutic group run by Siegfried Heinrich Foulkes, the distinguished psychoanalyst and pioneer of group analysis. Redgrove later
remembered these sessions continuing for about eighteen months,
and being treated by two analysts in London and Cambridge. He
had read Freud's *Psychopathology of Everyday Life* which 'opened
up a new world to a very conventionally-educated boy' and was
fascinated to meet real live psychoanalysts. (Curiously he seems to
have completely forgotten his analytic sessions with Dr Spaul at
Netley.) His later judgement, when he had experience of a very
different kind of analysis, was that these doctors were 'concerned
to maintain the status quo'.

There could be no question of his starting his Cambridge career
immediately on discharge from hospital: aside from his mental
condition, there was still the 'Previous Examination' to be retaken.

As an appropriate way of occupying himself before going up the following October he took a job at Whiffen's laboratory in Fulham. Whiffen's was a well-established chemical and pharmaceutical manufacturing business, which when Peter went to work for them had recently been taken over by Fisons. In a later CV he describes this job as 'Research Assistant', which sounds rather grand for a school-leaver; it seems more likely that he was a laboratory assistant.

While he worked at Whiffen's he resumed his Latin studies for the Previous Examination, studying again with Frank McNulty. By February McNulty was anxious about the strain Peter was putting on himself by working and studying at the same time. He wrote to Jim expressing his worry that Peter might be heading for another breakdown, that he wasn't progressing with his Latin, and that he was in danger of forgetting his theoretical chemistry. In the event he passed the examination in June.

There is no evidence of Peter having had a girlfriend before this time. Certainly he was still a virgin. It was while he was working at Whiffen's that he met the woman who was to change all this. Barbara Sherlock was a student of Kingston Art College, two years older than himself. She was a tall, strong-featured young woman – long-faced, not conventionally beautiful, but her daughter thought her 'stunning'; her features were more austere than Nan's, but she had a captivating smile, and her attractiveness is more obvious in movie images than in still photographs. In character she was both strong-minded and forbearing, qualities that were to struggle for predominance over the years of her relationship with Peter. Her father, John Sherlock, was a vigorous and practical man who had fought at Gallipoli at the age of seventeen and made a very successful career as an engineer, forming what became the British Thermostat Company. He insisted that Barbara take a secretarial course before allowing her to study art. He and Jim together formed a phalanx of dynamic but socially orthodox achievement, which allowed them to provide a financial safety net for their children, but made an oppressive family ethos from which Peter and Barbara wanted to escape.

Barbara was the first artist Peter had ever met. One day when they were travelling together on the top deck of a bus she said to him that being an artist means you never have to be bored. He wanted to be like her, and like her art-student friends who didn't wear ties. She opened up a new world to him, which was a revelation. She was also his first muse or (since he might have given this title to his mother) the first woman who directly inspired him to poetry. Their first lovemaking is a foundational event in Redgrove's story of his formation as a poet. His parents went away for a month, and he and Barbara took the opportunity to make love in their bed at Orchard End. There are, one would have thought, quite strong taboos against making love in one's parents' bed. Perhaps it was simply a matter of convenience: the only double bed in the house. But especially in Peter's case revisiting the primal scene for one's own sexual initiation seems fraught with meaning: sympathetic magic to heal his parents' relationship; or, less benignly, a usurpation of the father.

Redgrove did not record his thoughts on this matter, but he more than once made it clear that this experience was for him even more momentous than a first sexual experience usually is. After he and Barbara had made love 'a great peace' and 'a silence' came into his head, and into that peace and silence came his first poem. It was 'a call to vocation' which inaugurated his life as a poet and also, in retrospect, inaugurated the great theme of his poetry: 'a coming together of bodily happenings and mental happenings in a way I had never known before'. He got out of bed to write it down: the whole story neatly encapsulates both the fundamental role of sexual experience in Redgrove's poetry, and the stresses that his 'vocation' was to place on his relationship with Barbara.

What Peter wrote down on that memorable occasion was this, or something very like it:

> Caught in a fold of the living hills he failed.
> Extending his amiable senses he found
> The mist that glittered like a skin
> The horny rocks and the alien soil.

This is the earliest surviving draft of 'The Collector', eventually to be the title poem of his first book. The opening line, in particular, has an alluring sound pattern that might well have made the young first-time lover jump out of bed in the belief that he was a poet. These lines obviously comment directly on the sexual initiation he has just experienced. On the evidence of the poem this was not the triumph that Redgrove's self-mythologising recollection makes it seem, but the ability to make genuine poetry, rather than self-pitying complaint, out of such a moment testifies even more strongly to his 'vocation'.

The whole poem, in fact, is unusually cool in tone for Redgrove, portraying its protagonist with a distance approaching irony: a man whose senses fail him and who lives by reason, watching with 'reasonable curiosity' the vivid lives of birds, flowers and other people, he is an epitome of what Redgrove was later to call 'onlooker consciousness'. In a journal entry twenty years later he wrote that the poem held 'knowledge about me and about my situation with her'. He copied the poem out and beside these lines –

> And with reasonable curiosity he saw
> Crows fall from the sky, lilac tongues
> Of death in the square-cut hedge: such omens
> Were full of interest

– he wrote 'Netherne'. These lines perhaps evoke the apathetic state of mind to which he was reduced by the insulin coma therapy, and which may still have afflicted him. The poem concludes:

> At the end, as he would have wished, the Divine
> Fingers plucked him from his skin
> With much pain for both;
> For he was interested in his illness,
> And the world, strange to relate, had grown fond of him.

The young poet's debut, not unusually, enacts a desire for extreme experience: romantic enough, but in Redgrove's case distant and controlled in expression, so that in the half-century since its publication there has never been a problem about accepting it as an accomplished and adult poem. But the complete draft is dated May 1953, when he had been writing poetry constantly for the best part of a year. We shall return to the question when exactly the first draft was written, and whether it was literally his first poem, a little later.

Clearly the poem contained knowledge about himself, but what did he mean by saying there was also knowledge about his situation with Barbara? He wrote this note after their marriage, like the Collector, had failed, and we are entitled to be sceptical about such hindsight. Thinking about the poem in 1972, still wounded by the end of the marriage, he saw that what the poem desired was incompatible with the domestic life he and Barbara had tried to create. At the time he wrote it, however, and despite the 'failure', he surely felt that the woman he had just made love to and the poem she had inspired were parts of the same ecstatic new life.

His relationship with Barbara was another death blow to the youthful scientist: as he was to say later, 'Hormones ceased to interest me as I fell in love. To be a good scientist I would have had to hold the two kinds of knowledge apart, and I could not.' By the time Peter went up to Cambridge in October 1951, he and Barbara were engaged.

Queens' is one of the most picturesque colleges in Cambridge, a cluster of strongly contrasting buildings on either bank of the river Cam. It was founded in the fifteenth century, first by Margaret of Anjou, the wife of Henry VI, and refounded by her successor Elizabeth Woodville, queen of Edward IV: hence the position of the apostrophe, signifying two queens, a Cambridge shibboleth. The buildings date back to the original foundation, but Peter first had rooms in the Victorian Friars' Building, and later in the massive modern red-brick and rather ugly Fisher Building, across the river from the old college. From his ground-floor window in the Fisher Building he enjoyed peaceful views across meadows where horses grazed towards Newnham, then one of only two women's colleges. Queens' boasts two sites of particular interest to tourists. One is a wooden bridge that joins the two halves of the college across the Cam. This is known as 'Newton's Bridge' and 'the Mathematical Bridge'. In fact it was built in the eighteenth century, and Newton had nothing to do with it; its other name is based on the equally erroneous legend that it was constructed without the use of iron bolts and held together by geometrical calculation. 'Newton's Bridge' may have superficially appealed to the scientist in the young Redgrove. The older man, thinking about his college, is more likely to have been drawn to the memory of a remarkable sundial in Old Court. This dial is an extremely complex construction, which tells the days of the year as well as hours of the day; moreover, if you know the day of the lunar month, and the moon is shining, you can (not very accurately) tell the time at night. This would have had a strong imaginative appeal to the man who would later record the day of his partner's menstrual cycle in every entry in his journal. It may have inspired the clock that 'measures the lunations' in 'Rev. Uncle' (*WNP*). Across Silver Street from Queens' is the Anchor pub, which has an important place in the mythology of Cambridge poets of the early fifties.

Redgrove's own account of his Cambridge career is that he had no interest in his official scientific studies and spent his time instead writing poetry and attending lectures in the English Faculty. 'The science departments which I had joined were not places where one explored with a sense of wonder, but rather machines for producing limited knowledge in identical formats, which were known as degrees.' This was epitomised by a young American post-doctoral tutor 'draping his lanky figure on a bench and talking about a kind of chemistry that was competitive, not contemplative'. In fact it was precisely during Peter's time at Cambridge that one of the greatest scientific discoveries of the century was made there, in the Cavendish laboratories: Francis Crick and James Watson's deciphering of the structure of DNA. Who knows if Peter's attitude to science might have been different if he had been aware of this exciting work? But he was not aware of it: it was happening in a different world from undergraduate lectures. His attraction to English, and particularly to the teaching of F. R. Leavis, may partly have been attributable to the fact that Leavis did not believe in withholding his most developed thought even from first-year undergraduates, whom he regarded as members of a 'collaborative community'.

During his first year, however, Peter applied himself to his studies in an orthodox way. In correspondence with Jim he was already thinking about the courses he would take in his final year, balancing career prospects against his aptitude and inclination. For a scientist he was poor at maths, and after consultations with his supervisor, tutor and the University Appointments Board, and reading government careers booklets, he favoured biochemistry. However, the level of his enthusiasm for science at this stage is betrayed by the fact that he was gearing his options to an administrative rather than a research career. The background of this correspondence with Jim may be deduced from Peter's insistence that 'a man speaking solely from the angle of appointments and not personal happiness' stressed that a student should follow the subject he likes most. Jim was taking a close and possibly intrusive interest in Peter's studies, and the text of one of these letters is actually an 'extract' typed up by Jim himself, as if to be used as evidence. Peter thanks him for his help with suspicious effusiveness: 'I thank you from the bottom of my heart . . . there's nowhere [sic] I can stop thanking you.' He was attending lectures on the history of science as well as those required by his course and, in a more surprising conformity with Jim's inclinations, was going to meetings of the Cambridge Old Tauntonians.

The Cambridge Bachelor degree, or Tripos, is divided into two parts. Part One is usually taken after the second year and Part Two after the third. In order to proceed into the second year students have to pass a Preliminary exam. Peter took this and passed in the Second class. (The Second class was usually divided into Upper and Lower, but this division was dispensed with for the Natural Science Prelims.) This was a respectable result: in his year there were 78 Firsts, 222 Seconds, 186 Thirds, and 24 candidates who were required to resit papers. As the holder of a College Scholarship, however, he might have hoped for a First.

The first sign of Peter's decisive turn from science to poetry is a remarkable flurry of book purchases in the summer and autumn of that year. In July and August he bought Eliot's *Collected Poems*, *Four Quartets*, *Murder in the Cathedral* and *The Family Reunion*: with the sole exception of *The Cocktail Party*, this is Eliot's complete poetic and dramatic works up to 1952. Eliot was the presiding genius of Cambridge English at the time, as both poet and critic, but it would be an unusual English student who bought all of these books at the end of his first year. Peter bought them on different days, and one can trace here the growth of a passion, the young man devouring one volume and rushing out to buy another. During the same period he bought *The Oxford Book of Mystical Verse*, evidence that he may have felt a spiritual affinity with Eliot as well as poetic admiration. Barbara's parents had a holiday home at Selsey, a strange, isolated peninsula on the Sussex coast, and Redgrove later remembered reading *Four Quartets* there:

> Eliot was the first poet who made me feel I might write something like poetry. I remember reading 4 Quartets lying on a bed at Selsey, where my first wife had taken me to meet her parents – I often stayed there and it was a mystical place – the height of the sky, the sands, the beaches of pebble and their sounds. I was seeing correspondences between the small circular seashore umbellifers arranged in their circles, with Dante's Celestial Rose, and this mediated by the restless sight and sound of the place – indeed near Selsey where Blake saw the angels rising into the sky and heard the ploughboy say 'Father, the gate is open' from the cottage at Felpham. But I couldn't understand Blake, really, while Eliot seemed luminous and clear with his pool filled with water out of sunlight, the movement of darkness upon darkness, the white light still and moving. I have the copy of Four Quartets by me, marked with Langland-like stresses . . . and

when I bought the book marked on the flyleaf 22-7-52. All came together in a place like Four Quartets 'Now the light falls / Across the open field' and the seashore chapel far out among the fields and on the edge of the sea. It was one of the places where the scales dropped away, and 4 Quartets was its book.

The 'seashore chapel far out among the fields' was at Church Norton, on Pagham Harbour a mile or two north of Selsey, where in September 1952 Peter walked with Barbara and on the way back began to compose these Eliotic lines:

> Rain whose drops with the sunlight
> Filled the air
> Seep beneath the surface, sudden quiet and green.
> Into life from sunlight not refracted beams.
> In love, the pattern of the self
> Its opposing cells of self-regard, lust
> Coalesce become aware of more than one

He recounts another epiphanic experience in a Cambridge bookshop, looking for a scientific textbook, but preferring the smell, feel and look of the poetry books, 'anthologies that felt better between the fingers, contained more irregular and exciting structures of type, and whose ink smelt better'. He picked up the first volume of the Auden and Pearson anthology, *Poets of the English Language*, and read the first lines, Langland's 'In a somer seson when softe was the sonne . . .' His 'hair stood on end' and his 'skin felt sunny' inside his clothes. He 'bought the first volume (being short of money) and then could not resist the whole five'. He did indeed buy the Auden and Pearson anthology, in October, back in Cambridge for his second year, but his account of the naive young scientist lured to poetry books by their sensory appeal is a transparent piece of mythologising. This was a young man who had read the whole of Eliot, eager for more poetry. It is really interesting, however, that Eliot leads him back to Langland. Throughout his career he espoused the alliterative metrical tradition of English poetry, exemplified by Langland, and subtly transformed by Eliot in *Four Quartets*, against the more courtly iambic tradition inaugurated by Chaucer. (Note the 'Langland-like stresses' that he marked in his copy of *Four Quartets*.) Near the end of his life he incorporated a modernised version of lines from Langland in an elegy for the Cornish tin-mining industry.

Several of the poetry books that Peter bought in the summer and autumn of 1952 are inscribed 'Peter and Barbara Redgrove', in the hands of both of them, though they were not to marry till 1954. His retrospective account of his first marriage portrays himself as the victim of 'tribal values', brainwashed into marrying the first woman he slept with. Inscribing himself and Barbara as a married couple in the books that symbolised his new direction in life suggests that at the time he enthusiastically embraced the married state, and felt no conflict with his poetic aspirations. At some stage during his student career Barbara came to live in Cambridge, lodging with the artist Cecil Collins. Having acquired a secretarial qualification at her father's insistence, she got a job at Pye Telecommunications, which at that time was one of the few large employers in Cambridge outside the university. The poet Harry Guest, who became friends with Peter in their second year, was confident that he and Barbara were lovers, and she was 'a fixture', though the university regulations would not have allowed them to live together. Guest recalls them as being enormously affectionate. This relationship partly accounted for his feeling that Redgrove was more mature, more adult than himself, and certainly not a 'fractured soul': evidently Peter did not confide in his new friends about his psychiatric history. To Guest, Peter was an entertaining and stimulating friend with a lovely sense of humour. Certainly the relationship with Barbara exempted Peter from one of the most neurotic aspects of Cambridge University life at that time: the grotesque gender imbalance in the student body. As another student poet whom Peter knew, Daniel Huws, put it, to most male Cambridge undergraduates women were 'exotics'. Redgrove's freedom from this artificially induced othering of women may be a further reason, in addition to his closeness to his mother, for his strong sympathetic identification with the opposite sex. But he paid a price for this advantage. His fellow students, especially those with literary aspirations, had open futures, and their dreams ranged widely. Ted Hughes, for example, dreamed of emigrating to Australia and living a free life there. It is hard to imagine Hughes seeking advice from the Appointments Board. Indeed, it would have been unusual for any student so assiduously to gather information about careers in his first year. But Peter had a pressing motive, which he made clear when he thanked his father for his help because of the difference it will make to 'the sort of home Barbara and I are going to have'. Bourgeois domesticity squatted on his horizon.

When exactly did Peter start writing poetry? Unfortunately that early draft of 'The Collector' is undated, but he did put dates on most of his early drafts, which he kept assiduously, even of poems that remained unpublished. The earliest dated poem is an excessively long and laboured allegory called 'Venusberg', in which the speaker complains that nobody will visit his castle. Most of the poem is an uninspired description of the attractive furnishings of the castle, but there is some interest in the conclusion, where he explains that he is shunned because of his 'friends' who share the castle with him:

> Upright in their boxes, the skin fallen in
>   They would crackle like parchment to touch them
> Little dark spiders the eyes in their caves
>   But seeming to stare all the same.
>
> Alas, yes I know, I can't let them go
>   This furniture here of my castle.
> They don't like my friends, that's what it is
>   Why nobody comes to my castle.

The hidden, despised other who inhabits the self will haunt Redgrove throughout his life, and is the most pressing personal motive that drives him to write poetry. It is enough to show us that 'Venusberg' is not an empty exercise. The personal significance is more explicit in a poem he wrote a year or two later:

> When mists come whirling, and the adders creep
> Barbara comes twirling, swirl-shedding light;
> My dusty house, to my brooms I leap –
> And quickly sweep the bodies out of sight.

Peter wrote 'Venusberg' in 1951 – before or shortly after his arrival in Cambridge. But there is no evidence that he wrote anything else until the following summer – the summer in which he discovered Eliot. In July he wrote an accomplished pastiche of a metaphysical poem, 'To His Mistress's Bladder', and from September onwards he was writing prolifically. It seems likely therefore that the momentous simultaneous launch of his sexual life and his poetic vocation happened during this summer, and that 'Caught in a fold of the living hills, he failed' was not literally his first line of poetry, but the first that answered his deepest need, the 'coming together of bodily happenings and mental happenings'. To complicate matters further, in one of his last published poems ('Mementoes', *FVC*) he writes that his first line of poetry was inspired by the river at Kingston, and was 'Rolling habitat of such white ghosts as cold Ophelia', the opening line of the unpublished 'Lethe', first drafted on 8 August 1952.

He was still interested enough in scientific study to write poems about it. That autumn he wrote one on 'The Anatomy Lecture' and another, 'The Laboratory', where he even found beauty:

> And here there is a beauty
> In 'Imagination's other place'.
> A virility of thought.
> An economy of operation.

He had found the phrase 'Imagination's other place' in a review of James Kirkup's second collection, *A Correct Compassion*. Kirkup was in his early thirties and establishing his reputation: he was currently the first Gregory Fellow in poetry at the University of Leeds. The review quoted only four lines from the title poem, which was inspired by observing a surgical operation. Peter was so 'deeply moved' by these lines that he wrote to Kirkup, despite not apparently having read anything else by him, to ask permission to use the phrase 'imagination's other place', which was 'particularly evocative' for him, in a poem of his own which he hoped would eventually be published. Kirkup replied asking to see his poem, and Peter responded with a coy preamble that 'to send a poem, unfinished as mine is, to a person of your distinction is to invite disaster', but nevertheless enclosed a draft. By now he had heard Kirkup's sequence 'A Company of Fools' on the radio and was able to say, 'I hope I may one day write something half as fine.' It is difficult to tell if this correspondence shows the naive impulse of a tyro poet or a calculated attempt to draw attention to himself.

Shortly after this, in November, Peter read an advertisement in the student newspaper, *Varsity*: 'Undergraduates interested in private poetry readings contact "Gerrard", 31, Kimberley Road'. Whoever 'Gerrard' was, the advert had been placed by a group of English students at Downing College: Tony Davis, Neil Morris and Philip Hobsbaum. They were students of F. R. Leavis, in revolt against the 'elocutionary golden voice kind of speaking' then in fashion. The leading spirit was Philip Hobsbaum, then in his first term at Cambridge. Hobsbaum was six months younger than Redgrove, and like him had not done National Service: in his case, he failed the medical examination because of poor eyesight. He had grown up in Bradford, worked as a clerk in West Yorkshire after leaving school, sneaked into the Leeds University lectures of G. Wilson Knight (later a very important figure for Redgrove) and written some 2,000 poems before going to Cambridge.

Peter turned up with a friend from Queens', Rodney Banister, a Lancastrian who had taken a First in Part One English. In his own recollection he is greeted by 'a bearded man in a fine dark woollen double-breasted suit emerging with a cane polished like dark fire in his hand and an interested smile' (the beard, like his mother's blonde hair, is probably a back-projection) and introduces himself diffidently: 'I'm just a scientist and I need something else. The chemists are so cold in Cambridge.' Hobsbaum welcomes him, saying a scientist is just what they need. Redgrove calls this meeting his 'salvation', and he makes it clear that the crucial factor was Philip Hobsbaum's personal character. He could be prickly and dogmatic – he later had a long estrangement from Redgrove and an even longer one from another member of what was to become known as 'the Group', Alan Brownjohn – but Redgrove's memories are entirely of his intellectual generosity:

> All the Cambridge people I had met so far were competitive, no more – adversarial, as though their minds were so small there was only room for conflict and refutation; scepticism it was not, it was a habit of incredulity: only room for one person, ego. Hobsbaum's mind was not thrown into disorder by the presence of another. It had room for all of us, and all that he had read too, which was everything in the canon. But for him it was fresh and curious all the time.

Despite his diffidence, Peter made a strong impression on Philip, who thought he 'bore a resemblance to Frankenstein's monster, only better dressed', with a 'well-bred voice' that was 'at variance with his threatening appearance'. One vivid anecdote of Hobsbaum's suggests that Peter had already developed the humorous courtliness that was to be such a feature of his personal manner in later years: 'He said in comfortably middle-class tones, "Thank you, my foot is quite warm now", signalling that I had inadvertently placed my brief-case on his toes.' Somebody chose to read Henry King's 'Exequy' from Herbert Grierson's anthology *Metaphysical Lyrics and Poems*, and Peter said, 'You will find "The Exequy" on page 203.' 'Who was this person,' Philip wondered, 'who appeared to know the page numbers of every poem in the English language?' It was recently acquired knowledge: he had bought Grierson's anthology a few weeks earlier, on 2 October.

If Hobsbaum's group had remained a poetry-reading circle, it would not have played a very important role in Peter's life. Soon, however, it progressed to the discussion of new poetry (Hobsbaum recollects discussing Thom Gunn's 'Carnal Knowledge' which he thought 'a callow piece of posturing', but which Redgrove and Banister defended) and to 'the active production of creative work'. From the start, on the recommendation of Leavis's colleague H. A. Mason, Hobsbaum instituted a key 'Group' practice by typing the poems for discussion on his Remington 10 machine, which he proudly recalled could do 'eight to ten copies at one go', and circulating them in advance. The other well-known poets associated with the Group, such as Peter Porter, Martin Bell, Alan Brownjohn, George MacBeth and Edward Lucie-Smith, did not join until after it was resurrected in London in 1955, but there were some future academics at these meetings, notably Roma Gill, who was to become a leading authority on Marlowe. Redgrove was according to Hobsbaum the dominant figure, 'already prolific as a writer and correspondingly earnest in discussion'. But for Peter it was Philip himself who was the guiding spirit in these discussions. He disliked the word 'genius', but he made an exception for Hobsbaum's qualities as a teacher: 'that genius as a teacher that welcomes people on their own terms'. 'He could see that people spoke better than they knew.'

Hobsbaum's teacher F. R. Leavis was the dominant intellectual force of Cambridge English at that time (I. A. Richards and William Empson both having left for foreign parts) though never an institutional power. Leavis, then as always, was a controversial and divisive figure: Harry Guest thought his influence was evil, while Hobsbaum considered him, with Hugh McDiarmid, one of the two greatest men he had met. Leavis's core values are best described in his own words, in a retrospective essay about his magazine, *Scrutiny*, which ceased publication while Redgrove was at Cambridge:

> We recognised . . . that like the culture it represented [English Literature] must, in so far as living and real, have its life in the present – and that life is growth. That is, we were concerned for conservation and continuity, but were radically anti-academic. We were concerned

to promote that which the academic mind, in the 'humanities', hates: the creative interplay of real judgements – genuine personal judgements, that is, of engaged minds fully alive in the present.

Leavis took poetry seriously, believed in the creative importance of criticism, and that judgements about literature are inseparable from judgements about life. Redgrove was sympathetic to these core values: later he expressed to Hobsbaum his dislike for the phrase, 'It's all a matter of taste', which he called 'my father's favourite saying when he wants to make me prickle, upon which I accuse him of an intolerable blasphemous heresy – the heresy of saying that nothing is more excellent than any other thing'. The Leavis circle also provided him with a temperamental equilibrium between what he prejudicially called the 'scientific moles', only interested in getting a good degree, and the *jeunesse dorée* of the arts men, concerned with 'cutting a figure'. He greatly appreciated, as a 'barbarous scientist', being able to attend Leavis's lectures and join a tutorial group at H. A. Mason's house. From one of these lectures he noted:

> Realisation attained by unconscious recognition of image. Images in such realisation need not be *clear*. What is needed is an organised body of experience. Imagism was a reaction against Georgianism but the only images that matter are those which come after the poet has been stirred. Images cannot be calculated, it is the 'trap'.

He responded to the Leavis who was dedicated to exploring the nature of creativity – enough for him to have preserved these notes. Leavis's words undoubtedly appealed to a poet of Redgrove's temperament, who later wrote of the 'important unconscious component' in poetic creation, and devised a working method to enhance his access to it. But he never became a devotee of Leavis, who he felt 'was trying to steer one into something of his own temperament'. He preferred critics such as E. M. W. Tillyard, Muriel Bradbrook and (especially) A. P. Rossiter, who he thought 'wrote as scientists write, but better'.

A great paradox of Leavis's career is that despite his radical commitment to creativity he took no interest in new writing after *Four Quartets*. Another friend of Redgrove's, the Barbadian poet Kamau (then 'Eddie') Brathwaite, looked up to Leavis as a critical idol, but when he showed the great man examples of writing by Caribbean contemporaries such as Derek Walcott, George Lamming and Wilson Harris, Leavis dismissed them as 'not *"realized"*'. Ted Hughes had an extreme and idiosyncratic aversion to all forms of literary criticism, which led him to give up English after Part One and change to archaeology and anthropology, but there is some justice in his allegation that Cambridge English 'separated the spirit of surgery & objective analysis from the spirit of husbandry & sympathetic coaching', at least as far as new writers were concerned. Hobsbaum himself stopped writing poetry when he got to Cambridge, but he attributed this less to Leavis's influence than to his fellow-students, 'who felt that if you couldn't write *King Lear* next Tuesday, there was no point in writing at all'. Peter's great stroke of luck was that in Philip the Leavisian values *were* combined with 'husbandry and sympathetic coaching'.

As the Thom Gunn incident shows, Peter did not defer to his new mentor's judgement. A more important case is Dylan Thomas. Hobsbaum has an amusing narrative of Thomas's visit to Cambridge, when they were so disappointed by the appearance of the 'scruffy wee man' that Redgrove exclaimed, 'No, that cannot be Dylan Thomas.' Hobsbaum shared Leavis's low estimate of Thomas's poetry, and there is a certain *Schadenfreude* in his account. Redgrove's recollection of the same event is that Thomas was indeed an 'ugly puffy fatso', but in later years, 'This memory from my student days kept visionary poetry alive for me and kept me alive too.' Hobsbaum would also not have approved of Peter visiting the legendary George 'Dadie' Rylands for verse-speaking lessons, which may perhaps have been inspired by emulation of Thomas's orotund performance. He was such an adept pupil that he won the Rylands prize for reciting verse. Rylands epitomised the Cambridge establishment that Leavis loathed: he had been a member of the exclusive 'Apostles' and, as a beautiful young man, had been cultivated by the Bloomsbury Group, especially Lytton Strachey. He was also an important influence on generations of Cambridge actors and directors, including John Barton, Peter Hall, Derek Jacobi, Ian McKellen, Trevor Nunn, and Michael and Corin Redgrave. Here Peter was at least flirting with the world of the '*jeunesse dorée*'. He had a notably beautiful, resonant and, as Hobsbaum reported, 'well-bred' voice, but his manner of reading poetry was not to everybody's taste. I have heard it described as actorish and even 'vicar-like'. Peter Porter was impressed by his powerful delivery but thought his voice 'almost ludicrously posh' for someone from a middle-class background.

There were readings by other poets of whom Hobsbaum would not have approved, such as Vernon Watkins and George Barker, and it was at one of these that Peter met Harry Guest. Guest remembers their staying up till two in the morning with Barker in Robert Gottlieb's kitchen, Barker sitting on the kitchen table drinking, radiating uncondescending charm to the company of undergraduates. Guest knew Hobsbaum and recognised that he was an influential figure, but did not attend the Group meetings. He got on amicably with him but kept him at arm's length as a Leavisite, which Harry himself was not. Peter was soon having parallel, equally intense but quite different discussions of poetry with Harry. Between these two there was no mutual criticism: Harry was surprised by the critical atmosphere of the Group and would not himself have welcomed it. Meeting Peter in his second year at Cambridge it was obvious to Harry that he was 'not just a temporary undergraduate poet' but 'dedicated for life'. He was deeply impressed by everything that Peter showed him. He also provides first-hand witness of Peter's disenchantment with science: he was utterly contemptuous of the syllabus, and claimed never to attend a lecture or contact his tutor (though the poems 'The Anatomy Lecture' and 'Laboratory' indicate that there may have been some posturing here). Harry was reading modern languages and introduced Peter to French poetry, especially Racine and Mallarmé, which Peter asked him to recite into his tape recorder. This was the first tape recorder Harry had seen, 'a cumbersome wooden object very heavy to move'. Peter followed Jim in his enthusiasm for new technology. They also read their own poetry into the recorder, and Guest particularly remembered and admired 'Guardian', which Redgrove published in his final year at university but never collected. His recollections suggest that Peter was not as averse to 'cutting a figure' as he later claimed, and was not without his own undergraduate affectation. He remembers that Peter carried a swordstick with him everywhere. They went together to a talk by David Piper, then assistant keeper at the National Portrait Gallery, later to be its director. Peter became involved in an altercation with Piper, and as they left the building said, 'Don't worry, Harry, I had my swordstick at the ready.'

Guest was engaged in starting a new poetry magazine, *Chequer*, with a group of fellow-students including Karl Miller, later to be an influential literary editor and founding editor of the *London Review of Books*; Ronald Hayman, the future biographer and playwright; and Michael Bakewell, who was to be Head of Plays at the BBC and a distinguished radio drama director. Over the next couple of years *Chequer* was to be one of the first magazines to publish Ted Hughes and Peter himself. Nevertheless, Rodney Banister suggested to Peter that they start a poetry magazine of their own. Peter admired Rodney for his 'great style and . . . immediate clarity of thought, which was taken to be a sign of absolute intelligence at that time', and was flattered to be asked. They called the magazine *Delta*. Jim was anxious about this venture; Peter wrote reassuring him that he would not get too deeply involved financially and, more revealingly, about the character of contemporary poets:

> Now it seems the artist has found his niche in society. He usually does something else besides write – has to – starving in a garret is no longer a meaningful gesture – and he now believes that he must have something valuable to write about besides himself. There are no esoteric cults or crusades – Sitwell is out. Nobody sleeps between black sheets and nobody says Black Mass – not even at Oxford.

Evidently Jim thought poets were self-absorbed and decadent. Peter goes on, attempting to meet his father on his own ground, to say that a poet is not unlike a journalist. He is skating on thin ice here, as his subsequent attempts to combine the vocation of a poet with more commercial kinds of writing will reveal.

The conception and launching of *Delta* are recorded in an article Rodney Banister published at the time on the 'Undergraduate Page' of the *Spectator*, in which this piece of literary history is lacquered with heavy layers of undergraduate facetiousness. Banister describes Peter as 'in his Disraeli period, and a virulent Royalist'. If true, this is an intriguing parallel with Peter's future Cambridge friend Ted Hughes, who at about the same time (the Coronation was in June of this year) wrote a dialogue between Elizabeth I and II, in which the old queen mocks the new one for her diminished role. Banister represents the venture as an attempt to 'become capitalists', which sits uneasily with what he calls 'our avowed aim . . . to destroy the clique, to become catholic, to print all that superior poetry no one knew about, but which was only waiting for an enlightened editor'. Despite the facetious tone he does provide useful information about the economics of magazine publication. A print run of 1,000 cost £25; selling the run at sixpence a copy would cover costs, and advertisements at £5 for a full page represented profit. They sold the magazine by the usual Cambridge method of hawking it in the street and around colleges, and persuading bookshops to sell it without profit. Banister also records a mysterious episode in which Peter took him to 'fix the London end' at a 'kind of Poets' Pub moored in the Thames', but the details of this are swamped by whimsy. They only sold two half-page adverts, to the Cambridge bookseller Heffers and the Arts Council, at £2.15s each, but managed to sell the whole print run, so were not out of pocket.

Surprisingly there were no poems by either Redgrove or Banister in this first issue. Peter had not yet published at all, but Banister (who was a year his senior) was well enough regarded to be included in Thom Gunn's *Cambridge Poets 1951–1952* anthology later that year. Nor was there an editorial. Banister says that they originally composed a 'slashing editorial', at a time when they planned to call the magazine *Tonic*, along the lines of acting as a tonic for Cambridge writing. They abandoned it partly because it would add to the cost. Banister and Redgrove 'made pilgrimages to men reclusing near Cherry Hinton, to unfashionable men who did not believe in "form"', but reinforced the magazine 'by harrying the Old Gang and by begging a contribution from a distinguished elder poet'. Peter had capitalised on his correspondence with James Kirkup, the 'distin-guished elder', who contributed one of his most popular early pieces, 'Summertime at Leeds', reprinted in his 1954 collection *The Spring Journey*. The most obvious representative of the 'Old Gang' was Thom Gunn, the undisputed star of Cambridge poetry at that time, whose first collection, *Fighting Terms,* was to appear the following year. Gunn contributed 'Here Come the Saints', which he included in *Fighting Terms,* and 'Hide and Seek', which remained uncollected. Redgrove later said that he admired Gunn's poetry 'from a distance'. In person he thought the rising poet (four years older than himself) had 'a dark sort of sexiness which was pleasantly disreputable', and Gunn's 'pock-marked porcelain-pallid face like coral' reminded him of a Chandler gangster. This appearance contrasted piquantly with his 'exquisitely polite' manners and 'smile of great sweetness'.

Philip Hobsbaum thought the first *Delta* contained little but the 'Old Gang' and dismissed it as 'a huge disappointment' which 'did little except follow the existing fashions in Cambridge'. Indeed, Banister's claim about destroying the clique must have been tongue-in-cheek, since all but one of the student poets – Alasdair Aston, L. E. (Kamau) Brathwaite, Norman Buller, Frederick Grubb, Thom

Gunn, P. J. Head and John Mander – were also published in one or other of the *Cambridge Poets* volumes. The sole exception was Claire Delavenay, who nevertheless figured with Gunn, Peter Hall, Karl Miller, Judi Dench, Ronald Bryden and others as a star of the 'metropolitan centre' of Cambridge life according to Daniel Huws. The group to which Huws and his friend Ted Hughes belonged gathered at the Anchor pub and observed the 'metropolitan' set with a sense of upholding 'unpretentious provincial values'. Delavenay soon decided that she was not a poet, despite which Peter was to recall her poems in his journal forty years later. She was to achieve greater distinction as the biographer Claire Tomalin.

The most intriguing figure among the contributors to the first *Delta* is Brathwaite, who was later to become, with Derek Walcott, one of the two most celebrated anglophone Caribbean poets and the champion (in opposition to Walcott) of an African-centred conception of Caribbean cultural identity, expressed in what he called 'Nation Language'. Brathwaite had published in Frank Collymore's Caribbean magazine *Bim* in 1950, the year he went up to Cambridge, but felt 'culturally marooned' there and would have been surprised to be considered an instance of 'the existing fashions' at the university. He contributed his important early poem 'The Day the First Snow Fell', which he later said symbolised the 'pain & separation & Xile loneliness (my first Christmas away from home) . . . & the Xpression of the stark (black/white) racial prejudice I was Xperiencing in . . . literary Cambridge'. He called the poem a 'suicide note'. However, he considered that the 'one original' among the Cambridge poets of his time was 'my friend Peter Redgrove', who encouraged him to experiment with what he called 'a prose-style technique', helping him in his resistance to the formalism of what was soon to be called Movement poetry. He later visited Redgrove in Falmouth, to give a reading at the art college, and his continued warmth of feeling towards his university friend is marked by the dedication to Redgrove of his poem 'Letter from Roma'. It is a sign of how rapidly Peter developed in accomplishment and authority during his years at university that a poet such as Brathwaite, two years older than himself, who was publishing before Peter began to write, and from such a different cultural background, should have cited him as an early influence.

By the time the first *Delta* was published, at the beginning of May, Peter had abandoned any serious attempt to study for his degree, and over the Easter vacation he had confided to Jim his fears that he would fail the Part One examination. He told his father that he thought the insulin therapy had diminished his enthusiasm and aptitude for science. On his return to Cambridge he also went to see Dr McCullagh, who took a sympathetic approach, referred him to the college doctor, and assured Jim that, in the event of Peter being unfit to take the exam, he would apply to Senate for the maximum possible allowance in respect of illness. The doctor thought that he might be starting a schizophrenic episode. As we have seen, Harry Guest, who got to know Peter well during his second year, saw no signs of psychological disturbance. It may be that the severity of his earlier collapse enabled him to pass off his disinclination for scientific study to his father, the college authorities and the doctor as a recurrence of his illness. Jim wrote to Dr Dalberg at Netherne about the concern that Peter's mental state was causing, and expressed his distress at the thought of a relapse, a possibility that the medical staff at Netherne had warned him of. On 4 May Jim spoke to Dalberg, who told him that Peter might have to undergo electro-convulsive therapy, but should be kept away from hospital unless diagnosed as actually psychotic. Dalberg thought that Barbara was good for Peter 'but must be told of illness. Just as well to wait year', which raises the questions of how long it was before Barbara was told of Peter's psychiatric history, and how they could have reached the stage of considering themselves effectively married, if she had been kept ignorant. Dalberg warned Jim and Nan not to let Peter think they were worried, or that he was under surveillance. McCullagh also wrote to Dalberg, in terms that suggest he was unaware of the true state of Peter's studies, describing him as 'academically an extremely promising young man, who, on his present showing, ought to be placed either in the First Class or high up in the Second Class in Part I'.

Whether Peter was really suffering a relapse, or faking it, his university record card shows that he was absent from the Part One examination in 1953. McCullagh told Jim that a return to residence would depend on a satisfactory medical report in September. Despite these difficulties, Jim and Nan accompanied Peter and Barbara to the May Ball, an event which Jim commemorated by cutting out a photo and facetious report from the *News Chronicle*.

If Peter had suffered a breakdown in the summer term it did not stop him from taking what must have been almost the perfect vacation job, as editorial clerk with the *Times Literary Supplement*. Here he made the acquaintance of the distinguished poet Edmund Blunden, who was working as assistant editor before taking up the Chair of English at the University of Hong Kong in September. He felt agonies of envy seeing the acceptance slips for poems in the office. He was ambitious enough to want to publish his first poem in a national journal, not a student magazine, and vain enough to find it 'insufferable' to be asked where he had published and have no answer. He offered some poems to Blunden, who accepted one, and it appeared in the *TLS* on 16 October. The *TLS* did not publish poems every week, and when it did there were never more than two. Poets published in immediately preceding issues included such established names as John Betjeman, Roy Campbell, Robert Graves, James Kirkup and Vita Sackville-West. There were newcomers such as D. J. Enright and Adrienne Rich, but even they were far more advanced than Peter. For a twenty-one-year-old who had been writing poetry for little more than a year this was a remarkable debut. Redgrove himself later described the poem as 'very crypto-erotic'.

Notturno

While the dark-blooded mermaid sang
like sea stiff roses in the crowded room
tanned shadows held in silent mirrors
turned on each other for acceptance.

Across the tawny beach they strung
their salt blood on the pacing
loom in darkness
the dark water striding in
tall silence moved
from thigh to thigh scooping up

the night like clouds while the divine
assault of the sea reached on
to pull and wrinkle in the clear
tube of dusk, cry
fly through rest and sink
a vein in dying amber.

Wounded the tree sang drops
for love and left the warmth to die.

From its precious Italian title to its inflated rhetoric – 'the divine/

assault of the sea' – it is almost uniquely unrecognisable as a Redgrove poem. Edmund Blunden is to be congratulated for seeing promise in it – perhaps the 'sea stiff roses' are the most notable instance. It is telling, however, that in both his first two published poems Redgrove picks up motifs from what was then the first known poem of his great example Eliot. Prufrock has 'heard the mermaids singing, each to each' but does not think that they will 'sing to me'. Redgrove feels no self-conscious inadequacy to the eroticism and creativity that the mermaids represent, just as, in his much better second published poem, he does not, like Prufrock, hesitate to say, 'I am Lazarus, come from the dead'. His connection with the *TLS* ensured a review of *Delta* (blandly favourable with no poets specified) and to his being commissioned to write reviews himself. His critiques of collections by Elizabeth Jennings, Lucien Stryk and others are firm and judicious, and his rebuke to one poet for lack of 'realisation' shows Leavis's influence, but his review of Thom Gunn's anthology *Cambridge Poets 1951–1952* is a banal and constipated performance ('while only some of the verse in this volume stands out by reason of its quality as poetry, all of it is pleasant to read'), suggesting that he was anxious about offending his contemporaries.

Peter satisfied the medical authorities and was allowed to take up residence again for his third year. He was now, however, completely devoted to poetry. Towards the end of the summer, on the strength of his success at the *TLS*, he asked to see Dr McCullagh about transferring to English in his final year. The Tripos is designed to allow students to change subject for Part Two but – whether because he had not completed Part One or because this change was considered too extreme – his request was refused. He saw Dr Dalberg again in October. She reported to McCullagh that he was 'somewhat vague and unrealistic' but much improved since his discharge from Netherne. There was no active psychosis and she felt it would be 'a terrible blow' if he were not allowed to return to Cambridge. He maintained that he could concentrate well, and that 'he would have mainly to revise for the tripos', having now agreed to continue with science. The strong likelihood is that he succeeded in deceiving both academic and medical authorities about his intentions, and was desperate to stay at Cambridge for the literary life.

In the autumn term of 1953 he followed up his *TLS* triumph with 'Lazarus and the Sea', 'Phlebas the Phoenician' and 'Lie' in the third and fourth issues of *Chequer*, now edited by Ronald Hayman. The idea of Lazarus resisting rebirth may have been suggested by Thom Gunn's 'Lazarus Not Raised' (which Redgrove had read in *Cambridge Poets 1951–52*) but Redgrove owes nothing else to this poem, which is an example of Gunn's brittle formalist early manner ('The scheduled miracle did not take place'). Much more important is Eliot: Redgrove takes on his early inspiration by narrating the Bible story from an unorthodox angle (compare 'Journey of the Magi'), echoing 'Prufrock' ('a soft argument / Of such measured insistence'; 'a tedious argument / Of insidious intent'), indeed boldly doing what Prufrock hesitated to do: 'Would it have been worth while . . . / To say: "I am Lazarus, come from the dead, / Come back to tell you all, I shall tell you all."' Peter draws both on his experience of insulin coma therapy, and on his transgressive sexual obsessions, to create a completely achieved work that is not dependent for its effect on any knowledge of its personal origins.

'Phlebas the Phoenician' declares its allegiance to Eliot in its title, and shares a phrase, 'holy simplicity', with 'Lazarus and the Sea'. Redgrove experimented with a six-part version of 'Lazarus', which incorporated 'Phlebas', 'Notturno' and 'Lethe', and the importance to him of the phrase 'holy simplicity' almost certainly comes from the world of his 'Game', rejecting the patriarchal social persona and immersing himself in the 'mother-world' of nature. This poem is not as authoritatively achieved as its companion, but it announces Redgrove's promise in the way it combines what he later called 'the strength of the sentence' with a vivid imaging of the relationship between human and natural worlds:

> Her cold lips lying on the shore, the beat
> Of her heart against that ribbed and inverted chest
> That brave men launch on her icy motherhood.

The sea is a central motif in these two poems and in 'Notturno', recalling the profound effect of Selsey on Redgrove, and his association of that place with Eliot. His fourth published poem, 'Lie', treats sexual relations in a way that anticipates poems of Ted Hughes such as 'The Dove Breeder' and 'Parlour-Piece', but with an assurance Hughes himself had not achieved by this stage:

> He showed her the butcher's where blood painted
> partly canvas aprons. A white slab grinned
> at them, a saw spat, thin knives in ranks

climbed out above the counter. How skeleton
met like stained teeth in the meat; red jelly
writing insubstantial lives on creamy bone.

This may be one poem that gives us a glimpse of anxiety about his relationship with Barbara. The protagonist makes these melodramatic gestures because 'The beauty was not comfortable / . . . He knew his love / As slender as a willow, as white as milk / Would fall, oh, fall into the moulds they made for her.' The protagonist himself however 'feared freedom' so 'comforted her with his own person, / From womb to womb.' This suggests that sexual intimacy is a retreat from his fear both of her susceptibility to convention and of the freedom that is its opposite. The poem concludes, 'The chief concern, the comfort, was assured.' Like a number of early poems that approach their protagonist with an ambivalent sympathy this ending is dubiously reassuring: another example is 'The Collector', which ends: 'the world, strange to relate, had grown fond of him'.

The second issue of *Delta* did not appear for nearly a year after the first, in the spring term of 1954. Rodney Banister had graduated and Peter's co-editor for this issue was one Miles Atterton. He may already have recognised that 'Lazarus and the Sea' was exceptional, because he published it again in *Delta*, along with another poem 'Dr Immanuel Rath'. Redgrove was a lifelong filmgoer – he went twice to Powell and Pressburger's *Tales of Hoffmann* in his first year at Cambridge with his Tauntonian friend John Ryland. This poem takes its subject from an earlier cinematic masterpiece, Josef von Sternberg's *The Blue Angel* (1930). Immanuel Rath, an old-fashioned, scholarly and repressed schoolmaster, unforgettably portrayed by Emil Jannings, tries to rescue his pupils from the decadent seductions of the eponymous nightclub by visiting the place himself; he becomes ensnared by the erotic but coldly manipulative singer/dancer Lola-Lola, even more unforgettably played by Marlene Dietrich, loses his job and sinks into a life of humiliating degradation.

As 'Lazarus and the Sea', 'Lie', 'The Collector' and this poem show, Redgrove was already beginning to master the ability to create poetic personae at a variety of angles to his personal preoccupations, anticipating later masterpieces such as 'The Widower', 'The Case' and 'The Haunted Armchair'. The repressed middle-aged bachelor

Rath, 'slow in the flesh', is very different from the young student already sleeping with his future wife, but there is a sign of identification in Redgrove's emphasis on his persona's obsessiveness: 'his life / Consolidated by small ceremonies. Time to make sure / Of a sufficient amount of sugar in his tea, his canary fed, / Of the small pocket notebook carrying his list of daily requirements.' The first stanza seems to be settling for an easy shot at an easy target, but the poem – which presupposes a knowledge of the film, and only hints at Rath's downfall – shifts into a surprising celebration of the scholar's celibate existence: he is 'fresh as a schoolboy', 'bred his applications in the warmth he made' and 'weigh[s] his teaching in a golden scale'. But the main surprise is reserved for the final line:

> And before this angel came to spoil
> His breviary, and to crack his seal,
> He loved his words, no woman flowered for him,
> Sheer multiplicity chuckled in his loins.

The suggestion of sterility in the penultimate line is cancelled by the last, especially the word 'chuckled', an early example of Redgrove's facility for vigorous, idiomatic and bodily suggestive diction. The flowering of a woman may (it is implied) be one kind of fulfilment but it may also (as in the case of 'this angel') be a destructive entrapment. 'Chuckled' implies a joyful sublimation rather than rigid repression, and may allude by contrast to the terrible scenes in the film where Rath, enslaved by his desire for Lola-Lola, dresses as a cockerel and crows, first as a comedy act and then as a ghastly outcry of despair. For some reason Redgrove never collected this superb poem, though he liked it enough to be thinking about including it in his fourth collection, *The Force*, thirteen years later.

The second *Delta* also carries a reproduction of a pencil and wash drawing by Barbara Sherlock titled 'The Good Listener'. Significantly this is a female figure, in modernist-inflected but representational style, perhaps influenced by African art, standing on sturdy legs, with pronounced abdomen, small breasts and flattened head with slightly African features, tilted back. Despite the stylisation, the figure gives an impression of intelligence. This is perhaps the one comment we have from Barbara about what it was like to be a woman in the company of undergraduate poets, but it is also a sign that, in these early years, they shared an artistic partnership: Peter wrote a poem with the same title, though we don't know who was responding to whom. In another case, Peter's poem 'The Dance', he is explicitly inspired by Barbara's sculpture, and 'For a Sculptor's Birthday' is a tribute to her art.

Peter published another poem in *Chequer* this term: 'Basilisk' which, though he omitted it from *The Collector*, he included as the second part of 'More Leaves From My Bestiary' in his second volume, *The Nature of Cold Weather*. This poem is at one level a blow against the scientists whom he was more materially defying by neglecting his studies, concerning as it does an 'idle naturalist' who dissects the apparently dead 'fabled bird' only to be struck dead when the light catches it. However, the poem is memorable not for this rather tired motif but for the controlled grotesquerie with which Redgrove evokes the beauty, horror and fearsomeness of the legendary creature:

> Rising above the fringe of silvering leaves
> A finger, tanned and scaly, gorgeous, decayed,
> Points to the shivering clouds, then turns down
> Most slowly, towards you. The light catches, cold and hard
> Pulls round the polished bone of fingernail
> Arrests attention, the prey falls dead.

There was to be one more issue of *Delta* before Peter left Cambridge, but he dropped out of the editorial role. Miles Atterton was still nominally editor, but *Delta* 3 carries a curious statement that 'Philip Hobsbaum edited the poetry'. Since, apart from an editorial by Hobsbaum himself, the magazine is all poetry, this doesn't leave much room for the other editor. Hobsbaum was to leave a much more lasting mark on *Delta* than Peter had: it was under his editorship that *Delta* published Ted Hughes and Sylvia Plath, but he also gave the magazine its critical, specifically Leavisite, cast, which it still had in the 1960s when it was edited by Simon Gray and Leavis's future biographer, Ian MacKillop. Hobsbaum lost no time in making clear his contempt for Peter's editorial policy: *Delta* was 'no longer trying to be just another university magazine . . . The editor has tried to collect verse which has immediacy, definition and contact with reality.' But if Hobsbaum thumbed his nose at Redgrove the editor he gave strong backing to Redgrove the poet, printing three poems including what was to become the title poem of Peter's first book. Hobsbaum singled out 'The Collector' and 'Joseph of

Arimathea' by David Ewart as 'excellent minor poems' that 'require reading and criticism at a serious level' (Ewart's poem merits Hobsbaum's praise, though its author seems to have disappeared as a poet).

This issue of *Delta* also included 'Guardian', an early instance of Redgrove's elaborate allegorical poems such as 'At the White Monument' (which Hobsbaum also thought outstanding), about a man who 'provided first / Of all for his family and for his wife' before planting the 'dedicated grove' in which 'a god grew'. An unspecified 'they' 'regarded it all as an intolerable folly / In the domestic shade' and coerced the man to 'tell his sacred story', upon which 'the tender god hid / And would not be discovered again among the flowers'. Again there are signs of anxiety about combining domesticity with poetry. Harry Guest greatly admired this poem and writes that lines such as 'the sun's green fingers' and 'the thickness of a great tree / Rippling out through time like a rod thrust into water' are evidence that despite Redgrove's rejection of his scientific studies they 'lent his poetry a unique dimension as he *knew* about chemistry and anatomy and magnetism and could therefore draw firsthand upon a rich store of imagery less familiar to the uninitiated'.

According to Hobsbaum, Ted Hughes offered poems for this issue of *Delta* but they were rejected. Peter's early friendship with Hughes at Cambridge is obscured by contradictory reports and unreliable memory. He told Hughes's biographer Elaine Feinstein that Hughes was two years ahead of him, whereas they were exact contemporaries. This is a symptomatic error. Redgrove once said that he thought of Hughes as the elder brother he had never had. Hughes was in fact older by eighteen months, but his entry to Cambridge had been delayed by National Service. Redgrove's recollections of the beginnings of their friendship consistently inflate and predate Hughes's reputation and achievement as a poet, casting him from the beginning as the senior partner in the relationship.

They almost certainly met in their final year. Hughes had gone up to read English at Pembroke, and achieved a 2.1 in Part One, but he progressively felt that the academic study of literature had a 'torturing destructive effect . . . on some essential part of [his] psyche'. He was writing all the time, but felt that what he wrote was 'total confusion'. He had published several poems in his school magazine, but did not publish again until the summer of his graduation, 1954. He dramatised this crisis memorably in his account of a dream in which a burnt fox appeared to him while he was writing an essay, put a bloody pawprint on the essay, and said, 'Stop this – you are destroying us.' He changed to archaeology and anthropology, and got a Third in Part Two, in ironical contrast to Peter's unsuccessful attempt to change to the English Tripos.

Redgrove described their first meeting to Elaine Feinstein as if Hughes were a celebrity: 'Someone said there was this marvellous poet and personality, Ted Hughes, who you must meet.' According to this account he called on Hughes at Pembroke. As he approached Hughes's rooms up the steep staircase he heard 'a strange yowling' coming through the door. Hughes explained that it was Beethoven's last quartet, which Peter had never heard before, and told him that 'the whole of the music is crushed into the first few bars, which are then unravelled'. (Redgrove was later to compare the openings of some of his own poems to 'the apparently discordant beginnings of certain of Beethoven's last quartets' in which there is a 'blare of noise which is then, as it were, rectified or demodulated into various harmonies . . .'.) Hughes had Beethoven's death mask on the wall, which he took down and carried across the room towards Redgrove at chest height, with a waddling walk, telling him that this was Beethoven's height and gait. Hughes's physical presence made an impression on Redgrove that he had never experienced before. Redgrove felt that Hughes was able to express 'a kind of knowledge' in his physique, and that this meeting was 'in continuum with his poems' in which 'something real has arrived. There is real presence.'

Probably many people responded to Hughes in this way, but Redgrove's sense of a continuum between his physique and his poems particularly recalls Sylvia Plath's famous account of her first meeting with her future husband: 'The one man in the room who was as big as his poems, huge, with hulk and dynamic chunks of words.' In later years Redgrove said that he both admired and loved Hughes, whose 'person' was dear to him. Peter Porter thought that this love was not reciprocated. I do not think that these feelings are, at least primarily, a matter of veiled or repressed homosexuality on Redgrove's part. He explored the conflicting aspects of his sexuality exhaustively in his journals, and more than once asked himself if certain responses were symptoms of repressed homosexuality, but never with reference to Hughes.

Moreover, Peter himself had an imposing physical presence, was at least as tall and strong as Hughes, and so would not have been impressed by Ted's mere size. However, whenever he experienced strong feelings towards another man he invariably invoked the figure of his father. The marked masculinity of Hughes's personality very probably played into Redgrove's complicated feelings about his own masculinity, that of his father ('so virile a man obsessed with manliness'), and his 'feminine identification'. He sought all his life for 'guest fathers' including, as we have seen, Aleister Crowley, and was attracted to the figure of the maternal uncle, who in many tribal cultures plays the role of initiator, as an alternative to the father. Hughes could not be a father or uncle but he did fit the role of elder brother and, when he died in 1998, Redgrove linked his grief with that which he felt at the deaths of his son Pete in the same year, and of Barbara four years earlier, and wrote that Hughes had been 'quite brotherly to me in the past'. Discovering that such a masculine person could also be sensitive and answer to the poet in Peter may have been a revelation to him. There is another aspect of Hughes's persona that may also have stirred the psychological mudpool of Peter's family drama. Philip Hobsbaum (admittedly a little maliciously) describes Hughes's 'smelly old corduroys and big flakes of dandruff in his hair'; this chimes with Plath's more smitten account of him wearing 'always the same black sweater and corduroy jacket with pockets full of poems, fresh trout and horoscopes'. Peter and Philip, Hobsbaum affirms, wore suits and ties, in contrast to the scruffy appearance of Hughes and his circle. Immersed in his Game, Peter was unlikely to be as complacently comfortable in his suit and tie as Philip was, and may well have regarded Hughes's shambolic appearance with more envy than disdain.

All this may partly explain the undoubted distortions in Redgrove's accounts of his early friendship with Hughes. He told Elaine Feinstein that he regarded Hughes 'very much as a senior poet'. Feinstein interprets this as evidence that Hughes had 'already acquired a large reputation as a poet even though he had published nothing under his own name'. But it is really very implausible that Redgrove, who had published ten poems including one in the *TLS*, and edited *Delta*, should have thought Hughes the 'senior poet' when they were still at Cambridge. In fact, *pace* his own account, it is unlikely that when he first met Hughes he knew

that he wrote poetry at all. Daniel Huws, who had known Ted
since the autumn of 1952, and had been a regular member of the
group with whom Ted gathered in the Anchor pub, had no idea
that his friend wrote poetry until the sixth issue of *Chequer* was
published in the summer term of 1954 (Peter and Ted's last term).
Daniel published his first poem in this issue and, shortly afterwards
in the Anchor, Ted asked him what he thought of another poem
in the same number, 'Song of the Sorry Lovers' by Peter Crew.
On getting a favourable reply Ted declared that the poem was
his. He had also published a poem under another pseudonym,
Daniel Hearing, in *Granta*, but Huws is emphatic that none of
the Anchor group, including Hughes's closest friend Terence
McCaughey, knew of this. The same issue of *Chequer* included
Peter's poem 'Artist', and Ted said to Daniel, 'Let's go and see
Peter.' Huws says that Peter wasn't a close friend, though it is
likely that Ted knew him better than Daniel did. They went across
to Peter's nearby rooms in Queens' where, as he had done with
Daniel, Ted asked Peter what he thought of the pseudonymous
poem. Huws doesn't record Peter's response. Peter had six bottles
of German wine in his room, on which the three of them got
drunk; they then attempted unsuccessfully to gatecrash a party in
a room high up in Old Court. 'Ted got in a tussle and hurt his
thumb. For years after, that thumb gave him trouble.' Such drunken
escapades are commonplace in student life, but there are enough
anecdotes about Peter involving alcohol to suggest that it had
already begun to play a part in his life that was later to become
problematic.

Huws's anecdote tells a very different story from Redgrove's
reminiscences. It is not the behaviour of a 'senior poet' to wait
for a reader's response before confessing authorship. Hughes's
desire to show the poem to Peter, but still maintain anonymity
till he got his response, suggests that on the contrary he felt
deferential and even nervous towards the more established writer.
This was quite appropriate, since neither of the poems Hughes
had published at Cambridge compares remotely in quality with
'Lazarus and the Sea' or most of Redgrove's other early published
work: it was not until November of that year, after he had left
Cambridge, when he published 'The Jaguar' and 'The Casualty'
in *Chequer*, that Hughes began again to show what he was capable
of for the first time since his remarkable schoolboy poems 'Song'

and 'The Recluse'. Many years later Hughes wrote warmly to Redgrove of 'how important you've been to me. You've no idea how much – right from the first time we met.' He remembers at that meeting Peter talking about 'the imaginative possibilities of – an old man considered as an ant-hill'. He once told their mutual friend Frances Horovitz that he had known two geniuses: Sylvia Plath and Peter Redgrove. It was, in other words, the poet in Redgrove that appealed to Hughes from the start, whereas what Redgrove most vividly recalls is the force of Hughes's personality.

Hughes recalls that this first meeting was on 'the Mill Bridge'. This contradicts Redgrove's recollection, and accords with Philip Hobsbaum's reminiscences, which give further evidence of Redgrove and Hughes's respective standings in the Cambridge poetry world. Hobsbaum records that he and Redgrove met Hughes in the Mill pub, where they could drink pints of Merrydown cider, because they didn't like the beer in Cambridge. (He is probably confusing the Mill with the Anchor, which is in the next street and where Redgrove recalls drinking cider with Hughes. Both pubs are close to the bridge.) 'Whatever we talked about first,' Hobsbaum writes, 'it wasn't poetry.' But one evening Hughes said 'out of the corner of his mouth as usual – "I hear you and Redgrove are starting a poetry magazine. Here are some poems I'd like you to look at."' He handed over a 'wad of manuscript' that was 'greasy and typed in grey characters, as though the ribbon in the typewriter had been used a great many times over a period of years, and never been changed' and retreated to the Gents. According to Hobsbaum Peter looked at this typescript and said, 'Ted's a nice chap, but I don't think we ought to publish his poems.' Peter had of course already edited two issues of *Delta*, but was handing it over to Philip. In the event, Hobsbaum records that Peter came to him in the run-up to the fifth issue (by which time both he and Hughes had left Cambridge), with what turned out to be two poems by Hughes, which Peter had sellotaped together under the impression that they were parts of a single work. One of these poems, 'The Woman With Such High Heels She Looked Dangerous', was published in the fifth *Delta* in spring 1955.

In retrospect Redgrove wrote that Hughes's poetry before *Crow* (which he disliked) gave him 'a working sense (as did Sylvia

Plath's) of how much must be done by a contemporary poem before it *is* a poem'. Both Hughes's career and his poetic development advanced more rapidly than Redgrove's after they left Cambridge. By the time Hughes published *The Hawk in the Rain* in 1957, with poems such as 'The Thought-Fox', 'The Jaguar' and 'Wind', he undoubtedly was the 'senior poet'. But when he knew Redgrove in the summer of 1954 Hughes was the author not of these poems but of 'Song of the Sorry Lovers' and 'The Little Boys and the Seasons', about which he later ruefully wrote, 'Five years in which I tried constantly to write . . . Then all I could come up with was Little Boys and the Seasons!' Elaine Feinstein compliments Redgrove on his humility in his reminiscences and he is, indeed, admirably modest. In the intervening years his reputation had suffered in comparison with Hughes's, and this made him anxious about the way he publicly discussed his friend. But in reading back Hughes's later achievement and reputation into their first meetings there is something deeper than modesty, diplomacy, or simple forgetfulness. It was as a man that Hughes first impressed Redgrove, a sympathetic embodiment of the masculinity with which he struggled: the deference to the 'senior poet' is a mask, probably unconscious, over this primary emotional reality.

Peter's last year at Cambridge, then, saw the triumphal entry of the poet. His work was admired by Edmund Blunden, Ted Hughes, Kamau Brathwaite, Philip Hobsbaum, Harry Guest and Ronald Hayman; he had ten poems published between October and May, including three that were to be collected and one in a national journal. He was still only twenty-two years old: of his contemporaries perhaps only Thom Gunn and Geoffrey Hill came into their strength so young. But it is unlikely that his parents saw the year in this light. He had done no work towards his degree: he told Peter Porter that he got high on Merrydown and Benzedrine during the exams, and Harry Guest that he sat in them writing limericks. In a cancelled draft of the novel *The Terrors of Dr Treviles* he portrays a student lying in bed enjoying a masturbatory fantasy about mud while his tutor hammers on his door asking why he isn't in the examination hall. His record card this time shows not that he was absent but that he failed. On 22 June Dr McCullagh wrote informing Jim that the Council of the Senate could not approve the award of a degree, and asking 'that when you break the news to Peter you will tell him how much I admire his courage in coming back this year and making an attempt to complete his studies'. The phrase 'break the news' is eloquent about how Peter must have disguised the reality, to his parents and presumably to the college authorities. Jim desperately grasped at flimsy hopes. He wrote back to McCullagh that he had understood from him and another Fellow of Queens' that Peter could qualify for some form of degree. (They had probably discussed the Aegrotat, which in some cases can be awarded when a student is unfit to sit the exams.) McCullagh was on sick leave and it was not until January that he replied to Jim, 'I did what I could to further Peter's case with the Council of the Senate, but unhappily his examination performance was so very poor that the Council were unable under the Ordinances to make him the allowance of an Ordinary Degree.'* Then follows what must have been a sickening blow for the already bitterly disappointed father: 'I tell you this in confidence because I do not suppose you know that Peter in fact absented himself from a great deal of the examination.' McCullagh goes on to say that '[t]he danger that we feared in September 1953 did result and Peter broke down again some weeks before his examination'. If this were so it is surprising that the parents are only now being informed, more than half a year after the event. It seems more likely that McCullagh is trying to present Peter's behaviour in the least unfavourable light.

In later years Peter regretted not having a degree: he often dreamed that he was successfully retaking his exams and on one occasion (in a dream significantly involving his father) that he had 'two firsts'. He was deeply gratified when the University of Sheffield awarded him an honorary doctorate two years before his death: the first degree he had ever received. But at the time it was almost certainly a greater blow to his parents than to him. His stories to Peter Porter and Harry Guest may be bravado, but there is one independent witness to his state of mind during finals. Daniel Huws, who did not himself have exams at the time, was wandering down Trinity Street in the middle of the morning when he bumped into Peter, who had just walked out of an exam. They

---

* This conflicts with Peter's university record card which states that he failed Part One, not Part Two, in 1954, implying that he was retaking his second year, not that he had been allowed to proceed to the third. In practice, since he did no work, the difference is irrelevant.

went and had coffee. Huws can't remember what they talked about but he does remember being struck by Peter's 'high spirits, elation almost'. Maybe he was high on Merrydown or Benzedrine, but I think he was elated because the long pretence was over, the youthful scientist was finally dead and by however dubious means he had managed to stay at Cambridge for three years and use the time there to make himself a poet.

Marriage and the Group 1954–61

Failing to get a degree had little outward effect on Peter's life in the summer of 1954. He and Barbara were married in July, at St Mary's Church, Walton on Thames. It was a conventional middle-class wedding, inevitably recorded on film by Jim. Barbara had made a bust of Peter, against which the family propped a sign: 'LEAVING TODAY'. We see Peter in his wedding suit, making a speech by the three-tier cake, fiddling like any new bridegroom with his unfamiliar ring, raising a glass with David on the lawn at the reception, an elderly relative acting the fool, the car departing with an L-plate attached, a brick and tin can clattering behind. They flew to Jersey for their honeymoon.

But the smooth-running wedding arrangements belie a less comfortable story. Peter may have enthusiastically embraced marriage when he wrote 'Peter and Barbara Redgrove' in his books in 1952, but he later said the one thing he held against his mother was her insistence that he *must* go through with the marriage when he had cold feet. We glimpse the shadow of a painful scene in a journal entry written many years later: 'to get away from our families . . . her anger, breach of promise . . . her plea that she was nothing without me'.

In the absence of contemporary evidence we have to rely on Peter's inevitably biased reflections after the marriage had ended. There was much joy at first, he admitted, but the honeymoon was sexually disappointing. He wondered if he had blighted their sexual relationship by his fear of having children, but in one of his poems of this period it seems to be the male speaker who wants a child and protests against the 'dropped monthly egg'.

There is, in reality, no reason to suppose that Peter and Barbara were not happy in the earlier years of their marriage. Certainly everybody who knew them thought they were happy. They had known each other for more than three years, and Barbara must have been fully aware of Peter's depressions and obsessions, if not the depth and recalcitrance of his 'alternative' sexuality. She certainly had the measure of his alcohol dependency, and told him on their honeymoon what a poet he could be if he didn't drink. She was the woman who had inducted him into the life of an artist, both by example and by sexual initiation, and they were both in revolt against the conventional attitudes of their parents. Hobsbaum's fiancée Hannah gathered from Barbara that they enjoyed a 'hectic and happy' sex life.

Barbara's younger sister Hilary retained fond and vivid memories of the young married couple. The Sherlock parents often went away on business, and Hilary, as a teenager, used to stay with Peter and Barbara at such times. They were, she recalls, 'always there for me', and she had a great affection for Peter, though she thought he must have got frustrated with her, being on 'a different plane' and 'very erudite'. Despite this – though characteristically – he would indulge her by taking her to horror movies. Barbara was 'always fashionable and brave in what she wore' (though not as outrageous as Nan) and when Hilary was confirmed she was proud of the brilliant young couple who acted as her guardians at the service. The Bishop of Kensington made a beeline for Peter, mistakenly thinking he knew him, but Peter engaged the Bishop in conversation with magnificent aplomb.

Failing his degree did not seriously jeopardise Peter's employment prospects. By August he had started a job as a copywriter that he described in a later CV (maybe exaggerating slightly) as 'Group Head of Publicity Department' with Odhams Press. He was sufficiently well-paid to be able to turn down an offer of £850 a year from another firm, on the grounds of loyalty to Odhams, and desirable enough to have the trouble of refusing a raised offer from the same company over the phone. He was sanguine about combining with poetry a kind of writing that was totally, even 'ludicrously', lacking in the value of poetry. He hoped that this gulf would enable him to take the copywriting seriously on its own level, and to succeed at it without 'contamination'. He wrote 'Precious being!' after this word – a note of self-mockery that he wouldn't give in to later, when the gulf became intolerable. Now, however, at the start of his copywriting career, he believed that it expressed part of himself and, while he didn't regret the opportunities he had missed by failing in the army and at Cambridge, he would regret losing the job.

Initially he and Barbara lived in a flat in Potters Bar, eighteen miles north of London, but within a year they were, with parental help, able to afford a house in Grove Park Terrace, Chiswick, almost on the river. During the first year of marriage and working for Odhams Peter kept up his friendship with Ted Hughes who was now in London, and with Philip Hobsbaum in Cambridge, resulting in Peter mediating the publication of Hughes's poem in *Delta* in 1955. In the·summer of that year Philip graduated and moved to London, where he worked six months in television and then as a teacher at Tulse Hill secondary modern school (where one of the pupils he inspired was the future Mayor of London, Ken Livingstone). The Cambridge Group had faltered when Peter left, but in the autumn of 1955, when Philip had moved into a 'grubby bedsitter' in Kendal Street, off the Marble Arch end of the Edgware Road, Peter pressed him to resume the Group in London. As a result eight young people gathered in Kendal Street one wet October evening. They were Hobsbaum, Redgrove, Ted Hughes, Hobsbaum's eighteen-year-old fiancée Hannah Kelly, two actors – Patricia Hartz and Leon Cripps – Julian Cooper, an Anglo/Argentinian poet Hobsbaum had known at Cambridge, and his American wife Catherine. Redgrove read 'Bedtime Story for my Son', which was to be one of the finest poems in his first collection, and one that Hobsbaum himself particularly admired. It was a rare example of a poem that almost wrote itself, in a few minutes. Hughes read 'Soliloquy for a Misanthrope' and 'Secretary', which were soon to be published in the notorious *St Botolph's Review* (the short-lived magazine he and his friends started in Cambridge, which led to his meeting with Sylvia Plath) and later collected in *The Hawk in the Rain*. These are far more assured and memorable than Hughes's undergraduate poems, and one can see why Hobsbaum was now championing Hughes as well as Redgrove. They are also among the harshest and most misogynistic of Hughes's early poems, a sharp contrast to the tenderness and 'feminine identification' of 'Bedtime Story for my Son'. Despite the assurance and ferocity of his new poems Hughes was at this time, according to Hobsbaum, 'rather shy and introverted', and did not publish beyond student magazines until Sylvia Plath took him in hand in the summer of 1956.

Only Philip, Peter and Hannah were to be lasting members of

the Group, though other Hughes poems would later be discussed in his absence, and Catherine Cooper did the Group great service by introducing her young Australian friend Peter Porter. Despite his cultivation and scholarly demeanour, Porter never went to university, and had come to England in 1951 to try to make a career as a writer while doing various menial jobs. After an unhappy love affair he returned to Australia, but the draw of Europe was too great for the man who was to become the leading representative of what his compatriot Les Murray called Australia's 'Athenian' or urbane and cosmopolitan literary tendency (as opposed to Murray's 'Boeotian' or native and rural school) and he came back at the end of 1954. Soon Porter, too, was a regular member of the Group. Hobsbaum's first issue of *Delta* had included a poem by the Jamaican-born Oxford undergraduate Edward Lucie-Smith ('A Tropical Childhood', later to be the title poem of his first collection). Hobsbaum and Lucie-Smith didn't know each other, but Hobsbaum had seen a poem by the latter and invited him to contribute. Lucie-Smith was very flattered by this, since Oxford undergraduate poets felt inferior to their Cambridge counterparts because of the reputation of Thom Gunn. He did his National Service after graduating, but became a core member of the Group – and eventually its second convenor – after his discharge. Later still, when Hobsbaum and Hannah had moved to their marital home in Stockwell, the dapper young BBC producer George MacBeth began attending.

Shortly after the launch of the Group there occurred a meeting which, at least in the small world of the Group, accrued legendary status. Peter was drinking in a pub near his house in Chiswick. Across the bar he noticed a small man, somewhat older than himself, dressed in a shabby suit, with horn-rimmed glasses and a neatly trimmed goatee beard. What drew his attention was that the man was reading poetry. Peter approached him and a comically formal dialogue ensued. The tall, slightly portly young stranger said in his 'cultivated and resonant' voice, 'Excuse me, Sir, but does that happen to be a volume of verse that you are reading?' 'It is indeed, Sir,' the older man replied in a West-country accent. 'May I enquire what it is, Sir?' 'Surely. It is Norman Cameron's translation of Rimbaud's verse-poems.' The upshot of the meeting was that Martin Bell joined the Group, and Redgrove formed what was probably, after Hobsbaum, his second most important literary friendship.

Martin Bell's background was very different from Peter's. His father had worked for the Southern Railway and he had grown up in an environment of stifling respectable poverty. His parents couldn't afford for him to go to Oxford, so before the war he had studied at what was then University College, Southampton, his birthplace. Since his teachers included Vivian de Sola Pinto, the pioneer editor of Rochester, and J. B. Leishman, the distinguished translator of Rilke, he perhaps had as good an education as he would have got at the more renowned university, but he retained an oppressive sense of class-based marginality. The only other person Bell knew in Southampton who wrote poetry was the literate and cultivated cricket commentator, then a policeman, John Arlott (one of the first non-standard English speakers to break through at the BBC) but though they talked about literature neither confessed to his own compositions. He also differed from Redgrove in having been as a young man a committed Marxist and Communist Party member (he left the party after reading Koestler's *Darkness at Noon* during the war) and having served with the Royal Engineers in several theatres of conflict. Despite his disenchantment with Communism he remained a convinced man of the Left. He records the 'strenuous and successful tussle' he and Peter Porter undertook to persuade Redgrove to vote Labour in 1959. Although he was fourteen years older than Redgrove, he was hardly more advanced on a poetic career, which had in Peter Porter's words been 'cauterised' by 'shortage of money, pressure of family and the onset of war'. He was now 'languishing' as a teacher, an occupation which must have been purgatorial for someone with a pronounced stutter. The meeting was immensely significant for both men.

Many other poets brought their work to Group meetings over the years, especially in the later phase after Hobsbaum left for Sheffield in 1959 and Lucie-Smith took over as chairman. Notable names were to include Fleur Adcock, Alan Brownjohn, Zulfikar Ghose, Adrian Mitchell, Nathaniel Tarn, Anthony Thwaite and David Wevill. However, of 246 presentations recorded by Hobsbaum (admittedly an incomplete count) 103 were by himself, Redgrove, Bell, Porter, Lucie-Smith and MacBeth, and these six, later augmented by Brownjohn, formed the core of the Group.

Although the atmosphere was democratic and cooperative, Hobsbaum, Redgrove and Bell were in their different ways the dominant figures. Everyone who has gone on record about the Group has paid tribute to Hobsbaum's chairmanship. Alan Brownjohn has attested that, while Hobsbaum could show a 'Leavisite fierceness' in criticising slack writing, it was entirely without malice, and that a word of praise from him would 'send people away absolutely glowing'. Peter Porter was no Leavisite but he admired Hobsbaum's belief that Leavisian principles could be applied to new work, testifying in particular that Redgrove was a central part of Philip's belief in literature: 'a man he'd discovered, who he thought was a genius and who was a living proof of the continued quality and value of poetry'. We have heard already from Redgrove's experience in Cambridge that he valued Hobsbaum's largeness of mind, which was reliably on display in Group meetings if not in all aspects of his personal relationships. Lucie-Smith remembers that he was 'fond of argument in the way that other men are fond of food', and that his often hectoring manner concealed a genuine respect for intellectual democracy. Bell was respected for his quickness to understand a new poem, his sense of humour, generosity and erudition, and the way he combined this breadth of knowledge with a warm and passionate appreciation of particular poets. Years after his death Redgrove was still reflecting on his ability to 'see into the poems and discover for me new things'. But, for Hobsbaum, Bell and Porter at least, there was no doubt that Redgrove was the outstanding poet among them: indeed the finest, or certainly the most gifted, poet of the age. In Porter's words:

> Peter Redgrove is the only poet I know whose belief in [the] magic [of poetry] is emotionally and intellectually credible . . . It is hardly surprising that I consider him the most gifted poet working in Britain today. Not always the most successful or accomplished – he can be over-strenuous, hypertrophied or obsessional – but the poet with the largest vision and the most spectacular trust in language.

In Hobsbaum's recollection Redgrove 'dominated the whole show effortlessly; a big man with a big voice' who week after week read verse that Hobsbaum became convinced was of exceptionally rare quality. As Hobsbaum's comment on the size of Peter's personality implies, it was not only the quality of his poetry but his presence that commanded respect. Porter puts this more vividly:

> At the very first meeting of the Group which I attended, I was introduced to this tall, already formidably strong and seemingly entirely mature man. He did not look like any poet I had seen before, but then he didn't look like someone just down from Cambridge either

. . . Instead, he resembled a businessman, but with a very remarkable difference: he had, even at that time . . . an extraordinary aura . . . Peter was (and is) courteous, courtly even, but I had not been with him half an hour before I was convinced that I had met an absolutely original person, and that the form his originality took could only be called 'poetic'.

The best flavour of the Group is provided by Hobsbaum's transcript of the discussion of a Redgrove poem in 1958. The poem is 'The Archaeologist', later published in *The Collector*.

> So I take one of those thin plates
> And I fit it to a knuckled other,
> Carefully, for it trembles on the edge of powder,
> Restore the jaw and find the fangs their mates.
>
> The thorny tree of which this is the gourd,
> Outlasting centuries of sand and water,
> Re-engineered by me, stands over there,
> Stocky, peeling, crouched and dangling-pawed.
>
> I roll the warm wax within my palm
> And to the bone slowly mould a face
> Of the jutting-jawed, hang-browed race;
> On the brute strength I try to build up a calm,
>
> For it is a woman, by the broad hips;
> I give her a smooth skin, and make the mouth mild:
> It is aeons since she saw her child
> Spinning thin winds of gossamer from his lips.

PORTER: The poem is open, though, to the criticism of the last stanza, which Philip liked, that the 'Spinning thin winds of gossamer' – the very idea of the baby which is frothing at the mouth as babies do, including as they do in a famous advertisement – the trouble is that the transferred idea of the winds of gossamer coming out of the baby's mouth – to me, it doesn't really quite come over.

HOBSBAUM: Well, let me make it quite clear. I've been listening to the objections to this. Quite honestly, I mean, although it is an idea which might seem sentimental, don't you think something that's seen, as I think this is seen very precisely – I mean this is one of the most distinct and obvious characteristics of a young child, and it is a kind of energetic image anyway, a kind of pro-life image – I should have thought that that kind of distinctness and energy would have prevented it from being sentimental. Surely, isn't something that's sentimental a sort of vague idea in which you invest a vast amount of emotion which isn't really justified?

PORTER: I suppose why I think it's sentimental in this case is that – I'm not quite sure, I've been through museums and looked at skeletons, I looked at the re-created figures of Cro-Magnon and Neanderthal Men and that sort of thing – and it only worried me that the last stanza assumes a kind of automatic identification which I agree is probably, as you say, a sort of natural thing which you imagine the woman is being concerned with, that is, her child, but it's just a little bit too automatic, that she is *looking* for her child's spume. It's a bit too glib. 'It is aeons since she saw her child / Spinning thin winds of gossamer' – I mean, you really don't know enough about anybody in the past to sort of make this kind of automatic assumption.

HOBSBAUM: But one of the earliest instincts, surely, would be motherhood, I would have thought, maternal instinct? She's not looking for it, it's just that – Aren't you reading a bit too much into it? All he's saying is that it's aeons and aeons since she was alive and performing her natural reactions.

PORTER: I suppose all I can say is that I would have preferred it to be put less—

BELL: I can see the objection – it's giving this woman a fine aesthetic-appreciative attitude to the child.

REDGROVE: Oh, foul play, Martin!

BELL: I think this is how it's being read.

HOBSBAUM: It is not giving *her* the appreciation, it's the poet's appreciation not the woman's.

Bell: The point is she saw it, he says she saw it. She saw this like an image in Virginia Woolf, say. It could be read that way.

HOBSBAUM: Oh, I think that's a little perverse. If you say George Bloggs saw somebody doing so-and-so it doesn't mean to say that the way it expresses [it is] the way George Bloggs saw it. There is a writer here speaking to us, surely. In fact, explicitly, there is a persona, the archaeologist here, which I should have thought removes it even further from the possibility of it being a Neanderthal woman seeing her child with just that sensibility – I admit, it would be perverse if it was so.

MARGARET OWEN: I think it's rather a good image because it's one of the particular things about mothers and babies that they do – well she stares at the child.

The discussion is of its time, both in its strengths and in its weaknesses. The concern with, and hostility to, sentimentality and aestheticism testify to the influence of Leavis either mediated by Hobsbaum or as something diffused in the literary climate. However, it is Hobsbaum himself who shows the most definite Leavisite leaning in his belief that the 'distinctiveness and energy' of the image is a prophylactic against sentimentality. Leavis's keyword 'realised' is in the air here. (In his affectionate satire 'Mr Hobsbaum's Monday Evening Meeting' Bell has Hobsbaum exclaim, 'Not in the poem! It's not realised! / An abstract statement on the page!') Porter is not deflected by this argument and continues worrying away at his discomfort about the poem, which is obviously essentially moral: 'you really don't know enough about anybody in the past to make this kind of automatic assumption.' Bell's detection of a false 'aesthetic-appreciative attitude' is perhaps the most penetrating observation, despite Redgrove's protest: it cuts through Hobsbaum's rather platitudinous remarks about maternal instinct.

Margaret Owen's interjection is a reminder that, despite the undeniable male dominance of the Group, women were accommodated (the work of a dozen women is preserved in the archived papers). However, she does seem rather obviously to be putting the 'woman's point of view', and perhaps the most important omission from the discussion is any criticism of the speaker's assumption that a woman's face should be 'calm' and 'mild'. In his later reflections Hobsbaum acknowledges that 'like many women writers of those days' Owen 'eventually opted for domesticity rather than publication', though she continued writing and participated in the Reading exhibition devoted to the Group in 1974.

If Hobsbaum, Redgrove and Bell were in their different ways leading spirits, the other key members brought distinctive qualities to the Group. Lucie-Smith was impressively articulate and a gifted practical critic; Porter, whose early poetry is characterised by a satirical edge, deflated any tendencies of his friends to portentousness, and Hobsbaum likened him to 'an intelligent clown at a seminary'; MacBeth, 'always impeccably turned out in three-piece suit, tie, and neat moustache', was a gadfly who delighted in provoking the rest of the Group with knowingly outrageous attitudes. When he wanted to wind Redgrove up he would tell him that Ted Hughes was a better poet than he. These two had a long-standing friendship and MacBeth was very supportive in getting Redgrove's work on the radio, but at times Peter reacted with paranoid suspicion to what Lucie-Smith called MacBeth's 'cool, confident dogmatism'.

The procedure was the same as at Cambridge: each week one person's poems, about six in all, would be distributed in advance (occasionally two novices might be combined). These copies were called 'songsheets'. Initially, as at Cambridge, Hobsbaum duplicated them (or Hannah did so for him) by the primitive method of multiple carbons on his prized Remington 10. The result of this can be seen in the surviving copies, some of which are almost indecipherably smudgy. However, Hannah worked as a secretary and was soon able to produce much more satisfactory copies on a duplicator at her office. Hannah, who had grown up in India, was only eighteen when she met Philip at a Jewish society. (Philip's Jewishness was important to him, though he had no religious belief.) She was a very attractive young woman, and Peter called her eyes 'fishpools of Heshbon', quoting his favourite book of the Bible, the Song of Songs. He always treated her kindly: when Philip chided her about something he interjected, 'It's not a police state.' Although she wrote poetry later, when her marriage to Philip had sadly disintegrated, she lacked the confidence to do so at this time, but was happy to serve Philip and his poet friends, by whom she was somewhat awestruck. As a young girl she had read about Madame de Sévigné, and was entranced by the idea of holding a literary *salon*. Her role in the Group was more typical of a woman in the 1950s: as well as acting as secretary she was responsible for providing biscuits and coffee – medium-ground Kenya coffee of which she and Philip were very proud. When her sister sent money as a wedding present she spent it on a tape recorder that Philip used to record the Group's deliberations.

As at Cambridge, the poet was not allowed to explain his or her intentions till the end of the discussion. This reflects Hobsbaum's hostility – again characteristic of the time – to 'intentionalism' in criticism, a hostility that was later to set him at odds with William Empson when he went to Sheffield to study for a PhD with the great critic. In the second part of the evening, after the coffee and biscuits, members would read and discuss poems by other writers, from forgotten Elizabethans to obscure contemporaries or, in Martin Bell's case, translations of European poets, especially Rimbaud. Perhaps the most telling judgement of the Group, especially as it affected Redgrove, is Lucie-Smith's recognition that the process put psychic pressures on the members, that a critical observation about a poem's failure to resolve a conflict could imply an unacknowledged personal failing in the poet; but that this was handled with great sensitivity, in order for an atmosphere of mutual trust to develop, and that nobody would use the implicit revelations in ways that might be hurtful. Redgrove later acknowledged that he suffered 'severe mental trouble' during his association with the Group, but had been able to conceal it from his friends. Writing poetry, with the support his friends gave him, helped him to 'unravel these difficulties and (I hope) turn them into expressive work'.

Alcohol was not allowed at the meetings and this helped to foster a widely shared image of the Group as earnest, cocoa-drinking, polo-necked-sweater-wearing devotees of D. H. Lawrence. The truth was that many of the Group, including Redgrove, drank heavily, and as their friendships naturally migrated beyond the formal meetings, they would gather in pubs and in the afternoon drinking clubs common in Soho at that time of stricter licensing laws, which Peter Porter says should have had written over their doors, as over the gate of Dante's Hell, '*Lasciate ogni speranza voi ch'entrate*' (Abandon all hope, you that enter). Of all the Group members, Martin Bell was to be the saddest casualty of this drinking culture.

Bell's 'It Was a Violent Time', a kind of *poème à clef* which paints a bilious picture of literary London, asks, 'Who snapped whose umbrella, then /Tore down urinals, roaring?' The answer is Peter Redgrove, who denied demolishing a urinal but admitted putting his fist through a window and breaking the umbrella of Vernon Scannell, another legendary drinker among the poets of the time, who also happened to be a former semi-professional middleweight boxer. Predictably Redgrove lost the ensuing fight, but then took up judo, partly inspired by this humiliation, and partly by having drunkenly asked Ted Hughes what would happen if they fought, and got the grim reply, 'that he would tear off my head'. Redgrove and Hughes never fought, but there was a second Redgrove–Scannell bout in the pub next to the Royal Court Theatre (where, two decades later, the novelist, dramatist and ex-Rugby League pro David Storey chastised the critic Michael Billington for a bad review by punching him). This time – either because of the judo training or because Scannell was much the drunker of the two – Redgrove succeeded in throwing his opponent, who promptly fell asleep and was ministered to by his wife, who said he should stop fighting because he bruised too easily.

Alan Brownjohn, who joined the Group in 1958, was a teeto-
taller at that time and was dismayed when a party of them were
performing a collective reading of Wallace Stevens's 'Sea Surface
Full of Clouds' and Redgrove and Bell, who both loved the poem,
were asleep when their turn to read came round. In the same year
the two Peters did a reading tour together and found themselves
in Taunton where Redgrove persuaded Porter to spend the afternoon watching a western with a large flask of whisky. As a result
Porter lost his poems on the bus. Redgrove and Bell, in fact,
circumvented the no-alcohol rule by tanking up in the pub beforehand and rushing back there during the interval. When Lucie-Smith
took over as chairman he protested about Peter's bad manners in
turning up late because of this. Although Lucie-Smith was fond
of Peter and admired and supported him as a poet, he was a
shrewd judge both of his poetry and of his character at this time.
He thought there was a sense in which Peter was 'not quite grown
up', and that his friends indulged him as 'a kind of spoilt child'.
Of the poetry he said, 'What he was writing about didn't matter
to him much for its own sake – it mattered to him mostly (if not
entirely) as a pretext for a display of poetic skill.' This is a harsh
and sweeping judgement, and certainly not true of Redgrove's best
early poetry, but it does put tellingly into perspective his early
insistence that poetry is fiction, his refusal to be committed to
prose statement, and the major development in his later work
when poetry, prose discourse and ideological commitment are
integrated. This critical perspective probably affected Redgrove's
attitude to Lucie-Smith, which was never as warm as to other
leading members of the Group. He confessed to Hobsbaum that
he felt confused about Lucie-Smith, who was clearly intelligent,
but 'flawed by a kind of self-protectiveness or self-justifying' that
sometimes seemed to 'harden into a wall of conceit'. He acknowledged, however, that he could only see 'his own theories about
him', not the man himself.

Although the methods of the Group owed a great deal to
Cambridge English, there was no Group ideology. Of the key figures
only Hobsbaum was a devotee of Leavis and none of the others
(except Redgrove to a degree) shared his enthusiasm for D. H.
Lawrence. Porter and Bell were disciples of Auden, whom the Leavis
school judged to have failed after his early promise. Porter considered that only Gavin Ewart could challenge Bell as the inheritor of

Auden's mantle. Redgrove was, in Porter's words, 'sui generis' and the great poets were for him 'figures in a pantheon, but they were not really where he was coming from'. Indeed, Hobsbaum was the only product of Cambridge English – Lucie-Smith, MacBeth and Brownjohn were all educated at Oxford and none had read English. They did not even all share Redgrove and Hobsbaum's religious devotion to poetry. Porter has written that the only art he can take entirely seriously is music. Lucie-Smith, like Byron, did not want to be 'all poet', but preferred those who wrote poetry 'with the left hand', such as Rochester, Donne, Herbert and Marvell. Despite chairing the Group for longer than Hobsbaum did, he was detached from the core in more than his moderate drinking: with a passionate interest in European modernism, and a developing curiosity about contemporary art, he found Hobsbaum's perspective a little parochial. As a closeted gay man, though he did not find the ethos of the Group stifling, he was at a tangent to many of the preoccupations of his married colleagues (marriages that were, for the most part, doomed).

Bell may have been a frustrated poet but he was a mature man with a formed mind, unlikely to be influenced by the 'sui generis' genius of his young new friend. The importance of the meeting to him was the encouragement and companionship offered by Redgrove himself and by the wider group of young poets who not only accepted but looked up to him. There is a certain pathos in the fact that – immediately or soon after this first meeting – Redgrove asked Bell when he was bringing out a collection and Bell responded by spending a whole day filling a notebook with handwritten poems, and giving it to Redgrove, with the title 'Unfriendly Flowers: Selected Verse of Martin Bell 1947–56'.

Bell and Redgrove had indeed very different poetic personalities, as Redgrove himself implied when he praised his friend for 'the tone and movement of a common speech' and for writing about 'the social life of his time and the experiences of the poet in it as an ordinary human being'. (Redgrove would always protest that this was essentially his own subject matter too, but it is not the first description of his poetry that comes to mind.) Nevertheless, Redgrove was the one who benefited from the friendship in terms of artistic influence. Bell believed that poetry was, in Peter Porter's word, an 'intonation' – there is in his work always an element of dramatic utterance, of vocal gesture. His influence can be seen in the emergence of clearly

defined speakers even in early works of Redgrove that are autobiographical in origin, such as 'Against Death', 'Old House' and 'On
Catching a Dog-Daisy in the Mower', as well as more fully dramatised pieces such as 'The Play', 'Picking Mushrooms' and 'Mr
Waterman'. The very existence of the Group may also have fostered
this development. Edward Lucie-Smith has remarked that several
members started writing dramatic monologues, and that this may
have been a way of 'speaking out, and yet of preserving a screen
between oneself and these friends whom one knew perhaps too
intimately'. It was also through Bell that Redgrove developed and
began to turn to creative use the interest in French and German
poetry that had been kindled at Cambridge by Harry Guest and
Frederick Grubb. Bell was the 'onlie begetter' and first reader of
Redgrove's Rimbaud imitations, 'Fantasias', and, as a student of J.
B. Leishman, encouraged Redgrove's lifelong love of Rilke.

The two poets had a popular stand-up routine, performing
Redgrove's buffo dialogue 'The Play', in which one old man lures
and flatters another into accepting a part in a play that will culmi-
nate in his death. They gave a public performance under the auspices
of the 'Contemporary Poetry and Music Circle', a branch of the
Progressive League that organised events at the South Place Ethical
Society in Bayswater. Each evening's entertainment began with readings by promising poets and concluded with another reading by
'headline' poets. On the night of Redgrove and Bell's reading the
headliners were Allen Ginsberg and Gregory Corso, making their
first appearance in London. These American poetic stars hugely
enjoyed 'The Play', laughing and applauding enthusiastically.
Ginsberg patted Redgrove on the head and called him 'angel child'.
Obviously aware of Ginsberg's sexuality, Redgrove insists that this
was *after* hearing his poetry.

Peter soon acquired a reputation – surprising to those who only
knew the almost reclusive poet of his later years – as a self-promoter.
Bell's 'It Was a Violent Time' asks, 'What megalomaniac said,
aggrieved, / "You'rr the pushingest mon in poetrry today"?' The
answer is the Scottish-American poet Burns Singer (though presumably not in quite such a cod Scottish accent), and the occasion was
his refusal to let Redgrove into his flat to continue a poets' drinking
session. Lucie-Smith complained that Peter 'overpitches his claims
and overplays his hand', with the result that even people who
admired his talent ended up resenting him. Lucie-Smith was a shrewd

judge of Peter's character, and speculated that his 'creeping around and sucking up' was the effect of his trying to prove to his father that poetry could produce the kind of worldly, material success Jim respected. Even his good friend Peter Porter said that in the early years he was manipulative and worldly, but though he tried to work the system he was unsuccessful at it. Ted Hughes wrote to his sister Olwyn in May 1956 that Redgrove was 'obsequious . . . then asks for a favour', and it is evident from this letter that neither Olwyn nor Sylvia Plath liked him at this time.

Actually, as this same letter makes clear, Peter was 'pushing' largely on behalf of Ted, who announces that through Redgrove he is getting offers of work from the BBC. Peter made a tape of Ted reading from *Sir Gawayne and the Grene Knight* and sent it to Donald Carne-Ross in the BBC Talks Department. Despite Carne-Ross's early interest Hughes seems to have made only one broadcast, a reading of one of his own poems, before departing for America in 1957. According to Porter, Redgrove was also 'nobbling literary editors' such as Alan Pryce-Jones at the *TLS* on Hughes's behalf. In November 1956 Ted acknowledged Peter's generosity in this respect and cited his efforts as the main reason why he hoped soon to be able to sell his work in England. Whether through Redgrove's influence, or by dint of Sylvia Plath indefatigably sending poems out, Hughes was published in the *TLS*, *Spectator* and *Nation*, as well as American magazines, by the summer of 1957. Porter, admittedly a hostile witness where Hughes is concerned, said that 'Peter adored Ted, and Ted treated him very off-handedly'. However much truth there is in the second part of this judgement, the first is indisputable, and Hughes's increasingly and conspicuously greater success was to put a never-resolved strain on Redgrove's feelings for the 'big and famous poet' whom he 'loved and envied'.

As far as the BBC was concerned, however, Peter was initially much more successful than Ted, perhaps because of a persisting prejudice against non-RP voices. He appeared twice on literary discussion programmes in June 1956, and was soon regularly reading his own poems. His first appearance was a review of Peter Brook's production of Eliot's *Family Reunion* at the Phoenix Theatre, on 'Comment' on the Third Programme, in which his admiration of Eliot didn't deter him from sharply criticising the play's weaknesses: he insisted that the play is stylistically insecure, and attributed this to 'Mr Eliot's inability even to be interested in ordinary people.'

He lamented the direction that Eliot's verse drama had taken, and that he hadn't developed the style of *Sweeney Agonistes*, 'which arguably has more vitality than the rest of the plays put together' – a judgement that Eliot's later critics would agree with. His first poem on the radio was 'Without Eyes', which he read in February 1957 on 'The Poet's Voice', produced by Donald Carne-Ross. Soon this programme passed to George MacBeth, and during his years in London Peter was to broadcast eleven poems altogether, including the Redgrove–Bell performance of 'The Play'. His earnings from the BBC in this period were £130 – until the publication of his first collection in 1960, his main income from writing.

Hobsbaum's group was unique in its methods but it was not the only gathering of poets in London in the 1950s. Alan Brownjohn, an Oxford graduate a year older than Redgrove, began attending the monthly poetry evenings organised by George Fraser, a distinguished elder poet and critic whose name was, to his long-term disadvantage, associated with the neo-Romantic 'Apocalyptic' school of the 1940s. The Apocalyptics, with whom George Barker was also associated, were to be shifted to the margins of literary history (or at least fashion) by the successful campaign on behalf of the self-consciously unpretentious 'Movement' and the brilliant example of Philip Larkin. But Fraser was still a respected figure who presided genially over his monthly gatherings, which unlike the Group meetings were lubricated by the alcohol that the participants brought with them. According to Brownjohn there was no close critical scrutiny of the kind Hobsbaum encouraged. Several poets would read their work (in contrast to the one-poet 'songsheets' of the Group), and some discussion might or might not follow, in which Fraser would make discerning and encouraging comments. From the point of view of this social and easy-going norm (which the notoriously unclubbable Leavis would have called 'flank-rubbing') it is easy to see how the critical rigour of the Group would have been ridiculed as Leavisite Puritanism.

Brownjohn had published a poem by Redgrove in his magazine *Departure*, but they did not meet until some time later when four new arrivals came together to Fraser's, sat in a row on hard-backed chairs, and spoke vociferously about the poems that were read. They were Hobsbaum, Redgrove, Porter and Bell. Fraser was tolerant and welcoming and showed no overt impatience, but may have felt some irritation at their dominating presence. Group representatives, reinforced by Lucie-Smith, continued to attend Fraser's evenings, and one of their favourite provocations was to read a poem by Hughes, then a bugbear of Fraser's circle. Later Porter invited Brownjohn to the Group, and he became a regular member.

Fraser was also invited to the Group soon after the occasion Brownjohn records, and a letter of Redgrove's to Hobsbaum about this shows that by now Ted Hughes had certainly stepped into the role of 'senior poet'. Redgrove admired Hughes's refusal to compromise, staying mobile and 'living on his wits' in contrast to his own 'treaties and arrangements with the world', consequent on his marriage. Redgrove clearly wanted Fraser to be favourably impressed by the Group, and to this end he recommended that Hughes should be on display for the visit: 'With Ted I think we are likely to be at our best, without the personal interest of some other member present who would be anxious to catch the great critic's notice, and the rest of us who might feel we ought to help him.' Evidently Redgrove thought Hughes was above such anxieties.

'The great critic' may have been ironic: a pseudo-typo in the same letter refers to Fraser's 'sill (beg his pardon) differently aligned remarks' about Redgrove's own poetry. Contrary to Brownjohn's account of the tone of his meetings, Fraser had evidently criticised the form and rhythm of Redgrove's poetry. Despite the pseudo-typo Redgrove says that he respects Fraser, and demonstrates this, not only by his anxiety that the Group should make a good impression, but also by defending his methods against Fraser's invocation of 'traditional forms': 'For myself, I think that the form came out of the language, not the other way round, and that the process is of continuous growth, listening to the patterns the language makes and the ways in which it produces expression or arrives at it.' This is typical of the way Redgrove discusses his own work in these early years, and may surprise readers of his later work who regard him as an inspirational poet for whom form is unimportant. His notebooks at this time include word-lists, rhyme-schemes and lists of rhyming words, and he experimented with sonnets, villanelles, sestinas and other traditional forms. But for many years one of his main preoccupations was hostility to (or at least avoidance of) the Chaucerian iambic tradition and defence of an alternative metric, inspired by the accentual metre of Langland but not mechanically imitative of it, which he found more congenial. It may not be too fanciful to suggest that the rule-bound regularity of iambic metre reminded him of his father's world, of business suits and ties, and regulated sexuality. His rebellion against all of this, so far latent in his poetry but powerfully active in his consciousness, could not be contained within 'traditional forms'.

Not long afterwards Redgrove met the critic Bonamy Dobrée, who had recently retired as Professor of English at Leeds, and was to be an important mover in the young poet's career. Porter was surprised that Dobrée, a 'very fastidious' First World War veteran, 'spine permanently standing at attention', should have admired Redgrove's work – he thought he warmed to Peter because he was 'very English and ebullient'. Dobrée also challenged Redgrove about his rhythms, though Redgrove evidently found him more sympathetic than Fraser, describing his admission to the latter's 'nursery' as 'not . . . a very nutritious transplantation'. (He remembered Fraser's evenings with affection, however, and said that he had 'met people there who I would not have missed for the world'.) In contrast to Fraser, Dobrée told him that he thought the iamb 'a bore' and Redgrove was a lifelong admirer of his 1925 pamphlet *Histriophone*, a dialogue on dramatic verse, which dismisses metrical analysis as 'trochaic inversions, acatalectic lines, and all the elaborate frivolity of the text-books' and takes as its yardstick the spoken word.

Peter stuck at the Odhams job for two and a half years – the longest he was to stay at any salaried job until he went to Falmouth School of Art. He felt that he had no talent for advertising and, as he insisted to his father, he 'did well enough at Odhams' by 'being as personable and pleasant as I could, and getting as much help as ever I could', finding it an 'intolerable grind . . . to think up any acceptable idea at all (often failing and having to be rescued)'. He felt that he cheated his way through the job, and would eventually be found out.

In February 1957 he resigned from Odhams and travelled to Malaga, where he worked part-time as a language teacher. He had planned this venture at least a year beforehand, when he was making detailed notes about letters of recommendation, arrangements for accommodation, learning the language, healthcare, what clothes and books to take with him and how to manage Odhams so that he could return to his job if necessary. The earnings from teaching hardly covered his rent, and the trip was made possible by an earlier legacy (of which he had obviously saved something) from a mysterious 'crippled girl who never left her bed, and who died leaving me money enough to buy a tape-recorder, a certain amount of independence at Cambridge, and seven months (as it should be) in Spain'. What is most startling about this move is that Barbara did not accompany him, yet there is no evidence of estrangement. In his planning notes he envisaged her visiting him for holidays and conceiving their first child in an orange grove. His stated reason for going was that 'it would be an excellent thing for me to live in a foreign country as part of my education'. Barbara's own voice is inaudible during this period and for most of their marriage, and reminiscences of her are disappointingly bland – as Peter Porter said, people one met in Redgrove's company tended to be 'out-dazzled' by him. Lucie-Smith describes her as 'a nice, sweetnatured, rather ordinary (ordinary in the sense of wanting what most people want, home, family etc.) suburban girl, with an equable temperament and a lot of common sense'. Brownjohn hints at more robust qualities when he calls her 'strong-minded' and 'plain-speaking', and Porter concurs with this impression, adding that she 'believed profoundly in Peter's talent'. Unsurprisingly the young Hannah Hobsbaum formed a more vivid impression of the married sculptor eight years her senior. Hannah thought Barbara very talented and intelligent and once refused an invitation to go with her to an art gallery because she wouldn't know what to say to her. Barbara was committed to Peter's vocation as a poet, and may have agreed that he needed this experience of travel. She may already have begun to find the frustrations building up in Peter as he tried to combine poetry with commercial employment – and, more secretly, to integrate his sexuality into their marriage – difficult to live with. He didn't keep an intimate journal at this time, but an abandoned verse draft dramatises the conflict in the marriage:

> What have you got to fear? why run away like that all the time?
> We're friends. I love you. Sit down here. Let's talk.
> Foolish, oh foolish to waste you [*sic*] time like that.
> Let's face up to things. You're not a fool. We're friends
> And lovers, and occupy the same space, are one.
> That is the way to see it. It's not obscene.
> Give me your hand, I'll start to show you so,
> Then you'll be asking me, and not the other way around.

The Game was evidently causing trouble between them. He later told Penelope Shuttle that the Spanish trip had been part of a quid pro quo: this time of freedom for him before they started a family.

While he was away Barbara had to deal with a problem with the mortgage. Her father had helped them to buy their house, but the building society was pressing for payments. Whether this was a direct result of Peter giving up his job is not clear, but his Skimpole-like vagueness about money difficulties, at his safe distance, must have been infuriating to those who had to tackle the problem:

> I do hope this Building Society will take this sudden debt that has happened to us, and that they're not going to be harsh about it. It was one of the reasons that we were so much beholden to Mr Sherlock for making it possible to us to have such a nice home, that it would be in the family and we could have a certain freedom (although a business-like one) about our payments, so that if for some reason we couldn't manage it at a given time, we could have credit to manage better at some future date.

He lived in a little whitewashed room ('so you can see the mosquitoes', he said) with a walled garden outside with gravelled walks, little hedges and trees. He had 'quite a lot of electric light, for Spain', but the water supply was erratic, despite which he bragged of doing his own laundry. Initially he didn't boast of any great poetic achievements, but devoted his efforts to translating poems by Ali Chumacero, Silvina Ocampo, Alberto Quintero Alvarez and Octavio Paz: he called these 'rather exercises in sympathy with the author than linguistic understanding'.

He recorded little of his social life in Malaga, but he did recollect 'a rather frivolous English colony there' and meeting the American writer, journalist and photographer Guy Murchie, whose ideas that there are gradations of sex, rather than a polarised masculine and feminine, and many senses beyond the recognised five, might already have appealed to the author of *The Black Goddess and the Sixth Sense*. Another Malaga contact was Gamel Woolsey, the American poet and chronicler of the Spanish Civil War. She was married to the English writer Gerald Brenan and had formerly had a passionate affair with Llewellyn Powys, brother of John Cowper and Theodore. Peter reported a proposal to collaborate with her on translations of Spanish poetry for the BBC, but this proved abortive partly because, belatedly, he became absorbed in writing his own poetry. During this period he composed 'Fiesta', 'Our Friend', 'Holy Week', 'Control', 'Flies', 'Malagueño', 'Thirteen Ways of looking at a Blackboard' (the last inspired by his experience of teaching English in Spain), and forty-seven poems that he never collected. On his return he bound all these up in card wrappers and distributed them to his friends. Through the notebook he kept at this time runs an anxiety that he is spoiling his poems by revising them – he keeps referring himself back to the first versions: 'feeling should be the guide'. He also tells himself to avoid making prose notes: 'cannot think in prose'. But he never abandoned the practice of frequent revision and in later years he was to develop a systematic method of composition by stages, including prose drafts.

At some point Jim and Nan must have visited, because many years later Peter wrote a poem, 'At Malaga Cathedral', in which his mother touches the body of a carved Christ and exclaims, 'What a man!' Peter was almost certainly faithful to Barbara while they were apart, though there is evidence that he was tempted by the invitation of an older woman (probably not Gamel Woolsey who was over sixty):

> Mrs X of fourty-four [*sic*] and over
> Professes to invite
> Mr twenty-four or younger
> To her bed this night.

This is followed in his notebook by several pages of more heated writing, and a transcription of Benjamin Franklin's 'Advice to a Friend on Choosing a Mistress', in which he recommends that if the young man cannot keep chaste, he had better choose an older woman. None of this writing is overtly autobiographical, and Redgrove was evidently planning a poem on the theme of Franklin's letter, but the relevance to his own situation is obvious: 'Mrs X' says to her young man, 'That feat / Will add something to your life / That'll help you when you bring back your wife.' However, the dominant note of all this writing is frustration rather than guilt:

> To pace about one's room all night,
> To take the weight upon the feet and wear
> A blister in the carpet. To avoid the handy method
> And keep it strictly at the side because
> There's nothing in that meeting but a hand.

It goes without saying that he was missing Barbara – 'every day is awful without [her]' – and eventually she joined him at the end of July, after a separation of more than five months. 'Spain is wearing a very different complexion,' he wrote to Hobsbaum. 'My naturally gloomy nature is buoyed up by her . . . I'd felt little of the beauty, but a lot of the scumminess; but this evening, with Barbara in the room, I am excited by the liveliness of something that pervades Malaga.'

By October they were back in Chiswick; her sister Hilary had the impression that Barbara had had a bad time. An unpublished poem in dialogue form has an implicitly male speaker rather condescendingly trying to reconcile his companion to the dirt and poverty of 1950s Spain:

> A. 'You won't explore this track, or that street
>   Where the dust is sifted by canvas feet
>   Or in the gutter the children fight
>   Or on the sills dogs bathe in the light?'
>
> B. 'Or where the skin of the baby bakes in the heat,
>   And cracks, or the child snatches the dusty goat's teat,
>   And the quaking udders spread the blight
>   Of people dying out of the light.'

To his credit Redgrove gives 'B' the last word. The poem strikingly anticipates the portrayal of the conflict between Hughes and Plath in Hughes's 'You Hated Spain', which refers to their visit in 1956, but was not written till the 1970s: 'You saw right down to the Goya funeral grin / And recognised it, and recoiled.'

Lucie-Smith observed that Peter was convinced he could change everything by altering his external circumstances, and as a result was always meeting with disillusionment. He undoubtedly enjoyed his time in Spain, and it was a creative stimulus, but it did not solve anything, or make a long-term difference to his life. When he returned he again had to submit to uncongenial employment and, despite his plans beforehand, returning to Odham's doesn't seem to have been an option. His and Jim's letters at this time are good-tempered and at least in Jim's case affectionate, but their minds struggle to meet. Jim accepts that sales is out of the question but cannot understand why Peter won't apply his undoubted creative gifts to advertising, as he had done at Odham's. There is an undertone of controlled exasperation about this, and in Peter's attempts to explain that his compulsion to write poetry is inimical to the production of advertising copy. For a time there was hope of work in television, but Jim had to report from his contacts that the BBC was cutting back, while the recently formed ITV was too crass for a writer of Peter's temper – an opinion pretty universal among educated people in the 1950s. Eventually he found employment as writer and sub-editor for the Education and Technology supplements of *The Times*.

One of Peter's letters to Jim is signed, 'Your eldest and most difficult son'. These words would soon have an agonising resonance for the parents. David, now just short of his twentieth birthday, had developed in a direction that seemed almost designedly opposed to his elder brother. Peter had loved David as a small boy but believed they had been driven apart by Taunton: in later years they couldn't talk to each other. It may be that David would have chosen a different direction in life from that of his brilliant elder brother anyway. Peter records that Jim used to call him 'poor David', and spoke of him as 'retarded'. If this was the atmosphere in which he grew up he would certainly have wanted to avoid comparison with Peter. The route he chose, as if electing to triumph where Peter had collapsed, was to join the Household Cavalry (Life Guards). He planned to spend three years in the army (the minimum permitted in the Guards) before joining his father's company. Photos of him in Mounted Review Order, with red tunic, spiked white-plumed helmet and thigh-length boots, tightly strapped in by white waist- and cross-belts, riding a bay horse and shouldering his sword, wearing a mask of grim masculine resolve, could not be more remote from his brother's persona. He was only nineteen. Hilary thought he throve in the army. A couple of years younger, she had a teenage crush on him, despite or because of which she was intensely annoyed by his cockiness and apparent self-confidence. The Redgrove and Sherlock families were on close terms, and the Redgroves used to visit at Selsey. One time David insisted on Hilary getting up early to go duck-shooting with him. He ordered her to go round the edge of a field, where ducks were settled, walking in a muddy ditch so as not to alarm them, and then fire a shot to send them in his direc-tion. She stayed out of the ditch, disturbed the ducks and they flew away. She was pleased to have frustrated the cocksure young man, but he was so furious that she jumped on her bike and cycled off home. His friend Chris Harding thought that he struck an extrovert manly pose in imitation of the father he hero-worshipped and feared.

Just before Christmas 1957 David went to a party with a group of friends. Some of the guests stayed in a hotel and, in the early hours of Christmas Eve, one of them, a young woman, found that she was locked out of her bedroom. The room was next to David's and he gallantly offered to climb out of his window, scale between the rooms and get into hers. While carrying out this exploit he lost his grip, fell to the ground and was killed.

This is the version of David's death that was unquestioningly accepted by the family, including Peter. Is there anything suspicious about it? Probably not: if David had wanted to get into the girl's room for other reasons he needn't have gone to such risky lengths, though it is possible that in a mood of drunken bravado he wanted to make a romantic appearance, in keeping with his 'Loopy' reputation from Taunton. As far as Peter was concerned, the official story suited his construction of the family's sexual dynamic. For him it was a tragic recapitulation of the chivalric rescue, which was his reading of the spirit in which Jim took responsibility for Nan and Mimi. David's comrades in the regiment sent a wreath in the form of a sword in flowers. When Peter saw 'this severe emblem relenting in death and bursting in bloom' he wept.

In the following months Peter's notebooks are haunted by David's death, but it is hard to judge how much this is inner compulsion, and how much family duty. Jim, who struggled to understand Peter's vocation as a poet, could see the point of a poem commemorating his son. Three weeks after the tragedy, Jim sent Peter a poem of his own:

Queen's Guard

They rode down the Mall on that soft Easter day
Old and young heads turn to watch as they wheel
And a happy young face was there leading the way
His eyes shining bright as that of polished steel

Daily past 'Horse Guards' the holiday crowds wind
And little hands reach up bravely with sugar held ready
Do the blue eyes under that proud white plume grow even more kind?
Then an admiring smile from beneath a saucy spring hat – 'Steady
  Trooper, steady!'

The planes have lost their green – the window boxes their flowers
Cavalry scarlet is cloaked as grey as Whitehall's facade.
And those gentle blue eyes no longer watch the slow passing of Ben's
  hours
Called to greater Guard.

The accompanying letter was appropriately self-deprecating, but it also issued a challenge: 'I have an inarticulate kind of feeling that I would like our love for the boy to be expressed in words that will live longer than the sheaf of letters and tributes which just now are heaped around us. I believe you can do this.' Peter could not fail to do what his father had done, however feebly and conventionally.

Peter's first attempt commemorates David as someone who was anxious to do right: putting out a cigarette is a task he felt 'somebody might / Get at him for not getting right'; in a photo he smiles for the camera 'as if he likes / Being told what's right'; in the army 'He did his guard as he was told was right'. In these verses Peter seems to be pressing on the difference between himself and his brother – not just difference, but something in David that he himself had decisively rejected. In a poem written so soon after the death, and partly for his parents, he could not pursue these thoughts very far, and consequently the poem seems patronising. As we have seen, in later years the brothers were unable to communicate, and Peter has the task of trying to speak out of that silence: 'When I write of you it goes cold and dead / You who died leaving most unsaid.'

Other attempts are conventional elegies, at times feebly dutiful:

> To comb this despair
> Out of my hair
> When I see my face:
> It resembles his;
> And I meet my mother:
> She is sad for the other;
> And my father's hand
> Is lighter far.
> Because of my brother
> There is only one son
> And I am their last one.

More successful are two pieces recalling incidents from their childhood: an attempt by the two of them to destroy a wasp's nest, and a sword-fight that ended with Peter wounding David's nose. But neither of these poems effectively makes the anecdote a channel for feeling about David's death. It was not until the following summer that Peter found a metaphor that brought into focus both his grief at the death and his sadness about the way their relationship had developed:

Memorial

(David Redgrove: 28th December 1937–24th December 1957)

Two photographs stand on the dresser
Joined up the spine. Put away
They fold until they kiss each other,
But put out, they look across the room.
My brother and myself. He is flushed and pouting
With heart, and standing square,
I, already white-browed and balding,
Float there, it seems, and look away.
You could look at them and say I was the one of air,
And he the brother of earth
Who, in Christmas-time, fell to his death.

Fancy, yes; but if you'd seen him in his life
There'd be his bright blond hair, and that flush,
And the mouth always slightly open, and the strength
Of body: those muscles! swelled up with the hard hand-springs at night
Certainly, but strong. I, on the other hand
Was remote, cross, and disengaged, a proper
Bastard to my brother, who enjoyed things,
Until he was able to defend himself. It's June;
Everything's come out in flush and white,
In ruff and sun, and tall green shoots
Hard with their sap. He's ashes
Like this cigarette I smoke into grey dryness.
I notice outside my window a tree of blossom,
Cherries, I think, one branch bending heavy
Into the grey road to its no advantage.
The hard stone scrapes the petals off,
And the dust enters the flower into its peak.
It is so heavy with flowers it bruises itself:
It has tripped, you might say, and fallen,
Cannot get up, so heavy with dust.
The air plays with it, and plays small-chess with the dust. (C)

Redgrove successfully translates into a modern idiom traditional elegiac themes of lost youth, the passage of the seasons and the fate of the mortal body. But its real originality and poignancy of feeling is in the first few lines, and particularly the image of the photographs, figuring the actual estrangement of the brothers and the hidden, suppressed, desired or remembered intimacy. It became one of his most popular early poems, and if it was composed partly out of familial duty it succeeded in these terms too, as it was one of Jim's favourites. Later Peter skilfully adapted a translation of 'Alma Ausente', one of Lorca's elegies for the bullfighter and writer Ignacio Sanchez Mejias, to make an elegy for David: he omitted all the Mediterranean detail in Lorca's poem, and a line about '*La madurez insigne de tu conocimiento*' (the distinguished maturity of your knowledge), which would have been inappropriate to the nineteen-year-old soldier, but retained references to Sanchez's daring – 'Your appetite for hazard and the taste of death'. He published this poem as 'Variation on Lorca', the first of 'Two Elegies' in his second collection *The Nature of Cold Weather*.

Whether or not the trip to Spain was a quid pro quo, Barbara conceived immediately on their return, and their first son was born in July. The situation of a young couple desiring, conceiving and giving birth to children recurs in numerous early poems and is perhaps the keynote of Redgrove's first collection. The finest of these is 'Bedtime Story for my Son', which beautifully evokes the half-conscious desire of a young couple through images of haunting, which they track down to 'just underneath both our skins', and the wife's pronouncement, 'I couldn't go and love the empty air', is the basis for an effectively modulated refrain. More commonly the expected child is the focus of a disturbance in the relationship or in the husband's state of mind. 'The Pregnant Father' is explicitly about the husband's fear that the child will be a 'cuckoo' and that the birth will be 'The start of one love and ending of another'. In 'Against Death' and 'Old House' the commitment to life shown by bearing children struggles against an 'agony of imagination' feeding on all the deaths that have occurred in the house. If these poems raise questions about Peter's commitment to family life, they are also successful examples of dramatising his preoccupations: they declare and objectify, rather than neurotically betray, the anxieties that motivate them: he said that 'Against Death' was 'rather a beastly poem perhaps: the impulse seems to be an obsessional avoidance of death by the means every man has'.

Bill was born on 6 July. Seeing Barbara in labour Peter wept; he thought this was because he couldn't participate, but could only stand and watch. But as the poem 'Expectant Father', in which he is woken up by a phone call from the hospital, suggests, he didn't see the actual birth. In the following weeks Peter showed every sign of paternal fondness for Bill, including boasting about the baby's vocalisation and reading poetry to him. He declared himself very glad that Bill looked more like Barbara than himself, and that 'the family face' was not being reproduced – ironically, since as an adult Bill grew to resemble his father uncannily.

Bonamy Dobrée thought highly enough of Peter's poetry to offer his support for the Gregory Fellowship at Leeds. Peter refused because he didn't want to prejudice his position at Times Newspapers. Nevertheless the job there lasted little more than six months: he left because, although it was more suited to his temperament than advertising or publicity, it required him to be away from home during Barbara's late pregnancy. Edward Lucie-Smith suggested that he should capitalise on his scientific background by presenting himself as a specialist copywriter; he followed this advice and was appointed Senior Scientific Editorial Assistant with Glaxo Laboratories. His interviewers told him that he was being engaged as a 'star writer', and he hoped that if he made a good start they would 'treat me as a sort of consultant to be called in for "high class" work'. Except for having to get up at 6.30 to begin his day's work he was very content with his working conditions and hopeful of 'settling down for a fair time at Glaxo'. He hoped to flout the supposed rule about domesticity being bad for artists.

His later reflections on this and all the other jobs he took between 1954 and 1961 are uniformly baleful, and he dismissed his attempt to reconcile art and domesticity as capitulation to the 'tribal values' of a post-war era, when 'one's woman expected one to work in this fashion, whatever it did to one'. He resorted (as during his finals) to Benzedrine and alcohol, the former to get through his paid work quickly, the latter to 'deregulate [his] senses' to work on poetry, including his versions of Rimbaud. A door in the building was known as 'Redgrove's Entry' because he used it to sneak out and back during the working day. His very last prose writing, left unfinished at his death, was a contribution to a Dylan Thomas commemorative issue of *Poetry Wales*, in which he wrote:

> I often left a pair of spectacles open on my office desk to declare my absence. Who was to know that I was out at the pub reading and imitating Rimbaud and Dylan Thomas, my only refuge from the pharmaceutical firm where I worked then, palace of pills that did not and could not understand these strange phrases that changed the world, in which creatures of the imagination flourished.

By September 1959 the Glaxo job, or Peter's reaction to it, was causing a 'rough passage' for him and Barbara:

> However willing I am in myself, or however much I acknowledge it necessary, more than a certain amount of sitting in an office, translating words into words, facing literary problems that are capable only of second-rate solutions, more than a certain subscription to the high-flown artificiality of hack-writing, produces a mental chill that I have little power of myself to warm.

He took an unauthorised holiday and when he returned was called into his boss's office and asked to leave. He did little work, kept bad hours, walked about the office with a gloomy face, his restlessness was bad for office discipline. In an example of long-vanished commercial humanity his boss allowed him time to find another job before enforcing the sacking. By the following month he had secured a job with the British Standards Institute, dealing with the press and publications, but not writing. It was less well-paid than the Glaxo job, and he thought it would be dull, but more acceptable because 'less exigent'.

Peter had good reason to be cheerful at this time, because he was looking forward to the publication of his first collection. Though he hadn't been able to take advantage of Dobrée's patronage for the Gregory Fellowship, Dobrée was a friend of Herbert Read who was on the board of Routledge. Routledge had a small poetry list including John Wain and D. J. Enright, and through the Dobrée–Read axis they offered Peter a contract. He had wanted to call his first book 'The Nature of Cold Weather', after a long poem that he wrote in 1958, but the publishers found it 'a bit hard to swallow from a new poet', and took the poem out. His editor Colin Franklin suggested that 'The Collector' 'would offend no one with violence and might please most people after only one reading', and so his first volume came to be named after what he considered his first poem. Peter thought the title rather weak, giving the impression that he might be a retired parson, and that the book should have a subtitle such as 'Leaves from my Hedgerow' or 'Gems from my Rockery'.

He was expecting the book to be published in the autumn, and it bears the publication date 1959, but it was held back in the hope that it might be published as a Poetry Book Society Choice (it wasn't) and it actually appeared in January. This was an epoch not only for him personally but for the Group as a whole, since it was the first collection by a member. Philip was now living in Sheffield, studying for a PhD with William Empson, but Peter was delighted that he of all people was able to come to the party he and Barbara threw for the occasion. With Philip's withdrawal as chairman, the first period of the London Group, its most vital period as far as Peter was concerned, had come to an end. *The Collector* was an appropriate marker of this period, and Philip wrote a warmly appreciative review which was, however, only published in a Sheffield student magazine. Peter sent the review to Jim, whose pride in his son's achievement could not suppress his temperamental hostility to certain aspects of his imagination. He wrote, 'Here and there, your subjects strike me as unattractive to the ordinary man, even if he is not at times rather revolted by them.'

Peter was grateful for Philip's review, but more hung on the national newspapers and magazines. Larkin wrote rather condescendingly in the *Guardian* of 'a talent at present spending itself excitedly on all sorts of sensations and ideas, some of them acceptable, but too many trivial or disagreeable'. Much more enthusiastic were the American poet Donald Hall in the *New Statesman* and the fellow Routledge poet John Wain in the *Spectator*. Hall wrote that Redgrove's way of making metaphors was similar to that of Gunn and Hughes, and that he was good enough to be considered their peer rather than an imitator. Wain praised Redgrove without recourse to easy comparisons, saying that he 'writes boldly on important themes, and where he succeeds, succeeds memorably'. The poems had 'undeniable power and sense of purpose' and his failures, such as the Hopkins pastiche of 'A Leaf from my Bestiary', could be forgiven as the result of critical blind spots.

Redgrove must have been encouraged by Wain's review, in particular, but the most eagerly awaited notice was that of A. Alvarez in the *Observer*. Alvarez might not yet have had the influence he had a few years later, when he published the era-defining anthology *The New Poetry* and lampooned Movement poetry for its 'gentility', but he already had the power to make reputations. Alvarez's review came out on 27 March, and it was titled 'An Outstanding Young Poet'. Sadly for Peter, this prodigy was not himself but Ted Hughes, whose second collection, *Lupercal*, Alvarez reviewed in the same article. This was indeed the review that did more than any other single notice to establish Hughes in the public eye as the most important poet of his generation. In *Lupercal*, Alvarez announced, Hughes had 'found his own voice, created his own artistic world and . . . emerged as a poet of the first importance'. His achievement was 'to take a limited, personal theme and, by an act of immensely assured poetic skill' to broaden it until it seemed 'to touch upon nearly everything that concerns us'.

Any praise Alvarez might have given to *The Collector* would have been obscured by this monument of critical acclaim. But the reality was far crueller than mere overshadowing. Alvarez chose to cast Redgrove as the failure that threw Hughes's success into relief. His poetry was 'a poor man's version'. Instead of coming to terms with violence he exploited it. The verse was technically uncertain, wavering between 'clipped he-man colloquialisms' and 'poetical bluster'. It was a 'vulgarisation', a mechanical exploitation of sensationalism.

Alvarez was a gifted and perceptive critic, and he unerringly picked out examples of Redgrove's writing at its worst. Redgrove's poetic voice was still too often uncertain, and his tone in writing about horror and violence often betrayed a failure to integrate his deepest concerns into his poetic persona. *Lupercal*, in which Hughes gave to the world poems such as 'Hawk Roosting', 'Pike', 'An Otter', 'The Bull Moses' and 'View of a Pig', is undoubtedly a far more assured volume than *The Collector*. Some readers still consider it the pinnacle of his achievement. But a critic has a responsibility to identify what a new poet is capable of, where his strength and promise lie, not to take the easy option of lampooning his failures. Hughes's first collection, *The Hawk in the Rain*, contains at least as many bad poems as *The Collector*, but Alvarez received it warmly, if with more reservations than *Lupercal*. At least two poems in *The Collector*, 'Lazarus and the Sea' and 'Bedtime Story for My Son', are outstanding achievements, and many others are promising. There is an accomplished variety of tone from the sombre elegy of 'Memorial' to the sensuous precision of 'Without Eyes' and the comic high spirits of 'The Play'. But Alvarez was apparently blind to all this. Even with the weaker poems that he singles out, he seemingly wilfully misconstrues. He quotes these lines –

> I'll clear it up; so white a flesh
> Against the green; I'll let it char,
> But tuck the mangled neck back again –

and exclaims, 'That, believe it or not, is "On Catching a Dog-Daisy in the Mower"', without divulging to his reader the explicit fact that the speaker is repressing the knowledge of a 'friend's' death in a fall (the poem was of course inspired by David's death). Alvarez quotes as typical of the book the very poem, 'A Leaf from my Bestiary', that Wain had cited as a forgivable lapse.

Peter immediately drafted a riposte. He rightly protested against Alvarez's misrepresentation of 'On Catching a Dog-Daisy', but it is clear that what was most wounding was being portrayed as the poor man's Ted Hughes. He phoned Lucie-Smith, who talked him out of sending the letter, but he, Hobsbaum and Bell leaped to Peter's defence and wrote on his behalf. None of the letters was published, but Alvarez took the trouble to reply to Hobsbaum privately. He agreed that some of the detail in the poems was successful, and that in this respect his review was partial and unfair, but maintained that the overriding issue was that the book was 'full of hatred of life, of disgust & horror, combined with a certain gloating exploitation of these qualities'. 'Bedtime Story for My Son' was the only poem he acknowledged to be an exception. He appealed to Hobsbaum on his own ground by invoking 'the Lawrence–Leavis criterion of "health"'.

It is unlikely that a single review would cause lasting damage to a writer's reputation, but comparing him to Hughes in this way made an easy tag to justify ignoring Redgrove. More certainly, the review was far more personally wounding to Redgrove for the fact that it was Hughes (rather than, for example, Vernon Scannell, who is casually dismissed in the same review) – Hughes, whom he 'loved and envied', whom he had outshone poetically at Cambridge, but whose career he had so devotedly fostered – on whose altar he was being sacrificed. When he rang Ted himself about the review, he took care to appear 'very philosophical', and he may have been comforted by his friend's opinion that his poetry was 'much better than Alvarez made it out to be'.

Soon afterwards Redgrove was introduced to Alvarez by Anthony Thwaite. Alvarez repeated in more conciliatory terms what he had said to Hobsbaum: he was sorry he had been so violent in the review, and though he still thought Redgrove was a sadomasochist, 'he wished he had dwelt on the means I used to accomplish such an effect in my verse'. To that extent he admitted that he had been unjust. Surprisingly he told Redgrove that he would like to include

Jim Redgrove,
Peter's father,
1925

Nan and Mimi Cestrilli-Bell,
Peter's mother and grandmother

Nan on honeymoon, 1926

Peter and Jim, 1932, from home movie

Peter aged about 4,
from home movie

Peter in his laboratory,
*c.*1946, from home movie

Taunton School

Orchard End, Kingston upon Thames, Peter's childhood home

David, Jim, Nan and Peter at Jim and Nan's silver wedding, September 1951

TED. - Pembroke College Cambridge. 1952

Ted Hughes at Cambridge, 1952

Peter and Barbara's wedding, July 1954

David in Guards' uniform

David and Peter 'joined up the spine': the 'Memorial' photos

Martin Bell, 1950s

Philip Hobsbaum, early 1960s

Peter Porter, 1980s

Peter, Barbara, Bill and Pete in
Buffalo, February 1962

Drawing of Peter
by Barbara, 1964

Jim (with ever-present
movie camera) and Nan,
February 1964

Peter and Barbara,
February 1964

Dilly Creffield,
1962

some of his work in the Penguin anthology that he was editing. Astonishingly, in the light of the review, he chose ten poems for *The New Poetry*, six of them from *The Collector*, including 'Lazarus and the Sea' and 'Bedtime Story for My Son'. Only Hughes and Gunn were more generously represented.

But a disturbance had been introduced, or perhaps exposed, in Redgrove's feelings about Hughes – a disturbance which was never to be fully resolved. (Seventeen years later the episode of the review was to be reprised when Craig Raine similarly treated Redgrove as a foil to Hughes.) He analysed his feelings with remarkable object-ivity in a letter to Hobsbaum. On the one hand he recognised 'Ted's personal excellence' and 'earnest desire to be helpful', together with the fact that there was a great deal in common between their outlooks. Moreover, of course, Redgrove admired Hughes's poetry – he cites in particular 'November', 'The Bull Moses', 'To Paint a Water-Lily', 'Pike', 'Relic' and 'Hawk Roosting', all in *Lupercal*. But he hated being compared to Hughes (almost always to his own disadvantage) and could not bear the fact that Hughes was, as he saw it, fawned upon, rather than having his merits justly appreci-ated, and seemed to lap this up. He cited an American who was visiting to arrange recordings of British poets for the Library of Congress, who could only 'croon at Ted "Sure, I admire your judge-ment, Taid; say, Mr Redgrove, I truhst this man's judgement"', while Ted 'put on a princely, pleasant face and gave this nonentity the benefit of a long urbane discourse'. No doubt being sidelined himself sharpened his distaste. Above all – as a result of this 'fawning' – he saw Hughes enjoying the privilege of developing his talent free from the burden of a salaried job. These things in combination 'poisoned' his feelings about his friend.

Hughes and Plath had returned in December after more than two years in America, and had settled in London. Redgrove looked forward to a renewal of their earlier intimacy, and to an extent his hopes were fulfilled: in an episode immortalised in Plath's biography, he went with her to see the Aldermaston march, and found both of them 'as friendly as they had ever been'. But he now accused Hughes of 'receiving me into his intimacy and dropping me like a Yo-Yo'. Twice Hughes had been an hour and a half late for a meeting, and when Peter invited Ted and Sylvia to join him and Barbara at Selsey, Ted promised to ring back, but failed to do so. The gulf that had now opened between the two poets' public standing is thrown into sharp relief by Hobsbaum's suspicion that there was a 'venal' motive behind this invitation: presumably Hobsbaum thought his friend cultivated Hughes for professional advantage. Peter was mollified when he learned that this last discourtesy was caused by Sylvia suffering from mastitis (her daughter Frieda was born in April), but Ted's failure to keep promises to visit is a recurring theme. In 1972 Peter's journal tersely records, 'TH said he was coming and is not.' The two poets did see quite a lot of each other in the short period before Ted and Sylvia left London for Devon, and Peter and Barbara left for America. Much later in life Peter was nostalgic about the hours they spent in a pub at Oxford Circus talking about Shakespeare, and Ted records spending a whole day drinking with Peter, and consuming nine pints – a feat more characteristic of Redgrove than of Hughes.

As the correspondence about Hughes shows, Redgrove's intimacy with Hobsbaum was undiminished by the latter's removal to Sheffield. Hobsbaum continued to comment on Redgrove's poetry but a more intriguing development was that he again began writing poetry himself. Through all the years in which he had chaired the Group he had written only fiction – an unpublished novel that he later described as 'sub-Amis' and 'absolutely dreadful'. Whether it was the liberation from school-teaching, the contact with William Empson, or even distance from the talents of his London friends, the move to Sheffield opened a new creative vein, and he completed four collections in the nine years it took him to complete his PhD. (He had no grant but Hannah worked to support them, and he didn't need to take a full-time job until he was appointed to a lectureship at Queen's Belfast in 1962.) Later, reflecting on his subsequent estrangement from Hobsbaum, Redgrove thought that 'some of us let him down, in not being as good at criticism as he was, at practically-useful criticism'. But his letters to his friend in this period give the lie to his self-judgement. He offers Hobsbaum constant support, and the letters are full of detailed, candid, perceptive and encouraging criticism.

By the summer of 1960 Peter had changed jobs yet again, joining Peter Porter and Edward Lucie-Smith at Notley's advertising agency. He exploited his scientific background again and was employed to produce 'ethical' copy for pharmaceutical products. No satirist could have exposed the irony of this term more savagely than the fact that one of the contracts Peter worked on was for Thalidomide. He was relieved that his copy wasn't used, and even more so that, having given Thalidomide to Barbara when she was pregnant and unable to sleep, they escaped the consequences.

He thought the work at Notley's was undemanding, but even his friends were startled by how little he did. Both Porter and Lucie-Smith remembered that he worked as little as he possibly could, and the latter's response, at least, was not entirely benign, since other people had to pick up the work that Peter neglected. Lucie-Smith thought that Peter despised any work that did not have to do with poetry. He once made the reasonable suggestion that Peter should try his hand at science fiction: 'He gazed at me with big tragic eyes and exclaimed: "But that would be work!" End of conversation.' Lucie-Smith also witnessed the extremity of the frustration that Peter suffered at this time, and the potential for violence beneath his courteous manner: 'I remember him gripping and rattling the lift cage at Notley's, and literally roaring like a caged lion.' Their boss told Edward that the quality of Peter's work would be acceptable only from a trainee at less than half the salary he was getting, and Edward was anxious that Peter would get the sack, even from a firm that he considered tolerant and easy-going. When he tried to raise his concerns with Peter in the pub one evening, his friend flew into a rage mixed with threats of what he would do to the directors of the company. Edward realised that Peter was much more emotionally involved with his work in advertising than he pretended to be, and was as sensitive to criticism of his efforts as he was about his poetry. As Lucie-Smith recognised with regard to Peter's self-promotion, his relationship with Jim was undoubtedly the root of this sensitivity.

Probably Barbara was no stranger to this anger at home, but Peter was still trying to reconcile domestic life with the disruptive energies that drove his poetry. In December their second son was born. In contrast to Bill's birth, this time Peter saw the baby being born: forty years later he recalled the 'turquoise flesh' of the child 'speedily flushing' out of his mother's womb. The boy was named after his father, and was always known as Pete. Of all the children of the marriage to Barbara, he was to be the closest to his father's heart.

By the time Pete was born, Peter had the prospect of liberation from the life he had been living since 1954. Since early 1960 he had been trying to find a university post in America. He was offered a one-year teaching post at the University of Buffalo in New York State, and with the help of references from Herbert Read, George

Fraser and Philip Hobsbaum (though a graduate student writing a reference for a university teaching post is a little bizarre) he also got funding from the Fulbright Commission. Hobsbaum probably finessed Peter's lack of a degree, since the letter thanking him is signed 'BA (Prelim), Fulbright Scholar'. By the time he left for America in June his second collection was accepted and in press. He was never to live in London, or work in the commercial world, again.

VI

The Gregory Fellowship 1961–66

The next four years were the only time in Peter's life when he was attached to the English Department of a university. He taught for a year in Buffalo; during that time he was approached again by Bonamy Dobrée about the Gregory Fellowship, and this time he eagerly accepted. The three years of the fellowship were to be the only time in his life when he was paid to be a writer, the only time until his fifties that he did not have to juggle his writing with a salaried job. He was free for ever from the worlds of advertising and journalism, but the obvious conflicts caused by earning a living had masked deeper trouble. The freedom of full-time writing was wonderful for his work, which developed at Leeds more than at any time since Cambridge, but the strains in the marriage became more severe.

He sailed for America on the *Queen Elizabeth*, alone, on 15 June. Six weeks later the family, accompanied by Jim and Nan, flew out to join him in Buffalo, on the eastern tip of Lake Erie, close to the Canadian border and Niagara Falls. They lived in a typical American one-storey clapboard house surrounded by a lawn and wire fence, within walking distance of the campus. The houses reminded him of seaside resorts on the south coast of England. Edward Lucie-Smith, who visited in November, was more vehement in his response: he thought Buffalo was like 'a gigantic, extra-vulgar, brilliantly neon-lit version of Greenford, Middlesex'.

The English Department was housed in Crosby Hall, one of a number of neoclassical buildings that distinguish this site. Peter taught Shakespeare ('helping the Professor', Oscar A. Silverman), modern literature, freshman English and – obviously most to his liking – creative writing. For the first time he put Hobsbaum's Group method into practice himself, and was to continue to do so, in Leeds and Falmouth, for the next twenty-two years. He threw himself enthusiastically into his teaching, offering more than the scheduled hours by inviting students to his home to practise reading Shakespeare aloud. Nevertheless he had some reservations about the students: they were bright but passive and often ill-prepared. This may explain the odd complaint he later made, that he had given Shakespeare away to his students, and it took him years to get him back. He had a principled objection to the way freshman English was taught: 'the extraction by main force of *the* abstract idea from the tissue of thought and emotion and memory in the mind, and writing with the "thesis" as taskmaster'. Obviously, nothing could be more alien to his own approach to writing.

Peter wrote to Dobrée that he felt more at home in a university job than he had done in any other, and he was certainly prepared, if necessary, to stay in America and teach for a second year (the terms of his Fulbright grant limited his stay to two years). Over the year, however, complaints about the university, and about America, grew. He found American culture 'decadent', by which he meant 'an insistence on the form of things rather than the spirit', exemplified by the narrow specialism of both academics and doctors: he complained about not being able to visit a GP and accused American doctors of having 'abandoned the art of medicine – by which I mean the idea of the whole man, of total functional health'. Curiously, on the credit side, he praised Americans for their large families. By the spring he was saying that Buffalo was 'not what you'd call a very *good* American university' and that the year had not been 'an easy time for any of us, and a considerable disappointment'. Apart from his mild complaints about the students and the professionalised narrowness of his colleagues his main grouse was that, because he didn't have a degree, he was paid the lowest possible salary, $5,000, but there is no evidence that he was suffering financially.

Despite his teaching duties he was able to set aside several days a week for writing. Like Ted Hughes a few years before him, whose *Lupercal* was entirely written in America but showed no trace of it, Redgrove's work was little affected by his change of location. The only influence, perhaps, was the weather, the winter that was 'terrific (in Blake's sense) . . . with the snow blowing and drifting like sand-dunes'. (Bill, who was three at the time, remembered only 'horizontal snow' from his year in Buffalo.) This may have inspired the snow scenes of poems such as 'The Wizard', 'Virgins' and 'Winter Lightning', published in *At the White Monument* and *The Force*.

Probably the most notable event of the year took place back home: the publication and reception of his second collection, *The Nature of Cold Weather*. Most of the poems in this volume were contemporary with those in *The Collector*, including the title poem which Colin Franklin had thought too challenging for a first collection. Almost all the reviews weighed Redgrove's undeniable virtues against qualities that the critics found difficult or repellent: on the one hand his 'vitality', 'highly-tuned responsiveness', 'richness of sensibility' and (especially perceptive from Charles Tomlinson) 'committedness to a range of neglected experience'; on the other 'mania, tension, fantasy and confusion', 'the most inchoate type of metaphor imaginable', 'mere violence of diction and manner'. Peter's friend George MacBeth (always a more moderate admirer than some of the other Group members) summed up the general views starkly: 'The quality of his work ranges between extremes of goodness and badness rarely approached by his contemporaries.' More unreserved praise came from Donald Davie – a surprising supporter, the poet–critic of the Movement and author of *Purity of Diction in English Verse*. Davie asserted that 'by comparison with him nearly all [his contemporaries] inhabit a strikingly *unfurnished* world'.

But the really great event was Alvarez's review in the *Observer*, an astonishing volte-face after his treatment of *The Collector*. Alvarez began his review by saying that he felt he owed Redgrove an apology. However, he does not rescind his attack on *The Collector*. That volume still, in his view, 'showed Redgrove as the Bard of the Nasty, of sadism, wounds, murder and the cellarage of violence . . . translated into rather over-wrought, mannered language'. *The Nature of Cold Weather* by contrast shows 'a nerve-end fineness of description made stable by precision of language'. In a prescient foreshadowing of Redgrove's later concerns, 'masculine violence and aggression' has been supplanted by 'a more passive feminine experience'. Alvarez is puzzled by this because he is aware (the jacket says so) that many of the poems are contemporaneous with *The Collector*, but he doesn't revise his earlier estimate: the first book 'hopelessly misrepresented his talent'.

In truth there is no such vast distinction between the two collections. The most obvious difference is that there are longer, more ambitious poems in *The Nature of Cold Weather*, but these are by no means the best. Only the prose poems, the 'Fantasias' derived from Rimbaud and the wonderful 'Mr Waterman', show a completely new side of Redgrove's talent. The 'feminine' qualities are plainly evident in *Collector* poems such as 'Without Eyes' and 'Bedtime Story for My Son', while 'nerve-end fineness of description made stable by precision of language' fits the latter poem, 'Lazarus and the Sea' and 'Memorial' as well as any poems in the second collection. The truth about Alvarez's response is revealed by the fact that he chose six poems from *The Collector*, and only three from *The Nature of Cold Weather*, for his anthology *The New Poetry*. He had changed his mind about *The Collector*, and didn't want to admit it.

In the New Year 'Mr Waterman' was broadcast on the BBC TV arts programme *Monitor*, performed by Kenneth Griffith. This interrupted monologue, in which the main speaker tells an unhelpful doctor how the pond in his garden, which he had always found disturbing, turned into an unruly, shape-changing usurper who invaded his house and threatened to seduce his wife, is a tour de force in which, for the first time, Redgrove combined imaginative brio and absurd comedy to explore psychological vulnerability. Arthur Calder-Marshall, reviewing in the *Listener*, thought it was a rare moment of 'television freshness' comparable with the work of John Mortimer, and recommended that it be repeated on a programme with a wider audience (a recommendation that wasn't taken up). Two years later another dramatic prose poem 'The Sermon' (published in *The Force*) was also televised with Michael Hordern in the main role, but these were to be rare examples of Redgrove getting his work on TV.

While Redgrove was in Buffalo, Bonamy Dobrée again asked him if he was interested in the Gregory Fellowship at Leeds. This time there was no obstacle and, since two of the four advisors for the appointment, Dobrée himself and Herbert Read, were his supporters, it was a foregone conclusion that he would get the fellowship.

The Gregory Fellowships in the Creative Arts were an enlightened and pioneering institution originally under the patronage of E. C. Gregory, a Bradford-based printer and, in Read's words, 'discriminating patron of the arts'. There were fellowships in poetry, painting, sculpture and occasionally music. As well as Dobrée and Read, the advisors were T. S. Eliot and Henry Moore. There was a stipend of £750 (somewhat less than Peter had been able to command straight out of university) which it was possible to raise to £1,075 by teaching.

By the time Redgrove became a fellow the money Gregory had originally endowed had run out but, to its great credit, the university itself continued to sponsor the fellowships until 1980. The scheme was a forerunner of the creative writing fellowships that sprang up in many universities in later years and, eventually, the introduction of creative writing into university curricula. Its most daring feature was that, while the fellows were expected to associate with academics and students to their mutual benefit, there were no formal duties. This freedom was potentially creative, but in practice the relationships of fellows to academics were often awkward. As Dobrée mischievously wrote, the fellows were 'regarded as rather strange fish, as of course they are in the University; they are meant to be'. The Leeds School of English was a distinguished one – it had been the academic home of G. Wilson Knight as well as of Dobrée himself, and one of Redgrove's most gifted poetic contemporaries, Geoffrey Hill, was currently a lecturer – but it was no exception in respect of its discomfort with living poets. When a fellow in painting, Dennis Creffield, who was to become a close friend of Peter's, told the Chair of English, A. N. Jeffares, that he thought of universities as 'hothouses of creativity', he was met with incredulous laughter.

It was not unusual, therefore, for the Gregory Fellows to feel somewhat isolated. Redgrove, however, had a special reason for discomfort. There was an existing, thriving and distinctive poetry scene at Leeds: in the words of one of its most prominent student poets, 'a tangible sense of committed debate and creativity that was not present in any other University at the time'. The most influential individual was Jon Silkin, and the ambience was well characterised by the title of Silkin's 1973 anthology *Poetry of the Committed Individual* which included, among Leeds-connected poets, Geoffrey Hill, Ken Smith, Tony Harrison, Jeffrey Wainwright and Silkin himself, but not Redgrove. The poetry scene that Silkin's approach epitomised was heavily politicised and Left-oriented. (Geoffrey Hill might seem a square peg in this company, but in the sixties he was writing poems such as 'Ovid in the Third Reich', his elegy for a Holocaust victim 'September Song', and his acerbic sequence about the Wars of the Roses, 'Funeral Music'. Silkin fell out with him in the seventies, when he became increasingly interested in religion.) Early in his time at Leeds Redgrove felt that in this environment 'nobody may write either a personal poem, or one that is a fiction. Social oratory is the ticket. So I live in a somewhat hostile and lonely atmosphere.' This is simplified and exaggerated: Peter had been a subscriber to Silkin's long-lived magazine *Stand* since its inception in 1952, and had (unsuccessfully) submitted poems in the summer of 1953, about the same time that he submitted his first published poem to the *TLS*. He was in cordial correspondence with Silkin before going to America and, in later years, was on friendly terms with him and with Smith, both of whom wrote some very 'personal' poetry. He co-edited an anthology with Silkin (*New Poetry 5*, 1979), contributed to *Stand*, and invited Smith to read at Falmouth School of Art. But there is some truth in his comment, as corroborated by a student poet of the time, Jon Glover, who recalls that he and his fellow aspiring poets were friendly with Smith and Silkin, and influenced by Hill, but 'had an ambiguous relationship with Peter and his own poetry'. Glover confirms that 'the sense that poetry should be . . . very expressive of what was going on in your emotional world' was at odds with the 'Leeds ideology'. In 1963 *Stand* published a conversation between Silkin and Anthony Thwaite, titled 'No Politics, No Poetry?', in which Silkin accused the typical contemporary poet of failing to understand the problems of the proletariat because 'he is turned inwards towards his own class and his own particular, and I think rather minute, problem – his own private relationships'. In the same year Ken Smith reviewed *A Group Anthology*, a collection edited by Hobsbaum and Lucie-Smith which played an important part in bringing the Group to public attention. Much of this attention was hostile, and Smith's review was no exception. He thought the anthology was tainted by 'an urbanity grown into showiness', and even questioned the principle of the poetry workshop: 'The temporary shelter of a small, if able, audience can produce out of a private and sparsely populated universe the illusion of a poetry-speaking world.' Predictably the exceptions he made were politically oriented poems such as Alan Brownjohn's 'William Empson at Aldermaston' and Adrian Mitchell's 'Veteran with a Head Wound'. According to Smith, 'What living means to those who are not poets is left out' of the work of the Group, and he concludes with a shot at Redgrove himself: 'The business of living is more akin to the world of Peter Redgrove's "The Secretary" than to that of the same poet's ephemeral "Mr Waterman".' Any implied compliment to 'The Secretary' (an unusually social-realistic piece for him) was more than outweighed – Peter must have felt – by the dismissal of a work much closer to his concerns and more characteristic of his gifts. Smith was an already accomplished poet in his mid-twenties when he wrote this, but if he ever looked back on it he may well have felt embarrassed by the juvenile dogmatism with which he instructed Redgrove about 'the business of living'. Certainly the review will have sharpened Redgrove's sense of working in a 'hostile and lonely atmosphere'. He was unable to confess his deepest preoccupations even to his most intimate friends, but at least those friends were sympathetic to the creative outcome.

Factors of class and region may also have formed barriers to Peter's integration at Leeds. It was proud of its status as a non-metropolitan poetry centre and Peter was, at that time, very much a 'London' poet. To a provincial working-class student such as Jeffrey Wainwright, Ken Smith's background as the son of a Yorkshire farm labourer made him easier to identify with than Peter, whose 'ludicrously posh' accent will have stood out more jarringly in Leeds than in London. Ted Hughes was a magnetic figure for these students, but his Yorkshire origins mattered here, and marked him off from a poet such as Peter. Silkin, it is true, came from a wealthy bourgeois London Jewish family, but his revolt against his upbringing took more visible, political and material form than Peter's inward rebellion, hidden behind his suit and tie.

Silkin, though temperamentally and ideologically so different from Redgrove, resembled him in making poetry the controlling principle of his life. He had founded *Stand* in 1953 and had been himself Gregory Fellow from 1958 to 1960. Extraordinarily he began a degree in English while still holding the fellowship, and was publishing Geoffrey Hill in *Stand* while the latter was his tutor. After graduating in 1962 he stayed in Leeds, a magnet for student poets, until he left for Newcastle in 1968. Ken Smith was still a mature undergraduate at Leeds when Redgrove arrived, graduating in 1963 and joining Silkin in the editing of *Stand*, and the two of them hawked the magazine round halls of residence and elsewhere, much as Redgrove had done ten years earlier with *Delta*, but with a greater missionary zeal. He left Leeds in 1965 for a job very similar to the one Peter was to go to, at Exeter College of Art. It is a pity that Peter didn't meet Smith a few years later, when Smith was influenced by Jung and wrote 'The Eli Poems', exploring dream-figures that he believed represented his *anima* and *animus*.

The student poets such as Jon Glover and Jeffrey Wainwright had a network of contacts which drew them to Silkin, Smith and Hill and enjoyed regular informal social contact with the former two, which they did not have with Peter. Relations with Hill were more constrained, but the gifted and serious among his students found his lectures on poetry 'mesmeric and brilliant' while his brooding presence, always dressed in black suit and shirt and bright-coloured tie, projected a powerful charisma that he affected to be unaware of. However, despite this element of marginality, Peter did play an important part in their lives. He was the only one of the Gregory Fellows to hold regular weekly poetry seminars, which (as he had done in Buffalo) he modelled closely on the methods of the Group. The students who were attracted to these seminars were mostly a closely knit group of serious and committed young poets who lived and breathed poetry and politics. They ran the remarkably enduring student poetry magazine *Poetry and Audience* (which a few years earlier had been edited by Tony Harrison and which regularly attracted contributions from nationally known poets as well as undergraduates), and their lives were 'a continuous process of editorial meetings and going on to Peter's group'. *Poetry and Audience* was produced weekly on a Gestettner duplicator in the School of English. A student who wanted to become involved in the poetry scene would begin by helping to staple the copies on Thursday afternoon prior to its distribution for one old penny. He or she might then graduate to the editorial meetings on Saturday mornings. Membership of the editorial board was the only formal requirement of the Gregory Fellow, and Peter was very conscientious in attending these meetings, with a group of students most of whom had been at his seminar the previous evening. The editors would then adjourn to the pub – the one occasion when Peter mixed with the students informally.

Despite not being ideologically sympathetic to Peter's poetry, or on intimate terms with him as with Silkin and Smith, the seminars played an important part in the student-poets' lives. The work of Jon Glover, for example, shows no trace of Redgrove's influence, but he learned from Peter's seminars 'the idea that whatever you do you have to be sure that it works on the page for other people'. This influenced Glover's practice both as a poet and as a teacher of creative writing. Jeffrey Wainwright, who was also much more sympathetic to the work of Silkin, Hill and Smith, nevertheless found the seminars demanding and valuable, and attended regularly for the best part of two years. He remembers that it was as easy to discuss Peter's poetry as their own. Glover's American wife Elaine, who was a visiting student at the time, was struck by the atmosphere of mutual respect in which the seminars were conducted, but found Peter intimidating and lacking in warmth. This perceived lack of warmth, which is very unusual in reminiscences of Redgrove, may be an indicator of his lack of ease in that environment. It wasn't until the final term of his fellowship that he felt the influence of those who 'believe poetry should serve the state and not the individual' was receding and the students were prepared to 'accept some kind of leadership' from him.

Redgrove also did not have an easy relationship with Geoffrey Hill, who had been a lecturer in the English Department since 1954, and whose first collection, *For the Unfallen*, was published in 1959. The two poets worked together on the committee of the Poetry Room, which was established in 1962 as a venue for readings and repository for audio recordings. Some years later, in a letter to Martin Bell (who also knew Hill at Leeds) Redgrove professed affection for Hill, but complained that 'he has shown me none'. This attitude is however maintained with difficulty, and later in the same letter he bursts out with: 'Actually I hate Geoffrey Hill for his secretive nature and smug conduct. I wanted friendship, and if not friendship, acknowledgement and he condescended to me like all the other academics up there.' Redgrove inveighs against Hill's 'pompous and costive work', and it is likely that Hill had at least an equally low opinion of Redgrove's poetry (he did not reply when I wrote to ask him for his recollections). But Hill and his work got under Redgrove's skin to some extent. Twenty years later he dreamed of a meeting in which he said, 'Our views on the reading and writing and the conveying of information are so different that I doubt whether we shall understand or like each other's poetry ever.' Hill agreed, but added, 'When I think of what is running around inside you unused it makes me feel pretty helpless.' In my last conversation with him, in the year before his death, Redgrove asked me if I thought Geoffrey Hill would last. When I said yes he asked, plaintively, 'Do you think I will last?' He frequently quoted the line, 'There is no bloodless myth will hold' from Hill's early poem 'Genesis', but may have had a mischievous intention in doing so, since he gave the line a menstrual significance that Hill surely did not intend. There might have been more fellow-feeling between the two men if each had been aware that the other suffered from OCD and depression – Hill, by his own account, even more severely than Redgrove.

Redgrove compensated for the lack of rapport with local poets by inviting his friends, especially Hobsbaum, Bell and Porter, to give readings and present their poetry at his seminar. He also made a new poet friend when a young lecturer called Don Thomas invited him to give a reading at a college in Hereford. Peter stayed at Don's house, and they formed an instant attachment. Don had started writing what he called 'science fiction poetry' which Peter was very enthusiastic about. He was especially impressed that Don had a telescope in his garden and made a close study of the stars for his poetic imagery – no doubt remembering his youthful revelations in the microscope. Don gave Peter a typescript of his poems and Peter sent one to Martin Bell: 'It's a *beautiful* book and he's an excellent poet of whom I do not doubt we shall hear more.' He wondered what they could do to help Thomas get published. He recommended his young friend as his successor for the fellowship but Jeffares and the new head of department Douglas Grant were unimpressed by Thomas's work. In 1968, as D. M. Thomas, he was to share a Penguin Modern Poets volume with Redgrove and D. M. Black. Peter was particularly impressed that Don was so devoted to poetry that 'he won't write prose, novels, short stories etc.' – ironically, in the light of the book that was to make Thomas famous.

Redgrove was himself especially resistant to writing prose at this time. He is dismissive of prose poetry (even though some of the most memorable pieces in his second, third and fourth collections are in this genre, and he was later to publish two volumes of prose poems), but more particularly it is discursive prose that he wants to avoid: 'A prose statement in this world is a flat invitation for people to read one's poems according to it. I seem to want to make a Fiction (of a poem) and then retire from it. In prose you're always there, and quite vulnerable.' This may be a reaction to the ideological atmosphere of Leeds but it also seems, in the light of his later writing, when he often invited people to read his poetry alongside his prose work, evasive. He was later to insist that there was always discourse in his poetry, but at this stage, even with three collections to his credit, he lacks confidence in his own discourse. He goes on to use a revealing metaphor: 'In prose I always feel I'm wearing the wrong tie, or no tie at all in the wrong place.' Thinking about prose brings out an image that evokes the uniform and standards of his father. Much later, when he had two books of discursive prose and seven novels behind him, he wrote: 'I started to write poetry because Poetry either was or was not, and couldn't be argued with by my father.'

Redgrove was to have a lifelong friendship with Thomas, but during his time in Leeds his most important new friend was not a writer. In 1964 Dennis Creffield, who had been a pupil of David Bomberg, was appointed to the Painting Fellowship. Just as Peter was attached to the English Department so Creffield was to the Department of Fine Arts (a rarity in English universities). His head of department Quentin Bell (the son of Clive and Vanessa Bell) suggested that the university commission him to make a portrait of Peter. Despite, according to his subject, having difficulty with 'this tiny little delicate mouth in this great chin', Creffield succeeded in making a number of powerfully expressive drawings, one of which can be seen on the Leeds Poetry website. The two men took to each other very strongly, and were soon inseparable companions. Peter wrote to Martin Bell that Creffield was 'almost as good to talk to as . . . oh well, I dunno, but very good', obviously meaning that he enjoyed Creffield's company as much as that of Martin himself, perhaps his most valued male companion. He goes on to say, 'just about the first I've met up here', confirming his sense of alienation from the Leeds poetry scene.

Creffield was the first professional artist Peter had got to know. As a youth, meeting Barbara had been a revelation to him of the world of art students, but Barbara, though she had continued to work as a sculptor, had not made art the centre of her life. In Creffield Peter met someone who was completely dedicated to his art. Creffield later said, perhaps ironically, that he was a 'bad influence' on Peter. Although Peter was now, for the first time since Cambridge, able to devote himself entirely to poetry (and grew his first beard perhaps as a sign of this) Creffield thought that he still led two lives, one of which was conventionally bourgeois. In his opinion Barbara very definitely belonged to the conventional life. The fifties marriages of the Group poets were now, in the sixties, beginning to unravel. In Belfast Philip had begun having affairs with his students and his marriage to Hannah was doomed; in 1965 Martin Bell, at the Edinburgh Festival, met the young Scottish woman who was to be the muse of his later years, Christine McCausland, for whom he would soon leave his wife Peggy; a few years later

Peter Porter's wife Jannice was to die of an overdose. When Martin was preparing Christine to meet Peter he told her that his friend looked respectable, like a successful businessman – echoing Porter's first impression ten years earlier. In a photo taken at Creffield's flat, on what is evidently an informal visit, Peter is wearing a suit and tie; in the background we see Dennis wearing roll-neck sweater and casual trousers.

In 1964 Peter and Barbara moved from a flat provided by the university to a three-storey detached brick house near Roundhay Park. On the second floor is an attic room which was Peter's study. Bill Redgrove remembers his father as a distant figure in his early years, shut up in this room, writing or talking to friends. When Creffield visited Peter they would go up to Peter's room together and spend hours talking, reading aloud, listening to music and drinking – Barbara was no part of this, and wasn't even mentioned. Dennis thought Barbara had nothing to do with their shared interests, and Peter did nothing to change his opinion.

This is not to say that Barbara had ceased to be involved with Peter's poetry. In a note on two drafts of a passage from 'The Old White Man' (WP) he wrote that she preferred the simpler first version, and this version was kept. But a split was opening in his life which, now he was free from the external strain of a job, was ominous. Equally threatening was the increasing evidence of out-of-control drinking; alcohol looms large in Creffield's reminiscences of Peter, and it is a constant theme of his letters to Bell: drinking in London, drinking again on the train back to Leeds, and carrying on drinking at home. Jon Glover once saw him staggering drunk in a university building site. 'Barbara behaved particularly well', he wrote to Martin about one such episode, but a happy marriage draws sparingly on 'good behaviour' of that kind.

During his time in Leeds his notebooks changed their character. Before then he had used them almost exclusively for drafting poetry, but from 1964 onwards the drafts share their space with fragments of intimate journal. He titled one such entry a 'Page of Troubles'. His life was barren without the 'openings' as he called them, moments of vision when the world seemed real, out of which his poetry came. At other times the world seemed 'solid, impenetrable', and these were his times of depression. Being called to act in an 'executive' capacity, to deal with money matters (being like his father, though he doesn't say this) causes the 'openings' to dwindle and disappear.

What troubled him most was that the devoted cultivation of his 'openings' seemed incompatible with the complete family life that he also craved. At such times he could not bear the cries of children; loved ones were 'kept aside'. A little earlier he had asked himself, 'Do children draw as heavily on one's life . . . taking the place of one's interior imagination?' He had analysed this condition ruthlessly in his poem 'A Silent Man' (*AWM*), whose speaker loves the cold:

> My heart
> Is cold and loves to stroll through cold,
> And seems to see a better speech
> Rolling in fat clouds of breath.
> I keep talk for my walks, silent clouds
> That flow in ample, mouthing white
> Along the paths. At home
> Where I've closeted my wife
> And instituted children in the warm
> I keep my silence, lest
> Those I love, regard, catch cold from me.

He quotes Kierkegaard – 'Not until passion is brought out of isolation in the solitary individual and brought into communal life with the marriage partner and children is it sanctified, baptized' – and his favourite Langland – 'Thus in three persones is perfechtiliche manhede, / That is, man and his make and molliere her children' (Thus perfect manhood is in three persons: man, his wife and her children) – to fortify him in his belief that he must reconcile poetry with family life. But the entry concludes, 'to reach the positive, leave obligation'.

Drink figures in these journal entries as a false friend. Drink enables him 'to have the ecstasies and insights of poetry – often in excess of any but the best of my waking states – without the trouble of writing them down.' In another mood he writes, 'Notes one makes in one's cups dwell on the obvious.' As he continued to do for the rest of his life he makes resolutions to give up drinking, but 'I'm so miserable & stiff sober.' He had started carrying little notebooks around with him and pasting pages into his journal. Some of these notes are written in the pub, and his intoxicated state is evident in the handwriting. One time he experimented with making notes after each pint and commenting on them: after the fourth pint (admittedly a small number considering his boasts of his capacity) he wrote in unsteady capitals, quoting Blake, 'EVERYTHING POSSIBLE TO BE BELIEVED IS AN IMAGE OF TRUTH'. In a later hand he wrote after this, 'And here I am. Lucky not to have offended / hit my wife or [???] my children. What a [???] to write. Mean, creeping.' In another notebook a pasted-in page has, in unsteady handwriting, 'The son exceeds the father, & there follows the holy ghost of charity', on which his later comment is 'messages to myself from Booze County'; and 'Evidently I can hear the liquor talk wittily' elicits the later revision, 'I can hear the liquor prattle everlastingly.' In these journals we also meet the first hints of the Game in Peter's private writing: trying to help an old friend who was suffering from depression he told him 'my own secret', and he speaks of his hatred for another friend in whom he detects 'that auto-erotic thing in myself too'.

A less double-edged resource than alcohol was judo, to which Peter applied himself seriously and effectively during his years at Leeds, rising to brown belt or First Kyu, the highest grade below that of teacher. Judo helped him to prevail in his return bout with Vernon Scannell, but it was more than functional. During the few years in which he practised it he ranked it with sex and poetry as a means of 'enlivening'. He wrote in his notebook, 'Joy is a terror that one trusts', and specified the enlivening terror that he felt before a judo bout. Dennis Creffield once saw him doing judo and was terrified by the vehemence with which he threw himself into the combat, which Creffield thought was nothing spiritual, but all to do with power – steam literally came off his head.

Just as Peter had never met an artist of Creffield's calibre, Dennis had never met such a poet as Peter. He found Peter's company, and that of his poet friends, thrilling and inventive: 'Everything was transposed into magic.' But the magic of Peter's company was inseparable from drinking. 'He taught me how to drink,' Creffield says, meaning that it was not just boozing, but a gateway to eloquence and unfettered imagination. Drinking was a serious and perilous exploit: Peter told Dennis that before setting out on a drinking expedition they must dose themselves with vitamin tablets, for protection in case they passed out and spent the night in a gutter. In the absence of Soho-style drinking clubs, they would occasionally pass the difficult hours between the pubs closing at two and reopening at six with a bottle of vodka and glass of milk in the music department of Schofields' store, sitting on the floor of a cubicle, listening to classical records. When Peter's fellowship came to an end in 1965, he and Dennis threw an epic party to which two hundred people were invited and which lasted three days. They ordered ten gallons of wine plus a 'private resource' for the two of them. Silkin, Smith and Hill were all there, and a student photographer/journalist from Oxford was invited up to interview and photograph the poets. To this outsider, aware that Silkin was reputed to dominate Leeds poetry, Peter stood out from the other three by his easy and unaffected manner. Surprisingly he said he was looking forward to having to earn his living again because he had 'exhausted his latent creative energies'. Jon Silkin 'puffed cigarette smoke to hide his face', and seemed shy, but both he and Smith demonstrated a 'desire to make themselves felt', while Hill lived up to his reputation for brooding unapproachableness, and the visitor got nothing out of him at all. This was the only time Jon and Elaine Glover visited Peter's house and, at the height of the party, Elaine recalls Jon emerging from a room and saying, 'Don't go in there: Peter is kicking his wife and calling her a bitch.' Jon was drunk himself and later had no memory of the incident, so it remains for ever a disturbing and prophetic piece of hearsay.

If Peter taught Dennis to drink, Dennis initiated Peter in other ways. As a young man, studying at the Slade, he had met a young student called Diane Clutterbuck at a party; they slept together and she became pregnant. Although he didn't love her he married her, and they had several children together, perhaps because she loved him. According to Dennis she adored being pregnant. He renamed her Dilly, and this became the name that everyone knew her by. By the time Creffield got the Gregory Fellowship they were separated; however, after a few months in Leeds he was offered a large flat by the university and invited Dilly and the children to join him there. Peter was fascinated and disturbed by the Creffields' unconventional marriage. Much later he wrote in *Innocent Street*, 'He took me out and showed me the women. I had not met such a Cavalier. My own sex was all mixed up with loyalty. Could I see here a more "normal" response? . . . We were cruising, and he played the dangerous one, the initiator.' As often in Peter's memoir and journals, there is some projection going on here, and Creffield has no recollection of their 'cruising' together.

It wasn't promiscuity that friendship with Dennis led Peter into. Dilly was a beautiful, lively, intelligent young woman from the Forest of Dean with, Christine McCausland thought, 'a touch of Cider with Rosie' about her. She didn't wear make-up, dressed in a white smock, and was a wonderful cook – she conjured a relaxed, seductive ambience in her house. She loved reading, and had had to abandon a degree in English when she became pregnant. She was a man's woman with 'pretty ways': flirtatious, she liked to attract men, perhaps even to make them fall in love with her, just because she could, as Anna Karenina does with Levin. She laughed a lot and enjoyed drinking: compared to Barbara, and despite all her children, she had the allure of irresponsibility. She was seven years younger than Barbara and wore her hair long in loose plaits, making Barbara, with her short permed hair, look in Creffield's opinion by comparison like a conventional fifties housewife. Soon Peter was in love with her, and she with him. In a way he was in love with both Dilly and Dennis as a couple: certainly he was seduced by their way of life, and he told Dennis that he went to bed with Dilly to get closer to him. In fact Dennis was the only one of this three who did not love both the other two: he only loved Peter. When Dilly arrived in Leeds she was pregnant. The affair with Peter may or may not have begun before this daughter was born, but Dilly and Dennis agreed to call her Petronella as a sign of their shared love of Peter. Many years later, when Petronella was a grown woman, the affair with Dilly was long in the past, and Peter was married to Penelope Shuttle, she phoned him and asked if he was her father. Peter assured her, correctly, that this was impossible, that Dilly was already pregnant when she arrived in Leeds.

What Peter thought charming about Dilly only irritated Dennis, who thought she was just a clever girl, and that her bright, laughing ways had nothing to do with his work, which was 'heavy stuff'. He had no time for her intellectually. Peter and Dilly, by contrast, animated each other, sparked each other off, and Peter appreciated her in ways her husband never had. And he thought she appreciated him in ways Barbara didn't – at least any longer: 'Dilly said you're not fat, you're covered with muscle – this gave me the erotic feeling; Barbara ignored it, or said, you'll never be sylph-like.' They went on long cycle rides together which Peter commemorated, together with her enticing domesticity, in one of the poems inspired by their affair, 'Water-Witch, Wood-Witch, Wine-Witch':

I take her by the hips
And lift her down as from a tree. In the cornfield we make our love

And as we finish the air is thickly grassed with rain. Who was it
Who smelt even as she frowned in anger
Of blueberries and honey, in whose honour
Corn-lightning played over the horizon?

In an annotated copy that he gave to Dilly, Peter wrote that another
poem was 'about the blessed lascivious humour of women. A poem
of innocent surprise on the young man's part.' Creffield described
Peter as innocent when he knew him. This kind of 'lascivious humour'
doesn't figure very much in Redgrove's earlier poetry, but it is a
definite feature of his later work, and one of the ways in which his
poetry becomes more relaxed and personable.

These poems, however, were not to be written till after he had
left Leeds. His third collection, *At the White Monument*, which came
out in 1963, is disappointing. Hobsbaum was enthusiastic about
the long title poem, an instance (like 'Mr Waterman') of a quasi-
dramatic genre that Hobsbaum called 'interrupted monologue'.
However, the dramatic potential of its strange story of a man who
entombs his wife by pouring concrete down the chimney as protection against the wind is thwarted by the style: an overemphasis on
muscular diction combined with off-key colloquialism that sounds
like an unsuccessful simultaneous pastiche of Hopkins and Browning:

Trotted out a small circle, shambling spoke:
The mixer jarring and churning, shoulder to it,
Grey magma spewed and lolloped down the gap
That to my eyes widened and puckered
In the power of its shout! Up an octave on the first load!
(Great dignity here – ramrod back) throb to a gabble . . .

This is typical of the language of the book, which – with a few
exceptions such as 'A Silent Man' – recycles Redgrove's mannerisms
rather than developing the growing points of his earlier work. Later,
when asked about the comparative unpopularity of this collection,
he said that the poems were characterised by 'hesistance, lack of
commitment, alienation, and frigidity', and this was disturbing to
his admirers who expected him to be 'rather rejoicing in natural
things'.

But the poetry that he wrote in Leeds, collected in *The Force* in
1966, is a different matter. This volume is the first decisive advance
in his work since *The Collector*, and a dazzling testimonial to the
value of the Gregory Fellowship. As Redgrove wrote years later, 'For

a certain kind of writer, or almost any writer at a particular stage of his career, such fellowships are literally salvation.' The title poem, 'The House in the Acorn', 'The Contentment of an Old White Man', 'The Heir', 'The Widower', 'Decreator', 'The Sermon' and 'The Case' – to go no further – all rank among the best work he had done so far, and in some cases exceed his earlier achievement. He has developed (or recovered from 'Lazarus and the Sea') a more relaxed, fluent line and diction, and a more secure grasp of persona and narrative. At one extreme the title poem is one of the most concise, luminous and engaging representations of natural forces, and their relation to human life, that Redgrove ever accomplished:

> At Mrs Tyson's farmhouse, the electricity is pumped
> Off her beck-borne wooden wheel outside.
> Greased, steady, it spins within
> A white torrent, that stretches up the rocks.
> At night its force bounds down
> And shakes the lighted room, shakes the light;
> The mountain's force comes towering down to us.

The old-fashioned domestic generator is an inspired and beautifully handled metaphor. The same natural forces that create the light also threaten it, and this works both at the literal level and for the more abstract enlightenment of the house's human inhabitants. The poem balances figures of order and control, such as the 'Greased, steady' wheel, with intimations of potential danger, in the suggestions of a wild beast that 'bounds down' and 'Lashes its tail'.

At the opposite extreme is 'The Case', Redgrove's most ambitious poem so far, and his most powerful example of dramatic monologue. He also published this poem separately as 'The God-Trap', with an introduction in which he described various experiences that had prompted it. The first of these was hearing Verdi's Requiem, when he was violently affected by the tension between 'the plea for the eternal rest or punishment of all sinners' and the sensuality of the voices of the singers, who were not choirboys but 'the full-blooded singers of opera'. This led him to reflect that a person who loved both God and the creation would be 'split in two'. He found a text for what troubled him in Hermann Hesse's *Steppenwolf*, which he used as an epigraph: '[Man's] innermost destiny drives him on to spirit and to God. His innermost being draws him back to nature.' This was reinforced by reading about Manichaeism, and crucially by a sight that gave him the foundational image of the poem, an elderly woman wearing a floral dress in a walled garden, standing by a bank of flowers and saying, 'Oh, this is life . . . what a shame we have to die . . .' He began to imagine the scenario in which the son of such a woman, whom he supposes to be a widow, is 'sent on a mythic quest for God', and to wonder if he had ever met an actual person like this. The final prompting, according to the introduction, was reading case notes about a boy diagnosed as schizophrenic, who was close to his mother (a widow after an unsatisfactory marriage), suffered from hysterical blindness and liked to spend his time in a garden and be addressed as 'Father'. Drafts of these case notes in his notebook suggest that they are his invention.

Redgrove does not confess, in this introduction, that when he heard Verdi's Requiem he was drunk, passed out, and when he came round thought that he had been 'wandering through a store of great rolls of brocade and draperies' remembered from Bentalls in his childhood. He believed that his dream was a visual transformation of Verdi's music and, though it is not directly reproduced in the poem, it is a template for the way the effect of the music on him is transposed into the most overwhelmingly sensuous poetry he has yet written:

And I swam in the thunderstorm in the river of blood, oil and cider,
And I saw the blue of my recovery open around me in the water,
Blood, cider, rainbow, and the apples still warm after sunset
Dashed in the cold downpour, and so this mother-world
Opened around me and I lay in the perfumes after rain out of the
    river
Tugging the wet grass, eyes squeezed, straining to the glory,
The burst of white glory like the whitest clouds rising to the sun

And it was like a door opening in the sky, it was like a door opening
    in the water,
It was like the high mansion of the sky, and water poured from the
    tall French windows.
It was like a sudden smell of fur among the flowers, it was like a
    face at dusk
It was like a rough trouser on a smooth leg. Oh, shame,
It was the mother-world wet with perfume. It was something about God.

Of course the effect is not *merely* one of sensuousness. This is poetry of the highest order in which a consciousness is vividly and disturbingly represented through its response to an unscreened experience of the natural world. The hectic tone, the sense of strain, and the explicitly religious language promise a dramatic development that in this case, unlike 'At the White Monument', is fully accomplished. This poem preoccupied Redgrove more than any he had written since 'Lazarus and the Sea'. It was the last of the *Force* poems he completed, but he had been working at the theme for many months before a prose draft of this passage appears in his notebooks, and the poem begins to take off.

Redgrove also does not confess, of course, that he himself had been diagnosed schizophrenic, and that he had been close to his mother whose marriage, in his opinion, was unsatisfactory. His father was not absent – he was only too oppressively present – but Peter's rejection of Jim's love doomed him, like his protagonist, to search for a substitute. This is not to say that the poem is directly autobiographical, but it is an exploration of psychological and religious territory with which his experience had made him very familiar. As if by polarised reaction to the 'mother-world' of nature, the protagonist is drawn to a God who is 'silent and invisible and I loved him for it, / I loved him for his silent invisibility, for his virile restraint.' The epigraph from Hesse concludes, 'Between the two forces his life hangs tremulous and irresolute', but the poem dramatises a more violent and complex polarisation. Nature and God are not merely opposites between which the human subject hangs, but the very intensity of his response to nature drives him to seek God – a God who is not immanent in the world of sensuous excess, but is the antithesis of that world, inaccessible to the senses. Thrown violently from one extreme to the other, he blinds himself and aspires 'to live unseeing, not watching, without judging, called "Father"'.

If 'The Case' is informed by Peter's still unresolved Oedipal conflicts, another outstanding monologue, 'The Widower', may be a report on the state of his marriage:

> Yawning, yawning with grief all the time.
> The live ones are often alive in fragments
> And some of us scream as the weather changes.
> Or I raise a frequent steak to my pluming nostrils,
> Starving, or yawning, so hungry for air,
> Gasping for life. And a snowflake was her friend.
> And the sky of clouds hurrying and struggling
> Beyond the skylight, were her friends.

She was daytime to the mind,
A light room of trees, spray of water, high flowers
Over a cloudscape, and I brought her
Twelve-hour lyings down for fear of this world,
Head buried in pillows for perfect darkness,
And into this she walked with nothing but advice
And what I called her spells for company.

The editor of Redgrove's first *Selected Poems*, Marie Peel, wrote of this poem, 'He himself was dead, is now alive, which by too tight a logic turns an unchanged wife into a dead one, himself into a kind of murderer. Looked at more dialectically, the wife must have changed also because of him, as he has done in part because of her.' Redgrove congratulated her on understanding the poem as no one else had done, and gave her words a directly autobiographical slant: 'Indeed, it was like this, in Leeds where it was written; our lives had changed so much individually that we seemed like a demonstration of Relativity: moving apart with our combined speeds.' It is true he had the habit of interpreting his poems retrospectively, but it would be artificial to ignore the autobiographical resonance, and the generosity of feeling towards the wife, especially in the beautiful modulation, 'Gasping for life. And a snowflake was her friend', is very attractive. The stifling atmosphere echoes a smaller and explicitly autobiographical poem, 'Sweat', in which the family

                    breathe and burn
        We burn, all together in a hot room,
        Our sweat is smoking down the windowpane,
        Marks time, I smoke, I stir, and there I write
        PR, BR, a streaming heart.

The trouble in this poem is hinted at in the line, 'She loves me and she loves our children too'. It may not be exactly, as Peter feared in 'The Pregnant Father' a few years earlier, 'The start of one love and ending of another', but the way the line slides from one love to the other implies a feeling of dilution, a fading of the erotic into the domestic.

When *The Force* was published in 1966 most reviewers took it as more of the same, but there were a few discerning critics who registered a development. John Fuller noted 'a more radical probing of his chosen world than in the earlier books'; Michael Baldwin detected a 'more open rhythm' which emboldened him to compare

Redgrove to Eliot; Howard Sergeant judged *The Force* to be 'a distinct advance on his earlier work in that diction and imagery, energy and concern for accurate detail are all kept carefully under control and integrated within the total experience communicated'. The most gratifying comment was Ted Hughes's response to 'The Case' in letters: 'the best & biggest thing you've done by far – in an altogether new dimension'. The passage beginning 'It was like a door' he thought 'a wonderfully sustained piece of truly musical writing'. It was one of a small number of poems in *The Force* where Hughes perceptively detected a new direction in Redgrove's work: 'they seem to come from a different personality, your better self'. The following year he had another boost when the American critic M. L. Rosenthal wrote in his influential book *The New Poets* that Redgrove 'stands with Ted Hughes as the poet of greatest vividness and intensity now writing in England'. He met Rosenthal in the late sixties and they became lifelong friends, though meeting rarely.

'The Case' is not just one of Redgrove's finest poems, but the harbinger of the major phase of his work, in which he comes consciously to grips with the knot of familial, sexual, psychological and religious trouble that has nagged at him since his adolescence. His meeting with John Layard in Cornwall two years later was to be the crucial catalyst, but in Leeds he was unknowingly preparing himself for that meeting by immersing himself in the works of Jung. He had first discovered the Swiss psychologist as a young man, recovering from his breakdown and insulin shock therapy, when he read *Modern Man in Search of a Soul*, which he found more sympathetic than the Freudian analysis he was undergoing at the time. Jung's title reminded him of Keats's 'vale of soul-making', and spoke to his feeling that he had no soul, when he came round from the comas. How important Jung was to him in the fifties is unclear, but he certainly began reading him intensively in Leeds.

Perhaps the most important single idea of Jung's for Peter was that of projection: the human mind's tendency to project the 'shadow' and the 'anima' on to others. Someone who felt so divided as Peter, burdened by a shameful secret self and beset by 'feminine identification', was exceptionally liable to this tendency. Over the years one of the most impressive signs of his self-awareness is his ability to recognise, if not always control, his projections, and to be aware that his feelings in such cases had nothing to do with their ostensible object. He quoted in his notebook, 'To confront a person with his shadow is to show him his own light. Once one has experienced a few times what it is like to stand judgingly between the opposites, one begins to understand what is meant by the self. Anyone who perceives his shadow and his light simultaneously sees himself from two sides and thus gets in the middle.' Redgrove is popularly regarded as a poet of extremes and excess, but he was always preoccupied with getting his life into a proper balance: in a later letter he insisted that Jungians deplore one-sidedness. Avoiding this is partly a matter of withdrawing projections. It also involves another set of Jungian concepts, elaborated in *Psychological Types*. In that book Jung divides consciousness into four functions: thinking, feeling, sensation and intuition. People are further divided into introvert and extrovert. In each person's consciousness one function is dominant, another subsidiary and the others 'inferior'. 'Right action', Redgrove insists, 'is to see the other *three* sides of a problem, and the other attitude (extrovert if one is introvert) also.' At least during the Leeds period Peter considered himself an introvert sensation/intuition type, which he marked 'very unstable'. This would surprise the many people, including his children, who were daunted by his intellect, but he wrote in his journal at this time, 'O God, I am like my poor brother David, not a man of intellect at all, but one who wants to feel more than he wants to know.' Interestingly he thought Dilly was the same type as Ted Hughes: 'sensation and thinking'.

As well as dream analysis, in which Peter was to become an adept, Jung's practice of 'active imagination' is crucially important. Active imagination is meditation, reverie or daydream, allowing unconscious images to form in the conscious mind. For Jung this was a therapeutic technique; for Redgrove it became central to his creative practice. He often used this technique in combination with automatic or as he preferred to call it 'sealed' writing, a practice that he seems to have begun while at Leeds.

Above all Jung was a thinker who provided Peter with a model of mental wholeness. He was a scientist, Peter insisted, but a scientist who was also religious: not one who practised or believed in religion to one side of his science as it were, but in whom the two were integrated. That is what Peter aspired to. Jung, he wrote, 'gives you schemes whereby you may know kinship with the whole world'.

Peter's fellowship came to an end in 1965, but he stayed in Leeds for another year, supporting the family by part-time teaching at Bretton Hall, a teacher-training college near Wakefield, founded in

1949 by the pioneering educationalist Alec Clegg, and specialising in the creative arts. He supplemented his income by selling manuscripts. He was himself a pioneer in this respect, having sold three notebooks to the Lilly library for £100 and a larger collection to the Harry Ransom Center in Austin, Texas, for £595, in 1961. Now he made £1,000 for a further sale to Austin, committing his working papers up to September 1966.

Since 1962 Hobsbaum had been a lecturer at Queen's University Belfast, where he had cultivated a second Group, of poets who were to become even more celebrated than their London predecessors, including Seamus Heaney, Derek Mahon and Michael Longley. Heaney has credited Hobsbaum with bringing the Ulster poets together: he 'moved disparate elements into a single action'. He would shortly take up another academic post in Glasgow, where yet another Group would flourish. Despite this continued nurturing of creative talent, Peter was prickly and suspicious about Philip's becoming ensconced in the academic world. He himself by contrast felt isolated and unappreciated in the School of English at Leeds, and the fellowship was only a temporary respite from the anguish of reconciling poetry with earning a living. Another factor was Peter's increasingly assertive sense of artistic vocation, influenced by the community of the Gregory Fellowship. Creffield remembers him speaking of the guilt he felt if he failed to seize the moment when a poem presented itself to him. At any rate, Philip felt that he had to defend his chosen profession against Peter with some asperity, saying that in such company as Leavis, Empson, Yvor Winters, Philip Rahv, Wilson Knight and I. A. Richards he did not 'feel dishonoured by the profession'.

Around New Year 1966 this tension combined with alcohol to catastrophic effect, as far as their friendship was concerned. Peter, Barbara and Philip were drinking at the Creffields' flat. Peter wrote to Martin that Philip was spoiling for a fight all evening, 'having given in front of Barbara and I a run-down on thrombosis and the Pill, and further affirmed that people like ourselves in universities were all sex-starved'. In this letter he asserts that Philip picked a quarrel because 'I told him he had written two superb poems'. In later years he further finessed this to 'I told him his poems were excellent and he should write more of them and less criticism.' Philip stormed out of the house. Peter affected not to understand why Philip had been so angry, but what he almost certainly said was

146

that Philip had written *only* two good poems, and the reason for this was that he had sold out to the academy. Certainly Creffield's recollection was that Peter attacked Philip on these grounds, and shortly afterwards Peter wrote a letter to Philip that is decidedly more remorseful and less chipper than his tone to Martin:

> I hope the emotions of that catastrophic evening have subsided enough in both of us to make it possible for me to write to you again. I think I should be writing first, since it was I that gave the offence. And the offence to my sober mind was the manner of expression of my opinion of your verse. If there was other offence, still 'If Hamlet from himself be ta'en away,' etc.: – I was in drink, as you were.
>
> The trouble is that I have always had such a very high regard for you as critic and teacher, as I have often averred, to yourself and all comers, that it has from the first been difficult for me to hear your other voice. The two poems in question have always seemed to me very different from your other work. I preferred them, and awaited others of their kind with the keenest anticipation, never doubting your talent to produce them. If you look back among our letters, you will see how I have wished that. I may be a bad guide or a bad critic by the which of your poems I prefer, but I have been an honest one.
>
> My fault was in speaking of such difficult and delicate matters in drink. Clearly I expressed myself in a truculent and wounding fashion. And this I am ashamed of, and deeply apologise for.
>
> We may according to your wish not meet or correspond again. I should feel this as a deep loss. From our long friendship, I imagine you would feel this too. But if this wish remains, then I will respect it, with sorrow.
>
> Yours, as ever, Peter

Philip returned this letter in the same envelope, on which he wrote, 'REGRET CORRESPONDENCE CLOSED. RETURNED TO SENDER.' There was to be no more contact between them for fourteen years, but the quarrel did not stop Philip from generously promoting Peter's work. Later that same month he met George MacBeth, and mentioned the quarrel 'only in passing when talking very appreciatively' about Peter's poems.

The letter is an excellent example of how sensitively Peter could address another person in difficult and painful circumstances. The wound caused by the deliberately brutal rebuff is sufficient to account for the simplifying and self-serving way in which he later referred to the breach. But there were to be other examples of his being unable to sustain a whole and generous view of a distressing personal situation, with the result that certain memories haunted and obsessed him, repetitively and without resolution.

Peter could not continue to support the family with hourly-paid teaching indefinitely, and in 1966 he needed to start looking for a full-time job. Following the Coldstream Report on the teaching of art in 1960, art colleges had been encouraged to supplement their traditional emphasis on drawing skills, knowledge of anatomy, perspective and composition, with an element of liberal education. To this end departments of Complementary Studies were formed, but the definition of what this constituted was left vague. Dennis Creffield and Neville Boden, the Gregory Fellow in sculpture, encouraged in Peter the belief that a verbal artist had a role to play in such a department: his companion fellows had 'very strong conceptions of the artist and a fellowship of artists . . . in which fellowship they quite freely naturally and generously assumed that poets belonged'. Creffield gave Peter a list of recommended colleges, and he wrote around. In April he was called for interview at the School of Art in Falmouth, Cornwall. In his letter of application he had written:

> I feel that my particular qualifications may be considered especially suitable to the post advertised. I am a practising artist-in-words of some note; I am sure therefore that I could make a useful contribution to a modern College of Art in clarifying the relation of the literary and spoken arts' relation [sic] to the visual arts, and by extending the students' experience of making to the verbal sphere.

Peter was an unorthodox candidate: he had no degree (though he disguised this by writing in his CV that he studied 'Chemistry, Physiology; then English' at Cambridge) and no previous experience of working with visual artists. But Falmouth was, despite Creffield's recommendation, a small and remote college, and Peter had a more distinguished public profile than anyone on the staff there. He performed at the interview with some aplomb, and one of the panel told him afterwards that they felt as if he was interviewing them. He was offered the job, at just over £2,000 a year, considerably more than he had been paid as Gregory Fellow.

In the summer he and the family moved to Falmouth, nearly 400 miles from Leeds and Dilly. There is no evidence that he ever contemplated leaving Barbara for Dilly. Even in November 1965, when the affair was probably in progress, he sent a note to Barbara from London: 'I have been having such nice sex with you. I love you so much it hurts to think of you when I'm away.' He told her about the affair, 'otherwise we could not be proper lovers, moving down to Cornwall'. Dilly had been accepted to read for a degree in English at Leeds, and the distance gave Barbara some security. As a parting present Peter gave Dilly copies of his first three books with lengthy quotations from the Exeter Book of Riddles and restrained inscriptions which may have been intended for Barbara's eyes. The same may be true of a letter he wrote to Dilly at the same time, recommending background reading for her degree, with not a hint of more than friendly feeling. But it was not the end of their affair.

VII

Crisis 1966–70

The town of Falmouth lies on a promontory in the south-west of Cornwall. Along that coast there is only one other major town, Penzance, before Land's End. The promontory is guarded by Henry VIII's Pendennis Castle; to the south are sandy beaches and the Atlantic coast, to the north the Carrick Roads, a large natural harbour that is navigable as far as Truro, and which shelters the dockyards. The town rises inland from the water, and most of its white-painted houses overlook their neighbours to views of the sea or the harbour.

Beyond is the hinterland of Cornwall: to the south, the heathland and green serpentine churches hugging the coves of the Lizard peninsula; to the north, Bodmin Moor and Tintagel, with its wild coastline and Arthurian legends; to the west, the prehistoric landscape of West Penwith, heathy fields walled with massive stones and scattered with the remains of villages, stone circles and underground chambers. Everywhere are the ruins of the tin-mining industry, strangely congruent with the prehistoric remains. Cornwall is largely supported by massive granite shelves, and Peter was soon entranced by the continuity between this hidden geological identity, the visible contours of the landscape, an angel carved on a granite tombstone, and even a pebble picked up on a beach.

In July Peter and Barbara made an exploratory trip to Cornwall, and visited Perranporth on the north coast, where they took an evening walk among massive sand-dunes in the moonlight. Somebody had been riding a horse on the beach, and Peter associated the broken rings of the hoofprints with the marriage he and Barbara were trying to restore. She pointed out to him that the movement of the seagulls and the sand-dunes echoed each other, and he later wrote this down in notes for what became the poem 'The Moon

Disposes'. They made love among the sand-dunes, and Peter had a feeling of renewal. On the same trip they bought a case of stone samples. When they returned with it to Leeds the stones were 'Drab . . . specimens of a distant place . . . under the dull sky of Leeds', but when taken back to Cornwall they became 'awake' and 'had begun to think, in the place they came out of'. The poem that Peter wrote about this, 'Minerals of Cornwall, Stones of Cornwall', may be seen as a statement of intent about the renewal of their marriage in their new home: 'Kaolin, the white wife of Cornwall / Glistening with inclusions'.

These are two of Redgrove's finest poems, and in neither of them is the autobiographical background explicit. But he was also writing explicitly, in a way that seems to leave no doubt about his determination to restore his relationship with Barbara:

> *The Resolve*
>
> I cannot hold steady what may happen
> The child so powerful, the pang so sudden,
> Let him come where love is, let love come where it was.
>
> Our fate is forked, something gladdened me then
> And grieved me too, that's how it begun [*sic*]
> But let love come where it was, let love be where it was.
>
> Petals repeat and expose the sun,
> They seed and repeat, what's done is done,
> Let love come where it was, let love come where love is.
>
> The web-work torn, tattered by rain,
> The spider rebuilds a steady line.
> Let love build where it was, let love build where he comes.
>
> I so rebuild, and here I begin.
> Let children come where love is, and where love begun.
> Let the timeless not grow in time's sin.

When he returned to Falmouth to begin the job he was alone for a while, before Barbara and the boys joined him, and he wrote, 'All I seem to be doing really is waiting for you.' 'The Resolve' hints at their decision, later fulfilled, to have another child. They bought a house, 8 Tehidy Terrace, in the north of Falmouth. Despite being in a terrace it is an imposing house: the front door is deeply recessed in a pillared porch, approached by a flight of seven steps, with a balcony above, and the living room has two tall windows overlooking the water, an arm of the Carrick Roads that leads to Penryn. This is a house of the well-to-do middle class, comparable in status with Orchard End, though less suburban in style. Peter paid between £5,000 and £6,000 for it, which entailed a mortgage of £500 per year, a quarter of his salary.

Falmouth was to remain Peter's home for the rest of his life, despite several resolutions to move. The remoteness of this Celtic south-western tip of England was to be irksome to him, and it was one of the factors that he blamed for his lack of commercial success as a writer. But over the years the climate, landscape and pagan atmosphere of his adopted home infused themselves into his writing so that they became part of his poetic personality. Living in Cornwall magnified his sensitivities, especially his swings between states of depression and ecstatic vision. Writing three years later for a radio broadcast about Cornwall, he described standing on a jetty in Flushing, across the estuary from his house, and feeling 'as if something black and very very tall had reached down and touched the top of my head with a finger, releasing a swarm of black thoughts which swirled about me. A light suddenly left the landscape, and the trees looked flat, as though they had been painted on glass.' Another time, on a journey out of Cornwall, he felt an unbearable depression lifting as he approached the Tamar, the boundary with Devon. Such depressions would turn equally suddenly into 'a terrific mood of heightened sensuality, so heightened that the smallest action would seem visionary'. More ominously he writes that he began drinking and smoking more than usual after arriving in Cornwall. He was, it must be said, writing this after three years in which the life he had sustained since the early fifties had finally broken apart, and Cornwall might have been a convenient scapegoat.

In 1966 Falmouth School of Art was a very small college with only a few dozen students: it was possible for all the staff and all the students to know each other. The college gardens typify Cornwall's strange semi-tropical climate, with eucalyptus and tree ferns, like an Australian rainforest. Peter had a big room with a first-floor bay window that bellied out near the entrance gate. The Principal, Michael Finn, a distinguished abstract painter, was quiet, unassuming and gentlemanly: most importantly for Peter, he was delighted to have such a vivid creative personality in the school, and willing to give him his head. He had appointed Peter because he wanted the school to have a 'big name' on its staff, to save it from foundering as a little, isolated provincial college. Undoubtedly, for the first few years at least, the school was the most congenial and rewarding paid employment Peter ever had. His 'head of department' (there were only two of them in the Department of Complementary Studies), Lionel Miskin, who had been a fellow-student of Lindsay Anderson and Karel Reisz, was a kindred spirit, a Jungian enthusiast with a love of black humour and a Tolstoyan beard. He reminded one of his students of God in the Sistine Chapel, and the head of painting Francis Hewlett called him an 'extravaganza'. Hewlett, a painter and ceramic sculptor who had worked with William Coldstream and Claude Rogers, was another member of staff who was to become close to Peter, as was the school librarian Derek Toyne.

The atmosphere of the school was relaxed and informal: 'teachers were at the same level as students, the knowledge was a two way event'. To many of the students it felt more like a family than an institution, and they felt able to visit the lecturers at home, even at weekends. Peter himself rapidly became a magnetic and influential figure. One student who went on to become a professional artist, Andrzej Jackowski, had formerly studied at Camberwell, where he learned to be 'a measurer' and did no imaginative painting. He felt 'completely lost' until he went to Falmouth in 1968 and met Peter: 'the great revelation – for which Redgrove was the catalyst – was that I could get these images from inside me'. Another gifted student, Dennis Lowe, who went on to a successful career as a visual effects supervisor, notably on several of Anthony Minghella's most acclaimed films, described his first Complementary Studies class with Peter in 1968:

> There weren't enough chairs so we sat cross legged on the floor, he said 'What would you like me to talk to you about?' – we all looked at each other and after what seemed a few minutes we pretty much decided that the subjects would be sex and death!
>
> He started immediately to block out the fundamentals of these subjects in relation to various world cultures and gave a fantastic hour long breakdown connecting sex, death and religion into the soup. Every week in that first term he would revise and continue to drill down into the subject in great detail, we all came away from his lectures with brain storms and quite often he would come with us to the pub . . . and continue with his knowledge until closing time!

Naturally the students were sometimes inhibited and unforthcoming. Ray Hopley, who started at Falmouth in 1968, recalls being intimidated by the combination of Peter's formidable physical presence, which he seemed able to increase at will to fill a room, and his polymathic range of knowledge. Peter had unorthodox ways of trying to overcome the inhibitions. One time he took in home brew, which only made them soporific; another time he introduced them to the Ouija board. Ray also encountered what he considered the more destructive side of Peter's personality. When he had consumed a lot of alcohol 'he could bring his powerful intellect to bear on someone he disagreed with, and, in a calculated verbal attack, humiliate and demolish them'. One wonders if something like this had happened on the fateful evening with Philip Hobsbaum. Ray didn't think that Peter was a bully; he didn't 'seek out to destroy people weaker than himself' but was 'someone with strong convictions, who enjoyed debate, but who could be quite ruthless in dispatching opponents whose views he found reprehensible, or not thought through'. He at last abandoned the suit and tie, and adopted what one friend thought a rather 'contrived image of the poet', with T-shirt, jeans and sandals, often with a flask of whisky in his back pocket.

He clearly enjoyed a much more complete, informal and influential relationship with students than he had had at Leeds. Through Lionel, and later through Peter himself, there was a constant stream of well-known visiting lecturers and practitioners from across the whole range of the arts. One notable event was Peter's collaboration with Harrison Birtwistle, then at the beginning of his remarkable career as a composer. Students were set the task, in a week, of composing settings for Wallace Stevens's 'Thirteen Ways of Looking at a Blackbird' (chosen of course by Peter); since hardly any of them could read music, they were required to invent systems of notation so that their music could be read by Birtwistle and the musicians he brought with him. The exercise began on Monday, and culminated on Friday in a performance attended by most of the school. This is typical of the way, in Peter's early years at the school, Michael Finn encouraged non-visual forms of creativity.

However Barbara might have felt about Peter's relationship with Dilly in Leeds, the two women were on letter-writing terms. In the New Year Barbara wrote a friendly, newsy letter to Dilly, humorously commenting on the small-town atmosphere of Falmouth. Her choice of incident to illustrate this, however, is startling. Neville Boden, the Gregory Fellow in sculpture at Leeds, and his wife Helen had visited them at Christmas, and had gone for a drink with Peter. Helen had borrowed Barbara's coat and lost a button from it at the pub: the barmaid, who recognised Peter, contacted the Art School caretaker, who in turn phoned Tehidy Terrace. The main point of Barbara's anecdote is that when she answered the phone the caretaker asked for Peter, 'for as you can see, it *wasn't me* wearing the coat!!!' Consciously or otherwise, Barbara seems to be warning Dilly of the impossibility of conducting a secret affair in Falmouth. Peter's parents also visited at Christmas, and Barbara complains sharply about their rudeness to him: 'I feel like treating them to a crash course on manners.' Peter was later to accuse Barbara and his parents (or at least his father) of forming a united front against him, but at least for now her sympathies were with him.

Barbara may have felt secure that Peter's liaison with Dilly was at an end, but she was mistaken. It is unlikely that the lovers were able to meet, at least alone, for another two years, but the relationship continued in letters and phone calls. Peter constantly protests his love and longing for Dilly, and frustration at the constraints they are suffering under, but he is equally protective of his marriage: 'I want you to be happy, and as much yourself, and as gay, as you always were, and I want the same for Barbara. I want to do nothing to spoil it for either of you.' He calls their relationship a 'passionate friendship', which seems a carefully chosen phrase. She needed 'a constant, continuing relationship with the person actually there a lot of the time', but the actual circumstances may have suited Peter better than he admitted. His divided feelings made him, for the only time in his life, rail against monogamy as 'the bond of mutual possession', and yearn for 'love-communities', but he knew this was impossible, and just talking to Dilly on the phone made him feel that 'an oppression had lifted'. Daily life with Barbara and the boys, and Dilly flickering alluringly in the distance, was for a while a sustainable arrangement. Peter was so far from wanting to break his marriage for Dilly, that he and Barbara agreed to reinforce it by having another child. Peter was never such a devotee of Robert Graves's *The White Goddess* as Ted Hughes, but just now he was conforming to Graves's idea of the (always male) poet, for whom the muse could never be a wife.

Certainly Dilly inspired some of the most memorable poems Peter was writing at this time. They are radiant with the presence of an alluring, uninhibited and provocative woman who constantly challenges and amazes the slow-witted male speaker. Despite 'The Resolve', soon after it he was writing 'Water-Witch, Wood-Witch, Wine-Witch', annotated by Peter as 'Dilly, aware in the weather and impatient of a man's diffidence and ignore-ance'. The erotic witchy female in this poem is desired by nature itself:

> And when she came out it was raining, the night itself
> Wanted to touch her, a silver stillness
> Stood waiting, she was wet all through
> Like a willow in the garden, wet apron
> Shivering on an abyss

and she says to the male speaker, 'you know / The language we call "Crossing the River", do you speak / The older tongue called "Wallow"?' which suggests complicity in the Game.

Above all, in 'Young Women with the Hair of Witches and No Modesty' the image of Dilly is fused with a numinous instructress who challenges and chides the rigid masculine consciousness. The speaker claims that he has 'always loved water', but admits that he 'often wished water would stand still' because 'Changes and glints bemuse a man terribly'. His attitude to the woman is the same: 'I used to see her straight and cool, considering the pond' but as she turns the waves of her hair, naiad- or mermaid-like, 'betray . . . her origin'. The speaker praises her in some of Redgrove's most beautifully sensuous lines:

> In such a world the bride walks through dressed as a waterfall,
> And ripe grapes fall and splash smooth snow with jagged purple,
> Young girls grow brown as acorns in their rainy climb towards
>   oakhood,
> And brown moths settle low down among ivories wet with love.

Lovely though these lines are, there is a touch of self-regarding aestheticism about them, which the woman disrupts:

> But she loosened her hair in a sudden tangle of contradictions,
> In cross and doublecross, surcross and countercross,
> And I was a shadow in the twilight of her late displeasure.
> I asked water to stand still, now nothing else holds.

Peter annotated this: 'Dilly Creffield at her most glamorous and provoking, in the company of her children.' The slightly patronising phrase 'glamorous and provoking' seems like a return to the attitude of the speaker who wishes the woman, like water, would 'hold still' – an attitude that, by the end of the poem, she has shattered. If so, the poem reflects the tensions between them during the whole period after Peter's move to Falmouth – to 'hold still' being to accept, as Peter would like her to, the boundaries of their relationship. The poem has an epigraph, 'I loved Ophelia!', which was to prove shockingly prescient. While the poem casts light on its biographical origins, however, it isn't dependent on them. The woman in it is the strongest appearance yet of the 'Goddess' or feminine principle that was to transform Peter's poetry even more radically in the years to follow.

But these poems are also a warning against a too-ready biographical interpretation. Until I saw the drafts I was convinced that 'The Youthful Scientist Remembers' was also a recollection of Dilly. The mud on the woman's jersey pleases the speaker and her naughty joke about the lily being 'somebody's red tail inside their white nightie' opens him to the splendour of the stars and 'starlight glittering in the mud'. When I told Dennis Creffield about the Game he said, 'He would have enjoyed Dilly because she's the same.' But one of the drafts is annotated 'One of the beautiful good pounces on Barbara (in continuance of her dream)' and another is dedicated to her. It may be that, having been awakened to an aspect of femininity by his lover, he was able to respond to the same quality in his wife. More certainly, we should remember that these poetic females are fictional creatures, for whom the real women are models: as far as the meaning of the poems is concerned, the women *are* the same.

Peter's letters to Dilly are undated, and it is impossible to put them in order. In one letter he says he wants to do nothing to spoil things for Dilly or for Barbara; in another he writes, 'I must change my life somehow', and describes his present life as 'one belonging to a former Peter'. He was drinking heavily and suffering daily depressions: 'Drink was the only tranquilliser that worked, and infallibly removed the daily depressions . . . I have a good constitution and can drink myself sober . . . with some thirty pints of beer or more than a bottle of spirits. Drunk to bed not just for a week (which might happen to anybody) but every night for a couple of months, a day's pause, then the same again.' As we shall see, this was not an empty boast. The ending of his marriage to Barbara, and the events that led up to it, preoccupied him for the rest of his life. Despite the success and happiness of his partnership with Penelope Shuttle this was, like his feelings towards his father, an aspect of his life that he never resolved. Most of the evidence about what he felt at this time is retrospective and coloured by the collapse of the marriage. Many of the symptoms, if not the causes, of the trouble were sexual. Peter complained in later years that Barbara never had an orgasm and so they had never been real sexual partners. For reasons that are not obvious he was inclined to blame her for this, though he does once ask himself, 'Did D[illy] have orgasms – perhaps not', and when Dennis asked Dilly what Peter was like in bed she replied with a laugh, 'Hopeless!' Barbara once said that making love with Peter was like masturbation. Whatever the sexual response of either woman, it was clearly how Peter felt about it that made the difference. Barbara tried to be sympathetic about the Game and even to join in. Once she smeared a marmite moustache and beard on her face but for some reason that put Peter off. Another time she 'did the Odalisque' (it's not clear what this had to do with the Game but perhaps she was just trying to enliven their lovemaking by imitating Ingres's painting). This 'didn't work either' for Peter – poor Barbara! He complained that she only did the Game for him, and got no pleasure from it herself. He also insisted on making love when she was menstruating, which she found painful but submitted to because it pleased him.

Peter was also disappointed that Barbara did not devote herself more to her art: he claimed that they had allocated a room in the house for her to work, but she never used it. Perhaps, he thought, they would have been closer if she had. Francis Hewlett never saw her work, and thought that Peter didn't make it easy for her. In Francis's words Barbara 'felt pushed out all the time'. By contrast, her children testify that her art was very important to her – 'there was always clay around the place' – and Bill thought that she *was* working in Falmouth.

When, in later years, Peter's journals return to this period, he seems to re-enter the depression that he suffered from at the time. Or perhaps he only wrote about his first marriage when he already felt depressed. These reflections aren't a reliable account of what happened. But he was genuinely struggling with depression, and with compulsions that had accompanied his whole adult life. He wanted to work through these problems and stay married to Barbara; she tried to be sympathetic but in the last resort could not help: 'I could do nothing to allay her fears because of the games, she could do nothing to transform my games.' His state of mind made him an increasingly unsatisfactory husband and father. He loved his children but his difficulties with Jim made him resist the role of father: 'I'm not a good father, being afraid of my own Oedipal conflicts with my father.' This was in itself a cause of alienation from family life, and it may have led Barbara to assume an enhanced parental role, becoming more the mother and less the lover. This in turn alienated Peter still further. Bill has few memories of his father's participation in family life: perhaps the most important is that at Falmouth Peter taught him judo to yellow belt standard. This, Bill recalls, was probably the most time his father devoted to him, and he recollects thinking him 'extremely strong as if steel beneath the flesh'. Later, at a new school, judo helped him to overcome the school bully. His other most vivid memory is of Peter taking him and Pete to a muddy creek near Gweek on the Helford estuary, play-fighting with the boys and falling in the mud. Peter himself describes this incident with relish in a letter to Dilly, and Bill recalls that Barbara accused him of falling in the mud deliberately. This isn't surprising, since Peter once concluded an evening in the pub by taking Ray Hopley and three other students mud-bathing in the creek at Devoran, a few miles north of Falmouth. 'There was a wide expanse of mud, lit by a bright moon, and in we jumped, frolicking with abandon, fully clothed. We danced and jumped on one another in the moonlight, our laughter and shouts echoing across the mud-flats.' When the effects of the drink had worn off, with mud in every orifice, they climbed into Peter's car and he drove them home, leaving the car 'lagged with mud'. It was only in retrospect that Ray considered the implications of Peter 'staying out all night with his wife and family at home, his indifference to the state of the family car'.

Peter thought that he must change his life somehow, and soon after arriving in Falmouth he met someone who helped him to do that, though more painfully and destructively than he had hoped. John Layard was an anthropologist and psychologist who before the First World War had travelled to Vanuatu (then the New Hebrides) with W. H. R. Rivers (who was soon to treat Wilfred Owen and Siegfried Sassoon at Craiglockhart) and been left there alone, to become a pioneering anthropological fieldworker and eventually write the book, *Stone Men of Malekula*. Layard suffered considerable psychological distress himself and underwent therapy successively with Homer Lane and Carl Jung. Lane was an idealistic and optimistic libertarian who believed that children should learn and grow by being given responsibility rather than by submitting to authority, and Layard was strongly influenced by these ideas, which also inspired A. S. Neill to found Summerhill school.

Layard is best known today, to his great disadvantage, through his association with W. H. Auden and Christopher Isherwood in Berlin in the late 1920s. In biographies of Auden, and in Isherwood's *Lions and Shadows*, he figures as a crank – the 'loony Layard' of Auden's *The Orators* – who believed that all illness was psychosomatic, that one should follow God (one's desires) rather than the Devil (conscious control) and all that was necessary for perfect happiness was to be 'pure in heart'. According to Isherwood, he and Auden (both in their early twenties) swallowed these theories enthusiastically, and Layard's reputation was the price of their later reaction. Most damagingly of all, according to Auden's biographer Charles Osborne, Layard, who was bisexual, developed an unrequited passion for Auden and shot himself in the mouth. He botched the job, took a taxi to Auden's lodging still with the gun in his hand and said, 'Wystan, I've done it . . . But it hasn't killed me. Please finish me off.' Auden replied, 'I would if I dared, but I don't want to be hanged.' Layard's own unpublished memoir largely confirms this account, with one important exception: it was not unrequited love for Auden that drove him to attempt suicide. Auden was besotted with a sailor, 'the perfect boy', and Layard (in his own eyes) betrayed his friend by taking the sailor back to his hotel. He then found himself to be impotent, and it was this dismal mixture of personal betrayal and sexual failure that drove him to despair. It is debatable which version of the story is more humiliating to Layard (who called his autobiography 'The History of a Failure') but the element of moral remorse in his own version has some dignity, and contradicts the caricature of his views in Osborne's biography and Isherwood's fictionalised memoir.

Later, shortly before the outbreak of the Second World War, Layard presented himself for analysis with Jung in Zurich. Initially he was delighted that Jung spoke to him 'like a friend, like an equal', the two of them sitting in armchairs, unlike the impersonal chair behind the couch of Freudian practice. Jung even 'poured forth' to Layard about his own life. Layard was also impressed by Jung's interpretation of his dreams, and felt that he was making great progress. But

Jung worked strictly to 'terms' and, whatever stage the analysis had reached, when the term ended the relationship was interrupted. This was the first of a series of disillusionments that brought Layard to feel that Jung did not really care about his patients. He came to believe that Jung took too little account of the 'personal' level of the unconscious because he was obsessed with his knowledge of the archetypes, and most damningly that he was terrified of sex, which he refused to discuss with his patients.

Despite this disenchantment with Jung as a therapist, Layard kept faith with his method, and in 1944 he published an unusually attractive analytic case history, in his book *The Lady of the Hare*. The first half of this book is a detailed account of the interpretations of the dreams of one patient, whom he calls 'Mrs Wright'. The title comes from one of these dreams, in which Mrs Wright sacrificed a hare, and the second half of the book concerns the importance of the hare in folklore and mythology, which Layard did not know about when he conducted the analysis. Mrs Wright was a farmer's wife, uneducated but highly intelligent, of Ulster Protestant extraction, devoutly religious and a woman of strong and genuine moral principles. In accordance with his first experience with Jung, Layard writes in the introduction to the book that the Jungian analyst does not need 'the paraphernalia of defence put up by the Freudian', but faces his patient 'in ordinary human converse' resulting in 'a deep mutual respect'. The most striking thing about the analysis is that throughout it he shows the utmost respect for Mrs Wright's religious beliefs, and uses the language of Christianity itself to guide her into a more flexible moral attitude.

In the late sixties Layard, who had been living in Oxford, quarrelled with his wife who threw him out of the house. Lionel Miskin knew him, and persuaded him to come to live in Cornwall, and to lecture at the School of Art. He presented a puzzling set of contradictions, both physically and in personality. He was tall and imposing, but by this time a physical wreck, debilitated by diabetes. He was sexually impotent as a result of a collision with a milk lorry, but succeeded in seducing a friend's wife because, according to Peter, he knew 'the Secret . . . of the clitoris', a closed book to most men at that time. He was a deeply intuitive man who often acted with astonishing indifference to taboos and conventions, but absurdly sensitive about social status: he was upset not to be invited to the Investiture of the Prince of Wales, and had a reputation as a 'social creep', flattering influential people. By the time he came to live in Cornwall he had retired from full-time analytic practice, having been given an annuity by a wealthy family whose deeply disturbed son he had helped by unorthodox methods, including allowing him to play with his excrement. Michael Tippett had been a patient, and in the forties at Oxford Layard's lectures made a strong impression on as unlikely a person as Philip Larkin. Nevertheless he considered himself a complete failure, and was given to saying to his patients that only a failure can help a failure.

Peter was profoundly moved by these lectures. From his fragmentary notes on them it is clear that Layard was speaking on the theme that he had dwelt on with Mrs Wright: that 'that which has hitherto been most feared or despised may be . . . transformed into spiritual strength'. That 'evil was necessary (i.e. inevitable) as well as good, so that anyone who tries to do good all the time *must* fail, because the other side has not been allowed for'; that God rules over the night as well as the day, and 'it is as fatal to neglect the powers of darkness as to neglect the powers of light'. His treatment of Mrs Wright shows a far more sophisticated mind than Auden and Isherwood's account of him: either he had matured extraordinarily, or he was traduced by his young friends in Berlin. Among his explicit quotations from the lectures Peter noted, 'God feeds on our sins' and 'the serpent telling Mary that she was too clean, and how this started the journey through terror to excellence'. The man who had been struggling all his adult life with feared and despised obsessions must have thought his saviour had arrived.

Soon after hearing Layard lecture, Peter took an overnight sleeper train to London. His head full of Layard's ideas, he was unable to sleep, and as was his custom he tried to relax himself by masturbating. This didn't work, and he realised that he had to write a poem expressing his new-found insights. He began drafting what was to be one of his most important poems, perhaps the pivotal work in his oeuvre, 'The Idea of Entropy at Maenporth Beach'. Unlike 'The Collector', nearly half the poem came to him in this first draft. In the poem he indulges freely his sensual love of mud:

> The mud spatters with rich seed and ranging pollens.
> Black darts up the pleats, black pleats
> Lance along the white ones, and she stops
> Swaying, cut in half. Is it right, she sobs

As the fat, juicy, incredibly tart muck rises
Round her throat and dims the diamond there? . . .

The mud recoils, lies heavy, queasy, swart.
But then this soft blubber stirs, and quickly she comes up
Dressed as a mound of lickerish earth,
Swiftly ascending in a streaming pat
That grows tall, smooths brimming hips, and steps out
On flowing pillars, darkly draped.

The triumph of the poem is that it is not merely a cathartic confession – indeed, it is not a confession at all. Redgrove's art is fully engaged with his material, and the delight is as much in the language which, thick with sensory monosyllables, still manages to conjure a feeling of impressive ritual, as in the imagined action. As Peter liked to do when he played his Game, the protagonist is dressed in white, but she is of course a woman. Superficially this disguises the wish-fulfilment in the poem, but it really reveals a deeper level of the desire which is, as we have seen, both to be and to possess the woman: the female protagonist is an object both of desire and of identification. The poem ends with an affirmation that this celebration of what is feared and desired does indeed transform it into spiritual strength, and a prediction that this will be the new generating source of his poetry:

The black rooks coo like doves, new suns beam
From every droplet of the shattering waves,
From every crystal of the shattered rock.
Drenched in the mud, pure white rejoiced,
From this collision were new colours born,
And in their slithering passage to the sea
The shrugged-up riches of deep darkness sang.

Peter sent the completed poem with several others to Layard, and asked permission to dedicate 'The Idea of Entropy' to him. The other poems obviously included 'Water-Witch, Wood-Witch, Wine-Witch' and 'Young Women with the Hair of Witches and No Modesty', because he told Layard, 'I sometimes think that the witch may be the same woman in her power after her rite of blackness.' So this poem, too, may owe something to Dilly, but while the witch poems were imaginatively dramatised moments in a relationship, with an explicit male protagonist, in this one the female figure is much more an aspect of the poet's psyche. Layard accepted the dedication, saying that he liked the meeting of the personal and the archetypal, which 'arouses in me feelings about the mystery and the drama of life'.

After dedicating a poem such as this to Layard, it was inevitable that Peter would seek his further help. Like Rilke who refused an analysis by Freud, he was anxious that his poetry might disappear with his demons, but decided that 'if the Jungian analysis gets rid of my poetry, perhaps the poetry wasn't worth having.' He wasn't the only lecturer at the school to do so. Francis Hewlett suffered from Crohn's disease; this is a physical illness but in Francis's case it had a psychological dimension: it got considerably worse at times of stress at work. Francis came to believe that Layard saved his life. As with Mrs Wright, he worked entirely through dream interpretation, and his method was very simple. For example, Francis told him a dream about going on a train to a place called Sea Mills, where there was no railway station. In the dream he encountered a beautiful girl wearing a red scarf and beret. Layard said, 'The dream is you: you are the train that never ran, the blood red beret and the beautiful girl.' In Peter's words, 'he improvised on the dream'. At first Francis disliked him intensely because he seemed to be trying to find out how artists work – trying to see into Francis's inner self. Then they had this conversation:

> 'I know why you're frightened of me.'
> 'I'm not frightened of you.'
> 'You think I'm going to discover something, you think you've got a room where all your most extraordinary bits are locked up.'
> 'That is nothing to do with you – that is art.'
> 'Yes, but there isn't anything in that room.'

Francis felt this was the most extraordinary thing anyone had ever said to him, and he had a great sensation of relief: it was so much easier to know the room was empty, that he didn't have anything to live up to. Layard was equally bold in interpreting the dreams of people he hardly knew. Peter persuaded D. M. Thomas to have a session with him. Thomas described a dream that involved a cathedral, and Layard told him, 'The cathedral is the body of your mother, and what the dream is telling you is "Kill your mother".' Thomas recognised that his writing was inhibited by fears about what his mother would think of it, and he needed to overcome this.

The analysis of another friend of Peter's showed that in one respect *The Lady of the Hare* wasn't truthful. There Layard claims that the Jungian analyst, unlike the Freudian, does not need to defend himself against negative transference because he does not 'represent the personal parents' but concentrates on 'the impersonal factors that lie beneath the personal relationships'. It is true that Layard was not defensive – he would weep during an analysis for example – but this patient experienced such negative transference that he wanted to kill his analyst. He planned 'the perfect murder': he would stifle Layard then pour tea over him so it would look as if he had drowned drinking tea. Arriving for his session he said, 'I've come down to kill you,' and Layard answered, 'That's a natural thing to want to do,' whereupon the patient burst into tears.

Peter never threatened to murder Layard, but he responded similarly to his lack of defences: Layard responding with feeling, and weeping, 'opened up avenues and dissolved projections'. Francis did not know that Peter had been Layard's patient and Peter's later references to their relationship are deliberately ambiguous. He referred to it as a 'training analysis', described himself as Layard's 'pupil', and told one interviewer that Layard dispensed with fees in return for Peter agreeing to use his methods in teaching. But Peter certainly was Layard's patient, and he certainly did pay fees – or rather Jim did. He persuaded Jim that the purpose of his meetings with Layard was, like his earlier experience of Freudian analysis, to reinforce the status quo, to stabilise him and his marriage to Barbara. He probably half persuaded himself of this too, since he never consciously intended the break-up of his marriage. Since Layard was charging £40–50 per month, which was a quarter of Peter's salary, it is not surprising that he needed help with the bills. He later said that he saw Layard for a total of about four hundred hours over a period of eighteen months: excluding weekends, that averages at an hour a day. The fact that Jim was paying the fees made one sally of Layard's particularly cruel. Francis was talking to Layard in the grounds of the art school when he noticed Peter talking to an older, stout, balding man with a moustache. 'Who is that with Peter?' he asked. 'That's the putative father,' came the answer.

Though Peter's public comments on Layard were always affirmative and respectful, privately his attitude was ambivalent. He later wrote to a scholar who was attempting (unsuccessfully) to publish Layard's autobiography, 'John made many mistakes and caused much pain' but 'even his mistakes were an enzyme'. In a letter to his mother when he was still undergoing analysis he described Layard as 'such a fool, such a wise man, such a sinner, such a healer'. Given that Peter's problems were rooted in his relationship with his parents, and partly in Jim's character, an orthodox model of masculinity would have been less than no use to him. Anything resembling masculine authority would be an inevitable target for projections of his feelings about Jim, Taunton and the army. Layard was physically decrepit, emotionally vulnerable, morally suspect, sexually ambivalent and, in Francis Hewlett's word, 'soppy': in almost every respect the antithesis of Jim. He would take his teeth out during analysis, and Peter thought he knew when he was getting interested because he salivated. One of his (perhaps self-interested) insistences was on confronting one's 'homosexual shadow', and he was no respecter of the boundaries conventionally observed by therapists; on one occasion he and Peter got into bed together and Peter fondled Layard's penis: 'I felt his little soft penis and stroked it: his whole skin was penis-skin, soft as a gazelle's nose.' That such a man, who could not be mistaken for the enemy, was also an intuitive genius and a disciple of Jung, to whom Peter was already attuned, was a tremendous stroke of luck. There was much conflict between the two men: Layard was intolerant of Peter's drinking (especially of his turning up drunk at their meetings) and Peter thought he idealised Barbara. Most surprisingly, despite his response to 'The Idea of Entropy', Layard was hostile or at least unreceptive to Peter's poetry. One of Peter's letters begins, 'I can't seem to keep my temper about these poems when I'm talking to you', and he later reported Layard as saying, 'You are hung up *because* you write poetry.' When crediting Layard with turning his life round Peter most often cited the general dictum, 'Depression is withheld knowledge.' In *Innocent Street* he gives two more specific examples of the cure of neurotic symptoms:

> Two miraculous cures from Layard. I had jactitation, could not lie down without a spasmodic gasp of breath and a shout. He said when did you first shout. I said I've just told you every night last night included. . . . Just tell me when you first spasmed. When it began. No when you first gasped for air. He wrinkled his face up like a baby's. As he did so, the answer came out of my mouth: When I began. That's it, when you were born. The spasms ceased.
>
> I told him I was afraid of being in the house by myself. That's

your father, he said. My father? He lives in London. When did your father come into your house? When he last visited, a fortnight ago. How did you feel? He turned his back to me, towards my wife. You were jealous of the house then. When did your father give you cause for jealousy by entering your house? When I was the sole occupant in my mother, the answer sprang out fast and agile as a baby's turd.

Layard gave Peter permission to play his Game as often as he liked, and encouraged him to dream about it. It is in the late sixties that he began to paste Game-related pictures, such as men and (more often) women coated in mud, into his notebooks, and to write explicitly about it:

> My poor friend – nowadays his greatest pleasure, all that is left of his withering libido, is to sit in the bath and pour warm custard on his head. There he sits until it dries, and then he can unpeel the custard-skins off his scalp, unpeeling his head like an orange. Somehow, he says, there is great refreshment in this grotesquerie, and he emerges a new man, as if the scab had been peeled from his brain, the scab of prejudice and habit . . .

Layard said of the Game, 'That's your mother' (Peter later dreamed about having sex with his mother in mud) and 'You'll never get rid of that.' He never did get rid of it, and he never entirely rid himself of anxiety about it, but the years 1968–9, when he was working intensively with Layard, were undoubtedly an epoch for him psychologically, creatively and domestically. It was Layard who enabled him to feel that what he 'feared or despised' could be a source of 'spiritual strength'.

During his time in Falmouth Layard became fascinated by a beautiful, gifted and troubled young man called Malcolm Ritchie, who had dropped out of the art school, but returned at Lionel's request to organise the school's collection of books into a library. He later became Layard's amanuensis. Malcolm was subject to hallucinatory experiences which were signs not of psychosis but of mediumistic powers that he later learned to recognise and develop. One day he left a sheaf of writing on a piano in the school, and Peter came across it and read it. He was immediately enthusiastic about this 'plasm' as he called it and wanted to know who had written it. He invited Malcolm to dinner, and soon they were regular drinking companions. Malcolm too was married with a child, but the disorder of both their lives exploded in days of almost unbelievable excess, when they would begin drinking as soon as the pubs opened in the morning, carry on all day, take a bottle of whisky and a bottle of vodka with them into a late-night movie, and continue through the night drinking home brew at Peter's house. During these two-man carnivals they would go into a hotel, plug all the baths and leave the taps running, wreck gardens while declaiming poetry, or enter unlocked houses and suddenly appear like 'two demons', causing uproar in the owners' sitting rooms. Once Peter defecated on the sunroof of a parked car.

Like Layard, Peter developed an obsessive fascination with the younger man. He wanted to know all about him and would interrogate his wife and girlfriends, to their annoyance and his. Layard told Peter that Malcolm was 'the Christ child'. Malcolm believed that Peter projected a great deal on to him, perhaps because he was intrigued by, and envious of, a personality that was even more psychically gifted and troubled than himself. Peter would ask him to describe things, and he later acknowledged that Malcolm was an influence on his work. He also generously promoted Malcolm's writing, once recommending it on the radio. One particular projection concerned the character played by Terence Stamp in Pasolini's film *Theorem*, a charismatic, sexually polymorphous intruder into a bourgeois family, who seduces all of them. At one time Malcolm felt that he was being lured into a *ménage à trois*. If so, it may have been an attempt by Peter to authorise his own sexual adventures; it was also, of course, a replication of the Creffield scenario, with himself in Dennis's role. Malcolm thought that Layard created a homoerotic atmosphere around him and he himself, though straight, was inevitably a focus of this. On one of their drunken nights he and Peter found themselves enclosed within the hanging branches of a very old weeping willow, illuminated with a green glow by the nearby streetlights. Peter suddenly said, 'I love you.' Malcolm, who was terrified of homosexuality, froze and was silent. Peter parted the branches and disappeared. A little later Malcolm was wandering confused in the garden, which belonged to a house under renovation, covered in scaffolding, and was suddenly cut down by a blow from an iron-tipped builder's plank, which took a chip out of his shinbone. As he lay on the ground in agony holding his leg he heard a tiny voice: 'A little girl came out and did that.' In 1970, probably some time after this episode, and after Peter had terminated his analysis, Layard wrote to him interpreting one of his dreams as the 'birth of a deeply knowledgeable anima, in the form of a girl'. Peter's bizarre behaviour with Malcolm may have been partly a violent reflex to embarrassing self-exposure and anger at rejection, but also a recognition that the dark side of his personality was linked to his undeveloped femininity.

Layard's insistence on the 'homosexual shadow' haunted Peter throughout his life, and he often invoked it when struggling with projections, usually of a negative kind, on other men. In the early seventies a friend proposed a homosexual affair, and Peter felt guilty about turning this down, finding a series of excuses for doing so. There is no evidence that he was like, for example, D. H. Lawrence, who was physically attracted to men though committed to hetero-sexuality. Yet Peter seems to have felt that he failed in some way by not accepting a homosexual relationship. He speculated that the 'homosexual shadow' was at the root of his Game, and character-istically concluded that he 'couldn't be homosexual because of my father', whom he described, without any apparent evidence, as 'a strongman with an unfulfilled homosexual streak'. His preoccupa-tion with homosexuality is perhaps best summed up by the journal note, 'I must indeed sleep with a boy. Myself.'

In the middle of this chaos, in June 1968 Kate Redgrove was born. She was very much wanted by both parents, and she was to be a beloved companion to her mother, but as usual the plan to save a marriage by having a child was ineffective. When Barbara went into labour Peter was too drunk to drive her to the hospital, and she had to drive herself. Jim sent Peter an article about alco-holism, which predictably incensed him: he thought the article was moralising, and took no account of the reasons why a man might drink, such as disliking his job in industry and being 'nagged by his wife and relations to "do the right thing" and "snap out of it"'. If Jim really wanted to help he needed to give Peter unconditional 'emotional support'. Jim wanted to do this, as he showed in a drafted and probably unsent letter that summer, in which he 'wanted very earnestly to find out whether you shared my feeling that we had been able to get a little closer together last weekend', but confessed, 'Perhaps I'm not very good at this, or at helping you with your problems.' He was temperamentally unable to sympathise with feel-ings that contradicted his own code of self-restraint, and Peter's belief that he could improve his relationship with Barbara by *indulging* deviant desires seemed to him merely irresponsible, as when he asked for money 'to keep away from Cornwall for a bit'. Jim's refusal precipitated another quarrel. Yet only a fortnight earlier he had sent, unasked, £35 towards Layard's fees, and was to contribute at least £120 to the same cause over the next few months: 'Your health & welfare are very precious to me and I am delighted that you have found this contact worth while.'

The marriage was in crisis: Peter and Barbara were both uncertain whether they would stay together, and at the end of July Barbara took the children to Selsey for a fortnight. The trouble was no secret to the wider family: it is clear that Jim knew about Dilly, and he warned Peter of a 'sticky wicket' with Barbara's parents at Selsey. Jim sent Barbara a cheque for her travel expenses, which she returned, saying that she couldn't accept from him what he had refused to Peter. Even without money from Jim Peter got away for a 'holiday' during which he met Dilly in Leeds, almost certainly for the first time in two years. He told Dilly that Barbara was no longer jealous, and acquiesced in his coming. Since 1967 Martin Bell had been Gregory Fellow, and visiting Martin would have been a good enough pretext. But Barbara wouldn't have acquiesced in Peter sleeping with Dilly, which he certainly did. He was anxious even about being seen with her. Martin was now living with Christine McCausland, and when Christine met Peter and Dilly in the pub Peter said, 'I'm not here, you haven't seen me.' Christine thought they both looked shattered and that Dilly in particular was very subdued. Peter said they had 'been up all night talking, talking, talking', and fixed Christine in the eye as if to say, 'That's all we've been doing – nothing else.' But he later told his mother that the meeting with Dilly had been 'fine, in bed'. Christine had the impression that Peter ended the affair on that visit, and in another letter to Nan he ambiguously writes, 'I was better with Barbara after my time in Leeds last summer, not because I had given Dilly of Leeds up, but because I had been with her.' However, his later letters to Dilly don't have the tone of an ex-lover.

Early the next year Peter published a new collection, *Work in Progress*. This was his first full-length collection not to be published by Routledge but by a small press, Poet and Printer. The book is dedicated to Barbara, despite several of the poems in it being inspired by Dilly. There is an introduction by D. M. Thomas which plainly states, 'The witch-figure of the poems is unmistakably a real woman, having a real love-affair.' In the copy that Peter sent to Dilly he supplemented the dedication: 'For Barbara, for one; for Dilly for another. No tournament; no blame.' On the title page he wrote 'On this book/Only you may look' and altered the price to 'beyond price'. He annotated every poem, including explicit references to their affair, and on the final page wrote, 'I love you.' Not the gift of a man who has ended an affair.

The dedication of *Work in Progress* to Barbara is easily explained by the poems that celebrate moments in the attempted renewal of their marriage, such as 'The Moon Disposes' and 'The Youthful Scientist Remembers'. Peter drafted an introduction describing the poems as a sequence comparable to George Meredith's *Modern Love*, representing 'the breaking of an allegiance & the forming of it again after a night journey'. The comparison with *Modern Love* was all too apt, since that sequence is about the irretrievable breakdown of a marriage. By early 1969, when the book was published, the dedication to Barbara seems most meaningful in respect of the last poem, 'Quasimodo's Many Beds', where the conflict is close to impasse. The speaker has Quasimodo's deformity and bad teeth into the bargain: these things represent what the woman to whom the poem is addressed considers his sexual deformity, which is also directly represented in the poem:

> Here is couched black mud
> In rich satin cushions. It is a washable disfigurement.
> We are all mire, and we are all clean, and this is a Quasimodo's bed.
> Great things, like you, or water or sun, mire or ashes,
> Or any little thing, pull my heart out of shape
> Which is no deformity. I sit, enthroned in mud
> Like an opulent person watching.

Redgrove and Layard quarrelled about this poem, partly on the grounds of obscurity, as a result of which Peter wrote a letter which is, for him, a unique line-by-line explication. He concludes by offering two alternative interpretations:

> Either Quasimodo is revealing something important to the girl, that she should love more widely, and if she does indeed love, his quirks are no deformities; or the girl is waiting for Quasimodo to stop playing about and make love to her properly. *It doesn't really matter to the poem which.* The situation is there and it's the reader's business to decide which of the two persons in the poem he thinks is right, if either is. Also it may behove me as recipient of this poem

(or 'active imagination') to consider my own psychological situation as reflected in the poem. Nevertheless the poem tries to be a discrete entity, a little machine that tells a tale. All it wants to do is to tell the tale. The moral is up to the reader. As writer, I am still reflecting on the moral.

The ideas about poetry in this letter are New Critical commonplaces, reflections of Philip Hobsbaum's hostility to 'intentionalism'. Layard however clearly thought it an instance of bad faith, and put incredulous exclamation marks in the margin, where Redgrove writes that it is for the reader to decide, and refers to himself as a reader of his own poem. More perceptively Layard told him it was arrogant to write such a poem from the man's point of view, telling the woman what to do, and Peter wrote a reply in the woman's voice, 'Quasimodo's Many Beds II'. In this version she calls Quasimodo a liar and takes up his challenge to immerse herself in mud:

> I rise in satin of earth.
> I am the earth of life.
> I move like a wet mountain

But this frightens Quasimodo, and the poem ends sinisterly:

> You take one step towards me.
> Which is when I open the knife.
> I love to be dressed in living red.
> I wait for you in the rain-hiss
> My hair snaky.

If this poem was meant to reassure Barbara it was badly misjudged. She had recently read a story, from the woman's point of view, of a paranoid husband who attacked his wife with a knife, and she thought it meant that Peter wanted to kill her.

Work in Progress also contains the relics of Redgrove's one attempt at professional translation. Alvarez had asked him to work on translations of the Hungarian poet Sándor Weöres, for a volume in the influential *Penguin Modern European Poets* series, which was to introduce poets such as Zbigniew Herbert and Miroslav Holub to an English readership. This involved, of course, working with literal translations and, since Alvarez used the word 'imitations', Redgrove produced versions with as much of his own stylistic profile as of the original. He put a great deal of work into this project, filling several notebooks with drafts. It foundered, however, partly because he sent the translations to Hughes for his opinion. Hughes had recently co-founded the magazine *Modern Poetry in Translation*, had worked with Assia Wevill on translations of the Israeli poet Yehuda Amichai, and would a few years later publish versions of another Hungarian poet, János Pilinszky. Hughes was developing a principle of extreme literalness in the translation of modern poetry, to which Redgrove's versions were anathema. He replied that he liked them very much 'as Redgrove', but that the effect of publishing them as a book of Weöres's poems in English would be to deprive readers of the chance to find out what the Hungarian poet was really like. Redgrove submitted to his friend's judgement, and re-translated the work in a more literal fashion. For some reason the project still foundered, and Redgrove later regretted taking Hughes's advice. The poems 'Signs', 'Orpheus Dead', 'Flowers for the First Wife', 'Stitch in Time' and 'Rayfly and Nightshirt' were salvaged from the original versions.

Peter's visit to Leeds may have been encouraged by Layard telling him that he should sleep with other women to 'improve his feminine self-image' (this sounds a little like his mother sleeping with other men to 'open her womb'). He persuaded himself that he was a better lover to Barbara as a result, but she refused to believe in Layard's advice and said it was just his 'lust'. Jim also refused to believe that a 'professional man' would say such a thing (was this what he was paying the fees for?). This was the only time in Peter's life when his attitude to women could be described as promiscuous. I say 'attitude' because there doesn't seem to have been a great deal of promiscuous activity, and Peter had to confess to Layard that one promising situation ended with both parties realising that 'it wouldn't do', and instead spending the day 'getting to know each other in other ways'. He later objected when an article about him attributed his poetic development to 'a series of sexual affairs', saying that this portrayed him as a 'shabby sexual adventurer'. Apart from Dilly only one encounter resulting from Layard's permission left a lasting mark. He met a woman who in his journal he calls 'Perilla Wymark'. She told him that her last lover, two years earlier, had been a voodoo initiate, and after they had made love he had 'a vision of her womb, as an amphora with handles, a loving-cup, or the Horned God'. This was perhaps his first experience of visionary sex, and he frequently referred to it in later years. Over time he possibly mythologised this encounter, suggesting that it was a kind of formal magical initiation, and at different times describing 'Perilla' as a witch, a Kabbalist and a Sufi. She did, at least, recommend Kabbala to him and advised him to read David Bakan's *Freud and the Jewish Mystical Tradition*, which was to be important to him in later years.

By early 1969 Peter and Barbara were debating separation or divorce. A significant consequence of the marital crisis was that Peter's intimacy with his mother was renewed. While he had always felt closer to, and more comfortable with, Nan than Jim, he had never been able to confide in her about the Game. Now they started writing to each other, and arranged a meeting in London without Jim's knowledge. Nan's letters haven't survived, but she evidently confided in him, as he did in her about his troubles with Barbara, Dilly and the Game. The tone of his letters is romantic and even flirtatious: he tells her that neither Dilly nor Barbara is 'my girl', and this is because 'everything comes from you, all women – yet we can't cohabit! Pity we didn't meet earlier.' They start using nicknames: he calls her Thursday, which he says is 'the name of a certain friend in my dreams who turned out to be you', and she responds by calling him 'Thor'. He complains at length about Barbara's 'frigidity', as he has learned to call it having known 'the quality of response in some other women'. Nan tells him that he should '*do* my odd things & so I might be cured of them': it must have been reassuring to him that she was so accepting, but his response is to say that he has 'persuaded Barbara to them', but he '*cannot love somebody to whom they are not natural* – only then they wouldn't be compulsive'. He later recalled Barbara saying, apropos of the Game, 'You are a funny boy.' Like another comment that irked him, 'You'll never be sylph-like', this sounds like marital teasing but, despite his excellent sense of humour, he was too sensitive about the Game to accept such remarks lightly. One thing he did respond to was that, in a quarrel, she would say, 'Look at me.' Then, he acknowledged, 'if I looked at her with love, that love was returned, and became possible again'. At one point, writing to his mother in 1969, he acknowledges that in the past, 'It has been different with Barbara.' Their sexual impasse is likely to have been caused, not by some inherent 'frigidity' in her, but by a deterioration in their relationship, whose origins were not so much in the Game itself but in her inability to cope with the depression, drinking and infidelity that it gave rise to – these things might well have affected her sexual response, the resultant 'wincing' as he called it which made him angry, resulting in more wincing and so on.

The house was another cause of conflict: the cost of the mortgage, and of the central heating which Barbara needed but which gave him headaches. The more depressed he felt at home, the more he resented its cost, which made him still more depressed. The couple consulted an estate agent about moving to a smaller house, but in the current state of the market this would have been of no advantage to them. Nan spoke to Jim on Peter's behalf, and Jim's response was to make an investment whose dividends would meet most if not all of the mortgage payments. He also paid the central heating bill. As always, the only way Jim could show his love for Peter was by helping him out financially.

At the end of March Peter and Barbara had a short holiday in Dorset, alone together. Barbara looked forward to this, but the thought of it depressed Peter. She went beforehand to her parents at Selsey and left the children with them, while Peter had the abortive adulterous encounter he told Layard about. They met in Dorchester and immediately started talking about their future. She told him that she wanted emotional security from him, that she wanted to live with him, and that if he wanted otherwise he had to take the step himself. He called this 'putting herself in the position of victim if I do anything' – a comment that was to prove unpleasantly ironic. They went on an excursion to Maiden Castle and Cerne Abbas, but Peter's 'mental insides were like a see-saw', he had a bad cold, and he had to ask Barbara to drive him back to the hotel halfway through the afternoon. Then, surprisingly, there was 'good sex, a little like the old days', after which 'at last I could look at her without thinking how old she looked'. Barbara went prematurely grey, and by her late thirties her hair was pure white, though in Falmouth she wore it long, perhaps in imitation of Dilly, and looked more like an artist. This is how Bill remembered her, not at all the '1950s model housewife' that Creffield described, but he was puzzled by an 'Ideal Home' flavour in some of the earlier photographs of her. He wondered, persuasively, whether in the earlier years of the marriage she presented herself in a certain way to reassure her parents that she was still 'in some way anchored to their reality'.

Despite the 'good sex', in the morning Peter wondered if he would 'ever feel really well in this woman's presence' – another sign that sexual difficulties were a symptom, not a cause, of their estrangement. That night he had a dream in which he had to fight three antagonists, one of which was a baby. He killed the baby with an axe through the fontanelle, making 'a horrible mess of blood and brains over its face like black porridge'. He wrapped the remains in a parcel but was worried about disposing of it because he thought the name 'Redgrove' might be sewn to one of its little garments. But Barbara dealt with it for him, and he thought that killing the baby was all right but her helping him dispose of it was not. He concluded that she was 'too involved in my interior drama for the good of either of us' (Layard wrote 'Yes' in the margin here) and linked the dream with having to let Barbara take care of him the previous day: 'I feel swaddled in an unchanging situation, and I feel we are holding each other back.'

Meanwhile, in Leeds, Dilly's final exams were approaching. Creffield's fellowship had ended the previous year and he had taken up a lectureship at Brighton School of Art, so the two most important men in her life were both absent. Through Dennis and Peter she had been part of the faculty social circle; she hoped to go on to graduate work and to make a career for herself in the university. But a few months before finals she had a minor breakdown and spent all one night unburdening herself of a 'litany of despair' to Martin and Christine. In the spring she was still anxious and dejected about the exams. Peter wrote to her frequently at this time, and his letters combine emotional support with psychologically astute advice. He tells her that it is precisely the most intelligent examinees who are most likely to despair because they overestimate what is required – they might even see in a question implications that the examiner is unaware of, to which it is impossible to do justice in the exam. Just as an actor cannot succeed without stage fright, so a period of depression and 'the actual shits' is necessary for a good exam performance. He tells her that she has been 'examining them, writing as you have with your whole self and not selling out', and assures her that she is 'absolutely one of the most intelligent – naturally intelligent – and with cultivation – women this person has ever met.' Exams are beneath her: 'Cheer up, my dear, and be yourself and as superb as you are.'

We see Peter at his most engaging in these letters: his own anxieties and obsessions are put aside, and he applies his insight and intelligence to the support of someone he loves. It is to be hoped that they were of some comfort and help to her. But she did less well than she had hoped: she got a 2.2. Dennis drove up from

Brighton and tried to comfort her, telling her that this was a marvellous achievement for a woman with seven children to look after, but for her it was a devastating failure. Martin's friend the Cypriot painter Stass Paraskos called on her and found her 'crying, crying, crying'. She told Dennis that she was going away for the weekend and he could look after the children. He was happy to acquiesce as long as she was back by the Sunday evening, so that he could return to his classes in Brighton. She put on her best clothes, a green velvet suit with a lovely high-necked Victorian blouse, and hitchhiked the four hundred miles to Falmouth.

When Dilly arrived in Falmouth, and knocked on the door of Tehidy Terrace, Barbara answered: Peter was not there. This hadn't entered into Dilly's calculations. Barbara greeted her kindly and invited her in. Dilly had come to Falmouth intending to beg Peter to leave Barbara. Now, faced with Barbara herself, she asked her rival to let Peter go. Her disturbed state of mind must have been obvious to Barbara, and her desperate appeal might not have been a fatal blow to the marriage, except that she must also have revealed that the affair was still active. 'I fear for Barbara if she knew', he had written only a month before. Dilly's ill-judged journey brought the end of many things.

Dennis and the rest of them in Leeds had assumed that she was visiting friends in London, and expected her back on the Sunday night. When she failed to return he asked Christine to look after the children so that he could go back to Brighton. A young woman in her early twenties with no experience of children, she was at a loss, but managed with the help of the woman who cleaned the house for them. On the Monday morning the door burst open and Dilly appeared. It was soon obvious to Christine that she was seriously deranged: she raved about having gone to a church and thrown roses on the altar: she saw a priest for confession and he said to her, 'My child, you are made for love.' She insisted to Christine that she would be all right and told her to go and look after Martin (making Christine feel that she was 'only good for looking after alcoholics and other people's children'). Martin and Stass wrote to Creffield saying that matters were in 'serious disarray' in his house, and he had better come to Leeds immediately. He got another letter from a colleague telling him that Dilly was keeping the children off school and had a Christmas tree in the garden in the middle of summer. When he arrived at the house he found a pet rabbit on the kitchen table, and the burnt remains of pound notes that Dilly had been using to light cigarettes. By the Friday she was sectioned. Paramedics came from St James's Hospital, put her in a straitjacket, and one of them carried her out of the house over his shoulder. The epigraph to 'Young Women with the Hair of Witches and No Modesty', 'I loved Ophelia!', had proved horribly prophetic.

The hospital psychiatrist proposed to treat her with electro-convulsive therapy, and for this Creffield's permission, as next of kin, was needed. Knowing that Peter had experience of psychiatric treatment, Creffield contacted him for advice. But Peter wanted nothing to do with it. The generous sympathy of his letters to Dilly during her exams had been drained away by the shock of her visit and confession to Barbara, which he regarded as a betrayal. The delicate balance that Peter had achieved for the last three years was destroyed for ever: now Dilly directly threatened his marriage and, perhaps an even greater threat, continuing the relationship with her would burden him with a terrifying commitment. His panic cornered him into an ungenerosity and bad faith that contrast sadly with his letters of only a month before. His letter in reply to Creffield has not survived, but one sentence in particular incensed his friend: 'I am fond of Dilly, and so is Barbara.' In this short sentence he managed to lie twice. 'Fond' is a mealy-mouthed word for the sentiments Peter had so recently been expressing in his letters and annotations to *Work in Progress*. As for Barbara, Peter wrote shortly afterwards to his mother that she didn't mind him loving another woman, but had always felt that Dilly was bad for him and 'beastly' to Barbara herself: 'If your lover and wife are enemies, what then?' He is now saying that 'it was a poor relationship, getting worse', and complains of being 'used' by Dilly. The rejection of Dilly is one last sacrifice that Peter makes for the sake of his marriage. Barbara has been 'splendid' and 'we seem to understand each other much better'. If ever true, this was not so for long: later he wrote that 'the marriage cracked irretrievably from this moment'. It was also the end of Peter's friendship with Dennis: a friendship broken, not by the adulterous liaison, but by the failure to honour it.

Most of what I know about Dilly I learned in a long conversation with Dennis Creffield, on May Day 2009 – almost exactly forty years after the tragic end of her affair with Peter, and twenty years after her death – in his studio in Brighton, scattered with work in progress and with documents he had unearthed for the occasion, big windows looking out on the channel, and William Blake's life-mask propped on a volume of the OED, standing in for the spirit of Peter Redgrove. He felt he had killed Dilly by marrying her without love, and he wanted to make reparation. He loved her memory more than he had loved her person at the time, and he was anxious that she should not be remembered in the light of Peter's later bitterness. We talked for five hours, and after about three hours he produced a sealed envelope which he said he had found only a year earlier, and hadn't known whether he should open. Now, he decided, was the right moment. The envelope was addressed to Peter at the School of Art, in Dilly's hand, but with no stamp. Creffield opened the envelope neatly with a paperknife. Inside was a letter written in purple felt-tip, dated 9 September:

> My dear Peter,
>
> Just to say – although I probably shouldn't – that nothing said or done has changed anything as far as emotions go. Although everything does seem rather hopeless and I presume we have reached another impasse. However being the irrational creature I am I hope for a letter in every post and a phone call every evening. (Not to imply any request for same!) Do not think I blame you at all for your inability to help in the summer – knowing the restrictions imposed on your actions – I would not have had you involved at all. But even writing is possibly a foolish act on my part though I like to preserve my own freedom of action.
>
> Wish me luck for my birthday, as I grow older I may become more sensible. Keep well and cheerful if possible, and small comfort though it may be and I do not expect any reply from you, have no doubts of me – for the time being anyway. 'Star crossed' has become a very meaningful term now. I am much recovered, living a very quiet, chaste and sober life.
>
> Much love, Dilly
>
> I won't write again, not wishing to cause conflict.

The sealed, addressed but unstamped envelope, kept for the rest of her life, poignantly dramatises her irresolution about approaching Peter.

Where was Peter when Dilly visited Falmouth? It is just possible it was that very day – if not, it was very close in time – that he went to Zennor, in the far west of Cornwall, to see his former student, the artist Andrzej Jackowski, and his then wife the poet Nicki Jackowska. Nicki had invited Peter to a meeting about a poetry festival she was planning. They were living at Lower Tregerthan farmhouse, just below the cottage where D. H. Lawrence lived in 1916 and wrote *Women in Love*. Staying at the farmhouse, but not involved in the meeting, was a slight, shy, dark-haired, boyish-looking young woman whom Peter noticed sitting on a sofa, reading Hardy's poems. She seemed to him to be reading with 'such intense concentration' that she was 'totally oblivious to all the other people in the room'. This was at least partly a symptom of her shyness. She was Penelope Shuttle. She was visiting a friend, the Carmelite friar Brocard Sewell, who was staying with Andrzej and Nicki. Sewell had been living at Aylesford priory, where he edited the *Aylesford Review*, a surprisingly radical journal to come from such a source: at the time he was suspended from the priory for publishing an article that called for Pope Pius VI to stand down because of his hard-line views on contraception. The *Review* had published such writers as Muriel Spark, Gregory Corso, Angela Carter and D. M. Thomas. Penelope, who was only twenty-two, had published poems in the *Review* as well as a novella in Calder and Boyars' *New Writers* 6 two years earlier, a pamphlet of poems and, most recently, her first novel, *All the Usual Hours of Sleeping*. She had grown up in Staines, Middlesex, attended an academically incompetent private school of a kind that still existed in the 1950s, and failed the eleven plus. Now she was living in a house owned by her parents in Frome, Somerset, working as a typist but living for writing. She had been familiar with Peter's work since hearing 'The Case' read on the radio and being astonished that it was not by a Continental writer.

They spoke only briefly, but Penny followed the meeting up by sending him her pamphlet, *Nostalgia Neurosis*. The covering letter is politely friendly in tone, but one phrase, saying she liked the 'simmering fever' of 'The Case', Peter might have interpreted as a veiled come-on. The effect of meeting Penny and receiving her letter and poems may be judged from the fact that he wrote three versions of his reply. At first he launched straight into 'I was immediately attracted to you as I came into that strange room', and praised her poems while provocatively taking issue with them, discussing them in detail explicitly as the work of a woman who is 'under dreadful bursting control'. The tone is very intimate for a letter written after a single brief meeting – 'Penelope, you mustn't be cross at the above' – and he concludes, 'From that brief meeting I would really like to know you better.' He decided against sending this letter, and a few days later wrote another one, referring teasingly back to the first, in which he had made 'outrageous guesses about your life', and which he was now going to tear up (of course he didn't do this). Now he wrote only that he 'alternated between hopping madness and pleasure of admiration', and that he would 'prefer to meet again than to try and capture my feelings in a letter to someone I scarcely knew'. The third, written more than a week after the first, is the shortest and coolest in tone, but he still emphasises that he would like to meet her again, when he returns from a visit to Ireland.

This Irish trip was a consequence of a new friendship with the poet and novelist Patrick (or P. J. to distinguish him from his famous Irish namesake) Kavanagh, whom he had got to know a year or two before at the Cheltenham Festival. The two men rapidly forged a warm and affectionate friendship, though Patrick was a Christian whose scepticism about some of Peter's imaginative flights caused the occasional flare-up. Peter had been confiding in Patrick and his wife Kate about his marriage difficulties, Dilly and therapy with Layard, and he typically started his letters with 'My Very Dear Old Patrick'.

Peter and Patrick flew from Bristol to Dublin, where they joined Patrick's friend the poet (and soon to be Gregory Fellow) Pearse Hutchinson, did a reading together, went to a party at the poet Eiléan Ní Chuilleanáin's house, and the next day the three men borrowed her car to drive to the West of Ireland. This was perhaps recklessly generous on her part: Kavanagh's unpublished memoir of the trip doesn't say who did the driving, but does make it clear that all three of them were drinking at every opportunity. Peter characteristically drank even more than the other two: before they left Dublin Patrick and Pearse retired for the afternoon, and later met him looking 'stout-wounded about the eyes'. That night Patrick had to share a room with Peter, and was kept awake by him 'epically ingesting air, expending it thunderously, tearing, thumping, from every orifice'. They drove west via Galway to Connemara, and visited Richard Murphy, an 'awkward, withdrawn man' according to Patrick, who startled his guests by suddenly coming out with a scatological story. Patrick and Pearse were reduced to torpor by Murphy's polite coolness, but it made Peter talk all the more. Kavanagh vividly captures his manner at this time: 'the way he smokes, drinks, paces, a basic good nature, a surface rage of impatient disquiet, nerves howling for some impossible movement'. Peter mythologised this period of his life in his account of his meeting with Penny, giving the impression that he spent three weeks seeking oblivion with Guinness in Dublin, whereas the whole trip lasted only a week, and was full of sociable as well as alcoholic pleasures. We should therefore not take too literally his statement that at the end of the trip his 'turds resembled the graphite of pencils', or that he had to be put on the plane by a 'kind lady'.

It is true, however, that when he got off the plane in Bristol he didn't head back to Falmouth but phoned Penny and suggested that they meet at the George Hotel in Frome. Here she made quite a different impression on him from 'the absorbed person of the first encounter. She was dressed in an extraordinarily glittering manner' in a dress that had been made for her by her mother. She invited him back to her house in High Street (named for its elevation rather than importance – it is a narrow lane of stone-fronted terraced houses) and when he proposed returning to the George to sleep, she invited him to stay with her. This was the real beginning of their relationship. He told her that because he had a bear-like body, people often thought he had a bear-like personality, and worried that people would think he was insensitive. He said, 'I'm different inside.' Penny called this the moment of revelation for her.

Back home after this meeting, he wrote to her, 'you made me feel very happy, and real too . . .' and ended by calling himself her 'loving friend who wishes you to achieve happiness and reality . . . and will help you to do so if he can'. At the end of August he spent another week with her in Frome, and later in the autumn they stayed in Glastonbury together. But a decisive break had still not been made in Peter's life, and it was by no means certain that he and Penny would form a partnership to supplant his marriage. Writing to her during that autumn he calls himself 'dangerously indecisive' though he knows that his 'security is rapidly dissolving' and he needs to change his life. He doesn't want to catch her up in his 'flurry, my dartings, plunges and vertigoes', and make her leave her security when he has none to offer. She was not a married woman with seven children and a drink problem, but she was very young and sexually inexperienced, socially phobic with an eating disorder and menstrual problems: a vulnerable person to be drawing into his personal and marital maelstrom.

That storm reached its ultimate intensity in November. The

eleven-year-old Bill was in the house at the time. He could hear shouting and thumping in the next room, and tried to wrestle the door open while Barbara held it closed to keep him from witnessing the scene inside. Peter was drunk, inevitably, and whatever had started the row its defining moment was when she told him that, because of his drinking, or his games, or his need for analysis, he was 'sexually inadequate'. He hit her; she fled to the Hewletts with a black eye, and asked Francis's wife Liz to testify if there was a court case.

Was this the only time Peter hit Barbara? It was the only one he confessed to, even in his journals, but Liz Hewlett thought he 'beat her up a few times', Malcolm Ritchie thought it happened more than once, and we have Elaine Glover's second-hand report of his kicking her at the party in Leeds. Hilary reports Peter dragging Barbara by her hair up the stairs, which may have been the same occasion that drove her to leave. There was, however, something about this episode that made Barbara act decisively and finally. She later told Kate that Peter said his violence was an act of love, and she was afraid that he would harm his baby daughter. She phoned her parents, and shortly afterwards Hilary and her husband John arrived to carry Barbara and the children away to Selsey. Bill recalls walking home from school with Pete to find a large 'For Sale' sign outside the front gate of the house. Pete, whom Bill like the rest of the family considered the perceptive and sensitive one, was inconsolable. It was only looking back that Bill identified this moment as the end of his childhood.

Despite the developments with Penny, Peter didn't experience Barbara's leaving as a blessed release. He passed the next two months in anguished uncertainty about whether the marriage was truly at an end, or they could make a new start, with a more workable arrangement such as living with the family only in vacations, when he was free from the pressure of his job. He was torn between guilt and self-justification regarding his own behaviour, and between rational sympathy and vehement accusation towards Barbara. What is most remarkable is that these conflicts were never to be resolved throughout his life. As late as 1993 he wrote in his journal, 'Though it turned out as it did with Penelope I still can't help feeling hurt that [Barbara] gave up on my depressions and treated me as if I was guilty.' Even after Barbara's death he returns to the final violent scene, expressing remorse – 'That was terrible and I shouldn't have done that' – but with the unpleasant suggestion that there was some kind of symbolic retributive justice in his violence: 'I struck her on ears and eyes for not hearing or seeing.' He even once wrote, 'She had precipitated the situation she desired.' In the spring he had complained that, by saying that she would not leave him, she was putting herself in the position of victim if he left; ironically now that she has left despite that assurance, he sees himself as the victim.

He was truly shaken and shattered by her leaving him. He felt nervous alone in the large, newly silent house. When he wrote to Barbara in December his tone was affectionate and apologetic, addressing her as 'Dearest' and describing the presents which she is to open on Christmas Eve and those which she is to leave till Christmas Day. But his letter is almost incoherent. Not surprisingly it was difficult to talk to his father who was 'very touchy' – Nan in a letter to Barbara describes Peter as in tears on the other end of the phone while Jim shouts at him. She was not blinded to her son's responsibility for the break-up: he 'knows he is a stinker . . . killing himself in self-pity'. She drew a revealing parallel with Jim – Peter can make you feel a 'vegetable', while Jim had always made her feel like 'the village idiot'. Nevertheless she prophetically points out to Barbara that it will be difficult for her to find such an interesting man, and enjoins her to treat him with kindness.

Barbara was due to come to Falmouth at the end of January and, in advance of this visit, Peter wrote a long diary-letter explaining that he had decided not to be there when she came. This letter ended up pasted in his journal, so possibly Barbara never saw it. Its main tenor is that they should not try to will an outcome but wait to see what happens:

> I can see this going either way, Barbara, but it must be as it happens, as our real selves want it, not as we bustlingly will it. One way, completely new lives, me calling to see the children. Another way, me commuting . . . certainly I can't manage job and family and writing, it appears: maybe I could concentrate more on the family in the holidays when the job's not going, perhaps like the last, happy year in the Gregory Fellowship [presumably before the affair with Dilly].

The tone of this letter is sincere and reasonable: he suggests that they share the blame for the break-up, but there is no vehement accusation of her or of himself. He misses the children and, though he writes that 'I never say if I miss you or anything that might be construed as making love to you on paper because it wouldn't be fair', he does go on to say that he misses her.

There is no mention of Penny in this letter, or any hint that another woman is part of the equation. Nevertheless, within three weeks of his writing it, Penny came to join him at Tehidy Terrace.

VIII

A New Life 1970–75

When Penny arrived at Tehidy Terrace in February 1970 Peter had decorated the house with daffodils. There was little furniture, most of it having followed Barbara to Selsey. The life that they began together was an enormous gamble for them both. Peter acknowledged a year later that 'we are two ill people', and they had set out to cure each other. Penny's parents were outraged at her living with a married man, and she was estranged from them for some time. Peter had burnt even more boats. He was still addressing Barbara in his journal: 'Is it better without me? My first spring without you.' For all the difficulties between them, she had been his closest companion from the age of nineteen. He faced the prospect of estrangement from his children, a challenge that he was temperamentally ill-adapted to deal with. But his family was not the only close attachment that, voluntarily or otherwise, he sacrificed. Contact with Dilly, of course, was unthinkable, and this estranged him from Creffield as well. He had lost Hobsbaum, his first companion in poetry, four years earlier, and now his anxiety about association with Dilly was so great that he cut himself off from Martin Bell too, because Martin was in Leeds and friendly with Dilly. He was never to see Martin again, though there would be an important resumption of correspondence in the two years before the older man's death. Perhaps most revealingly, after a meeting in May Peter severed contact with Layard. Once, when out in Falmouth with Penny, he suddenly said, 'There's Layard, don't look at him, let's go this way,' and led her out of the street. Layard himself used to say that Peter 'ran away' from him. Much as he owed to Layard, he was suspicious about the old man's desire to know his intimate secrets, and fearful of his power over him. He did not want Layard interfering in his relationship with

Penny, and wanted to protect her against him. Above all this rejection is a sign that, although Peter was never 'cured' of the troubles that had driven him to seek help, he felt that he had progressed as far as he could in that relationship. Two years later he wrote, 'Tomas [his fictional name for Layard] the poor old man. I hated him for these past two years.'

When Penny walked into Tehidy Terrace that day she knew that she was taking a serious step, but she didn't know that she was to take over the roles of nearly every important person in Peter's life: companion, sexual partner, poetic soulmate and counsellor. It was as if Peter thought those who had been closest to him were tainted with the sickness he was trying to shed. Penny offered him the chance of a new life, and he wanted to forget as much as possible about the old. The thought of Dilly agitated him so much that he couldn't bear to see a Leeds postmark, and once the break with Barbara was irrevocable, he was terrified of contact with her as well. He felt anxious whenever she wrote or phoned, and the thought of seeing her was so painful that he tried to take out an injunction preventing her from coming to Cornwall. The price he paid for this feeling was that he was never able to develop natural relationships with his children.

Peter may not have been cured but life with Penny meant one enormously important change. His life was no longer divided. Until now his poetic world had been almost exclusively masculine. Not only were his poet friends all male, but they were all drinkers and, especially since he had ceased regular attendance at Group meetings, talk about poetry with Hobsbaum, Bell and Porter would typically go on in pubs. Barbara could not have entered this world even if she had wanted to. The time he had spent with Dilly in Leeds had somewhat tempered this male ambience, as the poems she inspired testify. But with Penny there was no division at all. She was as dedicated to writing as he, they became the first readers of each other's work, eventually co-authors, and they were both committed to making room in their lives for each other's work and their own.

But it was to be a little while before they were able to settle down to their life together. In April Penny had to fulfil a promise to visit Brocard Sewell in Nova Scotia. She was there just over a week, during which time Peter sent her eight letters and cards, and a message on a vinyl recording he had made in a booth. After her return they moved into Wodehouse Cottage, a strange little house next door to the School of Art, with a street door only four feet high. This had been the tradesman's entrance to the estate of Sir John Wodehouse, lord of the manor, who subsequently sold the main house to the prominent Quaker, owner of Glendurgan Garden and developer of Falmouth Dockyard, Alfred Fox. Even in 1970 an unmarried couple might have had difficulty finding rented accommodation in Falmouth, and they were lucky that their landlord seemed indifferent to their status.

In June Peter and Barbara signed a legal Deed of Separation. This provided that Barbara would have sole custody of the children, and that Peter would pay her £16 per week, more than a third of his gross salary. This document refers to Tehidy Terrace as Barbara's house, probably because of the contribution her father had made when they first bought a house in London. From the start there were emotional difficulties about visiting the children. In March he wrote to Barbara that he thought they had been upset the last time he visited, and that he would rather not come unless she was there and wanted to see him, or they needed to see him. She replied, 'It's certainly not going to be useful to the children if you come from a sense of duty towards them . . . and no particular feeling from you that you want to see them!' In his letter he speaks of his feelings of guilt, and this is probably the reason why he never felt comfortable in their or (despite this letter) Barbara's company. He visited at fairly regular intervals, but by the summer of the following year this was clearly causing the children some disturbance, because Barbara asked Peter not to stay at their house when he visited. This led to a miserable and prolonged situation in which Peter believed that Barbara was discouraging the children from contact with him, while they always felt, on the contrary, that she encouraged them to keep up communication with their father. Bill and Kate are both emphatic that Barbara never said anything to influence them against Peter.

In the same month as Peter and Barbara were formally separated, Jim provided £500 for a deposit on a new house for Peter in Falmouth. This enabled him and Penny to buy 8 Trelawney Cottages for £3,500, Peter taking out a £3,000 mortgage. This was a much smaller and less imposing house than Tehidy Terrace. Trelawney Cottages consists of two rows of terraced houses facing each other across gardens separated by a path, so the house fronts on to a footpath instead of a road. Their house was at the end of the terrace, with two small rooms and a kitchen downstairs and three bedrooms, one of them tiny. This was to be their home for the next seven years.

Though the relationship was such a turning point for Peter, it was Penny's psychological well-being that first engrossed their attention. She was suffering regular severe depressions, and at one point Peter confided to his journal the fear that she would be like Sylvia Plath. They soon linked the pattern of her distress to her menstrual cycle. One of the techniques Layard had used with Peter was to get him to draw pictures of his dreams, and he passed this method on to Penny. This is how they describe what happened in *The Wise Wound*:

> Peter Redgrove had studied analytical psychology and dream analysis for many years, and in particular had spent 1968–9 as a pupil of the famous analyst Dr John Layard, who himself had studied with Homer Lane, C. G. Jung and others and had published many distinguished contributions to psychology and anthropology. With the help of Layard's methods, Redgrove enabled Shuttle to draw pictures of the depressions, and then to dream vividly as a consequence. She dreamed every night for five months, and the dreams were analysed every day, in sessions often lasting many hours.

The American scholar Holly Laird wrote a very perceptive analysis of Redgrove and Shuttle's collaboration in her book *Women Coauthors*, in which she says about this passage: 'What could sound more patriarchal than this? The decontextualised Shuttle suffers emotionally and physically; Redgrove studies, and has done so for many years, with a lineage of famous male psychologists, and he ministers to Shuttle by directing and analysing her dreams.' Laird goes on to say that this impression is misleading, but she has put her finger on something revealingly inauthentic about this account. Peter usually described himself as Layard's *pupil* rather than patient, and he never revealed even to Penny that Layard had charged fees – probably because he didn't want to admit that Jim had paid. Moreover the *Wise Wound* passage gives the impression that Layard was a much more respectable and establishment figure than he was: someone who had 'published many distinguished contributions' rather than one who encouraged his patients to get into bed with him and fondle his penis. The truth about Layard, Peter's relationship with him and his own psychological condition when treating Penny, is much less 'patriarchal' than the version in *The Wise Wound*, but much more scandalous in more obvious ways. Peter acknowledged that analysing the person you are living with is not generally considered good practice; still less when the analyst himself is in the grip of unresolved obsessions. The danger of Peter projecting these obsessions on to Penny is obvious. Indeed it could be said, paradoxically, that the successful outcome was partly the result of projection. Penny 'found a fresh attitude to her period, which enabled her to enjoy that time for its particular qualities, and no longer reject it'. Shuttle and Redgrove went on to write *The Wise Wound* and *Alchemy for Women*. Although these were co-authored works, and the whole project began with Penny's menstrual distress, it is Peter who seems the more fixated on menstruation, for the rest of his life. The physical messiness of the period answered to the eroticism of soiling in the Game, and menstruation came to stand for a transgressive sense of the feminine, in opposition to what Shuttle and Redgrove came to call the 'values of ovulation', of sex for procreation, which Peter clearly associated with his marriage to Barbara: he later wrote that the witch poems inspired by Dilly had been 'the beginnings of menstrual imagery coming into consciousness'. He wrote in his journal that menstrual sex was 'like & yet not like a game – to get blood on my pyjama trousers – I would have liked to smear myself with it.' Penny learning not to reject her period is a model for Peter learning not to reject the Game. Menstruation takes on an ideological character in *The Wise Wound*, and Peter learns to adopt a similarly ideological attitude to the Game, as resistance to prescribed gender identity.

Peter's analysis of Penny's dreams and treatment of her menstrual distress was foundational to the life that they created together. Not only did it lead directly to the work by which they were best known; it cemented the exceptional intimacy of their relationship and confirmed them in the shared belief that creativity comes from the exploration of the unconscious, and is not merely an optional decoration of life, but a healing power.

Peter later wrote, 'In the first seven years we didn't speak a cross word to each other.' This is of course implausible even without the evidence of conflict in his journals. Even the dream analysis did not go entirely smoothly – Penny once complained that she felt 'experimented on'. More fundamentally, living with Peter presented her with many of the same challenges that Barbara had faced. He suffered less from depression when he started living with Penny, but realised that he got bad-tempered instead, and he thought this frightened her, though she denies ever having been afraid of him. One such time she 'sobbed in her pillow just like [Barbara] used to'. He also drank less than he used to, but still turned to alcohol at times of stress and depression. Penny was less tolerant of this than of the Game. In their early years together, after the successful dream analysis, Peter would sometimes complain that he had got her right, now it was her turn to get him right. There was no such dramatic solution to his problems, but undoubtedly her tolerance and support in respect of the Game, over many years, was crucial to his not only learning to live with his compulsions, but turning them into a creative resource. Penny's acceptance of the Game was also essential to the sexual harmony that was at the centre of their life together, and that Peter had not been able to achieve in a lasting way with Barbara. Penny not only accepted the Game but joined in it and made Peter believe she enjoyed it. He had complained of Barbara that even though she tried to join in the Game he couldn't love someone to whom it was not natural. No doubt Penny did enjoy sexual relations with Peter even if it involved being smeared with shaving foam, and didn't stigmatise his compulsions by calling them unnatural, but it was still to please Peter that she joined in the Game, and even she sometimes complained that it was repetitive and time-consuming. However, it was also crucial for her that, unlike many people with fetishistic compulsions, Peter did not depend on the Game to function sexually, and it was in straight sexual intimacy that they found their greatest emotional and creative fulfilment together.

At Christmas 1970 Jim and Nan invited Peter, alone, for a holiday with them in Normandy. He was reluctant to be away from Penny for any time at all, but glad for his parents to be able to see him, as they put it, happier than he had been for years. On this holiday he had more intimate conversation with Nan about her lovers, including a man she said was interested in black magic, and about her lack of sexual interest in Jim. She told Peter that Jim wanted to 'experiment', and had bought a book, but she refused to read it. She also confessed that 'if she liked somebody, she did so until they liked her, then she went off him'. Despite these conversations he was conscious of a 'regression into the former situation' in Jim and Nan's company. Even something as natural as their 'sympathy & delight in the children' oppressed him, showing how severe was his need to break with the past.

During his first year with Penny, Peter struggled to write poetry, and she would set him exercises in 'active imagination' or automatic writing on themes suggested by his dreams. In one dream he had an empty pistol which he put under his armpit and used as a crutch. After improvising on this dream he speculated that his poetry was a crutch, because he couldn't 'walk across the water' by himself: 'It's now finished, and the gun is empty.' If he ever wrote another poem it would have to 'come as a natural thing among my other natural things'; otherwise he must 'learn to walk across the water of my feeling without a crutch'. As it turned out, he was about to enter a period in which he was more prolific than ever before, and which was to last until the end of his life.

In February 1971 they moved into Trelawney Cottages, their own home for the first time, and Peter began a new experiment in writing, 'stirred up', as he put it, 'by love of [Penny], and [our] new cottage'. He started pasting one item per day into a big foolscap diary. Some of these entries were in verse, some in prose; sometimes there was both a prose and a verse draft (an anticipation of his regular practice in later years). The entries begin on 1 January, but he may not actually have started writing till later, because he dated the book 4 March. At some point he added the title, '365 Stories About Her'. He didn't get to 365: the entries finish on 1 August, where he writes 'ENDS', indicating that he has brought something to completion, rather than run out of steam. This is the first draft of his first 'novel', *In the Country of the Skin*. I put the word in quotation marks because, although it was published as a novel, when Peter sent the typescript to Norman Franklin at Routledge he accompanied it with a scattergun of generic parallels: Rimbaud's *Illuminations*, Lautréamont's *Les Chants de Maldoror*, Djuna Barnes's *Nightwood*, Lowell's *Notebook*, Coleridge's and Hopkins's notebooks, Jung's *Psychological Reflections*, even the Bible and the I Ching. Least of all is he offering it as a conventional narrative: the books he has listed, he says, can be opened at any point and 'read off into your own reveries'.

The most transparent piece of narrative in *In the Country of the Skin* is the fictionalised account of Peter's breakdown and insulin coma therapy, which I described in Chapter 3. The protagonist who undergoes this ordeal is called Jonas, but he is not a separate person. He is one aspect of a personality whose other side is called Silas. These represent Peter's own sense of a division in himself between the rational scientist whom he considered to be neurotic and obsessive, and the dark self that he released in the Game. Another way of putting it, reflecting his constant attribution of his divided self to the personalities of his parents, is the 'schizoid father' and 'hysterical mother'. Jonas/Silas approaches wholeness by loving Teresa, a black girl who obviously derives from 'The Idea of Entropy at Maenporth Beach' and anticipates the later prose work *The Black Goddess*. But if the symbolism of her blackness leads off into earlier and later writings, the figure of an actual sexual partner who offers the promise of wholeness is obviously indebted to the presence of Penny in Peter's life: he often referred to her as 'Teresa' in his journals. Other 'characters' include Tomas, a version of Layard, and a mysterious 'sandy-haired man' who Peter describes as 'the person who observed [Jonas and Silas], nearer to Teresa than either, a kind of soul, or child. This child is the person who matters.' An as yet unborn, or undeveloped self, perhaps, who carries the promise of making the division of Jonas and Silas redundant.

In the Country of the Skin was like nothing else Peter had written, and he was anxious and sensitive about its reception. Before publication he showed it to a number of people including, bravely, an evening creative writing class that he was teaching, run by Exeter University. This group, which later developed into the Falmouth Poetry Group, included some remarkable individuals, such as Derek Power, manager of the local Boots, who became the first Chair of the FPG; Abigail Mozley who later edited the magazine *Bananas*; Stewart Brown, a student at the School of Art who was to become an academic authority on Caribbean and African literature; and Vernon Rose, a multi-talented individual who wrote novels and poetry, painted (including a portrait of Peter), sang and played guitar, made a hurdy-gurdy, ran a Punch and Judy show and had a magic act in which he sawed his wife in half. As this group developed it acquired funding to run a programme of poetry readings and publish a magazine, *Bridge*. The FPG ran for many years, with Peter participating intermittently, and later members included the poet and Booker-shortlisted novelist Gerard Woodward, and the poet and surrealist scholar Sylvia Kantaris, both of whom were close friends. It still exists, the longest continuously running group of its kind in the country, and was to be of great personal importance to Peter in his last years. The most formidable individual in the early group was probably Vernon Rose, about whom Peter developed an obsession which foreshadowed later more powerful projections. It is notable that like some figures who troubled Peter later in life Vernon performed magical tricks, an accomplishment that he associated with his father. Peter confessed himself frightened of Vernon, and was 'swimmingly grateful' as he put it, when the latter responded enthusiastically to *In the Country of the Skin*.

His colleagues responded favourably as well: Francis Hewlett thought each word was 'an image & an object he could sculpture', and Lionel Miskin said Peter had 'been to the underworld & brought back ringing words, a treasure'. However, the book caused some turbulence in his friendship with P. J. Kavanagh. The proliferation of similes, in particular, was too much for Patrick's more sober literary temperament. He compared similes to double whiskies, saying that they put him to sleep and when he wakes up the 'sudden connections I made under their influence' have vanished. He goes on, however, to use a grotesque extended metaphor of his own to describe the effect of Redgrove's imaginative prose: 'I see you pulling a thick endless cord out of your mouth . . . Attached somewhere but otherwise floating free in an amniotic sky which is liquid, which is walls, which is sweaty-sheets, bookpages, beer, sperm, clear mud.'

Peter was aggravated by this letter because of its tone, which he thought 'de haut en bas, lightly amused . . . supercilious'. He wrote a riposte beginning 'Hi Bish', instead of his usual affectionate greeting, insinuating that Patrick was writing like a churchman. *In the Country of the Skin* was his first uninhibited work: he called it 'the record of an experience'. But it is too obscure to be confessional, and Patrick clearly didn't recognise how important it was to Peter. The Group had of course taught him to accept criticism when he had failed to communicate effectively, but he thought that Patrick was resisting Peter's authentic experience, out of fear: 'I think you are as shit-scared and at least as incompetent as I am . . . both of us have to remember that there is both a Jacob and an Esau [i.e. a Jonas and a Silas] in both of us, and from your letter, you despise all forms of madness . . . You speak as an angel to my devil . . . You may be the improved specimen you make out, for all I know. But I don't think so.' It didn't help that Patrick had caricatured Peter as the character 'Trevor' in his novel *A Happy Man*. Trevor 'claims he is driven by forces inside himself which he calls "dark" and which he enjoys although he pretends they fill him with holy dread'. Patrick reproduced verbatim passages of Peter's conversation, such as the following: 'Mother's a nymphomaniac . . . When I was about thirteen . . . my mother told me in detail about her lovers. See? Psychic rape! I suppose she hoped I'd tell my father . . . He's a repressed homosexual.' Patrick subsequently regretted doing this, and Peter was annoyed when Barbara phoned him and said she recognised him in the character.

Peter had the good sense to attach a covering note: 'Dear old Patrick, Enclosed is the letter you deserve to get from me (only better-written, of course) for your last. If I didn't love you so well.' He later thought that his letter seemed 'mad', and he invited Patrick to visit him so that they could reach a mutual understanding. He explained that Patrick's letter hurt him because he admired his friend's work, and he envied Patrick's freedom to develop it. Part of the problem was undoubtedly (as, on a larger scale, with Ted Hughes) that Patrick was, in a modest way, more commercially successful as a writer than Peter: he acknowledged to himself that he was 'grudging of P[atrick]'s small success'. When Patrick visited him in early February Peter thought he 'seemed well-proportioned in his personality and strong, open and intelligent'.

His friendship with Patrick was one that had survived the shedding of old associations. So did three of his longer-standing poetic friendships, with Peter Porter, Ted Hughes and D. M. Thomas. He usually stayed with Porter and his wife Jannice when he went to London, and the warm affection and mutual respect between the two men remained undisturbed throughout Peter's life. Peter always relished the wit and erudition of Porter's conversation. Hughes, as always, was a more problematic case. At about this time Peter was again disappointed when Ted failed to keep a promise to visit, and a new disturbance had entered into his feelings about his successful friend. In 1970 Hughes published his most controversial collection, *Crow*, a sequence of harsh – often harshly comic – poems influenced by what Hughes called 'primitive' literature, especially the tradition of the Trickster-hero. In contrast to the often rich and dense language of his earlier work, for *Crow* he adopted 'a super-simple and a super-ugly language' to write 'songs with no music whatsoever'. *Crow* divided Hughes's critics as never before. Alvarez even exceeded his praise for *Lupercal*, saying, 'With *Crow*, Hughes joins the select band of survivor-poets whose work is adequate to the destructive reality we inhabit.' Ian Hamilton by contrast described the book as a 'cosy, unperplexing wallow'. The controversy did no harm to

Crow's commercial prospects, and it sold in remarkable numbers for a volume of verse.

Peter had never spoken pejoratively about Ted's poetry before, but now he found himself sympathetic with *Crow*'s detractors, at least with those who had admired Hughes's earlier work and thought he had taken a wrong direction. He thought the 'violent, mistaken, argumentative rhetoric in *Crow* [was] a perversion of a lovely talent', and that the verse was 'thin and panic-stricken'. More seriously, as far as his friendship with Ted was concerned, he began to see him as the epitome of an exclusive and destructive masculinity. He speculated that *Crow* represented 'the dark side of a personal sexuality', and even woke up one morning with 'the thought that TH is a sadist'. Hughes was a fine nature poet, but he had ended up 'incarnating' the dangerous aspects of nature. Later Peter came to believe that Hughes had been badly served by critics, especially those who admired him, and who encouraged him to inflate the manifestations of his personal unconscious, believing them to be universal.

D. M. (Don) Thomas was still teaching in Hereford but was a native of Cornwall and had stayed a few times with Peter and Barbara on his visits there. He was still in awe of Peter, whom he considered remarkably intelligent and intuitive, with 'a bit of magic about him'. In 1971 he proposed a joint reading tour of the United States, and was prepared to make all the arrangements himself. Thomas had just published his first collection, *Logan Stone*, but Redgrove was still the senior partner in this team, and Thomas was, in his own words, 'going on his shirt-tails'. He got bookings at the Library of Congress (which paid $1,000 each), the University of Michigan, Notre Dame University, Northern Illinois University, the University of Arizona at Tucson and Colgate University in upstate New York. Peter was away for three weeks, the longest separation he and Penny were to endure until his last years. Altogether he was paid $2,000 or £800 for the trip, but had to pay his expenses out of this, which left just under £300 – one tenth of the cost of his house for three weeks' work.

The tour began in Washington at the Library of Congress, which Peter described as 'all stately and brittle'. Don didn't know how he found the nerve to read in the vast auditorium, but Peter loved having such a space to 'boom' into – he told Penny that he threw off the effects of jet lag by 'booming and vibrating' into the microphone. They followed the reading by making a recording for the library.

The two poets approached their three weeks on the loose in contrasting spirits. Peter later said to me, 'We agreed to a division of labour. Don did the fucking and I did the drinking.' Don didn't drink heavily, but though married he was 'playing the liberated guy'. He picked up a couple of women on the tour, one of whom followed him from Washington to Notre Dame. Peter by contrast was in Don's word 'obsessed' with Penny. He talked about her constantly, and wrote to her and phoned her at every opportunity. There's no record of Peter drinking to excess, but it is easy to believe that separation from Penny had this effect. For Don the tour was a very happy experience, which he felt cemented his relationship with Peter. Peter enjoyed Don's company too, but Penny's absence made him miserable and homesick: 'I long to open a suitcase and have you step out,' he wrote.

At Notre Dame the reading had been organised by students, and their accommodation was mismanaged. There was a huge football game in town, and Peter and Don had to drive fifty miles to find a motel in a little town called Niles. More annoyingly to Peter, he was announced as 'Redgrave'. Sharing a bedroom with Peter, Don sensed an 'enormous sexual energy . . . almost superhuman', which put him in mind of Aleister Crowley, though he knew nothing of Peter's obsession with Crowley. He connected this with a strange experience at the campus of Northern Illinois University at De Kalb, where the conversation was of a colleague who had been possessed by the devil (taken literally) and Don was warned off one of the faculty wives with whom he was flirting – 'Watch it, Don.' That night he vividly saw the image of a bird of prey on the wall of his room – a susceptibility that he attributed to Peter's influence as well as to the atmosphere of the campus.

They took a long flight south to Tucson, where the Arizona desert, and the sudden subsequent change of cultural and racial atmosphere on crossing the border into Mexico, were Peter's most inspiring experiences of the tour. The university had a flourishing poetry centre where they put Peter and Don up in a 'Poet's House', and produced a striking poster with overlapping outline images of Don in full-face and Peter in profile. Their final leg took them from the Mexican border almost to the Canadian. Two years earlier Bruce Berlind, a professor at Colgate University in Hamilton, New York State, had invited Peter to read to a group of his students on a summer school in London. He was sufficiently impressed to follow this up by offering Peter a visiting professorship. Peter was still havering about this invitation, but in the meantime had taken the opportunity to add Colgate to the tour. Bruce's hospitable welcome, and the articulateness of the students, revived his enthusiasm, and on his return he resolved to try to arrange a sabbatical for 1973.

Peter's enthusiasm about returning to America was fuelled by developments at the School of Art after his return from this visit. He had striven, under the umbrella of 'Complementary Studies', to establish writing as a strand of the school's work, alongside painting, sculpture, photography, textiles and ceramics. Michael Finn had encouraged him in this. He was proud of having 'rescued' students who were dismissed from other departments and developed their writing, some of whom also became better painters as a result. Several of these students had gained First Class degrees. He had also, more generally, fertilised the work of students across the school by introducing science, mythology, psychology and dream analysis into the curriculum.

But in 1972 Michael Finn left to take up another post, and his successor, John Barnicoat, was clearly determined to take the school in a different direction. In the summer of 1973 Peter wrote an anguished letter to the sympathetic vice-chair of the school governors, Mrs Hilda 'Jim' Trench, who had been on his interview panel. He felt threatened by a new atmosphere in the school, and excluded by plans for reorganisation. He reported a senior member of staff warning him to 'watch my step since he didn't want me turning the whole place into a writing school'. He felt snubbed by the fact that writing was hardly mentioned in the minutes of discussions about reorganisation, and by being pointedly reminded that the school was 'a *visual* arts college'. He even began to wonder if Lionel was an enemy when he exclaimed, 'I'm sick of your bloody poets.' Mrs Trench replied sympathetically, while trying to get Peter to see his situation in a broader context. She told him that the school was facing a crisis, 'a clash of values which could destroy the very things which have made it unique and which justify its preservation as an autonomous institution'. The governors, she said, had recently been summoned to a meeting at County Hall where 'propositions were made which were little short of blackmail'.

At one board meeting Peter stalked in with a sheaf of papers testifying to his achievements, flung them on the table and walked out again. But this was missing the point. There was no question about his distinction: in fact, the very power of his reputation and influence could be felt as disruptive, when he represented what many of his colleagues saw as a marginal part of the school's activity. The jibe about 'turning the whole place into a writing school' would not have had any force if Peter had not impressed his colleagues as someone with the power to wield such influence over the college's future.

Peter started applying for other jobs: at an education college in Matlock, an art school in Melbourne Australia, even in university departments of English. The most promising contact was Michael Finn himself, who was now Principal of Bath Academy of Art. Finn was enthusiastic about having Peter, but eventually had to write to tell him that the prospects for the post had receded. John Barnicoat stayed in post only a couple of years, but his successor, Tom Cross, was no more sympathetic to Peter's work. Despite numerous further attempts to find more congenial employment, the situation festered on for another ten years.

Evidence of Peter's difficulty writing poetry during and after the break-up of his marriage can be found in the Routledge volume that he published in 1972, *Dr Faust's Sea-Spiral Spirit*. Of the twenty-eight poems in this collection, sixteen had appeared in *Work in Progress* four years earlier. Admittedly some of the recent poems are much longer, but the most successful ones, which make *Dr Faust* an advance even on *The Force*, are shorter, more crafted and structured. At the heart of the collection are poems such as 'The Idea of Entropy at Maenporth Beach', 'Young Women with the Hair of Witches and No Modesty', 'The Youthful Scientist Remembers', 'Minerals of Cornwall, Stones of Cornwall', 'The Moon Disposes', and 'The Haunted Armchair', all of which were written before 1968. A few of the new poems match these. 'Intimate Supper' is a superbly witty portrayal of the deity as a refined dinner host, and 'The House of Taps' (a favourite of Hobsbaum's) is another fine example, like 'The Force', of Redgrove's ability to channel the elemental through the domestic. This poem was inspired by a tap shop in Frome, and Peter called it 'our first poem together'. The most interesting of the new poems is 'Christiana', dedicated to Barbara and a more effective riposte than 'Quasimodo's Many Beds'. Redgrove quotes from the episode in *The Pilgrim's Progress*, when Christiana is shown a spider by the Interpreter and asked, 'Is there but one spider in all this spacious room?' Bunyan's heroine recognises that she and her companions are spiders full of the venom of sin. Redgrove's Christiana by contrast:

> wept to have found so much of myself ugly
> In the trustful beasts that are jewel-eyed and full of clean machinery,
> And thought that many a spacious heart was ugly
> And empty without its tip-toe surprise of spiders
> Running like cracks in the universe of a smooth white ceiling,
> And how a seamless heart is like a stone.

Peter was to write many poems about spiders, and this poem (especially its dedication) suggests a link between his fascination with these creatures and acceptance of the Game.

However, most of the recent poems in the collection are very different in character from this, and from the poems recycled from *Work in Progress*, and none more so than the title poem. This is a long, wide-ranging, highly metaphorical and hyperbolic representation of natural forces. Redgrove did a lot of reading about whirlwinds for this poem, but he always maintained that it was 'an account of Penelope's orgasm'. It is unlikely that anybody has read the poem in this light unprompted, and Redgrove wrote on this theme much more engagingly in 'Coming-Lady', published in their joint collection *The Hermaphrodite Album*. The prominence of this poem, and the presence of several other long poems in similar style, heavily influenced the book's reception, in which the emphasis was on exuberant, undisciplined wordplay. Even Alan Brownjohn, who was always well-disposed towards Redgrove, confessed himself 'battered' by what he felt to be 'directionless and unfocussed' writing, despite which Redgrove was 'an unflinching, and valuable, original'. Clive Wilmer, on the other hand, recycled the old chestnut about an inferior (in this case 'emasculated') Hughes, and fired off a series of pompous insults like 'pretentious bombast', 'the worst kind of decadent periphrasis', 'welter of self-indulgence', suggesting that he simply hadn't bothered to read such finely crafted and varied poems as 'Young Women with the Hair of Witches', 'Intimate Supper' and 'Christiana'. Peter Porter, as always, was one of the most reliably supportive of critics, affirming that Redgrove had produced 'the most exciting body of poetry of any English poet under 45'. For the most part, however, by this stage of Redgrove's career reviewers seem to have made up their minds what they think about him, and to look for evidence to confirm their preconceptions, with little attempt to distinguish between his more and less successful work.

Brownjohn had the good grace to write to Redgrove and acknowledge that his response to his poetry was conditioned by temperamental limitations: 'There's never less than pleasure and admiration – and some envy, I might add, of the kind a poet like myself who feels a bit eggbound with his own subtleties and faint nuances might be expected to feel!' Peter may have been mollified by this, but he would have been more fortified by D. M. Thomas's rousing (if private) affirmation: 'For me, the best British collection (with Crow) for many years. And much more enjoyable, juicy, full-blooded, than Crow.'

More material encouragement was to follow. *In the Country of the Skin* was not only accepted for publication by Routledge, but won the Guardian Fiction Prize. This opened two new channels in Redgrove's work. Until now he had written almost nothing but poetry, except for a few short monologues such as 'Mr Waterman' and 'The Sermon'. Now he saw a future for himself as a novelist, and channelled a huge amount of energy into trying to build upon the success of *In the Country of the Skin*. Over the next nine years he published six more novels, all of them more accessible than *In the Country of the Skin*, but the commercial success he dreamed of was to elude him. These later novels had more clearly defined characters, vivid scenes (none more so than a terrifying account of DTs in *The Beekeepers* of 1980) and a great deal of humour. But Redgrove proved unable to create a compelling narrative, and the novels are often filled in with pre-existing material such as poems and, in one case, an extract from the Victorian Egyptologist Gerald Massey, whom Redgrove discovered in the mid-seventies.

The second new channel was more rewarding in the long term. Through the influence of George MacBeth, Peter was encouraged to adapt *In the Country of the Skin* as a radio play. It was broadcast on Radio 3, and Peter began a parallel career as a radio dramatist, having a play a year broadcast for the next fifteen years. He never wrote successfully for the stage or (with one exception) for television, but the medium of radio suited him very well. Partly, the more elite audience of Radio 3 meant that he had to make fewer compromises, but in the inner theatre of radio, throwing the task of visualisation on to the listener, the relationship between writer and audience is more akin to that of poet and reader. He once said that he wrote for people who listen to the radio, not for those who 'sit in a trance in front of television'.

Peter and Penny declared their creative partnership with two books in 1973–4: the poetry collection *The Hermaphrodite Album* and the novel *The Terrors of Dr Treviles*. The poems in *The Hermaphrodite Album* are individually authored but not identified as such in the text. It was their custom to get together every day away from the house to discuss the work they had done, and the separately authored texts were the result of a genuine creative exchange, not merely the works of two writers who happened to live together. Among Peter's contributions, the witty and erotic sequence 'Six Odes', tracing the man's development from dominance of his partner to submission to the feminine (derived from extracts of *In the Country of the Skin*) is outstanding. *The Terrors of Dr Treviles*, like a number of Peter's novels, centres on a magus figure not unlike himself, exploring his tendencies to genuine illumination (again, necessarily through submission to the feminine) and ego-inflation. Throughout his life he was suspicious of charismatic male guru-figures, and watchful of any tendencies to become like that himself.

Like *In the Country of the Skin*, the novel generated a radio play, *Miss Carstairs Dressed for Blooding*. But the most notable work that Peter produced for radio in this period was not a play but a monologue, 'Dance the Putrefact' (*FECA*). This is the most confessional piece that he ever placed before the public. The speaker has arrived in a village where people come to perform their 'dance': it is a place where 'nobody pries or condemns. Your dance is not mocked.' 'Dance' stands for fetish or, to use Redgrove's preferred term, paraphilia. The ritualistic, obsessive character of the dance is acknowledged: 'I am very strict, in order that I may be very grotesque.' The speaker is also 'dance-blind' – he does not know the meaning of his dance, and is therefore 'condemned to enact it . . . imprisoned within it'. The 'village' is a kind of therapeutic community in which people learn to understand their dance through acceptance. A dance floor has been prepared, but the speaker needs to perform his dance on the smooth mud of a beach, the 'black mirror'. He draws the crude outline of a woman in the mud, then immerses himself in this, covering himself with 'exterior cunt' – Redgrove's term for the exquisite skin-sensitivity that he achieved through the Game. As with the Game, the speaker's dance is an escape from gender identity: 'I am the black woman. I am petal-soft, and my surfaces are round and shining. The bosom of my shirt is heavy with mud.' However, dancing alone in this way is unsatisfying: the man-as-woman 'dances sadly on her own', and her lover (the speaker's male persona) can return only when she disappears. Like Peter with the Game in reality, the speaker craves for a real woman to join him in the dance, and this wish is gratified. When he repeats his dance, a woman joins him and makes love with him. But this lady too disappears, and leaves him alone in the mud. Finally he joins the other dancers in a communal dance where he meets a new partner, they bathe and make love in his bed. This lovemaking has a hint of the Game, in that the arrangement of the collar around the throat is dwelt on, but the narrative leaves the impression that, through enactment and acceptance, the Game/dance is left behind, the speaker is freed from his prison. This was only one of Peter's narratives of the Game however; another was that it was his greatest treasure, the wellspring of his creativity. This counter-narrative is betrayed by the fact that the most intense and memorable writing is in the evocation of the transgressive, auto-erotic mud-dances: 'Dance the Putrefact' encodes Peter's conflicting attitudes to the Game.

Peter submitted 'Dance the Putrefact' to the BBC at the end of 1973. The producer John Scotney responded enthusiastically, and the only problem concerned the word 'cunt', for which a substitute was found. When it was eventually broadcast in 1975, even Barbara wrote enthusiastically about it, referring to it as 'the other "Entropy"', thus showing that she understood its significance. Their correspondence had settled down to a tone of strained cordiality, which was only disrupted when Peter complained about being chained to his job because of the maintenance payments, or when he became anxious about the prospect of having to meet Barbara. He no longer visited Selsey, but Barbara facilitated contact with the children by holidaying in Cornwall: Bill was able to stay over with Peter and Penny (meeting Penny for the first time) and Peter had tea with Pete and Kate. Bill was about to start an apprenticeship with an engineering firm, beginning a successful career in complete contrast to his father's. Pete was more of a worry to his parents. He struggled at school, as evidenced by his laboured and immature letters to Peter, and was showing symptoms of OCD. But Pete was the favourite of nearly all his family: he was sensitive, perceptive, funny and affectionate. Everybody recognised that there was something 'special' about him. Kate was the only child who was successful academically, eventually becoming a lawyer.

Peter remained enthusiastic about returning to America and eventually, after one or two abortive attempts, he accepted an invitation from Bruce Berlind to teach in Colgate for the year 1974–5. The post was the Olive B. O'Connor Chair in Literature, and entailed teaching two courses per semester, with additional duties advising students in January between semesters, for a salary of $20,000. The teaching requirements seem clear from Bruce's letters, but later, when the visit had ended in acrimonious fiasco, Peter wrote on his copy of one of his letters, 'I thought it was 2 altogether at this stage.' This is puzzling, since he seems to be offering four courses in this letter: Creative Writing, Psychology and Literature, the Non-Chaucerian Tradition in Poetry, and 'The Grammar of Intuition: What Poets Believe'. In retrospect the fact that the invitation arose from a friendly contact, and the letters between Redgrove and Berlind are correspondingly informal, explains much of the difficulty that followed. There are also some casual references in these letters to the possibility of arranging some readings at nearby venues, which Peter later took as more of a commitment than they were.

Peter and Penny sailed to América on the *Queen Elizabeth II*, in August 1974. The voyage itself was a great creative stimulus for Peter: he was 'fascinated by the QE2, its material, its rituals, its social life, its engines and its spirit', and during the few months he spent in America, as well as teaching, writing poetry and researching for what was to become *The Wise Wound*, he wrote his third novel, *The Glass Cottage*, in which the central incident is a murder on an ocean liner. The novel was prompted by the voyage in a more material way too: Peter and Penny had underestimated the cost, and Peter thought a novel would help to cover the unexpected expense.

In the first semester Peter taught his creative writing course and 'Poetry and Magic' (a more student-friendly version of 'The Grammar of Intuition'). His first impressions were very favourable – 'Colgate has a very handsome campus, and people couldn't be politer or more helpful' – and after a couple of months he still seemed happy with the way things were going: 'The American young have good uninhibited vigour, and a definite idea of their relationships to the people who try and teach them, but their imaginations are less conscious, less attended to – I'm trying to help change that, and the response is quite decent.' There were only thirteen students taking the creative writing course, but forty-five on 'Poetry and Magic', and he was apprehensive about the marking burden that he would face in December. However, at this stage he merely groaned at the idea of doing it year after year, and thought that just the once it would be fascinating.

His mind may partly have been turned against his American employers by another contact he had made there. He had signed a contract with Oxford University Press to take part in one of a series of collaborations between poets and classical scholars to translate Greek dramas. Peter's assigned partner was the American scholar William Arrowsmith, who was then professor of classics at Boston University, and their chosen text was Euripides's *Ion*. They hoped to meet to discuss the project while Peter was in America, but this proved impossible. This may partly explain why the collaboration with Arrowsmith, like the connection with Colgate, eventually ended in acrimony, when Peter's translation was rejected. Peter told Arrowsmith that he was working from 10.00 to 5.00 three days a week, and Arrowsmith responded, 'Good God, I had no idea how badly you are being overworked! . . . about *twice* what is asked of any professor at any reputable American university.' If Peter was literally teaching twenty-one hours a week, as Arrowsmith interpreted him to mean, he was indeed being exploited. However, the proposed schedule for his spring semester course on psychology and poetry stated only that he would teach 3.30–6.00 on one afternoon, which is a normal load for an American university course, and it is unlikely that the autumn semester schedule was any different. Arrowsmith may have had a motive for taking Peter literally, since he had quarrelled with Berlind, and he made a point of saying that Berlind should have been more helpful. Peter replied to Arrowsmith that he had given Colgate an 'ultimatum' that he would not work like this in the spring semester, and this had been turned down. For the first time he says that he is thinking of cutting his visit short.

There was some compromise, however, since the chair of the English department, R. L. Blackmore, proposed cancelling the spring course on the non-Chaucerian tradition, and replacing it with 'Studies in Poetry', for students with whom Peter wanted to work individually, and it was agreed that 'Psychology and Poetry' would only be available to 'upperclassmen'. This term proved fatally ambiguous, since in Blackmore's mind it meant excluding freshmen, but Peter thought it also ruled out sophomores. A few days after the agreement about changing the schedule, Peter received a note from the Provost and Dean of Faculty, informing him that 'the amount of linen and towels which you are using exceeds that which we normally budget for in the 88 Hamilton Street apartment'. This is an astonishingly petty message from such an exalted source, and Peter commented that 'it is best not to put opportunities for satire and criticism into the hands of one's visitors, especially when they are professional writers'. His next collection did take some satirical shots at Colgate, but his immediate response was a scattergun of resentments: his letter of appointment had been delayed, he hadn't been sent information about tax, the academic calendar was sent late, he hadn't been given information about the administration of courses, he hadn't been told that the courses were only for undergraduates, nothing had been done about arranging readings for him, he hadn't been allowed to select students himself for his poetry workshops.

This is the kind of list of grievances that people make in the belief that it delivers a knockout blow, whereas the reader is likely to think it is only a symptom of the writer's state of mind. Certainly the complaints can't all be taken seriously – the letter of appointment and the academic calendar, for example, had been sent in March, which seems quite soon enough. Peter was to repeat and develop his charge that he had been misled into expecting that Colgate would have a graduate school, and that he would be teaching graduate students. There is certainly no evidence of anyone explicitly mentioning graduate students, and Peter had of course already visited the university and seen what kind of place it was. Not long before Bruce's first letter of invitation, Peter Porter had described Colgate to Peter as 'one of those private colleges for the sons of the rich and the drop-outs of the privileged', despite which Peter bizarrely persuaded himself that it was in the Ivy League. He was also to put repeated emphasis on the fact that nothing was done about arranging readings and, while this specific charge might be unreasonable, it points to a more general cause for dissatisfaction and resentment. While it was made clear to him from the outset that he would be teaching two courses per semester (and it is most unlikely that this amounted to eighteen hours), he assumed that he had been invited because of his distinction as a poet, and would be treated accordingly. He was disappointed to find that the university – collectively and individually – had little interest in his creative work. As he put it in an open letter to the university newspaper, he 'felt like an invisible person within the established situation'. Penny also felt ignored. They enjoyed little social life while they were in Colgate, partly because Peter was not drinking while they were there. He later satirically surmised that Bruce and his colleagues had been impressed by his performance as the drunken poet on his previous visit, and were disappointed when he didn't repeat it. He would not have been pleased to hear that Ted Hughes told Bruce that he was probably behaving irrationally because he was on the wagon. In reality, when not drinking he always felt uncomfortable in company where alcohol was flowing, and very likely this did inhibit him socially at Colgate.

Peter's equilibrium might have been affected by a terrible piece of news that he received in January. Peter Porter wrote telling him that his wife Jannice had died from an overdose. Of all his friends' wives, Peter had perhaps been closest to Jannice, whose hospitality he had regularly enjoyed since moving from London, and the distressing effect of the news on him can be judged by the fact that he condemned Bruce for not condoling with Porter, although he barely knew him. Despite the build-up of resentment since November, the decision to end the contract and return to England was quite sudden. On 8 February, only shortly before the second semester was due to start, they were intending to stay; eleven days later they were arranging their departure. A crucial factor may have been that Bruce himself left for England at about this time. Peter was suddenly without his closest contact in Colgate, and he felt that Bruce had deserted him, going off 'without telling anybody about our unhappiness, leaving the situation as before'. Bruce consequently became the main focus of Peter's resentment: he got reports from his wife of 'sheer hatred' in remarks Peter was making about him, and their friendship was destroyed.

Peter had made as powerful an impression on his students at Colgate as he had at Falmouth. Marguerite Feitlowitz, who went on to become a professional writer, admired the example both he and Penny set for 'a life of extraordinary intensity', and was in awe of his ability to combine an imperious demeanour with a quick intuition of the inward states of his students. At least one student sympathised with Peter enough to take the trouble of writing to the university newspaper in his support. Alan Sherman (who was not enrolled on either of Peter's courses in the autumn semester) wrote,

'A great injustice has been served by the untimely and controversial departure of Peter Redgrove from our midst; one that is most ardently felt by the students he had, in so short a time, so spiritedly touched with his thoughts, perspective, and emotions.'

Although Peter was to complain that the trip to Colgate wasted his opportunity of a sabbatical, in truth it was a very productive time for him. As well as *The Glass Cottage*, he wrote about forty poems while he was there, and his American experience makes a strong impression on his next collection, *From Every Chink of the Ark* – much more so than his year in Buffalo had. Even more importantly, he made extensive use of the university's library to begin research for *The Wise Wound*. It was in Colgate that he discovered the work of the neglected Victorian mythographer Gerald Massey, whose work fortified him, more than Robert Graves, Eric Neumann or even Jung, in the belief that revelation takes us into 'the marvels of the commonplace'. Massey was 'less haunted and overbearing . . . more learned and kindlier' than Graves. Redgrove interpolated an extract from Massey's *Natural Genesis* into *The Glass Cottage*, and frequently used phrases from the older writer's work in his poems, especially in *The Apple-Broadcast* (1981) and *The Man Named East* (1985), perhaps his two finest collections, both of which he dedicated to Massey.

Peter and Penny had now been together for five years. During that time he had, with varying degrees of collaboration, completed three novels and two collections of poetry, begun a new career as a radio dramatist and written most of the ninety-poem collection, *From Every Chink of the Ark*. Penny had independently completed two novels and several poetry pamphlets. They had also begun work on the project that was to produce *The Wise Wound*, which was to transform Peter from the poet who hated prose and was evasive about the meaning of his work, into the writer for whom poetry, fiction and polemical writing were all parts of a single discourse.

The Wise Wound 1975–79

Aborting the Colgate job meant that Peter was without a salary for six months, since his Falmouth post was being filled for the interim by the novelist Paddy Kitchen. It also meant that he had an unpaid sabbatical, which came at the perfect time. On 25 March 1975, 'Lady Day' as he noted on the typescript, he sat down to begin the first draft of *The Wise Wound*, a task that would have been much more difficult without this period of fortuitous leisure.

The writing of this book permeated Peter and Penny's lives for the next three years, and its theme was to occupy Peter's consciousness for the rest of his life. Its composition was a continuous process of conversations on long walks, exchanging notes over coffee in cafés, and sitting at the same desk with a typewriter. (Discussing their work on walks and in cafés was a lifelong habit – they made a point of getting away from the domestic scene to talk about their writing.) It is unquestionably a work of joint authorship, and would have been impossible without Penny's contribution (her name appears first on the title page). However, its theme was, paradoxically but significantly, of deeper and longer-lasting importance to Peter than to Penny. It was he who conducted the extensive scientific, anthropological and mythological research – including literally dozens of unpublished dissertations – which gives the book such a formidable air of authority. The structure of ideas was his, and though he was very anxious not to take the project over, Penny recognised that he could not help doing so unconsciously. In the 1950s Peter's scientific writing, for Glaxo and others, had been at odds with his poetic vocation. Now for the first time he was able to integrate his scientific education and interests with his imaginative work. But this does not mean that *The Wise Wound* is a work of science in any orthodox sense.

The main argument of *The Wise Wound* is that the subjective experience of the menstrual cycle, and hence the unity of mind and body and of humanity with nature, has been systematically suppressed in most cultures, especially Christian culture and its secular scientific successor. This is obviously a matter of crucial importance for women, and *The Wise Wound* claims to be, and by many has been recognised as, a work of feminism. But the book also argues that the cycle exerts a profound subliminal influence on the psychology of men, through the women that they live with and – even for gay or celibate men – through childhood experience of their mothers. Even after the sexual revolution of the 1960s menstruation remained a largely taboo subject: it wasn't until ten years after *The Wise Wound* was published, for example, that adverts for tampons and sanitary towels began to appear on television. But Shuttle and Redgrove argue that, even when menstruation is openly discussed, it is invariably in a medicalised and negative way. They ask the question, how can a normal, healthy function be the cause of so much physical and emotional distress? They answer that this is largely for cultural reasons, and make the unprecedented suggestion that the cycle might confer *benefits*. The human reproductive cycle is almost unique in that sex is not merely a function of reproduction, but men and women are sexually interested in each other most of the time. This encourages closer and deeper bonds between individuals, and sexual relations have a much more extensive emotional, psychological and imaginative aspect than if, as with most animals, sexual activity was confined to the fertile phase of the oestrus cycle.

Redgrove believed that orthodox scientific method, by excluding subjectivity, produces a false and alienating idea of humanity's place in the world. Contemporaneously with *The Wise Wound* he wrote a short article in which he aired his cherished notion that Einstein's famous account of imagining riding a beam of light at the age of sixteen was actually a record of a wet dream. He links this with speculation that Einstein suffered from OCD, and his recorded nervous breakdown during adolescence, to produce a narrative remarkably like that of his own early life, in which he traced the Game to his first wet dream. In Redgrove's account, the theory of relativity turned Einstein's schizoid condition into an alienating universal world picture and so 'infected our age with his particular illness'. He thus constructs Einstein as a kind of anti-self. Despite the numerous citations from primary scientific sources, and the impressive command of reproductive biology, *The Wise Wound* is positively anti-scientific in its method. A scientist is trained to be open to all possible interpretations of data, and to represent the evidence without pre-judgement. *The Wise Wound* marshals evidence to point to one particular set of conclusions. When George Eliot, in *Middlemarch*, made her famous metaphor of random scratches on a glass surface that look concentric when a light is pointed at them, she was championing objective scientific enquiry against the preconceptions of egotism. Redgrove argues that the picture is not complete without the subjective element.

Argument in *The Wise Wound* typically proceeds like this: Shuttle and Redgrove describe experiments by Edmond Dewan, using artificial light to synchronise women's periods with the cycle of the moon.

> Dewan's work has been repeated by a clinic in Boston with excellent, but not invariably successful, results. The samples are as yet small, but the possibility is evidentially there. We believe that when a moon-religion operated, that it is likely that this 'Dewan effect' was used practically to entrain the cycle to the Moon, to point the analogy both for religious reasons, and for all the practical advantages that come from physical self-knowledge. Great feminine mental power may also have been the result. There may be a survival of this practice in modern witchcraft, in the ceremony called 'Bringing Down the Moon', which may have this practical and literal meaning.

Despite the gestures here to the scientific criteria of repeatability and statistically significant samples, the argument is fundamentally conjectural: 'the possibility . . . it is likely . . . may also have been the result . . . may be a survival'. Other possibilities are not considered and, though technically the grammar is tentative, the passage moves unerringly to conclusions that support the overall argument: knowledge of the menstrual cycle gives women mental power, and witchcraft preserves vestiges of such knowledge (one whole chapter, 'Nine Million Menstrual Murders', is devoted to the belief that the witch-hunts persecuted women who had gained power and wisdom from the study of their menstrual cycles).

This is not a criticism of *The Wise Wound* but an indication that it is a work of ideology, not of science. A reader who knows about the most important events in Peter's life will recognise that some of the contentions are personally motivated, if not self-interested.

For example, the contrast between the 'values of ovulation', which belong to the species and dictate conformity to social roles, and those of menstruation, which promote erotic and imaginative fulfilment, the creation of 'mental children' instead of biological ones, clearly echoes Peter's attitudes to his two marriages. The strong emphasis on the influence of the mother's period on her children, specifically boys, owes more to Peter's childhood intimacy with Nan than to any scientific research – even Penelope Shuttle has said, 'It was more about Nan than about me.' We can be confident that it was Peter who wrote the sentence, 'A child may resemble a lover encountered when the mother was pregnant from the husband', in which his Oedipal conflict and fantasies about alternative fathers are barely concealed.

This personal element may make a reader suspicious, and there are certainly some highly questionable assertions in the book, such as 'Western Protestant Capitalist culture is arguably the most woman-hating that has ever existed, and it is certainly the most bellicose.' But *The Wise Wound* is a great book because of its revolutionary ideological purpose: it explores and makes possible new ways of thinking and feeling about one of the most fundamental aspects of human life. The reproductive cycle is 'real magic . . . in so far as it provides images that can arouse and make use of the undiscovered energies of the human personality'. A more general quality is that, unlike many authors who insist on the oneness of the mental and natural worlds, Redgrove and Shuttle are profoundly humanist. Unlike Ted Hughes, who once argued that the development of the human brain was an evolutionary mistake that banished us from the paradise enjoyed by Neanderthals and baboons, for them the 'immense evolutionary change' from the oestrus to the menstrual cycle brings about 'the enhancement of life produced by shared sexual experience between individuals' and 'all the evolutionary developments which have been seen as specifically human: viz. the development of mentality, symbolism . . . recognition and valuing of the individual, and social organisation'.

Penny later called the menstruation work 'a life-raft' for Peter. When he was in Leeds he had aspired to emulate Yeats's ambition in *A Vision* to construct 'a system of thought that would leave my imagination free to create as it chose and yet made all that it created, or could create, part of the one history, and that the soul's'. At the time he thought that this must not be a prose book but a poem like

Rimbaud's '*Saison en Enfer*' or *A Vision* itself (which he evidently regarded as a prose poem). A little later he noted that Hughes had 'a less broken & confused intelligence than I' because (perhaps quoting Hughes himself) '"mythology protects the imagination"'. In a sense Peter began writing his own mythology in poems of the mid-sixties onward, such as 'The Case', 'Young Women with the Hair of Witches' and above all 'The Idea of Entropy at Maenporth Beach'. But it is in *The Wise Wound* and its successors that he finds his system of thought and, despite passages such as the wonderful poetic riff on the symbolism of the apple on pages 137–8, *The Wise Wound* is a prose work in a way that *A Vision* is not: a work of argumentative discourse, albeit subjectively coloured. He had reconciled the two sides of his intelligence, which was no longer broken and confused. It is no accident that this is when he begins the long final phase of his career, when his poetry becomes exceptionally prolific and consistent. He can no longer be accused, as Lucie-Smith had accused him, of using his themes merely as a pretext for poetry: his work is now sustained by a coherent vision.

Peter had written to Norman Franklin, proposing the book, before going to America. Franklin was initially enthusiastic, but when he read a specimen chapter in December 1975 he reacted with 'despair', recommending that the book needed more psychology and physiology and less overtly personal content. This was an astute judgement, and the final version shows that the authors paid attention to it. But relations with Routledge were becoming strained. Peter had engaged the writer and literary agent Giles Gordon to represent him (the first time he had used an agent) and Gordon wrote to Franklin saying explicitly that Peter wanted to sever his relationship with Routledge. Nothing came of this, but his dissatisfaction with his publisher rumbled on for another decade. Routledge were primarily an academic publisher with a small poetry list, and they were not geared to the kind of publicity operation that Peter felt other poets (especially those published by Faber) benefited from. In the case of *The Wise Wound*, he and Gordon stuck out for an advance of £3,000, and when this was not forthcoming sought another publisher. Eventually it was published by Gollancz, where Peter and Penny found an active and sympathetic editor in Liz Calder, who helped to bring the book to its final form, and in paperback by Penguin. Ironically, from the point of view of Routledge, it turned out to be the most commercially successful book Peter ever wrote.

The Wise Wound was published in 1978. Inevitably, for such an ideologically charged book, critical response was polarised. The authors were particularly incensed (rightly so) by a review that accused them of treating women as 'hormonal robots', and engaged in a lengthy correspondence about this charge. But there were numerous gratifyingly favourable responses. In print Margaret Drabble, Colin Wilson and Marina Warner praised the book, and the Australian poet Les Murray, a less predictable admirer, made it one of his books of the year. There were enthusiastic letters from the noted American feminist and author of *The Woman's Encyclopedia of Myths and Secrets*, Barbara Walker, and from Ted Hughes. Peter's feelings about Ted were still conflicted: in August he refused to review *Cave Birds* because he thought Hughes was continuing in the wrong direction that he had taken with *Crow*, and he didn't want to write unfavourably about a poet he still admired. Nevertheless Ted's approval still meant a great deal to Peter, and it could not have been more emphatic: 'far & away the most convincing & persuasive re-establishment of the real dignity & sacredness of woman . . . that I've read'. He compared it favourably to Graves's *White Goddess* and with characteristic insight told Peter that it provided a 'real system for your poetry'. This letter (which was quoted on the dust jacket of the American edition) may have encouraged Peter to reread *Cave Birds* with a more sympathetic mind, because in October he wrote to Ted describing the book as 'real Hughes, beautifully firm native English, colloquial yet wide-worded; sombre and serious'. Even more important than any of these endorsements were the many letters Peter and Penny received from ordinary readers, for years after the book was published, often testifying that it had literally changed their lives.

During their work on *The Wise Wound* Peter and Penny's partnership, hitherto dedicated to the creation of 'mental children', faced its biggest test so far. Peter had no desire to start another family. He was in his forties, had failed as a father and had still not resolved the difficulties with his own father that underlay that failure; he attributed the breakdown of his first marriage partly to not coping with the irruption of 'the values of ovulation' into the relationship when Barbara became a mother. He was more dependent on Penny than he had ever been on anyone: almost literally his life hung on the all-encompassing intimacy that they shared. Would the arrival of a child in their lives be, as he had feared many years ago, before

Drawing of Peter by Dennis Creffield, 1964

Peter and Dennis Creffield, 1965–6

Lionel Miskin, 1968

8 Tehidy Terrace, Falmouth

'A boggy wood as full
of springs as trees'.
('The Idea of Entropy
at Maenporth Beach')

PR and Kate, 1969

John Layard, early 1970s

Peter and Penelope Shuttle, 1970

Penelope Shuttle, 1971

Peter and D. M. Thomas in America, 1971

Peter with Coleridge at Ottery St Mary, 1972

8 Trelawney Cottages, Falmouth

Penelope Shuttle, late 1970s

Ted Hughes
dehorning a bull,
taken by Peter, 1970s

1 Arwyn Place, Falmouth

Peter and Zoe, early 1990s

D.Litt at Sheffield, 2001

A 'menstrual
mandala'

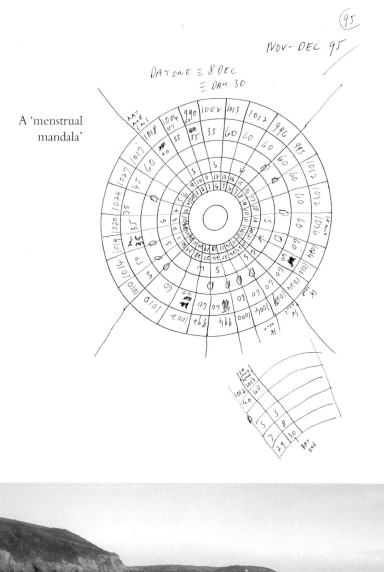

Maenporth Beach, where Peter's ashes were scattered

the birth of Bill, 'the start of one love and ending of another'? Quite early in their time together he records his anger at the thought of what a child would mean, and dreams of Penny throwing crockery at him because he refuses to discuss her desire for one.

By the time they were working on *The Wise Wound* Penny was approaching thirty and the issue had become more pressing. In the summer of 1975 Barbara visited with Bill, Pete and Kate, and the following day Penny became upset and talked about wanting children. Then, one evening that autumn, when they were walking on the beach, Peter suddenly said, 'Yes, we should have a child.' He had just visited his mother, and Penny believed that Nan had led him to accept what he had always resisted. She became pregnant the following spring. The time of her pregnancy was one of great happiness and sexual harmony. For Penny the preparation for motherhood supplanted the creation of 'mental children' and she wrote little, but for Peter it was the most prolific time of his life. He would get up at four in the morning to write, and during 1976 filled two notebooks with drafts of 441 poems, from which he selected the bulk of his 1979 collection, *The Weddings at Nether Powers*. Of course these poems were not written *ab ovo* during this period: for Peter the process of composition was always lengthy, and he was beginning to develop a systematic method of revisiting drafts after long 'fallow' periods, but this was the start of two decades of astonishing productivity, lasting till the mid-nineties, in which he had literally hundreds of poems ready for publication every two or three years.

If the pregnancy was a pleasure, childbirth was an ordeal for mother, father and child. Penny described the birth as 'like being in a road accident'. Labour was induced because she was overdue, but still prolonged and unproductive: Zoe was a large baby, lying transverse. After eighteen hours, with pethidine and an epidural, the baby was delivered by emergency Caesarian under general anaesthetic. She needed resuscitation and was taken away to an incubator.

Despite the ordeal of the birth, Zoe came through unharmed. Peter went into Truro cathedral and thanked 'Them', adding that 'something there as I kneeled accepted I think.' But mother and daughter didn't leave hospital for another eleven days, and the new phase in Peter and Penny's partnership began. Peter's thorough psychoanalytic training didn't save him from severe jealousy at this intrusion into the magic circle of his life with Penny but, as with the shadow-projection that he sometimes suffered with powerful male friends, he was conscious enough to be able to control it. He wasn't good at forming relationships with very young children who couldn't speak, and Zoe reciprocated by keeping her distance from him. Penny understood that he was bereft of the closeness they had shared, and gave him permission to have an affair if he wanted it: 'I instigated having the baby and I couldn't expect you to revert to a bachelor's existence so I said if any other experience comes along, well, you know, make up your own mind. I was involved with Zoe . . .' He did go away for a couple of days but no affair could compensate for what he had temporarily lost. He had been monogamous for most of his marriage to Barbara and was even more so now: he could only wait patiently for the slow return of their intimacy: not sexual relations merely, but their shared creative life. Peter and Penny had always slept in separate rooms, because he was such a restless sleeper. Now, Penny would take Zoe into her bed when she woke, and willingly accepted the whole burden of childcare. Zoe soon learned 'Daddy upstairs and Daddy writing', just as Bill and Pete had. There was a change when she began to talk, when he would take her out for walks and tell her long stories.

But Zoe was never in any doubt that she was much closer to her mother than to her father, and that Peter would have been happy not to have a child. She accepted her family relationships as given, and regarded Peter with affection as a 'benevolent, amused presence'. As she grew older she appreciated being 'in the middle of that creative relationship'. It was probably lucky that Zoe was a girl. Peter certainly thought so. Father and son was the cursed ground for him. He had not known how to be a father to Bill or Pete; with Kate there had not been time before the marriage broke up. The almost exclusive bond that developed between Zoe and Penny would have been more problematic for a boy, even though Penny would never have repeated Nan's violation of boundaries. Above all, for Zoe Peter was *there*. Kate, a mere eight years older, was the only child in her class who did not have two parents at home; Zoe was in a minority whose parents were still together.

Zoe's arrival enforced a move from Trelawney Cottages, the tiny house where Peter and Penny's partnership had been forged. In 1978 they moved to 1 Arwyn Place, a tall narrow end-of-terrace house, with views of the harbour. This was to be their home until Peter's death, and Penny's for years after. Many visitors have described the steep road up to the house, the narrow passageways lined with books (so that you had to walk sideways through them), the harbour views and, in the early years, Peter's study in the attic, where he installed a negative ioniser to control his weather-sensitivity. But horror struck as soon as they moved in, when they realised that, in Peter's words, the house was afflicted with 'tumours of galloping dry rot', which the surveyor had failed to detect. It had to be partially gutted; Penny and Zoe were evacuated to her parents' in Staines, and Peter had to live alone in a B & B for several weeks while he organised the repairs and tried to claim compensation from the surveyor. No local solicitor would take on the work, and the London lawyer whom he engaged had a nervous breakdown and neglected his cases. Peter came close to breakdown himself.

This was not an auspicious background for the most serious test of his strained relations with his first family, especially Bill. There had been visits to Falmouth by various members of the family in 1975 and '76: Bill brought his newly acquired moped on the train, and Pete stayed for Christmas. The tension that these visits – or more accurately the contact with Barbara that was necessary to make them happen – caused can be judged by three drafts that he wrote of a reply to a letter from her, proposing a visit to Cornwall in 1976. His first response is vitriolic: 'I want to ask you very seriously once more to leave me alone. The news that you're coming to Cornwall rouses all the old trouble and is making me ill.' A second version says merely, 'I'm afraid I'll not be here when you're due to come.' In the final version, written three days after the first and presumably the only one to be sent, he writes, 'I would certainly like a sight of you while you are down here,' making it clear that he proposes meeting Barbara as well as the children. This is the most striking example of something he often did in his correspondence: a cathartic release, after which he does what he knows he has to, once his feelings are under control. In this case it is notable that Barbara's letter says nothing about seeing him herself.

The circumstances of Bill's childhood had helped to ensure that he grew up with a temperament almost opposite to Peter's. As the elder son with an absent father he embraced the masculine role, and felt a quasi-paternal responsibility for his vulnerable younger brother and much younger sister. Despite not shining academically at school and leaving at sixteen, he throve in an apprenticeship and showed great promise as an engineer. He was confident enough of his future to marry at twenty, in 1978. Peter of course was invited to the wedding, and this brought the tensions in the family to a crisis. He wrote a letter to his father in which his anxiety is almost tangible. The date is not convenient; Bill has not communicated with him properly about the arrangements; he fears that Bill is repeating his own mistake by marrying too young, and is succumbing to family pressure. But the real reason comes through clearly: he feels he is the family scapegoat; his feelings towards Barbara, far from mellowing in the nine years since the separation, have become more painful, and he 'cannot contemplate a meeting with her without great distress'. He can't face 'an apparent family reconciliation over Bill's wedding, with all the falseness of [Barbara's] attitudes paramount', which would 'produce a fresh load of anxiety over the weeks preceding'. The continuing financial burden of the separation agreement, which he thought tied him to the increasingly uncongenial School of Art job, partly explains this failure to resolve his feelings towards Barbara. But his complaints about her conduct after the separation, especially that she had influenced the children against him, are groundless, and the idea that he is a scapegoat is a projection, partly caused by his inability to fully acknowledge that Barbara left him because of his violence towards her.

All this, of course, doesn't mean that the feelings he avowed in his letter to Jim weren't real: he would have suffered severe anxiety if he had gone to the wedding. Jim replied very moderately and diplomatically to Peter's letter, and tried to keep open the possibility of his going. But he didn't go. When I asked Bill how he felt about his father not being at his wedding he said he 'wasn't bothered'. I was sceptical, but undoubtedly this failure was overshadowed in Bill's mind by another, not long after.

From early childhood Pete had given his parents more cause for anxiety than the other two children. He suffered from OCD and struggled at school: until well into his teens his letters to his father are childish and stilted in expression. He was highly intelligent, sensitive and a gifted craftsman – Peter had helped to pay for an apprenticeship as a boat-builder, and he had won an award for seamanship – but he had none of his brother's confidence and independence. Whereas Bill had witnessed the violence between his parents, and Kate had only been a baby, Pete felt somehow responsible for the failure of the marriage, and thought it was unlucky that he had the same name as his father. To add to his misfortunes, in his teens he was diagnosed with the form of cancer known as Hodgkin's lymphoma. The treatment for this exacerbated his psychological symptoms, to the point that he was considered borderline schizophrenic. Barbara took over running a church youth group, largely to give Pete the opportunity to make friends, and it was here, at the age of nineteen, that he met a fifteen-year-old girl called Claire, who was a budding artist and loved the creativity and perceptiveness of the withdrawn young man. She also recognised that he frequently over-interpreted other people's words and actions, and suffered unnecessarily because of this. Claire responded warmly to Barbara's sympathy, insight and counselling skills, as well as her devotion to art. Eventually she and Pete were to be married.

The late seventies, however, were a bad time for Pete, as he struggled with his physical and psychological illnesses. Bill and his wife Sue looked after him for a time, but the strain became intolerable for the young couple, and Bill phoned his father to ask if he would have Pete to stay for a week or two, to give them respite. He refused. Peter himself has left no trace of this episode – he did not record it in his journal, or even tell Penny about it – so we can only guess his feelings and motivation. Pete was the child of that family for whom Peter felt the greatest tenderness, and he was perfectly conscious of the similarities to his own youthful ordeal. He was probably worried about the effect on Zoe of having a mentally ill young man in the house. Whatever his reasons, they did not impress Bill: this refusal, more than the absence from his wedding, was what defined Peter's failure as a father in the eyes of his eldest child. Peter 'walked away' from his family's crisis, he was 'far too interested in his own problems and difficulties', and this was what Bill 'had a lot of difficulty forgiving'. As far as Bill was concerned, the awkward relations of the previous ten years soured into a positive estrangement, and he hardly saw his father after that. Pete, by contrast, was always the one who defended his father against criticism by his brother and sister. As it turned out, many years later, in tragic circumstances, Pete was to be the agent of Bill's partial reconciliation with Peter.

Working on *The Wise Wound* did not inhibit Peter's other literary activities, and his writing as a poet, novelist and radio dramatist was prolific during this period. In 1975 his profile as a poet was enhanced by the publication of his first selected volume, *Sons of My Skin*, which outlined the development of his poetry from *The*

Collector to *Dr Faust's Sea-Spiral Spirit*. This book owed its existence to the enterprise and enthusiasm of a college teacher, Marie
Peel, who wrote to Peter volunteering to edit a selection. Peel showed
excellent judgement in making her choices, and supplied an introduction that is very perceptive in recognising both the qualities of
the poems and the underlying autobiographical narrative. It still
stands as an ideal introduction to the first two decades of Redgrove's
career. In 1977 he published his seventh collection, *From Every
Chink of the Ark*, the first of a series of exceptionally generously
proportioned collections. It contains several of Redgrove's finest
poems. 'Tapestry Moths', inspired by the great Elizabethan house
Hardwick Hall, which Peter visited on a reading tour of Derbyshire
in 1973, is one of his most engaging fantasies, in which an image
from one of the Hall's famous tapestries is eaten by a moth, imprinted
on its wings, then passed through the food chain till it is eaten by
a man who reproduces it in a dream. As in many of Redgrove's
most successful poems a delightful fiction guides the reader to
contemplate the dissolution of the boundary between subjective and
objective worlds. 'On Losing One's Black Dog', a mysterious poem
which Redgrove later clarified by explaining that its title referred
to the menopause, is the most ambitious of the poems inspired by
his menstruation work, in which he gives rein to his 'feminine
identification', creating an effect that is both alluringly erotic and
disturbingly transgressive as he explores various aspects of female
mystery. Other outstanding poems include 'From the Answers to
Job', a favourite of Hobsbaum's, and 'The Half-House', in which a
thrush rustling in the bushes is memorably transformed to a 'small
brown Christ sprinting among the pine-needles'.

Peter was always grateful to Routledge for allowing him to publish
fat collections like *From Every Chink of the Ark*, *The Weddings at
Nether Powers*, *The Apple-Broadcast* and *The Man Named East*.
But, whereas its successors are very consistent in style and quality,
this one might have benefited from a more rigorous editorial hand.
There are a lot of casual-seeming, jokey and list-like poems, which
were a gift to reviewers all too ready to dismiss Redgrove as a careless and self-indulgent writer. As with *The Collector*, all reviews of
From Every Chink of the Ark were overshadowed by one, and for
the same reason. In the *London Magazine* Craig Raine reviewed it
alongside Hughes's *Gaudete* and, like Alvarez seventeen years earlier,
used the occasion to portray Redgrove as a poor imitation of the

master: 'Hughes has a genuine respect for magic; Redgrove uses it frivolously. Where Hughes is hieratic, he is a conjurer, merely tricksy.' This was a more painful blow than Raine could have realised, not only because of Redgrove's sensitivity about comparisons with Hughes, but because he took magic very seriously indeed, and figured his father as the tricksy conjurer. Raine also followed Alvarez by focusing on some of the more vulnerable poems in this generously proportioned collection, and missing its genuine achievements. This time Peter did charge in and respond, at length, but he fatally weakened himself by unwittingly revealing that he had mistaken the colour of bramble flowers in one of the poems, allowing Raine to deliver a *coup de grâce*. Raine had not yet published his own first collection, and Peter identified him as a conventional don. Raine's subsequent emergence as the figurehead of the fashionable 'Martian' school of poetry, whose trademark was the very metaphorical inventiveness in which he himself excelled, was particularly galling. However, Peter always spoke generously about Raine himself who, despite his attack-dog manners as a reviewer, is warm and courteous in person, and responded in kind. A few years later he spontaneously sent Peter a card saying he had just read his poem 'The Visible Baby' in an anthology and thought it was a 'cracker'.

Ironically, only a couple of years later, Hughes was complaining at length in a letter to Redgrove about the way he (Hughes) was treated in reviews and, in a magnanimous reply which showed the warmth of his love for his friend and rival, Peter attempted to console him. Ted was upset by the personal hostility to him of someone like Peter Porter, whom he personally liked, but who accused him of arrogance. He went on to complain about a critic speaking of his barbarism, and then more generally about the destructive conceit of reviewers. He accuses reviewers of lacking self-knowledge, but he shows a curious lack of awareness in choosing Peter of all people as his confidant in this matter: he can hardly have been ignorant of, or forgotten, the Alvarez and Raine reviews. Peter's reply is masterly in the way it combines great sympathy with a courteous reminder of their respective public standing. He begins, 'Your cry goes to my heart, both for the things we share and the things we do not. I want to say something that will make you feel more confident, and better all round.' He defends Porter, emphasising the struggle he has to make a living as a writer. Hughes appears arrogant to someone like Porter because his well-deserved success is a 'mask' of the social and financial pressures under which the less fortunate writer labours. He confesses that at times he himself has been 'blinded to your work by envy in my own situation of your freedom, like Porter'. He shows sympathy with Ted's anguish about critics by satirising a bloodless and unfeeling type that he calls 'University Man', but suggests that there are some genuine critics who have shown understanding and appreciation of Ted's work. He concludes by saying that he has faith in better times to come. Where does he get his faith? 'Why, I re-open my Hughes, or my Blake, or my Langland, and the bitter fragments slide together again and become true reflection once again.' Hughes was moved by this response and replied, 'God bless you.'

This was also the period in which Peter built on the success of *In the Country of the Skin* to establish a career as a radio dramatist. In 1974 he sent a script to John Scotney, titled *The God of Glass*. Scotney passed it on to a young regional drama producer based in Bristol, Brian Miller, and thus began one of Peter's most fruitful creative collaborations. Miller thought that Peter was being passed on to him because he was considered an 'erratic genius' who was difficult to work with. His experience was mostly with popular drama and he had never worked with a poet before. He didn't at that time think of himself as an intellectual (though he later became an academic), but he responded very positively both to Peter's gifts as a writer and to his personality – what he described as 'a commanding leadership quality'. He attributed the success of their partnership to a strict division of roles: he never questioned Peter's script, but concentrated entirely on realising the aural dimension. Peter for his part never interfered in the production process – he never even came to the studio. It helped that Brian thought Peter was a genuinely shamanic personality, and was very receptive to his belief in poetry as magic. He described their collaboration as 'a sort of prophet–disciple relationship' but, though they met and were on friendly terms, the heart of their friendship was in the work they combined to produce – 'a relationship of the ether'. Working with Peter was the best thing that happened to him as a radio drama producer: the experience was invigorating and inspiring, and Peter stretched him as no other writer did. The feeling was mutual: Peter told Brian, 'Your enthusiasm for my work is one of the best things that has happened for a long time!' and after Brian left the BBC in the late eighties, Peter looked back on their collaboration as a golden age for his radio drama.

The God of Glass is a powerful and disturbing work, inspired by the popular horror movie *The Exorcist*, in which a young girl is possessed by demons. One of the most original sections of *The Wise Wound* is its last chapter, which explores the sexual psychology underlying vampire and other horror movies. Peter had a lifelong fascination with such movies and was completely free from cultural snobbery in his approach to them. *The Exorcist* was condemned by critics and clerics alike for its exploitation of mental illness and the occult. Shuttle and Redgrove acknowledge the exploitative aspect, but analyse the film as an allegory of the repressed psychic powers of the menarche (a girl's first menstrual cycle), 'ignored and deritualised' in Western culture. Like *The Exorcist's* Regan, Redgrove's Mary Ann develops multiple personalities, some of them masculine, hurls obscenities at the adults who try to help her, and kills the exorcising priest. The hero of Redgrove's play, Geoffrey Glass, is an African who has served eighteen years in prison for flaying a man alive, and spent the whole of the first ten years sitting at a table in his cell, repeating the words, 'Mr Glass sat at a table.' This experience is the equivalent of a shamanic initiation, and Glass the shaman is a kind of anti-exorcist, who controls the demons by entering into dialogue with them.

The God of Glass was recorded in July 1975 but wasn't broadcast on Radio 3 till two years later. In the meantime Miller had proposed that Peter do an adaptation of Thomas Mann's *The Holy Sinner*, which went through much more smoothly and was shortlisted for the Imperial Tobacco Radio Drama Award in 1976. Miller assured Peter that the delay to *The God of Glass* was for technical reasons, but Peter became convinced that he had enemies in the BBC who wanted to suppress his work because of its sympathetic portrayal of 'witchcraft'. There were indeed powerful voices in the corporation that were hostile to Peter's work, though not necessarily for the reason he supposed. In 1978 *The God of Glass* won the Imperial Tobacco Award, beating in the process one of the most popular radio dramas of all time, Douglas Adams's *The Hitchhiker's Guide to the Galaxy* (Peter may have been helped by the fact that Peter Porter was one of the judges). Despite this the play was not repeated and, when challenged about this, the controller of Radio 3, Ian McIntyre, wrote, 'It's not for nothing, in my view, that the Imperial Tobacco Awards are made of plastic.' Peter hoped that income from radio drama would help him to give up the art school, and the loss of substantial repeat fees understandably aggrieved him.

Hearing *The God of Glass* on the radio first prompted me to write about Redgrove, and in 1977 I published an essay comparing it with Hughes's *Gaudete*, which appeared that year in the still thriving *Delta*. This was the beginning of my correspondence and subsequent friendship with Redgrove. At the time I did not know that resemblances between the two works were a sore point with both writers, owing to the long delay in both cases between first drafting and public dissemination. Redgrove showed Hughes the script of *The God of Glass* when he assumed the latter was writing *Gaudete* and, when he read Hughes's poem, found 'too many emotional similarities to please me all that much'. However, Hughes had written a first version of *Gaudete* in the sixties, and he too complained of 'reminiscences' in both Peter's and John Fowles's work.

Peter adapted *The God of Glass* as a novel (without, unfortunately, reproducing the powerful effect of the radio play) and swiftly followed it with another novel, *The Sleep of the Great Hypnotist*. This book was the result of an experiment: Peter wrote it in ten days, using auto-hypnotic suggestion. He hoped to break into a more commercial, specifically paperback market with these novels, which was one of the reasons why he employed Giles Gordon as an agent. *The Wise Wound* was a modest success commercially, but Gordon got nowhere with the novels. *The God of Glass* was rejected by Gollancz, Secker, Michael Joseph, Futura, W. H. Allen and Granada. Gordon also tried to realise Peter's long-cherished ambition to be accepted on to Faber's list. He sent a large selection of new poems to Faber's chairman Charles Monteith, with the rather pompous title, 'This Ceremony Moulded Me'. Monteith's letter of rejection remarks that 'this particular poetic "tone of voice" becomes rather wearisome when one is exposed to large doses of it!'. It might have been wiser to send a smaller selection, with the much more engaging title *The Weddings at Nether Powers*, which was eventually used. These failures put a strain on the relationship of author and agent, leading Gordon to declare his resentment at 'feeling all the time that I have to prove myself to you'. Within a few days Peter had given up his hopes of commercial publication and offered the two novels to Routledge, who published them both in 1979. The two men managed to remain on personally friendly terms, but they agreed to end their professional relationship. Gordon wrote, poignantly but ominously for Peter, 'You are . . . the only writer of quality and originality and genius I think I've failed, as an agent, with totally.' The following year both Peter and Penny entered into a new arrangement with David Higham Associates, and Jacqueline Korn became his trusted agent and professional confidante till his death.

Peter was anxious that Franklin might be offended by his attempts to publish elsewhere, but his fears were unfounded and in 1979 *The God of Glass, The Sleep of the Great Hypnotist* and *The Weddings at Nether Powers* were all published by Routledge. Once again, though this time for a different reason, a single review blighted the reception of *The Weddings at Nether Powers* for Peter. For some years he had enjoyed a warm and friendly correspondence with the poet and novelist Robert Nye. In August 1979 Nye wrote, 'Without doubt you are the most genuine poetic force writing in English at the moment . . . I admire your commitment, your energy, your dedication, and your mastery of the craft. Who else, since poor old Rilke, has dared to listen so carefully to the "angels"? . . . At the same time I'd be less than honest if I didn't say that the magical element disgusts me.' Peter was grateful for the affirmation of his poetry, but felt obliged to retort, 'I wish you could get it straight about this magic business. I am not and never have been, in the occult business.' As we shall see, this disavowal is not entirely ingenuous, but Peter was justifiably sensitive about being labelled an occultist. What upset him more, however, was Nye's review of *Weddings*, which he declared to be full of 'all manner of visceral incantatory stuff, no trace of a sense of humour, and a solemn commitment to his own genius which would be embarrassing did not Redgrove, every once in a while, come up with an image which no-one else could have dreamt of'. Peter felt this review was a betrayal, and it is indeed hard to reconcile with Nye's letter: is this how one describes 'the most genuine poetic force writing'? Two years later he was still 'very hurt' by the review, but he was molli- fied when Nye revealed that it had without his knowledge been cut almost by half, omitting the assertion, 'At best, Redgrove seems more *inspired* than any other living English poet.' Even so, Nye's praise of Redgrove is unconvincing if he really thought the poetry has 'no trace of a sense of humour'. What did he make of the title? Or the dream of God as a Frenchman with a beret jammed on his head in 'God Head Gear'; the clergyman 'singing quadratics' in 'Rev. Uncle'; the mud-shop with fifty-seven varieties of bath in the title poem? Nearly every poem is infused by this kind of humour, which is essential to what Nye called the 'energy' of Redgrove's writing.

During the early seventies Peter had maintained sporadic contact with Martin Bell, but their friendship was compromised by Peter's paranoia about Dilly. After Martin's Gregory Fellowship ended in 1969 he had remained in Leeds, suffering from ill-health and alcohol problems and, after the latter had undermined his relationship with Christine McCausland and he was made redundant from a teaching post at Leeds Polytechnic, increasing isolation. On one occasion a friend of Martin's, John Milne, wrote to say that he wanted to cheer Martin up by taking him for a trip, and suggested bringing him to Falmouth. Peter's draft reply tells us more about the continued fragility of his state of mind, even in his new life with Penny, than about his real feelings for Martin:

> My marriage broke up quite largely because Dilly Creffield wouldn't let go. I've painfully knit a life together again, and I've fought off alcoholism but am subject to fits of nerves and sometimes can't meet people. One of the reasons for my friendship with Martin lapsing was that he discussed me with Dilly in his cups quite often as far as I can make out, and this so far as I could see helped the disaster along. I can't answer for the consequences if I discovered that he or anybody else were in any sense obliquely spying for Dilly – I just don't know what would happen to me and I suppose it would be bad for Martin too. I don't think Martin should read what I've just written here because I may be exaggerating [margin: 'though I had a letter not too long ago from the lady saying that he had discussed "my new circumstances" with her "quite indistinctly"']. But I must make it a condition of our meeting that neither you nor he are in any contact with Dilly.

He did not send this, and there is no evidence of any other reply. To another correspondent he wrote that Martin had 'intervened disastrously' in his relationship with Dilly. The logic, if it can be called that, seems to be that by talking to Dilly about Peter at the time when Peter himself was writing lovingly to her, Martin had somehow encouraged her disastrous visit, and by maintaining contact with her he might provoke another debacle. 'Paranoia' doesn't seem too strong a word for the fear of friends 'spying' on him, and anxiety about their speaking of him. Above all, feeling that Dilly was still able, in his 'new circumstances', to do him harm is revealing of his continued fragility, and of how strangely and exceptionally difficult it was for him to master, tame and distance painful past experiences.

However, in the final two years of Bell's life their correspondence flourished with a renewed intensity which was of inestimable importance to Martin. This began with a routine request to Peter, to sponsor him for an Arts Council grant. Peter was still sensitive about Martin's association with Dilly and, when Martin hinted that he would like to be invited to Falmouth, replied with uncharacteristic rudeness, reeling off a list of reasons why this was impossible, some of which – such as the claim that 'Penelope will not countenance any contact whatsoever with my Leeds life' – were fictitious. Martin was able to say truly that he had himself fallen out with Dilly at this time, and diplomatically omitted to tell Peter when their friendship was later restored. But the request happened to correspond with a dream about Martin and, true to his faith in Jungian synchronicity, Peter was happy to revive their intimacy in writing.

Martin was now living alone in a bedsitter, subsisting on invalidity benefit, holding alcoholism at bay largely because he couldn't afford to drink much. This situation did have the advantage, for a man of unworldly tendencies, that practical life had shrunk to the barest simplicity, with no bank account or utility bills. Christine McCausland compared him to Rembrandt's 'Philosopher' which hangs in the National Gallery, and in these eremitic conditions he devoted himself to translating Pierre Reverdy and other French poets. He also had the solace of his abiding friendship with Christine, which had survived their separation. In the short time left to him his material circumstances did not improve, but the renewed contact with Peter ensured that he did not end, in the words of Wordsworth that he quoted in one of his letters, in 'despondency and madness'. Bell had flourished as a poet during his years in London with the Group, between 1956 and 1967. The fruit of this period was his *Collected Poems*, published in 1968, and his inclusion in the Penguin Modern Poets series. The achievement of these years had been propelled by his chance meeting with Peter in the pub. The award of the Gregory Fellowship, far from liberating him for still greater achievement, as it had Peter, cut him off from regular contact with the Group and heralded a period of personal troubles, health problems and a creative block regarding his original verse. In 1976, when the friendship with Peter was re-galvanised, he was working mainly on translation and an autobiography.

To Martin, Peter embodied an ideal of the heroic, world-challenging creative imagination, a kind of negative projection of what he felt himself to be. Peter's prolific creative output, resonant personality and robust physical presence were indeed enviable, and Martin, like most of Peter's male friends, had little inkling of the nervous agitation, night terrors, sexual conflict and obsessiveness. He wrote to Christine:

> I shall call upon the most powerful weapon of all, who is Redgrove, who is not as the scribes & pharisees, but a man of power, who when he says 'Come!' they cometh. His reputation is at its height now, and Porter and I have agreed that he has finally pushed Ted Hughes to one side of the picture. You have some idea of how he writes letters – this time it will be on the same scale, in fully detailed arguments and rhetorical power, as Michelangelo's Sistine Chapel.

Peter used the request for support to persuade Martin that he should not be expending his energies on translation, but devote himself to original work. In the last years of Martin's life his relationship with Peter was, together with Christine, one of his two life-supports: Peter was his 'blood-brother'; he addressed him (only half jokingly) as 'Magus' and told him that they must exchange the roles they had in the fifties, with Peter now the 'guru'. It is not surprising that a man of Peter's personal and artistic powers should have deeply influenced students and other young people who encountered him; but here we see a mature, gifted and profoundly cultivated man with significant achievements to his name, rereading Jung at Peter's instigation and, in his late fifties, starting a dream diary that he kept up till his death. He recounted a dream of Peter as his 'analyst, confessor, literary critic and friend'. Peter gave some excellent advice about Martin's hostility to Roy Fuller for his influence at the Arts Council, and to a former lover of Christine's, being projections of his own unacknowledged darker self. Perhaps less helpful, to a man in Martin's circumstances, were his instructions for the sexual stimulation of a menstruating woman. This later flowering of a friendship between two men of such contrasting temperaments and destinies, but shared commitment to the poetic imagination, can claim some of the credit for the new original work that appears in the last pages of Bell's posthumous *Complete Poems*. But the intense correspondence lasted only two years: Martin's self-induced physical decline was remorseless, and he died in February 1978, on the eve of his sixtieth birthday. Peter wrote a fitting epitaph in a letter to Ted Hughes: 'Did you know that Martin

Bell has died? A great stylist, a humourist, and a man with a better understanding of French surrealism than possibly anybody else on this side of the channel.'

The loss of one old friendship was partly compensated for, the following year, by the recovery of another. The occasion was not, at first, propitious. In 1979 Philip Hobsbaum published his major critical book, *Tradition and Experiment in English Poetry*, in which he singled Redgrove out as 'the most imaginative and vital poet of the last thirty years', whose achievement puts into perspective the limitations of Philip Larkin, D. J. Enright and, most significantly, Ted Hughes. Hobsbaum devotes several pages of detailed appreciative analysis to Redgrove's poetry, but it becomes clear that his high valuation is based almost entirely on the earlier work. The later poetry is distorted by 'grotesquerie' and 'obsession', and the novels in particular suggest that 'Redgrove's obsessions have at last got the better of him'.

Peter understandably suspected a subtext: that he had succumbed to obsession as a consequence of their estrangement, and his best work was done under Philip's mentorship. He had several times contemplated writing to Philip during the previous decade and a half, and now he sat down to compose a letter that would almost certainly have confirmed the rift. He wrote of how hurt he had been by Philip's termination of their friendship, and that this was compounded by Philip having 'killed me and buried me in your book'. Fortunately he did not send this draft. As with Barbara, Peter discharged his feelings of anger and bitterness in the first draft, then returned to the task when he had conquered them. In this case he waited six days before trying again. In the redrafted letter he praised Philip's book, embedding a defence of his later work in an appreciation of his friend's 'exceedingly generous essay', and followed his expression of sadness at their estrangement with the conciliatory: 'I am sure that the cause was some deficiency in my own spirit, which I hope you will give me the opportunity one day to understand and repair.'

Fate could still have baulked the rapprochement. Philip replied by return of post, but somehow his letter went astray, and for six months Peter assumed that he was still obdurate. Only when Penny wrote to Philip in October were the lines of communication established, and Peter wrote, with undoubted sincerity, that he was 'overwhelmed with pleasure' at this outcome. It was to be a few years before the old friends met again – Peter and Penny visited Glasgow for a reading and stayed with Philip and his second wife Rosemary – and the meeting cemented their renewed friendship. There is no reference in any of their surviving letters to the cause of their quarrel, and no evidence that they ever discussed it.

X

Breaking Connections 1980–85

Throughout 1979 Nan's health was failing. She suffered a stroke, was frequently in and out of hospital, and was afflicted with aphasia. Her speech problems improved with therapy, but her granddaughter Kate remembers her as someone in mental decline, struggling to keep up her glamorous appearance but unable to put on her lipstick straight. At such times Jim would patiently usher her out of the room. Peter sent his parents his autobiographical essay 'A Poet in Teaching', which Jim read aloud to Nan, but only in parts, because she tired so easily. Less than a month later, on 25 May 1980, she died, sitting in her armchair. Jim sat watching her body all night, because he was unable to call the doctor.

Nan had been deeply important to Peter. He considered her the original guarantor of his imaginative life, the centre of the erotic 'aura' that 'opened doors' for him in the physical intimacy that he enjoyed as a child; she was also his ally in his resistance to Jim's world. She had supported him at the time of the crisis in his marriage, and welcomed Penny as the partner of his new-found happiness. She literally represented, for him, 'the goddess-priestess of the old religion'. He naturally grieved for her loss, and wept at her funeral, but the effect of her death was not as devastating to him as Jim's was to be, nine years later. He was of course prepared for her death by her long illness, but more importantly his relationship with her was completed, there was no unresolved conflict. Significantly the poem he wrote about her funeral focuses more on his father than on himself, in perhaps the tenderest words he ever wrote about Jim:

Since mine were sprouting I was able to see
The wings of others, such as my father's, standing next to me,

And his were ragged and tattered like those of an old moth
Close to drying up and drifting away, it seemed my duty
To merge my birth-wet wings with his, and this I did,
Entwining them in an embrace with him that he would never
    know . . .

('The Funeral', *MNE*)

As a later elegy for his mother, 'Joy Gordon', reveals, Peter visited
a spirit medium after her death. In that poem he reports that
the medium told him, whenever he thought of his mother, to
greet her image kindly and say, 'I'm glad to see you.' He doesn't
reveal in the poem, which was written before Jim's death, that
the medium also passed on a message from Nan: 'He's a monster.'
This doesn't seem the most helpful of messages for a man who
was still struggling, in his late forties, to come to terms with
powerful feelings of hostility to his father. But Peter was not a
superstitious man, and did not believe that this was literally his
mother speaking: he recognised such messages as revelations
from his own unconscious. His attitude to this, as to all matters
broadly termed 'occult', was highly sophisticated, as he illustrated
in an interview with the American poet Philip Fried, given at
about this time. Here he recalls an earlier visit to a spirit medium,
whose performance he analyses as a series of 'conjuring tricks',
offering the audience fake insights in the form of generalities,
in order to lower their defences and solicit their 'agreement',
which makes him capable of genuine insights: for example, Peter
reports that after a series of such 'tricks' the medium told him,
'The dead are helping you, and they are like bees in all the
flowers,' which he took as an insight into his preoccupation with
bees and spirits when he was writing *The Beekeepers*. As he said
in a letter written at the same time, 'The tricks are tuning devices
in which the mind is accustomed to reverie in trance, or waking
dreaming.'

The ground of all magic, for Redgrove, was the experience that
came to him involuntarily, of vision, enhanced senses and sexual
reverie. He wanted to live more fully in such experience, and not
in the depression that was its obverse. He also sought support and
companionship in his religious beliefs: a sense of religious community. He was especially drawn to the modern version of witchcraft
known as Wicca, and several times expressed a wish that he could
join such a group. He corresponded for a time with the Wiccan

practitioners Stewart and Janet Farrar, who were based in Ireland, and (most unusually) had them to stay in the house. As always in his correspondence he was seeking common ground, but he distanced himself from them when he wrote, 'I think I know some secrets, which present themselves directly to the senses, and with that possibility open, so much of the magical theorising around seems to be a waste of time!'

In 1982 a young student from Sheffield, Cliff Ashcroft, wrote to ask if he could interview Peter. They formed a close bond. Penny thought that this friendship compensated for Peter's poor relationships with his own sons (whom he never mentioned to Cliff). Cliff went on to write a graduate dissertation which was, surprisingly, the first full-length study to be written, and Peter was both moved and encouraged by its author's enthusiasm, devotion and insight. It was partly Cliff's questions that prompted him to write his second book of discursive prose, *The Black Goddess and the Sixth Sense*. But Cliff had a more than literary interest in Peter's ideas; he contacted a Wicca group, and asked Peter to check this group's credentials, which he did by consulting the Farrars. Cliff believed that Peter's ideas were too distinctive and individual for him to be comfortable in any group, and possibly that he was afraid of the effect such a connection might have on his reputation. However, once Cliff himself joined the group Peter became much more open in discussing his ideas, even suggesting in 1987 that they might join together to form a 'Society for Creative Occultism'. Eight the the years earlier he had protested to Robert Nye, 'I am not, and never have been, in the occult business.' We might deduce, either that his position changed in those years or that he was deliberately deceiving Nye. The first was certainly not the case, since during the year before writing to Nye he had conducted an intensive correspondence with William Webb or 'Frater Damon', the leader of an American organisation called Q.B.L.H., and would shortly afterwards accept the offer to establish an English branch. This correspondence began when Webb contacted Peter and Penny to congratulate them on *The Wise Wound*. Q.B.L.H. was one of a number of groups that claimed inheritance from Aleister Crowley, and was based in Peter's words on Kabbala and sexual alchemy. Peter and Penny took the Q.B.L.H. names Frater S.C. and Soror S.M., whom he later pretended to interview in *The Black Goddess*. We might have good reason to believe that Peter was deceiving

Nye, who was preparing to review *The Weddings at Nether Powers*, and any suggestion that he was an occultist could further marginalise his work. But it is not as simple as that. Peter adapted his posture and his language with *every* correspondent to whom he wrote on this subject. Even when writing to people who openly espoused Wicca, Kabbala or other occult systems there is something evasive about his attitude – he is always keeping a loophole open. Even to Cliff, towards whom he felt paternally protective and supportive, and conscious of his responsibility as a revered elder, after suggesting that they might form a circle together, he wrote, 'It's possible though that I am so entrenched in my own way that I would just be a nuisance.' He told the Farrars that he couldn't join any group that kept its beliefs and practices secret, but he himself bound to secrecy several people to whom he wrote about the occult.

One of Peter's warmest admirers, with whom he corresponded for many years, was Kathleen Raine, the poet and scholar renowned for her work on the spiritual foundations of Blake and Yeats. Raine had founded the Temenos Academy, which espoused a universal spirituality, with specifically Christian, Platonist and Kabbalistic leanings. She had been a member of the Christian Kabbalistic Society of the Inner Light, founded by Dion Fortune. For a period in 1982 their correspondence became particularly intense, when they agreed at Peter's suggestion to 'form a link on the inner'. In this correspondence he writes as a member of one Order (Q.B.L.H.) to another, addresses her as 'Soror A.V.A.', and makes much use of Kabbalistic language. The 'link on the inner' meant agreeing at specified times to engage simultaneously in 'active imagination'. There are a number of letters between them, written on the same day, in which they share their experiences. There is no doubt that Peter had the utmost respect for Kathleen, that he wanted to learn from her – as he did from most of the people with whom he corresponded – and that he was completely sincere about the 'link on the inner'. However, the use of Kabbalistic language in his letters is startling. Here is a sample, in which he describes the work he has been doing with Q.B.L.H.:

> I have been working out of Geburah towards Chesed for a while now, subsequent to the Wise Wound, which came out of our Path

18, Hod-Netzach. . . . Every poem is an exercise in travelling the tree, either as serpent or lightning-flash; from the lower Sephiroth of material objects to their resonances on cosmic planes; or from intimations out of the higher planes; our perfected tree is with Malcuth at Daath.

Peter made a number of Kabbalistic 'trees' in which he translated Geburah as severity, Chesed as mercy, Hod as glory, Netzach as victory and Malcuth as the Kingdom. So far, he seems to be translating very general concepts into a language that he thinks will find favour with his correspondent. The word Daath, however, represents a fundamental evasiveness in Peter's correspondence with Kathleen. He had obviously read widely about Kabbala, but the one book that he used to recommend, and the only one specifically on Kabbala in his personal library, was David Bakan's *Sigmund Freud and the Jewish Mystical Tradition*, which had been recommended to him back in the late sixties by 'Perilla Wymark'. Bakan's book is a cool and scholarly analysis of the importance of Freud's Jewish heritage, and especially the Kabbalistic tradition, in the formation of psychoanalysis. What most interested Peter was Bakan's emphasis on the sexual aspects of Kabbala. Unlike the ascetic mystical traditions of both East and West, the Jewish mystics ascribed sexuality to God. The godhead incorporates the Shekinah, God's female aspect, and 'The Jewish Kabbalist saw in the sexual relations between a man and his wife a symbolic fulfilment of the relationship between God and the Shekinah.' The *Zohar*, the most important Kabbalistic text, portrays the original man as containing both sexes, which were later separated. Bakan points out that Daath means both knowledge and sexual intercourse, as is well known from the Bible – 'And Adam knew Eve his wife.' Peter marked both this passage in Bakan and 'Insight is *Daath* . . . knowledge that comes from union . . . and *this kind of knowledge is a deeply erotic experience*' (Bakan's italics).

For Kathleen Raine spiritual experience had absolutely nothing to do with sexuality. She later confessed to Peter that the direction her life had taken entailed a sacrifice of the sexual energies, which she likened to a castration, and for this reason she could not share his 'tantric studies'. She told him of a dream in which they were swimming together, in which he caught her by the feet, and tried to pull her down; she was afraid of drowning, but managed to pull him up instead. For Peter on the other hand sexuality is absolutely central to his occult interests. What attracted him to Q.B.L.H. could not have been more different from Kathleen's refined and Christianised spirituality. His correspondence with Frater Damon is almost entirely about techniques for enhancing sexual experience, especially making it a channel for vision. He several times spoke of his activities in Q.B.L.H. as 'research' and, while he certainly took sex extremely seriously and considered it the ground of his work, sexual activity is what his research consisted of. The emphasis in his correspondence with Frater Damon is on heterosexual union, though Peter is occasionally able to hint at the Game, as when he writes that 'at stressful times, physical substances are used to energise the skin, and a rite of re-clothing', or when he tells another member of Q.B.L.H. about a 'special rite of KPR [Hebrew for atonement]' whose 'inner meaning is extremely secret', and which is described in his novel *The Facilitators* – in fact, a revised version of 'Dance the Putrefact'.

Peter was too sensitive and courteous to write to a woman of Kathleen Raine's temper about sexual matters in the explicit way he wrote to Frater Damon. Hence the Kabbalistic language serves as a kind of code in his letters to her, and hence also their 'inner working' was bound to be limited. After a few months he wrote to her an obscure letter saying that he had 'noticed things about traditional procedure which have to be discussed in my Order . . . Until this is resolved I should not practise with another within the tradition I am questioning, I believe.' Either this is merely a form of words to enable him to slip out of an arrangement that he no longer found helpful, or it is precisely Kathleen's 'sacrifice of sexual energies' that he is questioning.

A more amusing example of Peter's interest in magic is a correspondence course that he signed up for in 1981, run by Marian Green of *Quest* magazine. He was sent course materials and wrote assignments which were 'marked', literally with ticks in the margin. In one of his assignments he describes what he calls his 'magical tools and symbols'. These include a black mirror, a crystal globe, a pentacle, paraffin wax, beeswax mixed with male and female sexual fluids, an alabaster chalice, his negative ioniser, an image of the Goddess, an ammonite fossil, a crystalline amethyst geode, a green serpentine vase, rings made of moonstone and silver and haematite and silver, a double spiral of copper, a knife, and tubes of sulphur and salt. He once described them as 'objects which are present in both worlds, in the unconscious mind or the unknown world and the conscious world as well'.

Bearing in mind who Peter Redgrove was, some of the comments by Marian Green (let alone the ticks) seem rather patronising. For example, when he writes that he has some skills in healing, the ability to see auras, and possibly mediumistic powers, she comments, 'Most people have these skills but like playing a musical instrument, need practice & training,' and she tells him that he is 'missing the point in all this complexity'. He responded to her comments with remarkable humility but, after completing two projects, withdrew from the course, explaining that he had found 'a very powerful teacher locally'. Unless it was Penny, this teacher is likely to have been a fiction.

We have seen a pattern of Peter forming connections on the basis of occult interests, but leaving himself a loophole for withdrawal: this happens with Kathleen Raine, Marian Green, even in a small way with Cliff Ashcroft. There is no evidence of a definite withdrawal from Q.B.L.H., though the correspondence lapses after the late eighties. Here too, however, the limits to his commitment are visible. For all his use of Kabbalistic terminology, both in correspondence and in his journals, he thought that Kabbala was potentially obsessive and – unsurprisingly as an English poet – felt incapable of 'free conversation' in its language: 'English is my magick mirror.' He was suspicious of the tendency of such groups to form around charismatic male leaders, and alienated by the humourlessness of much occult practice: 'When the senses open for me, what I experience is so extravagant and *funny* that I have to tell it laughing otherwise it's not true to what I want to say! This I fear is an unusual quirk, and most people won't have it, since they like solemnity in spiritual matters.'

Because he was so eager to learn whatever his correspondents had to offer, he was in the habit of writing ingratiatingly to people with occult interests, often in a way that was misleading about the nature of his involvement. For example, to the surrealist writer and artist Ithell Colquhoun he wrote:

> I was . . . the pupil of a great adept, John Layard; and had a sexual initiation with another whose name I can't give, a Sufi. Some eighteen months ago I had a Second Order initiation from a Soror A.V.A. who was trained in Dion Fortune's group. I have the present task of working within Q.B.L.H. as their English centre under a charter from Frater Damon of that Order.

His purpose here is to represent a series of important experiences as a regular programme of magical training. Layard had no known occult connections. He was certainly an adept, but not in the way Peter implies here. The 'sexual initiation' came from 'Perilla Wymark': an influential experience, when he had a vision of the horned God, which he later took to be an image of the womb, but in no sense a formal magical initiation. Soror A.V.A. is Kathleen Raine, and Peter certainly took his 'inner' connection with her seriously, but she too would have been surprised to learn that this was an initiation. Similarly the link with Q.B.L.H. was substantial, but Frater Damon's invitation to form an English branch was far more informal than the rather pompous word 'charter' implies. There is no evidence that Peter ever met another member of the organisation in person. None of these experiences involved a formal initiation, and the only training he received, from Layard, was Jungian rather than magical. He was more straightforward when he told the Farrars that Layard was his real basis, and deeper than that was the sexual trance.

For all his genuine exploration of Wicca and other pagan groups, Peter probably found his most fulfilling experience of shared religion in something quite different. Whenever he could he used to visit the 'Obby Oss' festival held in Padstow on May Day. From morning till evening, accompanied by repetitive accordion music, the two 'Osses' dance, wearing grotesque masks with little resemblance to horses, and capacious hooped costumes, beneath which, Peter liked to think, young women used to be taken and marked with a tar-brush. He found this celebration deeply moving: the first time he witnessed it he found that 'tears were spurting from my eyes like a child'. He felt that something was happening which had never happened for him in church: 'the kind of experience when trivial everyday life deepens and seems more solid and important', giving him 'a deep feeling of energy, harmony and contentment'. He clearly felt that he was witnessing an enactment whose symbolism spoke to him as Christian symbolism did not. One may even suspect a displaced Christian feeling in his emotional response to 'the Oss dying and coming to life again', and it seems no accident that when he writes that 'all matters are simultaneously and eternally present' he strongly echoes Eliot's 'Burnt Norton': 'If all time is eternally present / All time is unredeemable.' Redgrove would probably retort that Christ is not the only god to die and be reborn, and that a pagan-rooted ceremony such as the Obby Oss is closer to the religion of Osiris. Whatever the particular channel through which the religious symbolism spoke to him, he was able to respond so powerfully and uninhibitedly because of the open, spontaneous and popular nature of the event, and its ability to unite ritual and laughter, with none of the solemnity that deterred him from more self-conscious rituals.

A few months after Nan's death, in September 1980, Peter and Penny were married. Penny had finally overcome her distaste for the institution because it simplified their joint ownership of property. However, Peter was still paying £180 per month to Barbara, partly for the support of Kate who was still only twelve years old. At about this time Barbara asked Kate if she wanted to continue seeing Peter, and she chose not to because in her eyes 'he was a stranger and our meetings were rather formal'. She did, however, resume contact when she was older.

He was now at the height of his powers. His 1981 collection, *The Apple-Broadcast*, was the first to show the remarkable consistency that runs through his later work. There are very few weak poems in it and many, such as 'From the Life of a Dowser', 'Silence Fiction', 'Song', 'Pheromones', 'On the Patio' and 'My Father's Spider' are among his finest. Poem after poem is informed by a deep substratum of coherent and confident vision, with a new level of stylistic unity and narrative structure. The protagonist of 'From the Life of a Dowser' is one of his most perfectly achieved quasi-autobiographical personae, combining engaging humour – 'Water is bad for him, much too exciting' – with beautifully subtle sensation – 'The water is cool, and tin-tasting, / A spectre of earthy darkness brushes by / His throat, and disappears' – and the menace of fragile sanity: 'The frowning clouds in white coats came for him'. 'Pheromones', which imagines what it would be like to have a dog's sensitivity to smell (a favourite subject of Redgrove's) is one of his funniest poems. On the doorknob of the pub Gents the speaker believes he can smell a tennis champion, and inside the Gents:

> my own genius mingles with that
> Of the champion and the forty-seven assorted
> Boozers I can distinguish here in silent music,
>
> In odorous tapestries. In this Gents
> We are creating a mingled
> Essence of Gent whose powers
>
> To the attuned nose
> Are magnificent indeed.

The humour lies not only in the absurd scenario but in the nimbleness of tone and register.

The Apple-Broadcast was more favourably reviewed than any of his previous collections: the 'system' whose absence he had lamented when at Leeds, and which he had discovered with *The Wise Wound*, was bearing fruit. He was irked when, in the year following *The Apple-Broadcast's* publication, Charles Tomlinson wrote in the *New Pelican Guide to English Literature* that his poetry lacked '*charpente*' (scaffolding). A good-humoured correspondence ensued, in which '*charpente*' became a joke word between them, but in which Redgrove made a serious claim about his development. He acknowledged a 'tendency to Whitmannerism and unargued vitalism' in his earlier work, but asserted that with *The Wise Wound* he 'understood where the vitalism came from', and this gave him a '*charpente*' which was evident in *The Apple-Broadcast* where for the first time he 'felt able to take a standpoint from which to argue'. Tomlinson replied acknowledging that *The Apple-Broadcast* was 'a book which makes all the difference', and that he had written his critique before reading it. One of the favourable reviews was by the distinguished Cambridge academic Muriel Bradbrook, and Redgrove had other influential admirers in Cambridge: he corresponded with, and met, John Beer and Frank Kermode, and in 1985 was exploring with them the possibility of a temporary fellowship at Cambridge. But Bradbrook's review was in Kathleen Raine's small-circulation magazine *Temenos*, and the support of these well-known critics, like that of M. L. Rosenthal earlier, did little to enhance his reputation.

Another factor in the artistic success of his poetry at this time may be that he had brought to its fullest development a very distinctive and productive method of composition. By the late seventies he was composing poetry in a highly organised way, a system that was designed to make maximum creative use of his sources of inspiration. These he called 'germs', which have to be 'incubated' in the unconscious, before being developed by active work. By the time of *The Apple-Broadcast* the drafting of a poem took place in four distinct stages. The first, the 'germ', was strictly a pre-literary stage. It may take the form of a passing thought, a phrase read or heard, or the product of a dream or automatic writing. These 'germs' would be recorded, unedited, in notebooks or journals. By this time of his life he recorded every dream and every time that he and Penny made love, though this material rarely found its way directly into a poem (exceptions are 'Davy Jones' Lioness' in *Assembling a Ghost*, whose narrative follows that of a dream, and 'His Naiveté' in *Orchard End*, which reproduces the record of a sexual experience). More characteristic of 'germs' are passing phrases such as 'The sparkling well: Fenten ow clyttra', which was the origin of 'From the Life of a Dowser', and 'Horus comes to greet you through this oil', which he developed into 'The Proper Halo'. He always carried with him a small loose-leaf notepad, and would paste jottings from this into his journal. The journals also contain often cryptic and apparently obsessive references to the Game, and to the past experiences from which he could not free himself, especially his relations with his parents and with Barbara. Again, until his last years such material rarely formed the direct origin of a poem, but its presence in his creative matrix was clearly important to the working of his imagination. He would deliberately not look into the notebook for some time. He would then go through it and type out pages of imagery suggested by the 'germs' that had thus 'incubated'. These he pasted into a separate notebook from the 'germs' themselves. Although the process of composition was now a more literary one, it was still largely unedited. The contrast between the pages of undigested imagery and a finished Redgrove poem shows how much conscious work went into the drafting process. The same material would be typed out in this way several times, with slight alterations, and combined each time with different material.

The third stage, and the decisive advance towards the production of an identifiable poem, is a prose draft. In the last twenty-five years or so nearly every poem went through a prose draft, and although one can detect revisions made in the subsequent verse drafts for prosodic reasons, the implication is that the rhythm of the verse is already at least implicit in the prose. He usually pasted the first verse draft in the notebook opposite the prose draft. The mechanics of the method as he describes it in his essay 'Work and Incubation', with the different stages of composition kept in different notebooks, were only sustained for a few years, but the fundamental method of germ, imagery, and formal drafts, with periods of 'incubation' between, was always maintained. The startling consequence of this is that Redgrove was at work literally on hundreds of poems, at different stages of composition, at any time. It would only be a slight exaggeration to say that, in each of his published collections, he was at work in parallel on *all* the poems over the whole period covered by the book. This helps to account for the consistency of the collections from *The Apple-Broadcast* onwards, though it may also explain the difficulty many readers have experienced, in recalling individual poems rather than the overall effect of a volume.

He was equally well-organised about the preservation of his work. Two or three times a month he would visit the office supplies shop in Falmouth run by Keith and Carolyn Trickey, to have a few copies made of his journals, one of which the Trickeys would keep for security, and to get his fair copies professionally typed. He also had A4-to-A5 reductions made, to create portable little books that he could carry around with him or, in the case of final drafts, send to friends. Keith was in some ways a kindred spirit, interested in environmental studies, and he and Peter became friends; but irrespective of friendship, purely in a business relationship, Keith was effusive about how courteous, appreciative and easy to work with Peter was, always allowing plenty of time for the work, and paying as soon as it was done.

Peter's poetry was thriving but his attempt to make a more lucrative career out of writing novels foundered in the early eighties. In 1982 he published his seventh novel in nine years, *The Facilitators*, and it was to be his last. He always remained somewhat bitter about the commercial failure of his novels, especially in the context of the fashion for 'magical realism', a genre to which he thought his work belonged, and the celebrity of a writer such as Angela Carter, whose audience he thought his own novels should appeal to. Most difficult to take was the triumph of his old friend D. M. Thomas in 1981 with *The White Hotel*, a *succès de scandale* which combined psychoanalysis, masochistic fantasy and survivor accounts of the Babi Yar massacre. Peter was aware that he couldn't keep his judgement clear of personal feeling: 'It is not the bad book . . . I feared, but it's not *that* good when one thinks of the enlargement of consciousness one experiences with one's favourite authors . . . That's my opinion, anyway, so far as I can express it in my turmoil of envy of Don's success.' He might ruefully have recalled that a few years earlier Thomas had congratulated him on *The Terrors of Dr Treviles*, which he said had inspired him to plan a novel of his own, but he was too lazy to write one. Peter was no longer the senior partner in this friendship. The following year Don considered buying a house in Falmouth partly because Peter lived there, but Peter put him off: 'But why Falmouth, Don? It's so damp, and electrical; the winters are so muggy. If I had the choice, I would go for stone, on the North coast.' Don wondered, no doubt correctly, if Peter was partly motivated by jealousy over *The White Hotel* – it would not have suited Peter to have a more famous writer, especially one who was a former protégé, living in the same town.

Conversely Don had always been jealous of Peter's job at the art school but by the early eighties Peter's long-standing unhappiness with the job was reaching crisis point. Given the changes in higher education over the period since he was appointed, his dissatisfaction was to some extent inevitable. The student numbers had trebled, but there were still only two lecturers in his department, and the kind of familiar and informal relations that he had enjoyed with students were more difficult to sustain. But there were also special reasons why Peter's position had become virtually impossible. He had been appointed because of his achievements as a creative writer, and the creative stimulation of the students was the hallmark of his work. He had been recognised as an artist among artists – indeed, as the most renowned artist on the staff. It was his ambition to establish creative writing as a degree-level subject of equal status with the visual disciplines. Lionel Miskin supported him in this aim. But there were powerful forces opposed to him. The renowned Cornish-based painter Patrick Heron, a patron of the school, wrote a letter to the governors stating his *extremely strong opposition to the proposal*, comparing it to a university English faculty devoting its resources to painting. Peter believed that this letter was solicited by the Principal, Tom Cross. The proposal was rejected in 1978, a 'major snub' to Peter in the opinion of his friend and colleague Derek Toyne. Peter may have been wrong about Cross's part in Heron's letter, but there was nothing paranoid about his feeling of exclusion and hostility to his work. When a student included creative writing in her graduation exhibition Cross said, 'This must never happen again.' On a more petty level, Peter had invited Charles Causley to read at the school, and the Principal interrupted their lunch to tell Peter that the reading venue was a mess, and he must get it cleaned up. Peter took this as a public humiliation in front of a distinguished guest, and was convinced that Michael Finn would have handled the matter more sensitively. (When I spoke to Tom Cross on the phone he said that he didn't really know why Peter left the school, and assumed it was for 'personal reasons'.)

By 1982 Lionel and Francis Hewlett, another friend and ally, had retired, and Peter was feeling increasingly isolated. Complementary Studies was defined as theoretical, not creative, and he felt that the role for which he had been appointed no longer existed. This was reinforced by Lionel being replaced with a new head of department who was an academic, not a practising artist. Francis thought that Cross openly wanted to get rid of Peter, but hostility was not confined to the Principal. Peter wrote a letter to the new Head of Painting protesting that he had objected to Peter's influence on students; he heard that this colleague accused him of being 'mixed up in the occult' – a sensitive point, as we have seen. On one occasion a student of sculpture turned up late to his class and launched into a 'sarcastic parody' of his teaching, saying that this was how the tutors in his department regarded it, calling it a 'nuisance' and a 'tea-break'.

Derek Toyne thought with hindsight that Tom Cross was right, and that a department of creative writing would have become an 'imitate Peter Redgrove department'. It may well be that history had undermined the possibility of a job such as Peter had taken in

1966, and that a talent and personality such as he could no longer function in an institution. However, the belittling exclusion to which he was subjected in his final years at the school would have been intolerable for any teacher; for a major creative talent to be treated this way was shameful.

In May 1982 Peter contacted his union, the National Society for Art Education, whose representative, John Steers, gave him invaluable support. With Steers's help he was able to negotiate redundancy with an enhanced pension on the grounds that the nature of his job had changed – an arrangement that was just enough to enable him to continue to support himself, Penny, Zoe, Barbara and Kate. He retired the following summer. Derek Toyne organised a leaving party, and received many testimonials from former students. Perhaps the most pertinent is from Martina Edwards, one of whose paintings, done in 1982, is proudly displayed on the website of what is now University College Falmouth: 'In all the years I spent at Falmouth, it was Peter and no painter that taught me anything essential about Art and seeing.' University College Falmouth now teaches a degree in English and Creative Writing, but there is no mention on its website of Peter Redgrove's part in its history.

He had reasons to feel optimistic about going freelance. In September 1982 he was elected a Fellow of the Royal Society of Literature, having been proposed by his friend Martin Booth. More materially, in October, the day after handing in his resignation, he learned that his play *Florent and the Tuxedo Millions* had won the Prix Italia for radio drama – an award that Brian Miller described as 'the Oscar of broadcasting'. It was the first regional production that the BBC had ever entered for the competition, and Miller thought that Ian McIntyre had put it forward as a snub to the London drama department. Miller himself went to Venice to collect the prize, accompanied by the most senior members of the BBC management, and stayed on the Lido in a hotel opposite the one used for the film of *Death in Venice*, but Peter refused to go because he thought it would dilute his concentration. Winning the prize guaranteed a repeat for the play, which was a significant supplement to Peter's income, and of course enhanced his standing with the BBC. Even more timely, the following year he was awarded an Arts Council grant of £5,000.

The launch of Peter's freelance career was further helped by an invitation to judge the Arvon Foundation's National Poetry Competition, for which he was paid £3,500. Arvon had been established in the late sixties by the artist and poet John Moat and the poet John Fairfax, and since then had been running residential courses in creative writing at Totleigh Barton, in Devon, taught by a wide range of established writers. Peter and Penny had taught jointly there regularly and successfully since the beginning of their relationship, and were to continue doing so through the nineties. Ted Hughes was a friend of the two Johns, and had leased to them his house in Yorkshire, Lumb Bank, where a second centre was established. By 1983 John Moat, who owned Totleigh Barton, was thinking about withdrawing from the foundation and wondering about its future. He discussed with Hughes the idea of asking Peter to manage an Institute of Creative Research. It is testimony to Ted's belief in Peter's talents and trust in his practical acumen that he was enthusiastic about this idea, and Moat wrote to Peter proposing it. Ted's judgement was right in that Peter was a highly organised person who was good at handling money (though he didn't have much to handle). Peter used to boast to Peter Porter that unlike apparently 'straighter' characters such as Porter himself, he had always had a mortgage. But the proposal suggests that Ted did not understand some of the deeper-lying aspects of Peter's temperament. Managing an institute would have meant adopting the kind of 'masculine' public role that he abhorred. Unsurprisingly he declined the offer.

Peter had often complained about living in Falmouth, and claimed it was only the job that kept him there. Now he was free to live where he liked and, by a remarkable synchrony, in the very month when he handed in his notice he received an extremely tempting offer of another job. He was in correspondence with a lecturer at St Andrews University, Graham Bradshaw, who had written an article about Hughes expressing reservations that Peter shared. Bradshaw was keen to establish a writer-in-residence post for Peter at the university, and with Peter's encouragement went to a great deal of trouble working out details and persuading the university authorities. In October 1982 the Head of English wrote offering a three-year post at £6,500 with a university house. This is such a good offer that it is hard to believe Peter refused it, but he did, explaining that 'I should need to disassemble most of my present circumstances: my location, my contacts and conversation with the people who

have been kind enough to mount my work, my library, my accustomed methods of work, and in the change of place to produce
what I think would be a premature dis-location in the poetry that
is at present coming and coming, out of Cornwall (and I mustn't
refuse that spring while it still flows).' When put to the test, the ties
that bound him to Cornwall were stronger than his reasons for
dissatisfaction.

He was never to have a salaried job again but he did start a new
'career' as a counsellor and therapist. Over the next few years he
built up a practice with eight or nine clients at a time, charging £20
per hour. Naturally he based his methods on Layard's, but he
observed boundaries that Layard had ignored – there is no evidence
that he got into bed with his clients. The records of these consultations are of course confidential, but there is some evidence of his
approach in correspondence with a close friend, the poet Frances
Horovitz. She was a friend of Penny's from *Aylesford Review* days,
and in 1975 the three of them had collaborated on a presentation
at the Cheltenham Festival. By 1983 Frances was dying of cancer,
and she had an intense correspondence with Peter, much of it written
from hospital, in which she showed great trust in his sympathetic
powers. He gave her techniques for managing pain by meditation,
encouraged her to do spontaneous writing, and interpreted her
dreams. One dream that he interpreted at length was of swimming
in deep water with a whale and being nervous 'because I knew he
was going to make love to me and I thought it would hurt. But it
didn't and I enjoyed it! Then afterwards, as part of the ocean, coming
to the realisation that the taste of water is the most beautiful and
divine taste there could ever be.'

There are many dream interpretations in Peter's correspondence,
and his reply to Frances is typical of his approach:

The whale-dream is a wonderful hospital-dream, and compensates
for the first treatment by showing healing going on deep within. The
waters are sex, or feeling, or womb-sea, and the whale is your warm-
blooded companion of the womb, your brother of the womb, the
one who has been with you since you were conceived, and is now
uttering himself to you, through the taste of the water, which is his
love and his seed, which is also the taste of your own body. At last,
it says, you are doing something for yourself alone – how can you
be complete without this hugging of yourself? (Love thy neighbour
as thyself, and if you don't love thyself, how can you truly love your

neighbour?) In hospital you were forced to be weak, which is right, so that *things could happen of themselves*, the warm-blooded brother who swims in the beginnings; in your case so developed and strong, greater than human, human-brained, speaking more than human speech, as the whales in the sea do. I have seen dream-sequences in which it was a swimming-pool, the dreamer nervous on the edge, because in the water was a shark, and to gain the freedom of their own water, their own origin, they had to risk eating, or were eaten, before they got that freedom. A shark is a lower form of life than a whale, that is, the inner energies were feared more, were not developed so; but it is so in you because you are a poet; this is your Muse whose body is the whole ocean, full of his song; and this you must catch with your inner, silent ear, however strange and universal it may seem, however imperfectly at first you tune into it, listening with the spontaneous writing, which is at first so hard, and later so healing.

This approach to dream interpretation is startling, perhaps even shocking. How can he be so confident in assigning meanings to the dream of someone, however close a friend, with whom he is only corresponding by letter, and who is undergoing an ordeal whose harrowing nature he can only guess at? We might recall Layard telling D. M. Thomas, a complete stranger, that his dream meant he wanted to kill his mother. There is a revealing passage in Bakan's book on Freud and Jewish mysticism, which Peter heavily underlined: 'The interpretation of the dream had priority over the dream itself.' The meaning does not lie inertly in the dream, to be discovered by the interpreter: interpretation is an active, creative process, and in this case Peter is obviously trying to raise Frances's spirits, suggesting that there is a force of health and creative energy in her, that she can use to fight against the disease.

She also asked him to 'exorcise' the image of a dead rook which haunted her, tainting her memory of a beautiful place that was emotionally important to her. In this instance Peter draws upon 'magic', telling her that he has exorcised the image by 'traditional means', and sending her a packet to warm in her hands and smell while 'looking' for the rook. All this is essentially a prelude (akin to the spiritualist's 'conjuring tricks'?) to a process of directed active imagination:

You will see its white bones among the green stems of the plants, and this sign [he draws an ankh cross, a cross with a loop at the head], and planted in this ground a small ash-tree. Please listen to the wind in the ash-leaves. The raven's [*sic*] feathers have blown away.

You may notice the black buds breaking open. You may cut yourself a walking-stick from the tree, first explaining and requesting. It isn't necessary to take a stick, but one will be freely given if you would like it. It is most important to hear the sound of the leaves. You may notice that the black buds have broken into purple flowers; this happened long before the leaves came, and had you come here earlier, you would have seen that the leafless tree had a purple tinge from the flowers. Then you would have noticed the winged 'keys' of the ash, which stay in the branches in clusters rather like bats or birds waiting to migrate.

As this letter suggests, there was a strong overlap between Peter's practice as a counsellor and as a teacher of creative writing. After 1983 he no longer had a job in education, but he had an outlet for his teaching gifts in his courses for the Arvon Foundation and in private consultations. His old friend Nicki Jackowska worked for the American Antioch University's graduate creative writing programme in London, and recommended students to take week-long tutorials with Peter and Penny. One of these students, Renée Gregorio, a quarter of a century later, remembered her encounter with Peter as one of the most formative experiences of her life. She approached the meeting feeling a little fearful because Nicki had told her that Peter was a powerful man and poet, and she followed him into his study with the sense of being on a precipice, facing a leap that could be 'both deathly and exhilarating'. He introduced her to sealed writing, dream interpretation, active imagination, electromagnetism and the body, hypnagogic states and the creative importance of the menstrual cycle (she had previously read *The Wise Wound* which had been her first introduction to 'mind–body connectedness'). She found him to be 'immensely gifted at asking questions that would release a flood of words from the depths of me' and felt 'listened to, deeply heard, keenly felt, and challenged by the immense intellect sitting across from me'. He took an explicitly Jungian approach, emphasising the importance of cultivating all four functions, and it is evident from her account of him that this was not just words, but he exemplified for her that kind of completeness of consciousness. She thought that his greatest gift to her was 'a trust in my own inner life, its shape and validity and magic'.

An extraordinarily uncanny aspect of Renée's meeting with Peter was that she had been the victim of an impostor who pretended to be Ted Hughes. She had fallen in love with this man and the disillusionment had disheartened her 'to the point of my questioning my ability to perceive anything at all with any degree of rightness, never mind be a poet.' She was understandably embarrassed and angry about this experience, and careful not to mention it to Peter until their final afternoon together, when it all 'came tumbling out'. Peter's response was to turn the mortifying experience into a psychological image that she could work with positively. He wrote to her:

> The figure of Ted Hughes is that powerful inner animus that belongs to your poetry as it should be; he represents a kind of daemon or demon-lover who inspires. He will be active at the period (as *The Wise Wound* points out) so it is no wonder he began to emerge during the premenstrual week. He will have the power of the blood, and of the ovum not impregnated, its 'disappointment' and energy, and will speak, if you let him (i.e., please bring him into your relaxation and into your spontaneous writing; and please read his poetry also as you sit down to write your own poetry, let his poetry make you want to write your own . . .). He will also be projected outwards on male friends, and there's no harm in that, so long as you realize it, and realize that he is you, functioning in a special way, with all capacities and resources going, and with special energy, which is yours if you want it, but may appear violent in its urgency. It is especially good that you have this single figure to work with, which is conversable, and which is a poet's image; but you must approach him through the outer Hughes' poetry. I recommend fantasy conversations pursued in the spontaneous writing.

Probably Peter would have been able to work in this way whoever the figure happened to be, but the importance of Hughes in his own inner life must have helped him in counselling Renée. The week they spent together was in April 1984, and in the autumn of that year she attended an Arvon course by Peter and Penny at Totleigh Barton. Peter did not reveal until she had arrived that the guest reader at the course was Hughes himself. By his counsel and by this 'conjuring trick' he 'showed himself capable of bringing the real to life, of showing the difference, of allowing me to face my own demon-lover as image and as man as a form of healing, as the shape of knowledge and becoming'.

Peter equalled the outstanding quality and consistency of *The Apple-Broadcast* with another big collection, *The Man Named East*, in 1985. The title poem, 'In the Pharmacy', 'The Quiet Woman of Chancery Lane', 'Under the Duvet', 'Shells', 'The Proper Halo', 'The Funeral' and 'Lights in the Mist' are all outstanding poems. The title poem is one of his most beautifully tender expressions of connection with the natural world:

> I kneel and dip my hand in, it insists
>
> Into my palm with a slight pressure
> Like a baby's hand, which is still
> The elasticity of yards of water
>
> Reaching down the hill
> From the clouds on high: I crouch
> With my hand in that baby's hand
>
> Feeling the slight movement of its fingers,
> The light clasp which is love.

'The Proper Halo' is another of Redgrove's engagingly humorous narratives, in which the 'germ' 'Horus comes to greet you through this oil' is developed into the story of an uncle who brought hair oil from Egypt, with this phrase written on the label, and misheard 'Horus' as 'Horace'. It is Redgrove's most fruitful ground: the meeting of the occult and the familiar, so that whenever the speaker has his hair oiled at the barber's he feels 'In a halo of light and scent, godly contained'.

He also published two shorter themed collections with small presses: *The Work of Water* and *The Mudlark Poems and Grand Buveur*. But he was as dissatisfied as ever with Routledge's marketing of his work and, in the year *The Man Named East* was published, events conjoined at last to bring about the break that he had long contemplated. In September he wrote to Norman Franklin, one of many letters over the years on this theme, pointing out that 'your ordinary semi-unknown Faber author will sell from 5,000–15,000', while Routledge had printed only 1,200 of *The Man Named East*. I happened just at this time to have sent Franklin a proposal for a critical study of Redgrove's poetry, and Peter hoped he would accept this, believing (probably erroneously) that it would help his sales. Before his letter got into the post I informed him that Franklin had turned down my proposal, on the grounds that critical studies of individual authors were difficult to sell, and studies of living authors rapidly went out of date. Peter added a postscript to his letter to Franklin pleading with him to change his mind. Franklin did not answer Peter's letter for nearly two months, saying when he finally did write that he felt it was a 'bleat of complaint (probably very justifiable)' which he could not answer: what Peter said about his sales was irrefutable, but there was nothing he could do about it, and he held by his opinion about critical studies of writers who were still active.

In the meantime there had been a new and, to Peter, very exciting development. Earlier in the year he had written to Penguin asking if they would like to do a selection of his poems. Jacqueline Korn had been negotiating with Penguin, who were reluctant to bring out a 'new' paperback, but would be interested if a hardback came out first. At the same time their editor, Robin Robertson, moved to Secker & Warburg as senior editor responsible for fiction and poetry. Robertson was interested in publishing the Selected Poems with Secker and having an option on Redgrove's next collection. Peter responded enthusiastically: he believed that Secker, like Faber, was a publisher capable of marketing poetry, and he looked forward to working with a more active editor than he had been used to at Routledge. He exchanged sorrowful and gentlemanly letters of parting with Franklin, and by February he had delivered to Robertson the typescript from which would emerge his next collection, *In the Hall of the Saurians*. As we shall see, this was not just a change of publisher but an epoch in the way Redgrove's poetry was presented to the public.

Any sadness Peter felt about the break with Routledge was more than outweighed by the promise of more effective publication. But 1985 brought the end of another connection that was purely sad. For a number of years one of his devoted readers had been a retired biscuit-maker from Bootle on Merseyside, J. H. Barclay, who had left school at thirteen. Mr Barclay (as Peter always addressed him) collected all his publications including, when possible, poems in magazines, and travelled to London just to hear Peter read. He visited Falmouth to see the places Peter wrote about, always careful not to intrude; Peter and Penny would invite him for a meal, and each time he brought a soft toy for Zoe. In April 1985 he went to the launch of *The Man Named East*, caught flu, and died ten days later at the age of seventy-nine. He once wrote, 'I cannot express how much your poems mean to me. I hope that I am not being a nuisance in writing to you. I am terrified that I may lose the kindness you have shown me by being too forward.' That his poetry 'spoke directly' to such a man, who responded with enthusiasm and understanding, was, as Peter said on Mr Barclay's death, a great comfort to him.

XI

The Death of the Father 1986–89

In 1986 Pete, now aged twenty-six, and his long-time girlfriend Claire were planning to marry, but Pete's fortunes were blighted again by a recurrence of Hodgkin's lymphoma. Again he had to have chemotherapy, and again this affected him psychologically, with depression and OCD, though not as severely as the first time. In Claire's words, the effect of the chemotherapy 'took him away as a person'. He rode a motorbike and, when putting on his leather jacket, if the day before had been a good one he had to fasten the zip and poppers in exactly the same order. There was a street in Selsey that he would never ride along because it was unlucky.

However, this relapse gave Peter the opportunity to compensate – to Pete if not to Bill – for his failure to help when Pete had been a teenager. He consulted a complementary therapist in Devon called Michael Ash, and sent Pete copies of Ash's books on natural healing and respiratory exercises. He spoke to Pete frequently on the phone and wrote him encouraging letters, saying he was proud of him for 'standing up to the doctors'. He also paid Ash to engage in 'absent healing'. What form this took is unclear, but evidently it was at least in part aimed at curing the infertility that the chemotherapy had caused. Pete was receptive to the absent healing, and consulted a faith healer himself. There was no cure for the infertility, but Pete did recover again from the cancer and Claire thought his father's attention helped him to 'get himself back together' more quickly. He felt that he had got his father back. According to a spiritual healers' association website, absent healing can work even if patients are unaware of it, 'coming as it does from the love and concern their friends and relatives have for them'. In a case such as this, when Pete was very much aware, it is quite believable that he benefited from this unwonted attention from his father. Indeed, there is a curious and not entirely ironic fittingness in the absent father showing his love for his son by absent healing. As he explained to Ash, 'The family is estranged, and I must take care not to come in too heavily.'

Later that year Pete was well enough recovered to go through with the wedding, which Peter went to – the only one of his children's weddings that he did attend. This was important to Pete, and confirmation of the special tenderness that Peter felt for this son, even though he had failed him in so many ways.

During this period Peter was working on his second discursive prose book – this time as sole author – which was published in 1987 in Britain with the title *The Black Goddess and the Sixth Sense*, though I think the American title *The Black Goddess and the Unseen Real* gives a more accurate idea of its contents. This book was not to achieve anything like the notoriety of *The Wise Wound*, which is a pity since, while it doesn't have the revolutionary impact of its predecessor, it gives a more whole and wide-ranging idea of its author's preoccupations, and is less disfigured by the intrusion of partially disguised obsessions. He took the title from Robert Graves, who wrote of the Black Goddess as 'so far hardly more than a word of hope whispered among the few who have served their apprenticeship to the White Goddess'. Peter regarded Graves's *White Goddess* as 'a kind of war-poem to the cruel aspects of the Terrible Goddess', and he takes the Black Goddess, by contrast, as a symbol of an entirely benign natural force, though like all forces potentially dangerous if repressed. The symbol encapsulates his preoccupation with the feminine, with the dark aspects of the psyche, with mud of course, but above all with multifarious elements in the human environment that are felt but not understood, experienced only through what he calls the unconscious senses or 'blindsight'. There is nothing supernatural about this whatever, though some of it may be questionable to orthodox science. He places himself in the tradition of Romantic scientists and philosophers such as Johann Wilhelm Ritter who conceived of nature as a cosmic animal or *All-Tier*, Friedrich Schelling who 'identified the principle of life with an ethereal or electrical fluid', and Novalis for whom the galvanic current was 'the higher consciousness of nature – of the soul of nature'. His project can be summed up as the promotion of a science that embraces subjectivity, or a world view in which science and religion are integral to each other.

Much of *The Black Goddess*, like *The Wise Wound*, argues from the citation of scientific publications, but at its centre is a section titled 'Vision at Land's End', of which this is an extract:

> The feeling-in-the-air, which draws me again and again to this place as though it connected me to the whole world, I will call perception and not a subjective illusion; perhaps by study I may see more because I feel more. I know, as we two walk the cliff-path underneath, that the clouds are charged with that life-force we call electricity and, as they scud over, their fields press on our own, which press back. I see them beginning to build into a thunder-anvil, and I feel something in the sight which is more than an appreciation of their manifest forms; I begin to feel them vibrate with a faint seen-echo-thunder that leaves with a prickling of hairs as the high white castle blows out to sea harmlessly.
>
> The sun has come out, but there are still clouds in the sky. The sun beams down upon them, and its power charges up the water-vapour and ice-crystals of which they are composed, and in which are dissolved the essences of living things, drawn up from the land: the distillations of trees, flowers, animals and people which begin to re-radiate and add the tone of their lives to the light which excites these molecules: nature's memory, or one of nature's memories.
>
> This must be why I see so many shapes in the clouds! There, that one is shaped exactly like a map of this part of the coast; that one like a floating version of the woodland on the hill over there; that one like a crowd of faces. I know the clouds are the crests of the water-vapour that pours up from the land, and so, as the crests of the sea-waves echo off the rocks of the coastline in a visible shaped margin, their forms cannot be independent of their source. I know that just as every cloud has a light-shadow, it has an electrical shadow too, which I feel by my sense of touch, by my whole skin, for the ionisation of the ground alters as each cloud passes over, and my lungs breathe this charged air.

This passage epitomises the way that, for Redgrove, 'vision' is inseparable from sensation, and can be articulated in terms of knowledge. It is deeply personal, because experiences such as weather-sensitivity were a plague to him as well as revelatory: revelatory because he addressed rather than suppressed the painful symptoms. It is also a vivid instance of his Jungian beliefs: intellect, sensation, feeling and intuition all come into play in his attempt to convey the totality of the experience. Redgrove even suggests that the normally 'unconscious senses' that rise into consciousness in this passage are the foundation of Jung's most famous idea, the 'collective unconscious'. In the late seventies he had taken the bold step of writing a poem that was based on one of Jung's most important dreams: the dream which, he said, led to the discovery of the collective unconscious. In it the dreamer passes from the upper storey of a house, furnished in rococo style and hung with precious paintings, through the lower storey which has medieval furnishings, and a cellar dating from Roman times, to a lower level still which is scattered with 'remains of a primitive culture'. Jung interpreted the dream as a descent from consciousness through the personal layers of the unconscious to something impersonal and collective: the 'primitive psyche of man' which 'borders on the life of the animal soul'. In Redgrove's poem 'Silence Fiction' there are only two layers, but the descent is similarly into a realm more unadorned and fundamental; most significantly, the descent is marked by a much stronger sensuous awareness than Jung's original:

> We unlock and descend into the cellar-roots,
>
> Light in the chimney-roots our lower fires,
> And begin our lives on the unadorned earth floor
>
> Some of which is sheer sand, elsewhere silky clay.
> There we find shells of earliest cookery, and our fingertips
>
> In the dirt encounter marvels of red-ochre bones,
> Our torches tossing shadow like black potter's clay.
>
> The wind blows through the upper houses, and the rain blows,
> Cleansing hearth and porch, rinsing chimney. (*AB* p. 120)

In *The Black Goddess* Redgrove seizes on a Jungian phrase in an unpublished seminar work, 'somatic unconscious', and asserts that this is 'the physical, genetic basis for his "collective unconscious".'

Jung is also a crucial influence on the way Redgrove deals with the figure of Oedipus in *The Black Goddess*. One of Jung's quarrels with Freud was that he rejected the primacy and inevitability of the Oedipus Complex. In a passage marked by Redgrove in his copy of *The Development of Personality*, Jung asserts that the Oedipus Complex is a symptom not a cause, and that infantile incestuous feelings are a metaphor. What they are a metaphor of is elaborated in another passage that Redgrove quotes, in which Jung argues that the Sphinx's riddle was a trap for the hubristic masculine intellect: that the riddle of the Sphinx was *herself*, a feminine image who mediates between the conscious and unconscious, the mind and the body. By answering in the way he does, Oedipus overestimates the intellect and condemns himself to the crime of incest. For Redgrove Oedipus thus becomes a symbol of the fate of the 'questing, visualising modern scientific intelligence'.

The personal undercurrent in all this is obvious. But, unlike for example the notion in *The Wise Wound* that a son may resemble a lover encountered when the mother is pregnant, it is not merely the irruption of an obsessive fantasy, but a fully responsible working out in cultural terms of his own psychological experience. Peter had come to see the 'good boy', the youthful scientist he had been, as a kind of Jungian Oedipus who turned his back on the revelations of his own dark side – revelations that he traced to his early relationship with his mother. He reads his own experience in terms of his critique of technological society which 'advanced by a deliberate act of self-blinding in the presence of the living riddles of the Sphinx' when it preferred the mechanistic electricity of Volta to the 'animal electricity' of Galvani – and has done so ever since.

However, this does not mean that Peter's own Oedipal conflicts were resolved – far from it. In October 1986 I visited him to conduct an interview, and casually mentioned that Cliff Ashcroft had pointed out a resemblance between him and Aleister Crowley. 'Did you ever meet Crowley?' I asked. 'No,' he replied, 'but my mother may have.' He didn't tell me that in June of that year he had written the following letter to the Warburg Institute, where Crowley's papers are lodged.

> I have a close friend on whom is dawning the possibility that he may be the illegitimate son of Crowley. I have promised him that I will do what I can to settle whether this is a delusion or no; he is not at all distressed by this thought (as why should he be?) but would regard it as an honour if it proved to be so. It would also settle a number of personal puzzles in his life.
>
> His resemblance to Crowley has been pointed out by a number of friends, to an increasing extent. (He is in his early fifties.) This has caused him to remember various stories his (now deceased) mother told him in his childhood. The chief of these is that she married hoping to have a child, but was unable to do so until she had taken

a lover. There were parallel stories of engaging in black magic. She lived at Kingston, Surrey, and often travelled to Richmond. There was also some talk of a boat or boatyard. She used the word 'atavisms' a great deal. Her name was Nan, and this was what she was usually called, and sometimes she took the surname 'Gordon'. The time would be early 1931, possibly in the spring.

My friend has read that Crowley was active at this time in this area, and that he was attempting to have sons and daughters, to 'coin his image'. He would be very grateful for any information that might disclose this parentage, and which might even open up the possibility of his meeting his siblings, or nephews and nieces, in due time. I should say that my friend has strong intuitive, magical and clairvoyant powers, which he has not sought to exercise, but which have come upon him almost inadvertently, which have been influential on others' lives, and which have corresponded very closely to points of Crowley's doctrines without his prior knowledge.

A note on this letter says that Peter didn't send it but phoned instead. He kept it in an envelope with photos of himself and Crowley. We don't know the outcome of the phone conversation, but in 1988 he wrote to Francis King, author of *The Magical World of Aleister Crowley*, with a similar enquiry, saying his mother had told him 'that there was some particular operation or event during March 1931 [when he was conceived] which involved the "Master"', and in 1990 he wrote again to the Warburg Institute, enquiring about Crowley's whereabouts in 1931. This time he did send the letter, and the reply, that the evidence was not entirely conclusive but letters suggested that Crowley was in Germany, seemed to satisfy him. Nevertheless he was still juxtaposing photos of himself and Crowley as late as 1995.

In early June 1987, the year *The Black Goddess* was published, he dreamed about Jim getting cross with him because he didn't know something, and felt resentful about Jim 'always putting me down over such things'. The dream ended in an embrace between father and son, which gave Peter a 'great feeling'. Conflict was not so easily resolved in the outer world. A few days later Jim came to Falmouth for a visit, when Peter was made to feel intensely uncomfortable by what he called the 'smells & electricity off this bull of a man' (now in his eighties), which he thought were the source of his obsessions, and which made him feel he had to run to get away. Their difficult relationship was entering a new phase, because

Jim was beginning to prepare for his own death. He must have thought the visit went well because a few days afterwards he wrote asking if Peter would be an executor. He agreed immediately, but the commitment was to be a source of anguish to him.

He had already begun to suffer from a new and strange obsession, which he increasingly explained with reference to his feelings about his father. Earlier that year Cliff Ashcroft had introduced Peter to a friend of his who was the high priest of a Wicca coven. Cliff himself described R (as Peter calls him in his journal) as 'a lovely warm man', and not at all overbearing: on the contrary, R's wife, not he, was the dominant figure in the coven. Peter met him only twice, but over a period of about two years he was painfully disturbed by R's image intruding into his consciousness, arousing feelings of fear, hostility and jealousy. He describes R as a 'Public School homosexual bully', a type of the domineering male leader that was one of the reasons for his keeping clear of pagan groups, worries that he might have a bad effect on Cliff, and admits to jealous fear that R (who was older than Cliff) might be usurping his position as father-figure to their young friend. It is typical of Peter that he constantly reiterates his recognition that these feelings are projections – he instructs a future reader of his journal that R is 'an imaginary figure not referring to any actual person' – yet remains none the less in their grip. He analysed the figure of R as 'my own obsession and shadow-fight coming to terms with my homosexual shadow based on my relationships [sic] to my father who at this time was dying or preparing for death'. He thus linked the obsession with Jim asking him to be an executor. As Peter saw it Jim 'wanted to place his affection somewhere preferably with his son'. He asked Peter to accompany him to a commemoration at Taunton School. Peter refused: 'I would have been completely split and false by going to Taunton.' So he doubtless would have been, at least in Jim's company, but he came to see this refusal as an instance of 'the destructive rejection of my father's love'. Relations between them were so cross-grained that he could only have accepted Jim's love by doing something that was false to himself.

We should however admit a grain of salt in accepting this explanation of the obsession with R. The intrusiveness of R's image became really disturbing in May 1987 and, when he was reconstructing these events two years later, Peter dated Jim's request about the executorship on 8 May, a month before the correct date. His memory had adjusted the dates to create a causal sequence. The case of R was a particularly persistent and troubling one, and unique in that it focused on someone he hardly knew, but Peter thought there was a pattern of projection in his relations with men, especially ones who had been important to him, starting with Ernest Neal and including Ted Hughes, Dennis Creffield and John Layard. He was acquainted in Falmouth with the magician and showman Tony 'Doc' Shiels who had taken a famous photo of the Loch Ness Monster and claimed also to have photographed a fabled sea-monster called the Morgawr near Falmouth. Eighteen months after Jim's death, in the middle of one of his three-day benders, Peter went to the pub with Shiels and found himself on the floor, Shiels standing over him holding a broken chair, and with no memory of how this had come about. He tries several times to account for what happened, and comments that this is part of the 'pattern', attributing the violence with Shiels to an obsession similar to that with R. It is no accident that Shiels was a magician, R a Wicca leader, and he linked such charismatic men with his father's persona as card-sharper and Freemason.

He sent Jim the first fruit of his new relationship with Secker, his second 'selected poems' titled *The Moon Disposes*. Writing to thank him, Jim singled out some of his favourites, which included predictably 'Memorial' and also 'My Father's Kingdoms', written ten years earlier and collected in *The Weddings at Nether Powers*. This poem is a recall of his childhood consciousness for which the public world of London – the lions of Trafalgar Square, the policemen, the sparkling shoes of the city workers, St Paul's, the BBC, the trains and the clocks, 'Selfridges and Father Xmas and Richmond Park' – all 'belonged to my father'. A couple of years later, just before Jim's death, he would remind himself of the 'positive father also paternalistic maybe showing me so plainly how to do things, in the car, unreeling the world'. Even so, the poem is perhaps more double-edged than Jim was prepared to acknowledge, ending as it does, 'Even the bombs that fell on London / Belonged, he let a few in.'

In August 1987 Peter stayed over with Jim in Hampstead, en route for Edinburgh. Jim told him of a plan he had hatched for instructing his executors. He would make a tape itemising all his belongings, which the executors would take around the house checking items off. This very characteristic scheme shows how little, even at the end, Jim understood his son's temperament. Short of actually seeing Jim's ghost, nothing could be more guaranteed to spook Peter than having to wander around the house listening to the disembodied voice of his dead father. During the night he had a panic attack and called Jim out of his bed. Hyperventilating, on his knees, he sobbed and told his father he didn't want him to die. 'I said how he was too much for me. I said he is so strong.' Jim replied, saying something like, 'My mother's at the helm,' perhaps meaning that he owed his strength to the example or inheritance of his own mother.

It wasn't till eighteen months later, almost at the last minute, that Peter wrote to Jim withdrawing his agreement to act as executor. He gave as reasons the fact that he lived so far away, that he had no experience or 'capacity to handle business affairs', and that his health was 'delicate and unstable'. Even in his journal he later wrote, 'I would have done it badly through my fear and hatred of money.' But in reality he was good at handling money, though he hated it, and never lost control of his personal finances even when he was hard up. He came nearer the truth at the time when he wrote, 'Woke realising must cancel agreement to be executor, the approach of that relationship on [my] unconscious.'

Jim died on 27 April 1989. He cancelled the home help, paid his outstanding bills, wrote a note reassuring his survivors about a missing budgie, and laid out on the dining room table the documents that his executors would need to consult. Then he put on the St Christopher medallion that Nan had given him for their golden wedding, went upstairs to the bedroom and sat at the dressing table, with its three mirrors for seeing oneself at different angles. One can be sure that a woman as concerned for her appearance as Nan would have spent many hours in front of those mirrors, and perhaps, looking into them, Jim thought he was following her. Anyway, there he died. He could hardly have bequeathed his son a more striking example of resoluteness in death or, indeed, a more resonant set of images for his poetry. Peter called it a 'death-poem' and a gift to himself. It allowed him to respect his father in death and provided him with an 'emblem' or 'teaching-story', which was to inspire one of his most memorable poems, 'My Father's Trapdoors'.

The night after hearing of Jim's death Peter recorded a dream of his father in a helicopter, saying, 'Don't be afraid that by looking at both screens I shall fall out of the sky.' Peter had recently changed his system of writing. He gave up using notebooks, and from now on he bound the loose sheets with everything from unprocessed journal material to final drafts into monthly gatherings that he called 'fascicles' (the length of the month of course being determined by Penny's period). Into each fascicle he incorporated what he called a 'menstrual mandala': a circular diagram divided into segments representing days of the month and concentric rings in which he recorded the weather conditions, whether he dreamed, sexual activity including the Game, drinking and so on. The mandala for this month shows that he drank for four days after Jim's death, with G for Game on three days. But if this shows him descending into the worlds of the mudlark and *grand buveur* under the stress of his loss, he also made a remarkable resolution, which he kept to. He would undertake the complete course of pranayama yoga, and read the Bible through twice, once in the King James version and once in a modern translation. It seems as if, on his own terms, he was emulating Jim's disciplined approach to life. Penny tried to defuse his grief by saying, 'Your father tortured you all your life,' but Peter could not remain satisfied with such a simply antagonistic view. He wrote in his journal, 'Or was it that he tortured himself, and through himself, those closest to him?' At the funeral, probably prompted by Barbara, the officiating clergyman acknowledged that while Jim 'retained throughout his life his almost small-boy sense of fun . . . this did not exclude a strong feeling for what was proper, which could make things difficult with others, especially those close to him, who did not see things in quite the same way'.

Jim's net estate was worth just over £300,000. After some small bequests to his uncle, the Old Tauntonians and Masonic Lodges, Peter inherited £143,000; an equal sum was divided between Barbara, Bill, Pete and Kate. Provision in the will in case Peter predeceased Jim showed that Penny would have been left as much as Barbara, and Zoe the same as the other children. Peter could now be more selective about the paid jobs he took on. He also ran down his counselling practice. He could now afford to do without this income, but his reason was that the turmoil of coping with his father's death made it difficult for him to engage with others' difficulties.

In the late eighties a former student of Peter's, Gerard Woodward, returned to Falmouth and met Peter by chance in the pub. As with

Martin Bell many years earlier, Peter invited him to Falmouth Poetry Group. Thus began one of the most notable writing careers of Peter's protégés: Woodward published his first collection in 1991 and went on to become a Booker-shortlisted novelist. Gerard was amazed to see Peter 'democratically' attending the group, and was impressed by its relaxed atmosphere. However, he was innocently the cause of a rupture. One of the most forthright members of the group, and a good friend of Peter, was Sylvia Kantaris, a Derbyshire-born poet who had settled in Helston. She had published several collections including a collaboration with D. M. Thomas (who also attended the group at this time), and this may have made her more confident in confronting Peter than some of the other members. At a meeting in February 1988 she criticised one of his poems, resulting in what he himself apologetically called a 'flaming row', and shortly afterwards she annoyed him again by arguing that Gerard, then a tyro poet, was imitating him too closely. Peter stopped attending shortly afterwards, much to Gerard's disappointment.

Meanwhile Peter was adjusting to his new publisher. Early in 1986 he submitted 149 poems for consideration by Robin Robertson. Robertson replied, 'I like 23 enough to publish and would hold 9 as borderline. We might, therefore, need a few more over the next six months.' This was not what he had been used to at Routledge, where Franklin had taken a much less hands-on approach to compiling collections. In fact, only twenty-one of these poems made it to the 1987 collection *In the Hall of the Saurians*, though strangely a further twelve of them were published in its successor *The First Earthquake* (1989). Peter declared himself exhilarated by the 'feeling of whole-hearted enthusiasm and energetic commitment' from Robertson, and even by his editor's 'sharp scythe'. He was maintaining the same high level of consistency in his poetry, and some of his strongest work is in these collections. 'The Big Sleep' (*IHS*) is an outstanding example of his use of the supple-rhythmed long sentence to convey continuity between consciousness and the natural world; and 'Wooden Pipes' (*FE*), inspired by a dream about Zoe, is one of his most tender poems. But, whereas *The Man Named East*, his last Routledge collection, had contained 88 poems in 137 pages, *In the Hall of the Saurians* eventually had only 34 in 54 pages. Robertson thought that the Routledge volumes were 'baggy and under-edited', and believed that Peter should be represented by a 'tight group' of what he considered his best poems. Certainly, as a consequence, the Secker volumes have fewer weak poems than their predecessors, and are less daunting to a reader not already committed to Redgrove. But Peter had a natural affection for the bigger collections of earlier times, which he came to believe more fully represented the range of his achievement. He sent the remainder of the poems to Michael Farley's Taxus Press, which had published *The Work of Water*. Progress was delayed when Farley could no longer afford the time or money to keep the press going, but eventually the project was taken over by Rupert Loydell's Stride Press, who brought out *Dressed as for a Tarot Pack* in 1990. This was the beginning of a unique arrangement that continued for the rest of Peter's career: each volume from his major trade publisher was shadowed, as it were, by a Stride collection. Robertson's highly selective and decisive approach to publishing Peter's work was an invigorating change from Routledge, but it held at least the potential for conflict.

In the same year that *The Black Goddess* and *In the Hall of the Saurians* were published Peter's career as a radio dramatist reached its peak with a series of six plays adapted from the tales of the Brothers Grimm – the belated fruit of a project that he and Brian Miller had discussed ten years earlier. Unfortunately for Peter, Miller left the BBC in the following year and, although he continued to write for radio, he never recreated the rapport that he had enjoyed with his most sympathetic producer. These plays formed the basis for a collection of stories, *The One Who Set Out to Study Fear*, published by Bloomsbury in 1989. He got a £3,000 advance for this book – far more than he had received for any of his Routledge novels – and he was delighted when he read an enthusiastic review by Angela Carter, one of the writers whose success he had hoped to emulate with his novels, and whose *Bloody Chamber*, which he himself had reviewed favourably, had set the benchmark for enterprises like Peter's new book. She described it as 'a rather mad, wholly idiosyncratic, joltingly uneven collection that takes risks on every page, and crazily, marvellously, survives them by the intensity of Redgrove's vision, the ancient power of the material'. Her accolade, 'Redgrove's language can light up a page', was to have pride of place in critical assessments on the jackets of all his subsequent books. Peter hoped that Carter's review was an indication that his fiction in general was more accessible than people seemed to think, but in truth the short stories in *The One Who Set Out to Study Fear*, based on traditional sources, have a much stronger narrative coherence than his novels. It is mystifying that despite this they were no more successful commercially, and he published no more prose fiction.

XII

Decade of Mourning 1990–98

In the early 1990s Peter had a new preoccupation. Many years earlier he had sold a large collection of his papers to the Harry Ransom Center in Austin Texas, and now he hoped to make another big sale. He put his remaining archive in the hands of Sotheby's, through whom he tried unsuccessfully to sell it to the British Library and to Cambridge. Eventually he approached Sheffield where, because of my own interest, teaching and research on his poetry were more active than anywhere else.

A price was soon agreed, and he made £25,000 over five years from the sale, but negotiations were protracted for reasons that had nothing to do with money. This new archive was significantly different from the one he had sold to Texas. Those papers consisted almost entirely of the drafts of poems. Some personal material had begun to emerge in the notebooks during the 1960s, but the intimate exposure was limited. From the 1970s onward, by contrast, he had begun to record a great deal of personal material, including reference to the Game. This was an important aspect of his developing method of composition: the 'germ' origins from which the process of 'work and incubation' progressed. He believed – I think rightly – that this archive was of unusual interest, and could form the basis for a study of the psychology of poetic creation.

However, those very aspects of the archive that made it uniquely interesting were also the cause of great anxiety. He was very excited about the prospect of serious research into the hinterland of his poetry, but he was obsessively worried about unsympathetic readers exposing his secrets in a derisive and embarrassing way. He managed to control this anxiety by restricting access to some of the journals that consisted entirely of personal material – though at the cost of limiting the exhaustive evidence of the creative process which gives the archive its special value. An even greater anxiety arose from the fact that this archive, unlike the Texas one, includes a large amount of correspondence. Peter was told that, in the event of libellous material being published, not only the author of the libel and the person publishing it would be liable to legal action, but also the person who put the libel into the public realm – the creator of the archive. A large correspondence, especially among writers, is bound to contain libels, and the amount of material was too vast for him to go through it and make it safe himself. 'Supposing someone takes offence at X saying so and so writes poetry dressed in his mother's clothes,' he worried as he was packing up the last boxes to send to Sheffield. He consulted the I Ching: 'I have fear about the Sheffield Agreement. P[enny] is convinced that it is safe, and I would like to be convinced too, so that it does not worry me. Please advise me how to manage these matters.' (Like all his magical practices, the I Ching was a means of accessing his own inner resources.) This problem was resolved by an agreement that the library would make everybody who used the archive sign a statement indemnifying Peter (and the university) in the event of their being responsible for the dissemination of libellous material.

During one of his visits to Sheffield to discuss the archive I witnessed a poetic 'germ'. I took him to a Derbyshire pub where a petrified cat was displayed in a glass case, a victim of an old lead miners' custom of walling up live cats underground 'for luck'. Water seeping through the porous limestone gradually covered the cat in a coat of stone. Over the years Peter sent me drafts of what eventually turned into two completely separate pieces, a prose poem in *What the Black Mirror Saw* (1997) and a verse poem in *From the Virgil Caverns* (2002), both titled 'Limestone Cat'. Beyond the image of the stone cat, neither of these poems shows any trace of its origin, which in the case of the verse poem occurred eleven years before book publication.

Despite his anxieties Peter gained much satisfaction from the thought that his great productive organism was in the public realm: from the affirmation that this represented, and from the possibility of scholars working on it. Although, like most writers, he was often scathing about the academic study of literature, he maintained – perhaps because of Hobsbaum's influence – a belief in the possibility that his work might be taught and written about with sensitive insight. He showed this with his response to Cliff Ashcroft's thesis, to the many reviewers with whom he engaged in courteous correspondence, and he was heartened when I published the first book on his poetry, in 1994.

His method continued to be highly productive, and his work was still taking new directions. In the spring of 1991 he submitted to Robin Robertson a typescript of 468 pages and 280 poems titled 'Poems Sept 88–March 91': he had completed two poems per week over this period. Robertson would have been planning a publication of between fifty and sixty pages, so he was clearly presented with a challenge. The resulting book, *Under the Reservoir*, consists of only twenty-five poems, admittedly including the long sequence 'Buveur's Farewell'. Robertson wrote, 'After deep immersion in Redgrove I have surfaced, drunk, with list in hand; listing. I'm less sure this time that my choice is sound, so will value our lunch.' His metaphor of immersion vividly conjures the experience of reading large amounts of Redgrove's poetry. Despite his stated tentativeness, fifteen of the sixteen poems on his 'certain' list made it into the book.

Robertson added a further list of fifty-six 'possibles', and there ensued an elaborate negotiation in which Peter enlisted Penny's advice. Peter and Penny each made a selection, and Peter drew up a list on what he called a '"most votes" principle'. He used this list, forty-one poems estimated at ninety-four pages, to argue for a bigger book, closer in scale to his later Routledge volumes:

> I would be very happy if this could be the book. Its length may dismay but in defence of that it is the Sixtieth [birthday] Bumper Issue; it celebrates an active and what some people would call 'late' fertile period in which my work has changed considerably; from the reviews, people seem to like the longer books; I do prefer that if people are going to start thinking of me as an old man that [*sic*] I should be publishing like a young man, not as others do, offering notes from retirement; and maybe a broad, strong and confident collection will give me a better stab at the Whitbread for which I've been shortlisted twice!

The book eventually published was little more than half this size, and included only three poems that were not on either Robertson's short or longer list. Robertson asked Redgrove if he felt 'hard done by', and Redgrove replied that he was 'happy and proud of my Secker books', adding, however, 'I feel a few more pages might be more representative.' He was not just talking about quantity. He told Robertson that he did not think *Under the Reservoir* was 'a Gaia book' because 'both you and Penelope have favoured the "facetious" poems over the environmental ones: in these there is a mocking element as with short sharp jabs . . .' (It is unusual for him to associate Penny with this point of view, as she generally supported his judgement.) This is one of a number of comments in which Redgrove suggests that it was not only the comparative brevity of the Secker/Cape volumes that frustrated him, but their character. Robertson favoured 'something lyrical, something self-contained in its own narrative' and left out what he considered 'the slightly wilder, less disciplined' poems. In this he was not merely indulging a personal preference, but presenting Redgrove's work in the way that he thought would find most favour with the public. Peter continued to publish supplementary volumes with Stride Press, run by Rupert Loydell, who by contrast with Robertson liked poems that 'allowed the reader to get into and wade around within a subject', poems with 'a kind of obsession, a subject tackled from a hundred viewpoints'. Redgrove began to think of these small press publications as an 'alternative stream' of his work. It is very strange, however, that by submitting so many poems he effectively ceded control over his main trade collections to his editor: if Robertson's preference had been different, presumably a book like *Under the Reservoir* could have been a completely different set of poems.

Under the Reservoir includes many excellent and characteristic poems such as the title poem, 'The Small Earthquake', 'The Secret Examination' and 'Falmouth Clouds', but it is most notable for the long sequence 'Buveur's Farewell', in which a new note enters Redgrove's work. The sequence resurrects the figure of 'Buveur' from the earlier small press collection *The Mudlark Poems and Grand Buveur*, but these poems have a quite different tone from the earlier ones. *Grand Buveur* had been predominantly a celebration of its hero's drinking exploits, but 'Buveur's Farewell' has a much darker, self-lacerating tone:

> I have stolen my head from myself,
> I have stolen my hands, my legs, my liver,

Being stolen they are no good to me,
My hands cut off, my feet cut off,
My mouth sealed, my bride eloped . . .

I walk back
From the pub like blind Oedipus
Sockets weeping brown ale,
I will return again to these bars
In the town called Colonus, again and again
Until I can no longer be found;

Do you call these sanctuaries gracious
When they show me as I am to my lover and child first
And to myself only at the very last.

In the 1960s he had sometimes cited his family responsibilities as a reason why he drank. Now they are a reason for despising his drunken self.

These years were also occupied with Peter's complicated mourning for Jim. The father who had loved him without understanding, whose love Peter had therefore rejected, who had been consciously or unconsciously a living reproach to him for his sexuality, academic failure, rejection of a conventional career and the collapse of his first marriage, who had embodied the masculine persona and social conventions from which Peter was in flight, troubled him at least as much in death as in life. Now, however, he was able to approach the trouble directly in his writing. His next collection, *My Father's Trapdoors* (published in 1994 by Cape, to whom Robertson had transferred) has a strong backbone of elegies for Jim – 'Eight Parents', 'A Passing Cloud' and the title poem. Of these the title poem is the most complex and searching. It begins by narrating – in a transparently autobiographical manner unusual for Redgrove – his early alienation from his father, epitomised by his discomfort when Jim gave him a furtive but 'hungry' kiss while seeing him off on the train to school; Jim's extrovert masculine accomplishments, which his son both admires and despises; and, most poignantly, the son's search through his father's house for evidence of him, finding only abandoned objects – 'A neat plump wallet and a corroded bracelet watch / And a plate with a tooth which was hardly dry.' The father has left, in a highly charged phrase, 'Only material for a funeral' and the son's task, rather like a secular version of 'The Case', is to make contact with his spirit. The title refers to the stage-devices with which conjurers managed disappearances, recalling the opposition in Peter's mind between what he considered his father's manipulative conjuring tricks and the 'magic' that he himself encountered in poetry, meditation and sexual experience. In the poem Jim has 'disappeared' himself, a feat that the son seems to resent, recalling the father's ability to 'disappear' him as a child by the force of his dominant personality, including a somewhat parodied but nevertheless autobiographically resonant version of the Oedipal scenario: 'Once in bed cuddly with mother // He waved a wand in his voice / And I got out of the silken double-cabinet / For ever.' However, the poem concludes by transforming fake into 'real' magic, constructing a stage-conjurer's scenario of a silken tent which collapses to reveal the father 'stark naked', stripped of the conjurer's evening dress, with his 'lean rod floating out just as it should, // Floating like my own'. This fancy enables Redgrove to conclude the poem with the healing words, 'pleased to be like him'.

Peter was not done with difficult mourning. In February of the same year in which *My Father's Trapdoors* was published he had a phone call from Pete telling him that Barbara was in hospital with a lump on her gall bladder. She was suffering from pancreatic cancer. He had been thinking, only a few days before, that he needed to 'purify' himself of the anger he still felt towards her, and this news of her serious illness stirred again the long unresolved turmoil of his feelings about their marriage and its conclusion. A few days later he spoke to her on the phone and was shaken to find that her voice 'still had power' over him. The immediate anxieties he felt are not very flattering to him: he worried that when she died he would have to go to the funeral, rehearsed all the reasons why he did not want to go, and thought of excuses for staying away. It was to be several months before he was put to the test. In August it is evident that he still hasn't 'purified' himself: he interprets a dream with reference to 'B making me look bad so she could have an excuse to leave me, and this joining up with my father's love (preferential) for the children . . . a conspiracy to say what a bastard I am'. It is puzzling that a man who was so adept at recognising projection in other obsessive feelings never seems to have seen it in this persistent misconstruction of Barbara's behaviour.

By November her life was obviously drawing towards a close.

She was allowed to leave hospital only on condition that someone was on hand constantly to look after her, and Hilary came to stay with her in Chichester, where she now lived. Her sixty-fifth birthday was on 26 November, and she wanted it to be an occasion when her friends and family gathered to celebrate her life, 'like a wake' as Hilary put it, while she was still alive. She also wanted Peter to come. Her sister, daughter and daughters-in-law all believed that she remained in love with Peter till the end of her life. She never found a serious partner to replace him. She told Kate that she loved him but could not live with him. She was very excited at the prospect of seeing him once more before she died. Peter's feelings, as might be imagined, were much more conflicted. He couldn't face the 'wake' but he went to see her a couple of days beforehand, staying at a hotel nearby. Hilary was aware of how much it cost him, and admired him for it. He and Barbara spent about two hours together. In her white nightdress she reminded him of Violetta in her death scene in *La Traviata*, her favourite opera, and he was struck by the featheriness of her skin. Each of them expressed sorrow for the pain they had caused the other and, as he left, Peter spoke to her Horatio's words to the dead Hamlet: 'And flights of angels sing thee to thy rest.' She had a great fondness for angels, and believed she had seen one which forewarned her of her father's death: she had become a Christian not long after separating from Peter. Hilary believed that she was much more peaceful after the meeting. Afterwards Pete drove him to the hotel and had a meal with him in the evening. They had, for once, the experience of talking naturally as father and son, and Peter was reminded how like him Pete was.

Two days later Barbara had her party. She wrote on the invitations that it was a 'command performance', and wore a long silver dress. On the same day Peter wrote a long poem, 'The Levee', imagining the party:

> She holds her levee
> In her silver full-length dress
> Transforming the enzymes of cancer
> Into a great birthday party
> Between two houses, a street party . . .
>
> And as the fountain gains stature
> It becomes wings,

> She is being withdrawn
> Into the great Angel,
> The partygoers hold the doors open. (*OE*)

A week later Barbara was too ill to remain in Hilary's care, and had to enter a hospice; in another week she was dead, just too early to enjoy her daughter Kate's wedding.

For Peter, Barbara's death 'made part of the world very provisional indeed'. As after Jim's death he plunged into auto-erotic activity which he interpreted as a solstice ritual 'to make B live again, to make the sun live again'. He began to suffer from physical symptoms which he characteristically attributed to the psychosomatic cause of mourning for Barbara. He had shooting pains all over his body, felt constantly tired and regularly had to sleep two hours in the daytime, his legs went watery and he couldn't walk properly, his feet went numb and his sexual energy declined. In his journal the following May he reported, 'Sex not good since B's death,' and in February 1996 he wrote to Peter Porter that 'Barbara's passing hit me harder than I would have believed possible not having lived with her for 25 years.' A fortnight after this he was tested for diabetes. The doctor told him the tests were clear but then discovered that another patient's results had been substituted for his; he was tested again on the spot and registered positive.

He was naturally suspicious that the insulin shock therapy might have been a factor in the development of diabetes. His doctor assured him that this was not the case and, indeed, it is likely that his years of heavy drinking were a major cause. Despite his psychological vulnerabilities he had always been physically robust, and the marked decline in his health hit him hard. It probably made him especially sensitive during the negotiations about his next Cape collection, which were going on in the months after Barbara's death, when his symptoms were becoming noticeable. He submitted a typescript of seventy-five poems, by most standards a healthy selection from two years' work, but notably fewer than he had submitted for *Under the Reservoir* and *My Father's Trapdoors*. Robin Robertson later reflected that this period witnessed a falling-off of Peter's creative powers, which may have been related to his health. Robin made a selection of twenty-five poems, which Peter was very happy with, but on further reflection Robin was less confident that there were enough strong poems to sustain a volume. Peter sent another eighteen poems, but this made matters worse as far as his own confidence was concerned, because Robin did not like any of this supplement.

This response made Peter feel very anxious and agitated. Despite Jacqueline Korn's reassurances that Robin was 'genuine, sincere and a great admirer of your work', Peter became suspicious of his motives, fearing that he was hostile to his poetry and even that he wanted to remove him from Cape's list. He alleged that Robin favoured younger poets and that, as a younger poet himself, he had an Oedipal rivalry, based on envy of Peter's long list of publications. There is perhaps some humorous exaggeration here, but there is undoubtedly evidence that his illness made him feel for the first time vulnerably aged. He was reassured when Robin contracted the book in anticipation of poems to be submitted later, and after Peter had sent a new batch at the end of the year the collection, titled *Assembling a Ghost*, was completed. Harmony was restored to his relations with his editor, and maintained for the rest of his life, but there was no such prospect of his health being restored, and for his remaining years he was increasingly an invalid.

However, in terms of publication Peter's work flowed more prolifically in the 1990s than it ever had. In five years he published nine new books. *Under the Reservoir* in 1992 was supplemented the following year by its Stride companion *The Laborators* and a collection of prose poetry from Bloodaxe, *The Cyclopean Mistress* which reprinted some earlier pieces such as 'Lake Now-And-Again' and 'Dance the Putrefact' but was mostly new work. *My Father's Trapdoors* in 1994 overflowed into *Abyssophone* in 1995, and *Assembling a Ghost* (1996) into *Orchard End*, which Stride published in 1997 simultaneously with another prose poetry collection, *What the Black Mirror Saw*. Increasingly believing that only one aspect of his poetry was represented by the Secker and Cape volumes, and, with a parent's fondness for the overlooked child, claiming to prefer the Stride books, he agitated for a 'Collected Poems' that would bring both 'streams' together. This project remained on his mind till the end of his life, but he was to be disappointed in it. Ever since the publication of *The Wise Wound* in 1978 Peter and Penny had hoped for a sequel, and many proposals were made to publishers, with titles such as 'Creative Menstruation', 'Lucid Orgasm' and 'Deepening'. It wasn't until 1995 that they finally succeeded in bringing out another joint book, called *Alchemy for Women*. Focusing on the correlation between dreams and the menstrual cycle, this book covers similar ground to its predecessor, but is written in a more popular style, somewhat in the manner of a self-help book. However, it didn't emulate *The Wise Wound's* success, and was to be Peter and Penny's last formal collaboration.

In 1996 he received another affirmation, which brought a happy final act to an often difficult old friendship. The Queen's Gold Medal for Poetry was inaugurated in 1933 by George V. It is awarded only occasionally, for a book of verse by a poet from Britain or the Commonwealth, but in practice has always been given to a poet with a substantial record of achievement. It had last been awarded to Kathleen Raine in 1992. Awards are made by a committee chaired by the Poet Laureate, so Peter had the pleasure of knowing that he owed this accolade to Ted Hughes. Ted wrote telling him of the award and hoping that he would not be put off by 'Republican (or other) reservations'. Peter replied assuring him that his ideas on the monarchy 'are close to your own: that the archetypes must be embodied', though in truth he had nothing like Hughes's enthusiasm for the monarchy and had written to his friend M. L. Rosenthal that he 'felt a great sense of betrayal that [Hughes] accepted the Laureateship'. It was Ted's role to accompany Peter into the Queen's presence, and Peter pleaded, on the grounds of his illness, that he might stay with Ted in Devon on the way to London. This, he said, would be 'quite like old times', though he rather pathetically added, 'I hope you don't mind my suggesting this . . . I don't want to force myself on you.' When they parted Peter shook Ted's 'firm, dry' hand and thanked him 'for everything', which he glossed as meaning everything from Cambridge to the present. It was their last meeting.

A couple of years later the *Guardian* published a more double-edged recognition of his standing in the form of a strip cartoon by 'Biff' (Chris Garratt and Mick Kidd). At a drinks party in the Ministry of Culture, Chris Smith and Ian Trethowan, Culture Secretary and Director-General of the BBC, are lamenting the middle-aged, middle-class character of audiences for cultural events. Smith outlines his scheme for 'delivering culture to the masses', culminating, in the final image, with a football ground, resounding to the crowd singing 'Here we go here we go', and the voice of the announcer:

'And now for this Sat'day's half-time poetry reading, please welcome acclaimed wordsmith **Peter Redgrave!!**'

The direct handling of personal material in poems such as 'Buveur's Farewell' and 'My Father's Trapdoors' signalled an autobiographical turn in Redgrove's later writing. In April 1997 Jacqueline Korn suggested that he write a book of memoirs. He eagerly agreed and started writing notes immediately. A brief outline written at this time suggests the kind of orthodox narrative that Jacqueline was hoping for:

> 1. Prebirth & Birth. 2. War and Orchard End. 3. Cambridge, Hughes, Hobsbaum. 4. Chiswick – Martin Bell – Porter – Leeds Witches & Drink. 5. Cornwall Layard 1st Marriage. 6. Rebirth-Dr Faust's Sea-Spiral . . . ICOTS WW. 7. To balance accounts.

However, a note he wrote to himself reporting the project as 'an autobiography to convey ideas, or the converse' might have alarmed Jacqueline if she had seen it. By September he reported that he had written 50,000 words, but not as a consecutive narrative, which he insisted would be inappropriate. Eventually he produced a typescript of more than 300 pages, *Innocent Street*, which is very remote from the kind of book that Jacqueline had in mind. It is very fragmentary, and much of it is cut and pasted from journal entries. This is not necessarily in itself ominous for an early draft, since Peter characteristically worked in this way. But it is very clear that the core of the book is not a set of luminous portraits of people such as Hughes, Hobsbaum, Bell and Layard, or even an accessible narrative of difficult personal experiences such as insulin therapy (which is strangely absent). It is on the contrary a deeply introspective meditation on his relations with his parents, his sexuality and visionary experience. He prefaced it with the statement: 'I use events in my life to raise two questions: how is a person to decide if they were sexually abused as a child; and what is this Eden that haunts us.' Jacqueline was expecting 'the memoir of a poet' with an emphasis on the people he had known, not what she called 'philosophical musings'. When I described the typescript to her she had no recollection of talking to him about a book of that kind.

Innocent Street was a book that Peter needed to write, for himself, to dwell in a concentrated way on all the memories that obsessed him. It is unlikely that he would ever have developed it into a form that would appeal to a publisher. But there was, or at least he so claimed, another factor that brought work on the memoirs to an end. In March 1998 Pete died suddenly of a heart attack. His arteries were hardened – the family believed as a result of his earlier treatment for cancer. Though sudden, his death was not entirely unexpected. He and Claire had known they would not have a long time together. Another consequence of his treatment was that he was unable to have children. Claire knew this when they married, but entered the relationship without considering herself: she put all her energy into his needs. She eventually realised, however, that this was holding back Pete's psychological recovery: 'He spent a lot of time worrying about me. He couldn't be himself because I was in the way.' They separated, and she felt that this gave him the freedom to get better. They had remained very close after their separation, and when they walked together out of the divorce court Pete said to her, 'I don't feel like I'm divorced, do you?' She agreed, and didn't feel she had her own life until after he died.

When Bill phoned to break the news of Pete's death to his father, Peter and Penny were staying with her parents in Staines. Peter was sleeping; Penny waited till he woke before telling him. When he called back he said, 'I saw him born.' He wept about Pete for months afterwards, and associated him with Ben Jonson's elegy for his infant son: 'Ben Jonson his best piece of poetry.' After this he did not feel that he could continue with *Innocent Street*: he was sensitised to the pain that he would cause Bill and Kate by writing about their mother and grandparents in that manner. This sensitivity may have owed something to his seeing Bill at Pete's funeral. It was the first time they had met properly since their estrangement over Pete's ill-health. They hugged and talked for a few minutes. Bill felt that they were reconciled, that there were no 'issues that weren't already gone'. He took Penny to one side and said, 'Look after Dad.' He thought that Pete, always the one to speak up for his father, would have been glad to have been the agent of this coming together. But, if Penny was right, Peter's grief for his son had another more destructive consequence: it was from this time that she detected the onset of a new threat, Parkinson's Disease.

On 28 October Ted Hughes died. Peter recorded the loss of his friend with strange formality: he typed a line in his journal and underneath, in upper case, 'DEATH OF TED HUGHES ANNOUNCED'. A month later he dreamed of Hughes 'alighting from the little train at the Dell', his local station, and woke 'in disbelief that he's dead'. Hughes had not visited Falmouth for thirty years, and now he never would again.

XIII

The Final Years 1999–2003

His legs were increasingly stiff and painful, and the walks with Penny, such an important part of their lives, became more restricted. Friends noticed that he began trembling, and that he found it difficult to follow the thread of conversations. All this combined with diabetic symptoms such as numbness in his feet to age him rapidly, a sad and sometimes shocking contrast to the robust man of a few years ago.

He was mourning Pete, and again, as with Barbara, he associated his declining health with his grief. He wrote out a list of afflictions, in which the symptoms of his physical illnesses are mixed up with his grief and even with echoes of his youthful breakdown: 'horrors', 'no energy', 'menace of everything', 'unreal', 'lose train of thought', 'loss of confidence', 'grief', 'muted sensations'. He felt that he was mourning his own death. In April Penny was called for a routine breast-screening: Peter was sleepless with terror, remembering Barbara's illness, and unwilling to drive her to the test centre. He recorded in his journal: 'Penny sweetly took command.' As she so often had, when Peter's psychological vulnerabilities threatened to overwhelm him. But now she was faced with a new challenge, of finding strategies to help him to cope with his increasing frailty, and the restrictions that this was beginning to impose on both their lives.

One of these strategies was that, for the first time in years, he began regularly attending meetings of the Falmouth Poetry Group. Here he was able to meet once a fortnight with old friends such as Eleanor Maxted, whom he had first known in the Group in the late eighties, and with newer ones including Caroline Carver and Jane Tozer. He also renewed his friendship with Michael Bayley, who had chaired the Group in the 1980s and interviewed him for radio in 1993. This group of friends was to become increasingly important to him and Penny. He would always bring with him to the poetry group a 'bulging and aged brown leather briefcase, patched with mending tape and packed with anthologies and reference books of immense weight', from which he would quote appositely at intervals.

The autobiographical turn in his poetry continued. Poems flowed from the work on *Innocent Street*, but the most revealing ones, about his mother's abortions and his youthful discovery of the Game, remained unpublished. He wrote in his journal, 'I see myself as a child of about 12 [probably the age at which Nan took him into her confidence] – that is the continuity.' There was also one last experimental development. From 1999 onwards the final drafts of nearly all his poems were cast in what he called 'stepped verse'. This is very similar to the 'variable foot' pioneered by William Carlos Williams, but Redgrove claimed to have discovered it in David Young's translations of Rilke's *Duino Elegies*. It is best described by an example, from one of the poems that came from his recent immersion in memories of childhood, 'My Father's Rover' (*FVC*):

> Father's car
> > like the groans
> > > of Loch Ness
> Hyptnotises, his beams
> > sweep across
> > > the darkened ceiling,
> His rhythm as
> > a driver
> > > hypnotises
> He brushes his moustache
> > with a forefinger
> > > like a hypnotist

His attraction to this form was to do with both the aural and the visual aspects of reading. The breaking up of the line is a way of controlling the breath when reading aloud. He also believed that, when looking at the page, the reader's eye is carried in advance: 'One could sense the whole page in advance of the narrative.' He claimed that each column could be read vertically, so that there are four poems in one, but few readers have found much benefit in trying to do this. The breaking up of the visual appearance of the poem on the page, disrupting narrative, may come from the same motive as his refusal to write a chronological account of his life. He told Michael Bayley that poems in this form flow more freely, but Michael believed, on the contrary, that the stepped verse introduces a hesitancy which might echo the symptoms of Parkinson's.

In 2000 Victoria Field, who was at that time married to D. M. Thomas, joined the poetry group, and found that Peter was still 'vibrant'. Everybody deferred to him, in contrast to earlier days when Sylvia Kantaris used to challenge him. But worrying symptoms accumulated. In April his leg was very stiff and painful, and he went to a physiotherapist about it. His handwriting deteriorated, and Penny started to write entries for him in his appointments diary. In June the doctor delivered the verdict of Parkinson's. Already in the previous year Penny had been upset that they had 'lost so much' because of his declining health. Now she wept while describing his symptoms to the doctor. By August Peter feared that he would never be able to walk properly again, though he still benefited from the healing influence of places that were magical to him. One such was the church cove at Gunwalloe on the Lizard, where the church is built almost on the beach, you can see waves crashing on the rocks through the porch, and the pathway is lined with ships' ropes. My wife Christine and I took him and Penny there in August; he meditated a while in the church and felt an acute nostalgia for what he called 'Gunwalloe feelings'. The healing sands took the pain from his foot as long as he trod them. He was no longer able to travel to so many readings and Arvon Foundation events, so sometimes Penny went by herself, and Peter would complain of loneliness. Their creative intimacy, which had been such an emotional and poetic resource to them both for so long, was in danger of turning into a stifling dependency.

By February 2001 Penny was even more worried about Peter's health. He was dizzy and vomiting, unable to keep down his medication. Over the previous two years friends had become anxious about the demands he was making on Penny, and her ability to cope with them. At about this time Michael Bayley saw her in the street, and was shocked by the contrast with the last time he had seen her, only three weeks before. Then he had confessed to her that he was sometimes in awe of Peter, and Penny had replied, with her customary robust humour, that he should 'give him a good kicking'. Now he saw her weighed down by her shopping, and her appearance reminded him grotesquely of the downtrodden Lucky in

Waiting for Godot. She was hunched, harassed and exhausted, and seemed to Michael as if she were focused on some impossible task ahead. She was so different that he was lost for words when they parted at the doorstep of Arwyn Place.

She was indeed focused on an impossible task ahead. She was tortured by terror of the prospect that Peter would live for years with Parkinson's, their lives increasingly narrowing, and guilt because of course she still loved him and didn't want him to die. And this had happened at the worst possible time in her own life, when she was suffering from severe menopausal symptoms, which inflated her feelings and made her burst into tears all the time. The one who could have helped her through this, as he had helped her through her youthful menstrual distress, was gone, consumed by his own deteriorating health, making demands on her that she felt she couldn't possibly fulfil. She was angry and mourning and, because the person she was mourning was still alive, much of her anger was directed at him.

The crisis came in late March. Falmouth Poetry Group friends realised that their situation was serious and spent as much time with them as possible, though in Caroline Carver's case this meant concealing from Peter and Penny that her own health was poor. As well as the doctor, Caroline arranged a visit from a social worker, to discuss Peter's care needs. The social worker kept saying she could weep at the state they were in, and couldn't understand that they had not been referred earlier. The most urgent priority was to give Penny some respite, and Caroline invited her to stay a few days with herself and her husband in Flushing, across the water from Falmouth. Peter refused adamantly to go temporarily into a care home: to him this meant 'being shut up with senile people'. But actually he was resistant to any kind of professional care: being bathed was a 'violation', having food brought in was 'dreadful'. When Penny went off to Caroline's he said, 'I need a holiday too.' Throughout the long-drawn agony of their inability to succour each other, his response to the situation swung between extremes. At times, as here, he was childishly demanding and unsympathetic to Penny's condition. At others he was, as Caroline reported, 'unbelievably patient and gentle' with her.

It was obvious to friends, professionals and to Penny herself that the best single practical step to make things easier would be to move out of Arwyn Place. The tall narrow house with its awkward steps and cramped passages added hugely to the difficulty of caring for someone with Parkinson's, and its small, rather dark rooms deepened the emotional gloom that was beginning to settle on their relationship. They needed to move into a bungalow, but Peter stubbornly refused to consider moving. The thought of it filled him with anxiety, and 'What about the books?' he would exclaim whenever the suggestion was made. The pre-menopausal Penny, the Penny who said to 'give him a good kicking', would have fought him for his own good, but she was in no state to do so, or even to contemplate the necessary arrangements herself.

Penny stayed with Caroline for four days. While she was away Eleanor Maxted and Michael Bayley spent time with Peter. The couple had long telephone conversations every day, but Peter, in a reversal of the loneliness he had earlier felt without Penny, was frightened of her return and begged Caroline to have her for longer. Caroline thought it was fortunate that she was going away and couldn't continue to look after Penny. A few days after her return Zoe came home and was shocked at how depressed her mother was. The company of her beloved daughter comforted Penny, and for a few days she seemed to get better, but on 14 April Peter phoned Caroline with another emergency. Caroline drove to the house and found Penny huddled in Zoe's arms. A more drastic course of action was needed, and it was agreed that she would go for a lengthy break with her parents in Staines. Thus began their longest separation yet.

There were times when she seemed to be getting better in Staines, but there were many relapses, and her elderly parents were themselves struggling to cope. At one point the news was so worrying that Peter considered hiring a car (presumably with a driver) and going to Staines himself – which Caroline no doubt correctly thought a terrible idea. They spoke frequently on the phone and Michael Bayley saw what he called 'heartbreaking' postcards from her, telling him that she was visiting places where they had been together, trying to connect with happier times. Eventually, in early June, at her parents' expense, she went for treatment to the private Cardinal Clinic at Windsor.

During this long separation the FPG friends continued to give Peter support, and a kind of informal rota was organised. Eleanor was surprised, in a poet, at his reluctance to be alone. She took him out ten times during Penny's absence, always at his instigation.

Caroline tried unsuccessfully to persuade him to use a computer. Once he talked to her about missing his sexual relationship with Penny, but Caroline feared that the relationship could never be the same again. She took him to see a show about Sylvia Plath, which distressed him partly because he saw his and Penny's situation reflected there – a recurrence of his earliest fear that she would be like Sylvia. Caroline and Jane Tozer wrote on Peter's behalf to the Royal Literary Fund, as a consequence of which he was awarded a grant for writers in distressed circumstances – a lump sum and a small annual pension.

While she was in the Cardinal Clinic Penny was prescribed lorazepam, which she described as an 'addictive happy pill'. Perhaps it was a consequence of this that, when she returned with her parents to Falmouth in mid-June, Caroline observed that Penny had painted her toenails green, which she considered a sign of good spirits. In early July Peter and Penny went for a short holiday to the Lizard, but soon after their return, for the first time, the words 'Upset' and 'Frenzy' began to appear in Peter's appointment diary (where he had never hitherto written anything emotional). Over the next two years these words track the ebb and flow of Penny's depression and anger. She would wake at night shouting, and spend all day weeping, crouching in corners or screaming abuse at him. Eleanor for one was profoundly shocked by this change in Penny, whom she described as 'the kindest and most dutiful of women'.

Later in July they went to Sheffield for Peter to receive an honorary doctorate – the only academic degree he was ever awarded. Through a combination of lorazepam and a huge effort of will Penny managed to seem like her normal self on this visit. Peter invited Philip Hobsbaum as his guest for the ceremony. It was the last time the old friends were to meet, and the meeting must have been sweetened for Peter by an article Philip had published earlier in the year, which now laid emphasis on his later work as the peak of his achievement: 'These are no discrete pieces of writing but building blocks of a mighty temple of art.' After the ceremony Penny felt a tap on her shoulder, looked round and saw that Kate was sitting behind her. She had made the journey to Sheffield, with husband and children in tow, without letting Peter know, because she wanted to represent her mother who had loved Peter till her death, and the family that was never mentioned on the jackets of his books. Penny invited her to the post-ceremony lunch, but she declined because she thought it would make Peter uncomfortable. She had resumed contact with her father in her teens and, in the last years, visited him in Cornwall with her family. She always felt that these visits were rather awkward, and had to be arranged like appointments. On the final visit, however, her children were greatly amused that he was breaking wind but not seeming to notice: Kate thought that he was enjoying the attention and making the most of being an old man, getting away with such behaviour.

During the visit to Sheffield Christine and I took them to Hardwick Hall in the hope that he might be able to identify the tapestry celebrated in 'Tapestry Moths'. To our frustration the Hall was closed, but we walked in the gardens, where there are yew bushes shaped into niches for statues. Penny and Christine looked in one of these. As they came out Peter said, 'Did you see the stars?' They looked at each other, puzzled. He instructed them to go back in and they could see immediately that, on this bright sunny day, tiny points of light sparkled through the dense yew branches, exactly like a night sky thick with stars. It was a privileged glimpse of the imaginative harmony that had sustained their relationship, but that was becoming increasingly rare.

The visit to Sheffield was an oasis. Michael Bayley, who saw them regularly in this period, thought their creative relationship had changed. When he called on Peter, he hardly ever saw Penny, whereas in earlier years she would always pop her head round the door. Peter said she was 'working day and night', but Michael thought they were no longer comfortable being alone together. Whereas they used to meet every day in a café to share their work, now they left poems outside each other's door. As Michael put it, 'They seemed to be drifting into the separate realities of their illnesses.' Peter's favourite metaphor for the kind of creative sexual intimacy that he thought his relationship with Penny epitomised was the alchemical symbol of the 'double pelican'. This derived from the ancient idea of the pelican, which supposedly wounded its own breast to feed its young, as an emblem of self-sacrificing love. In the double pelican the beak of each is plunged into the breast of the other, creating a single circulatory system. This is indeed a powerful symbol of intimacy, but it also has disturbing connotations of mutual predation. Their feeding off each other became destructive when neither had anything to give. Each spent a lot of time worrying what the other would think or be distressed by, but neither was able to control the behaviour that caused the distress. Michael felt that Penny was being held under a kind of emotional house arrest. She told him that Peter resented her visiting friends, asking if she found them more interesting than him. Conversely, he was frightened at her anger, and Michael himself witnessed what he called '*Shining moments*', when she would suddenly appear at the door and he wondered what she was going to do next.

Peter was still recording the days of Penny's cycle in his diary and journal, even though it was becoming increasingly irregular. He even kept a record when she was away. After her return he tried to make a link between the cycle and her recurrent anger and depression. One gets the sense that the menstrual cycle is a structure that he is desperately holding on to, a relic of the world that he and Penny had shared, that he looks to for a meaning that it can't possibly any longer yield.

Another resource for Peter, in addition to the Poetry Group meetings, was a meditation group that he began attending weekly. He learned about this group from Eleanor, who was initially wary about his joining. The members were all women, and they practised 'insight' meditation: they meditated silently for forty minutes, followed by a forty-minute discussion. Eleanor had known Peter only in the context of the Poetry Group, where he was a dominant personality, and she feared that he would unbalance the meditation group. But his demeanour there opened her eyes to a new dimension of his personality: he hardly spoke, certainly didn't dominate, and seemed humble and gentle, words that she would not formerly have thought of using of him.

Penny's therapist said that she needed a break every eight weeks, and in early August she went to her parents again. The day before she left, Peter was taken out by a friend in a car. Getting into the car he fell, leaving a mark on his face, and he worried that Penny would be upset by this, but much more serious was an injury that he incurred at the same time to his foot, which never got better: it turned blue and he eventually developed septicaemia. She went away again for a short time in October, and between these visits she and Peter had a few days' holiday in Boscastle – their last. During this period, as an anniversary present for Peter, she wrote the title poem of what was to be her elegiac book, *Redgrove's Wife*. But this witty and teasing poem is not an elegy; it begins with a refusal of self-pity and ends with a reaffirmation of love for the man she had

spent the last thirty years with: 'Amaze Redgrove's Wife?/ Leave that
to Redgrove.' Despite the evidence of this poem, for the whole of
the last half of 2001 their life was a recurrent nightmare in which
short periods of recovery only intensified the misery of Penny's
descents into harrowing distress. One time, when collecting Peter
to take him to the poetry group, Caroline caught a glimpse of her
closing the door: 'Her face looked black with anger and I had the
strong impression that her head was an enormous black balloon.'
Peter lamented that he was 'living with a madwoman' and longed
for the poetry evenings as periods of sanity.

He sought comfort especially in the company of women. He made
a habit of visiting a particular bookshop in Falmouth, which was
owned by a woman, and would sit there 'like a little child', while
she held his hand. For his seventieth birthday Eleanor Maxted organised a party for him, to which he invited six local women. Eleanor
pointed out to him that he hadn't asked any men. 'But I don't know
any men.' 'What about Michael?' 'Oh yes, there's Michael.' Michael
was a good friend, but Peter only wanted to be with women.

Penny was taking pericyazine, an anti-psychotic drug, and valium,
for anxiety, insomnia and seizures. One side effect of the latter is
amnesia. After one three-day bad episode in October she could
remember little of what had happened, and in later years her memory
of the whole period of her illness was much diminished. She was
nevertheless tormented by knowledge of the effect her condition
was having on Peter. One time she begged Caroline not to leave
because 'I love him so much, but when you go I'll start getting at
him again.' By February it was clear that she needed to go away
for a long period again, and her brother came to take her once
more to the Cardinal Clinic. This time Peter paid (thanks to the
Royal Literary Fund), and while she was there she was helped to
get off valium (ironically, since she had been prescribed the valium
by her GP to help her off the lorazepam to which she had become
addicted on her first visit to the clinic).

This time Peter seemed to cope better with Penny being away.
He now feared that they would never be able to live together again,
which was a harrowing look at the worst, but perhaps also a strategy
for coping with his present circumstances. For the first time in ages
he saw Don Thomas at a poetry reading. Don and Victoria took
him out for lunch a few times, which Victoria described as riotous
occasions on which Peter would drink three or four glasses of red

wine (which of course he wasn't supposed to) while he and Don shared 'blokey' reminiscences of their trip to America, and of fist-fights. It probably did some good to the suddenly bereft, suddenly old man to be transported back to the masculine world he had inhabited before he knew Penny. He also yearned to recover the sweetness of the beginning of their relationship. He told Michael that, when she returned, he would fill the house with flowers, as he had done when she first came to Tehidy Terrace. Michael, however, was mindful that she had said she wanted a new kitchen, and told Peter this might be a better idea.

She returned in May, apparently completely recovered. Peter wrote in his diary, 'Sweet spontaneous joy – may it last.' She was smiling for the first time in more than a year, and to her friends it seemed a miraculous return of her old self. In gratitude and celebration Peter dedicated his new book, *From the Virgil Caverns*, to 'the Falmouth companions in poetry who saw us through'. It was his first book for five years, the longest gap in his whole career, but there is no decline in quality. The title poem is his last major large-scale work, a meditation on cave-painting and the slowly changing forms of limestone caves, which winningly declares its origin in a newspaper article, but more significantly draws on his childhood experiences at the Great Orme and Kent's Cavern:

> Shirikov reported
> > in the *Independent on Sunday*
> > > (2 May 1993) on the true
> Use of the cave paintings;
> > the theory is that the boys
> > > entered the Distant Hall
> Crawling on their stomachs
> > through the mud
> > > which represented dying
> Through the synaesthetic ordeal
> > of the lower death-passage
> > > where the animals seemed
> To come alive, prancing
> > in the extended senses
> > > of the Distant Hall
> Thus creating in the candidate
> > his own particle
> > > of shared subconscious

Unlike Dante, Redgrove isn't guided through his caverns by a Virgil: the caverns *are* his Virgil. The book also contains one of his most attractive poems which, unlike most of his work, started from a direct prose narrative of a personal occasion. On 3 March 1996, three days after his diagnosis of diabetes, he visited a café in Falmouth where he asked for a glass of tap water. He recorded the conversation with the elderly lady proprietor that ensued, and over the usual passage of years developed it into the poem 'Elderhouse':

> I requested tapwater
> > in an ordinary tumbler
> And this started a procession
> > of courtesy-gestures, in turn:
> > > ran the tap over the back
> Of her hand until it was cool,
> > turned it off, off on
> > > to give me the clearest
> Available; I thanked her
> > With my best smile, to which
> > > she replied 'Have you
> A pension-book? if you have,
> > go to the British Legion,
> > > they will give you a free
> Meal . . .' I smiled and said
> > I would do this in
> > > a couple of years, and smiled
> With more care and repeated thanks
> > keeping my voice slightly
> > > high and elderly
> Which it was anyway though I did not quite
> > have the pension-book, not quite

Redgrove wrote nothing more charming than this gracious turning of what could have been a mortifying experience into a delicate moment of courtesy, friendship and shared understanding.

But this was not what growing old was like most of the time for Peter and, while Penny's state of mind was so much better after her stay in the clinic, there was no alleviation of the challenges that his health faced her with. Once, as they were at the doorstep about to go out, she noticed that he was wearing only one shoe: the numbness in his feet made him oblivious to this. His walking was more and more painfully slow, because he had to concentrate so hard on putting one foot in front of the other. He had to wrap up against the cold on a warm day in July, and his head was covered in scabs and sores. He told Michael Bayley, without a hint of the gallows humour that might have been expected of him, that one of the side effects of his medication for Parkinson's was death. He was able to work on his poetry for two hours a day, and he kept this up to the end, leaving material for three posthumous collections, but his note-books in the last couple of years consist almost entirely of drafts of earlier generated material. Creatively he was living off his fat. He had always been able to write himself out of illness, he said, but now everything was 'too far gone'.

There were five months of restored harmony, but in October Penny collapsed again. Twice she went to hospital in Redruth, and at home she spent most of her time in bed. Once when Keith Trickey called he could hear her 'weeping and wailing' upstairs. Michael Bayley visited frequently at this time, and he often heard her singing wordless songs for hours on end. Peter asked him if he would 'tutor' Penny, which Michael interpreted to mean that he wanted someone to be there for her, as he could no longer be himself. Michael started to feel like a go-between. One curious incident suggests that old wounds still festered in the midst of new suffering. One day Peter 'flung' to Michael a copy of Dennis Creffield's book of drawings of English cathedrals, and asked him what he thought. Michael answered that he thought them good, though disconcerting. 'Take it, take it,' Peter insisted.

Zoe had been working in Chile since August, but towards the end of the year she sensed from phone calls that her parents were trying to pretend that everything was normal. She came home in December, to find her mother hysterical. Peter wanted Zoe to be in the house all the time, as a buffer, so she stayed at home, not working, occasionally getting respite by visiting her boyfriend's house. An old friend, Dorothy Coventon, had joined the FPG this year and Peter called her several times to come round and talk to both Penny and himself. The comrades in poetry were again trying to see them through, visiting and giving them lifts. By April Zoe thought things were a little better, and left for Spain.

But Peter and Penny were heading for a serious conflict. He was booked for an event at the Voice Box in the Royal Festival Hall, a conversation with Michael Bayley followed by a reading. He was anxious to persuade his publishers to bring out a Collected Poems, and believed – for reasons Michael found difficult to understand – that this project would be jeopardised if he failed to go through with his commitment. Penny was desperate at the prospect of being left alone, and angry with him for going. Peter asked Dorothy and another Poetry Group friend, Dominic Power, to keep her company. The Voice Box event was on the evening of Wednesday 7 May, but Peter and Michael travelled to London a day early because Peter had also arranged to do a recording at the Poetry Archive. (It would, in any case, have been difficult for him to perform after spending all day on the train.) However, when Peter contacted Jacqueline Korn about the event she told him that she had a prior engagement in the evening, so Peter cancelled the recording and arranged to spend the afternoon with her. This was a relief to Michael, who had found the previous twenty-four hours stressful because of Peter's lack of mobility and quickly changing moods. Peter told Jacqueline that he would like to be taken to see the new tessellated glass roof over the Great Court of the British Museum; she arranged for a wheelchair at the museum and collected him by taxi from his hotel in Gower Street. At first he seemed quiet and depressed, but gradually his mood improved and he became his old self, 'an absolute delight, stimulated by everything, thrilled at it all' as she wheeled him round the Court. The afternoon became one of her most treasured memories.

By the evening, however, when the time came for Michael to take him to the Festival Hall, his mood had worsened. He became visibly more irritable and nervous, harping on about the importance of the event for his Collected Poems, and unresponsive to Michael's reassurance that all he had to do was to answer his questions and read a few poems. When they got to the Hall they had to negotiate a staircase to get to the lift. Peter was furious about this and rudely vented his anger at the event organiser. There were thirty or forty people in the Voice Box, including Peter Porter and Robin Robertson, both of whom were saddened and shocked by his appearance. Robin was there, naturally, to support Peter, but his presence may have made Peter more nervous, given the inflated importance he attached to the event, and the influence he supposed it would have on the fate of his Collected Poems.

When Michael asked his first question, Peter didn't seem to hear it, then Michael realised that he hadn't understood it. He made some attempt at answering the first two questions, but to the third he replied, 'I'm sorry, but I really don't know what you are asking me.' There was a pause, and murmurs in the audience, who must, as Peter Porter and Robin certainly did, have found the performance deeply distressing. Michael tried to retrieve the situation by asking Peter to read a poem, but Peter said, 'No, you read it.' Michael read the poem, and then the audience seemed instinctively to know the right thing to do – they got up, came to the stage, and started casually to talk to Peter. The audience saved the show, though Porter, for one, was almost in tears. As for Peter, Michael thought that he just wanted to be comforted.

Back in Falmouth, friends tried to keep Penny occupied. Dominic took her out for a drive and lunch, she had tea with Eleanor, Dorothy took her to Maenporth and the bluebell woods at Swanpool; but Penny was sunk in depression. On the Wednesday evening Peter was worried about her and asked Michael to phone, but not to tell her what had happened at the Voice Box. Michael spoke to her, giving an edited version of the day's events, and was disconcerted by the quiet, almost spooky voice in which she replied, 'Thank you, Michael, for letting me know.' The following morning Dorothy rang to propose another excursion, but Penny said she was very tired and wanted to take it easy. Like Michael, Dorothy was unnerved by the eerie calm with which she spoke.

Late in the afternoon Peter and Michael arrived at Arwyn Place in a taxi, both exhausted. They found the house locked up, the blinds pulled down, and no answer when they rang the bell. For some reason they had only one key, which Peter had left with Penny. That she should have left the house locked up, knowing that he was due to return, was seriously worrying. After about twenty minutes Dominic turned up and told Michael that Penny had taken an overdose and was in Truro hospital, recovering. He had driven to Truro to retrieve the house key. Michael had asked the taxi driver to wait a little way up the steep road, and he walked up to the taxi with Peter before breaking the news to him. Peter was strangely calm: probably relieved that something worse hadn't happened. In the afternoon Dorothy, worried by the conversation in the morning, had phoned Penny, who told her that she had taken an overdose, and there was no need to come because she had called an ambulance, and it was at the door. She later described this episode as a 'cry for help', and her actions certainly confirm that she had no serious intention to commit suicide. She only stayed in hospital one night,

though both Eleanor and Michael pleaded with the medical authorities to let her stay longer, on the grounds that there was nobody
at home fit to look after her. The next day Eleanor brought her
home, and she threw herself into Peter's arms as if they were young
lovers. But it was to be several years before Michael told her just
what had happened at the Voice Box.

Remarkably, the following Monday Peter and Penny both went
to the Poetry Group and presented poems – in Peter's case, his poem
about his mother's abortions – but he had difficulty reading. On
Tuesday he was sufficiently detached from his personal travails to
call Caroline and commiserate with her on a car accident, but when
he spoke to Michael's wife Chris the next day he sounded utterly
depressed. On Thursday morning he couldn't pass water or get out
of bed. Penny thought he had broken his hip and called the GP. She
sat with him and waited for the doctor to come. She tried to give
him food but he couldn't eat. They talked but after a while he
couldn't understand what she was saying. Then he slept for a bit.
The doctor didn't come till 3 p.m. Later, confronting the guilt that
was mixed with her grief, she thought shouldn't she have called an
ambulance instead of the GP? Might it have come earlier, and made
a difference? Probably not. She had thought it was only a broken
hip, but it turned out to be a systemic infection. When the GP had
examined him he called an ambulance, and arranged for Peter to
be admitted to Treliske in Truro, where Zoe had been born. In
Penny's own words:

> The paramedics gave him gas and air to get him downstairs. The two
> men used a sort of hoisting chair, the bigger of the burly twosome
> squatting on his hindquarters behind Peter, gripping him as they
> bumped down from stair to stair. 'Have a nice time,' Peter murmured
> to me as he was lifted into the ambulance. These were the last coherent
> words he spoke.

When he reached the casualty department, Peter became, as the
doctor put it, 'combative', fighting with the doctors and nurses until
they sedated him with diazepam, after which he never fully regained
consciousness. Penny went home where Michael and Chris sat with
her, but was called back to Truro by the duty doctor who feared
that Peter was dying. The cause of his sudden collapse was septicaemia, perhaps originating in his foot injury two years earlier, that
had never healed, or maybe an infection picked up on his recent

trip to London. By the time Penny arrived at the hospital he had stabilised slightly, but he spent the next fortnight in the High Dependency unit, before being moved to the Renal ward.

He hung on to life, or was kept alive, for another month. Zoe returned again, and began a long period of supporting her mother. She and Penny visited him every afternoon and read to him. 'Sometimes he responded a little, at others he fretted and whimpered, trying to pull the drip from his throat, cowering away whenever a nurse approached, making inarticulate panicky sounds.' The only words he spoke were, 'Get me out of here.' Once Michael visited and saw Penny standing, as if in church, reading his poem 'Reservoirs of Perfected Ghost', which recalls the bluebells at Enys House near Penryn, one of their favourite places:

Acres of the sky having
        floated down and settled in the woods,
                the bluebell canopy spreads beneath
The green capes of the trees;
        heaven is so full of sky
            it cannot hold – it falls
Into the woods, and spreads, heaven
        skygazing in its woodland cavern;
                bend down and pluck with admiration
A juicy stem; the blue bell
     salivates glass-juice on your fingers;
            lift this flower to your nose
It smells not at all!
        it is all of them that smells:
            the sun reaches through the leaves
And lifts the perfume out, gently
        from these masses, so as not to break it, keeping
            the shock of the blueness
As it issues from underground;
        heaven must have gone deep,
          to arrive so. (*FVC*)

When she had finished reading the poem she turned and looked at Michael with 'the most ecstatic smile on her face'. He thought that she felt close to Peter again, even though he was in a coma, after two years of estrangement and isolation. Zoe thought she pulled herself together 'in an amazing way' to go to the hospital every day. When she got back home she would go straight to bed.

Bill made several journeys from his home in Kent. Peter knew that he was there; he kept trying to speak to him but couldn't, and his frustration was palpable. Victoria Field was working on a community project in the hospital, and visited him several times. He was unconscious with tubes and monitors attached, but she too thought he was trying to communicate, and that he was distressed. The last time however, a couple of days before he died, he looked 'incredibly peaceful'.

Towards the end Bill was spending the mornings with him, Penny and Zoe the afternoons and evenings. There came a point when the renal consultant had to tell them that there was no hope of his recovery. His feeding tube and antibiotics were withdrawn and the morphine dose increased. He died on the morning of 16 June, after a month of semi-consciousness, with his eldest child holding his hand.

Epilogue

The next day there were full- or half-page obituaries in all the daily broadsheets. Alan Brownjohn wrote in the *Guardian* and Philip Hobsbaum in the *Independent*. Philip attributed to Hughes and Porter his own view that Redgrove was 'the greatest poet of his time', while the anonymous obituary in *The Times* described his career as 'a sustained and heroic commitment to the creative imagination'. Philip, whose own health was undermined by diabetes, couldn't come to the funeral at Truro crematorium the following Monday, but wrote to Penny, 'It is like part of one's universe being taken away.' Bill stayed in Falmouth and took responsibility for the funeral arrangements, including phoning Peter's friends to break the news. Kate also came with her family. In Philip's absence the oldest friend there was Peter Porter, who had travelled with Alan, Robin Robertson and Jacqueline Korn on the sleeper from London. Don Thomas was there, old colleagues from the School of Art, former students such as Dennis Lowe and Ray Hopley, and numerous members of the Falmouth Poetry Group and the meditation group. As the crowd of mourners waited outside, and the time of the service got nearer, we became more anxiously aware of Penny's absence. Would she be too distraught to come? She arrived, exactly at the moment when the funeral was due to begin, in a car with Zoe and her parents, convulsed in grief, clinging to her daughter.

The funeral was a Christian service, which pleased some of his Christian friends, but which others thought incongruous. Three of his friends read poems: Michael Bayley 'Elderhouse', Robin Robertson 'A Twelvemonth' and Eleanor Maxted 'Reservoirs of Perfected Ghost'. As soon as the service ended Zoe supported Penny out of the chapel and into the car. She spoke to no one, and there was no 'wake' afterwards. It was to be a long time before people could gather to celebrate Peter's life. People drifted off in their various ways. The London group drowned their grief on the train journey home. The Falmouth Poetry Group gathered in the evening, with their funeral wreath in the middle of the circle, and read from his work. There was a bust of Lord Falmouth in the room, and at the end of the evening they hung the wreath round his neck.

But Penny's nightmare continued. Her depression 'intensified into inchoate misery'. She wanted to sleep all the time, and sometimes took sleeping pills in the daytime. Poetry disappeared from her life, along with other activities that had been deeply important to her, such as yoga and meditation. 'The cowed spirit in me wanted oblivion, sleep.' Zoe got a job locally so that she could be with her mother, and was her lifeline.

A month after Peter's death she went into a NHS mental health unit for three weeks. While she was there she felt that the menopause had come to an end, and this was the first tiny moment of light in her recovery. But in September, when Stride Books published Peter's *Sheen* (the 'overflow' collection from *From the Virgil Caverns*) alongside an anthology of poems commemorating him, *Full of Stars' Dreaming*, there was no Penny at the launch. In December she had to face another bereavement: her father died. She stayed with her mother for the funeral but couldn't get out of bed before midday. Through all this Zoe remained her constant support, though she had begun an MA in London in October, and Penny felt that she had no chance herself to mourn her father and grandfather.

She was seeing a Jungian counsellor, but in early 2004 she stopped these sessions and retreated to her bed for a month, living on little more than oranges, crippled by agoraphobia. Eventually she decided this couldn't go on, asked if there was a milder anti-depressant that didn't make her want to sleep all the time and, with the help of new medication, began her slow recovery. One turning point was a visit with her friend Eleanor to Enys, to see the very bluebells that Peter had celebrated in the poem she read to him in hospital:

> It was a sunny windy April afternoon. The bluebells don't just grow in glades and under trees but spread out in vast open acres. I walked round the perimeter of the bluebell field. In the warm sun a wonderful perfume drifted up from the bluebells. The flowers, the warmth and the reality of spring, the many other visitors visibly enjoying the gardens – all this unlocked the fetters of loss. Colours began to return.

I still felt grief like a violent hand at my throat, but time was no
longer made up of endless hours, began offering possibilities.

She had not been into Peter's room since his death, but now she
crossed that threshold and found his last poems on his desk. Reading
them 'brought poetry back into my life', and she began writing again
herself. Jacqueline Korn phoned her with the suggestion that she
and Robin organise a memorial event. Penny's first impulse was to
say no, but almost immediately her second was to say yes, and her
attendance at Somerset House that summer was like a public statement of her recovery. Peter Porter, Alan Brownjohn, Elaine Feinstein,
Derek Toyne, Gerard Woodward, Robin Robertson and I spoke and
read Peter's poetry. Bill and Kate were invited but didn't go: Bill
said that he would have felt uncomfortable at a gathering of people
who had known his father much better than he did.

The first poem Penny read that day when she ventured into Peter's
room was 'The Harper', which she thought vividly evoked 'so much
of Peter's personality, his fascination with all life, in this instance a
water beetle, and the exactitude with which he explored water,
nature, but always putting the human experience in balance within
it'. 'The Harper' became the title poem of his last Cape collection,
published in 2006. As usual there was a generous overflow,
and Stride also published a last collection, *A Speaker for the Silver
Goddess*.

The first sustained work that Penny did when she resumed writing
was a sequence of elegies, mainly for Peter but also for her father,
called 'Missing You'. These became the centrepiece of *Redgrove's
Wife*, also published in 2006, which many readers thought her finest
collection yet. It was as if she had not merely recovered but surpassed
her old self, and not only in her poetry. The woman who had loved
Peter and been his soul mate found her fullest expression in
Redgrove's Wife and the later *Sandgrain and Hourglass* (2010), but
another woman also emerged, whom her friends had not known.
For the last twenty-eight years of Peter's life the couple had never
travelled abroad and, though they journeyed widely in Britain for
professional engagements, took their holidays in Cornwall. Now, as
if the creative partnership had entailed a measure of constraint, she
travelled constantly, both professionally and for pleasure, in the USA,
Canada, France, Italy and Spain.

On a hot day in September of the year after Peter's death, the year of Penny's recovery, she went with Zoe and a group of friends to Maenporth beach. They carried with them Peter's ashes, not in an urn as Penny had expected but a plastic tub like an old-fashioned sweet jar.

> Zoe and I waded out into the waves. I unscrewed the lid and tipped the grey gritty ash into the sunlit water. The clear sea swirled them away with incredible rapidity. There was a sudden cloudiness in the water, and then his ashes were rushing away on the outgoing tide, as if Peter's mortal remains couldn't wait to become part of the sea, of the whole world's waters; as if he wanted to be part of the continuum of nature, and I'd kept him waiting too long (fifteen months! I hear him say). And the sea, it seemed, couldn't wait to welcome him.

Then Penny read 'The Idea of Entropy at Maenporth Beach' and they all retired to a friend's house nearby to drink a glass of wine to Peter.

References

Archive sources
Sheffield

Mss 171: Redgrove's personal archive 1969–99. Redgrove sold the archive to the University of Sheffield in two stages, 1993 and 2002. The 1993 portion is partially catalogued. Catalogued items are cited by number, e.g. 33.08; the uncatalogued boxes are recorded as 'Outstanding Box 1' etc. The 2002 portion is uncatalogued and recorded as 'II Box 1' etc. Journals and notebooks are prefixed 'N'; later journals in 'fascicle' form are prefixed 'F'. Sheffield sources are from this archive unless otherwise stated.
Mss 255: letters from Redgrove to Philip Hobsbaum, Martin Bell, James Kirkup and others. This collection was purchased separately from a dealer.
Mss 392: a small collection donated by Dennis Creffield in 2009; letters and books inscribed to Dilly Creffield.

HRC: the Harry Ransom Center, University of Texas at Austin

Redgrove Papers: Redgrove's archive 1952–69
Hobsbaum Papers: correspondence with Redgrove, Lucie-Smith and others

Leeds

Redgrove manuscripts: GB 206 Brotherton Collection MS 20c Redgrove, University of Leeds.
Bonamy Dobrée papers: Dobrée GB 206 Brotherton Collection MS 20c Dobrée

Glasgow

Philip Hobsbaum Collection, University of Glasgow

Reading

Papers of the Group, Mss 4457, University of Reading

BL

P. J. Kavanagh Papers, British Library

UCSD

John Layard Collection, University of California San Diego

Lilly

Redgrove Mss, Lilly Library, Indiana University

Tulsa

Martin Bell Papers, Collection 1979–020, McFarlin Library, University of Tulsa

Emory

Ted Hughes Letters to Peter Redgrove, Mss 867, Emory University, Atlanta
Ted Hughes Letters to Olwyn Hughes, Mss 980

BBC

BBC Written Archives, Reading

Surrey

Surrey History Centre: records of PR's treatment at Netherne hospital

Private sources

NR: Neil Roberts; PS: Penelope Shuttle; CC: Caroline Carver; DC: Dorothy Coventon; KT: Kate (Redgrove) Tomkinson; CM: Christine McCausland; CA: Cliff Ashcroft

Abbreviations

People

AB: Alan Brownjohn
BR: Barbara Redgrove
CC: Caroline Carver
DMT: D. M. Thomas
ELS: Edward Lucie-Smith
GJR: Jim Redgrove
JL: John Layard
MB: Martin Bell
NR: Neil Roberts
PH: Philip Hobsbaum
PP: Peter Porter
PR: Peter Redgrove
PS: Penelope Shuttle
TH: Ted Hughes

Works of Peter Redgrove

A: *Abyssophone*
AB: *The Apple-Broadcast*
AG: *Assembling a Ghost*
AWM: *At the White Monument*
B: *The Beekeepers*
BG: *The Black Goddess and the Sixth Sense*
C: *The Collector*
CR: *The Colour of Radio*
DF: *Dr Faust's Sea-Spiral Spirit*
F: *The Force*
FE: *The First Earthquake*

FECA: *From Every Chink of the Ark*
FVC: *From the Virgil Caverns*
GC: *The Glass Cottage*
GG: *The God of Glass*
ICOS: *In the Country of the Skin*
IHS: *In the Hall of the Saurians*
IS: *Innocent Street* (unpublished; II Box 16, Sheffield)
L: *The Laborators*
MFT: *My Father's Trapdoors*
MNE: *The Man Named East*
MPGB: *The Mudlark Poems and Grand Buveur*
NCW: *The Nature of Cold Weather*
OE: *Orchard End*
TDT: *The Terrors of Dr Treviles*
UR: *Under the Reservoir*
WBMS: *What the Black Mirror Saw*
WNP: *The Weddings at Nether Powers*
WP: *Work in Progress*
WW: *The Wise Wound*

Notes

Chapter 1: Oedipus in Kingston 1932–45

pp. 5–6   'bull of a man': PR N77, 9 June 1987, II Box 16, Sheffield; 'massive and distinguished duenna', 'pixie green nymph': *IS*, II Box 16, Sheffield; 'raped Mimi at knifepoint': N49H VI, Sheffield; 'sheltered by Mimi's mother and stepfather': GJR to PR, 6 February 1969, II Box 14, folder 'Personal', Sheffield; 'in those days on the shelf': *IS* p. 278, Sheffield.

pp. 6–7   'I married the only man': Nan Redgrove to BR, n.d. (late 1969/early 1970), KT; 'for a wonderful love': GJR's diary 10 October 1926, PS; 'a sideboard of cups for everything': 'My Father's Trapdoors', *MFT* p. 48; 'imaginative, poetic and very feminine': Nic Compton, 'The House Where I Grew Up: Peter Redgrove: Kingston, London', source unidentified; 'desire to run wild in nature': *CR* p. 258; 'capricious, outrageous, colourful and flamboyant': Kate (Redgrove) Tomkinson to NR, June 2007, and interview with Bill and Sue Redgrove, 20 May 2007.

p. 7   'proceeded to throw it': *IS* p. 255; 'all my life I have had to live': Nan Redgrove to BR, n.d. (late 1969/early 1970), KT; 'Jim was to mourn his wife': Kate Tomkinson to NR, June 2007; 'You must learn to be brave': *BG* p. xi; 'big head wouldn't slip out': Nan Redgrove to PR, 3 March 1972, N44B, Sheffield.

pp. 8–9   'Is this my earliest memory?': *CR* p. 34; 'Once in bed at ten': 'My Father's Trapdoors', *MFT* p. 51; 'loved the radio': PR to PH, 1992, Hobsbaum Papers, Glasgow; 'I *Mummy's* Peter': II Box 14, folder 'Peter', Sheffield.

pp. 9–10   'the destructive rejection of my father's love': N77, 29 October 1988, Sheffield; 'This triangle is so important': N44B, 14 February 1972, Sheffield; 'small and insecure', 'nurtured his sensitivity': 'The House Where I Grew Up'; 'rutting smells in the communal bowl': *IS* p. 8; 'convinced that the smells': N77, 9 June 1987, II Box 16, Sheffield; 'open her womb', 'sinister male lover': *IS* p. 258; 'like a whore': *IS* p. 248.

pp. 10–11   'waterman on the Thames': *IS* p. 253; 'her quest was freedom': *IS* p. 255; 'He told Peter Porter': PP interview with NR, 5 July 2007; 'embattled love life': 'The House Where I Grew Up'. This published text refers to 'an abortion or a miscarriage', but Redgrove's private writings make it clear that he regarded them as abortions; 'damaged in the womb': *IS* p. 44; 'Talked about it': N53C, Sheffield; 'an explosive mixture': *CR* p. 43; 'business voice and mannerisms', '*The War of the Roses*': F58, 11–12 May 1990, Sheffield; 'the man with his arms protectively': *CR* p. 43.

pp. 11–12   'monster': Chris Harding, telephone conversation, 30 January 2009; 'two conflicting atmospheres': 'The House Where I Grew Up'; 'choose between them': 'The House Where I Grew Up'; 'Does the mother abuse': *IS* p. 143; 'non-genital karezza': PR to Gerard Woodward, 6 November 1991, copy with NR; 'so virile a man obsessed with manliness', 'learn something of the truth of womanhood': PR to NR 26 November 1990, NR; 'much preferable': *IS* p. 98.

pp. 12–13   'became transformed just before her period': *CR* p. 258; 'wanted to smash open Jim's head with the clock': N44B, 4 February 1972, Sheffield; 'You wait till your father comes home': *IS* p. 98; 'the Misses Williams' kindergarten': *CR* pp. 13–15.

pp. 13–14   'favourite books': PR to GWR, 2 July 1941, II Box 14, folder 'Peter', Sheffield; 'matey with everyone': II Box 14, folder 'Peter', Sheffield; 'chilling kind of child', 'small Faust': *CR* pp. 13–15; 'robot obsessional automatisms': N50/54, 14–15 May 1975, Sheffield.

pp. 14–15   'At the first stroke': *IS* p. 1; 'open and close my doors': *IS* p. 217; 'seize the knot': *IS* p. 158; 'dressed for persona', 'You look cool': *IS* p. 23.

p. 16   'hero-worshipped his father . . . Jim bullied both his sons': Chris Harding, telephone conversation, 30 January 2009; 'a proper / Bastard': 'Memorial', C 40; 'mistake': F138, 10 August 1996, Sheffield; 'persuading him to take the blame': F50, 21 September 1989, Sheffield; 'game of climbing cupboards': N44A, 18 January 1972, Sheffield; 'fought with old sabres', 'tried to destroy': N6, 1958, pp. 9, 54, Lilly; 'involved taking apart the hooks': *IS* p. 93.

p. 17   'the sound of her approach': F93, p. 38, 15 January 1993; 'she used the wrong words': F78, p. 22, 30 September 1991, Sheffield; 'a poem in Mimi's voice': F133, pp. 2–5, 28 February 1996, Sheffield; 'There was an entrance': 'Bentalls Aubade', *WBMS*, pp. 33–35.

pp. 17–18   'project qualities in himself', 'How shall I become the master': *CR* p. 36; 'Here's the man': *http://www.homesweethomefront.co.uk*, accessed 17 November 2007.

pp. 18–19   'Will you be growing me': PR to GJR, 28 March 1941, II Box 14, folder 'Peter', Sheffield; 'wordsmiths': Bill Redgrove, interview with NR, 20 May 2007; 'drifted almost full': *IS* p. 235; 'crawled and slithered': *IS* p. 249; 'phoney': *CR* p. 45; 'being taken up and pressed': N42G, Sheffield; 'passing into a secret door', 'go down into magical realms': *IS* pp. 98–100; 'the piled and mutilated bodies': PR to Giles Gordon, 11 April 1977, 65.04, Sheffield.

pp. 19–20   'the whole of *Monte Cristo*': F106, p. 108, 25 January 1998, Sheffield.

Chapter 2: The Youthful Scientist 1945–49

pp. 21–2   'It was the world in the water-drop': *CR* pp. 15–16; 'people who called him a surrealist': *CR* p. 108.

pp. 22–3   'He loved to walk': *IS* p. 256; 'His bible at this time': *IS* p. 39; 'the green pods make you ill': *IS* p. 8; 'drew away, more interested': *IS* p. 256.

p. 23–4   'Once, the rain came thundering': *IS* p. 83; 'on a motorbike in leather black jacket': *IS* p. 160.

pp. 24–5   'a field of white wheat', 'It's immature semen': *IS* p. 111; 'vivid sensation', 'fed the imagination': J44B, 6–7 February 1972, Sheffield; 'penalties for being caught': *IS* p. 251; 'a skin of clothes wetted': F107, 16 February 1994, Sheffield; 'sharply ironed': F88, 25 August 1992, Sheffield; 'too like a man': N73, 1 April 1983, Sheffield; '"incipient" transvestism': F89, 22 Sept 1992, Sheffield.

pp. 25–6   'coprophilia': N44B, 15 January 1972; F89, 24 September 1992, Sheffield; 'because they're creating sensation in their bodies', 'connected with their senses by the menstrual cycle': *CR* p. 105.

pp. 26–7   'Laurel and Hardy': *TDT* pp. 13–15; 'imagine a woman getting it': N45D, p. 100, Sheffield.

p. 28   'minor public school': GJR to PR, 10 October 1975, II Box 23, Sheffield; 'wonderful-terrible': *IS* p. 82.

p. 28   'cut off the natural communications between people': F76, 9 September 1991, Sheffield; 'an instrument of wartime and post-war propaganda': PR to Anne Stevenson, 18 March 1985, copy with NR.

pp. 29–30   'a complete monastery': John Brown, *Independent Witness: One hundred and fifty years of Taunton School*, Taunton School, 1997, p. 169. I am extensively indebted to Brown's book in this chapter; 'brainy': John Ryland, email to NR, 24 March 2009; 'in the mould of the great idealist headmasters': *Independent Witness*, p. 19; '*Very* capable and hardworking': Taunton School archives; 'the high calibre of the science teachers': *CR* p. 11.

pp. 30–1   'conscientious objector': *Oxford Dictionary of National Biography*; other information about Neal from *Independent Witness*; 'I loved him so much': *IS* p. 125; 'so argumentative in class': F50, 18 September 1989, Sheffield; 'that ritual of fertile mud': F148, May 1997, Sheffield; squash at Taunton: *The Tauntonian*, vol. 30 no. 178, January 1947, p. 17; vol. 31 no. 188, April 1950, p. 47; 'promoted to the rank of sergeant': II Box 14, folder 'Peter', Sheffield.

pp. 31–2   'illustrated by specimens recently collected': *The Tauntonian*, vol. 30 no. 178, p. 26; 'a barbarian scientist': *CR* p. 17; 'remarkable for its wit and humour': *The Tauntonian*, vol. 30 no. 181, January 1948, p. 198; 'gave us his usual artistically worded views': *The Tauntonian*, vol. 31 no. 184, January 1949, p. 29; 'Tries, but is much below average', 'good type', 'pulled his weight in the House': Taunton School archives; 'Loopy': Chris Harding, telephone conversation, 30 January 2009.

pp. 32–3   'natural communications between people': F76, 9 September 1991, Sheffield; 'small boys in public schools': Chris Harding, email to NR, 29 January 2009.

p. 33   'How I loved him': F82, 5 March 1992, Sheffield; 'He hoped never to
          have to work like that again': N44B, 6 February 1972, Sheffield;
          Edward Heath and 'prize schoolboyism': N44A and 44B, 24 January
          1972, Sheffield.

Chapter 3: Lazarus 1950

pp. 35–6 'I hope you manage': E. G. Neal to PR, 1 January 1950: II Box 14,
          folder 'Peter', Sheffield; 'Oxford and Cambridge, however': Tom
          Hickman, The Call-Up: A History of National Service, London,
          Headline, 2004, p. 2; 'register for conscription': Trevor Royle, National
          Service: the Best Years of Their Lives, London, André Deutsch, 2002, p.
          39; 'neurotic': IS p. 256; 'No, you can't do that': Royle, p. 41.

pp. 36–7 'In March he went to Cambridge': GJR to G. P. McCullagh, 4 April 1950:
          II Box 14, folder 'Peter', Sheffield; 'Enlistment was always on a Thursday':
          Royle, p. 46; 'One RAMC recruit': Royle, p. 35; 'almost died on the spot',
          'If you don't swing that arm, laddie': Royle, p. 50; 'I've got an appetite for
          tobacco now': undated copy in GJR's hand: II Box 14, folder 'Peter',
          Sheffield.

pp. 37–8 'just stood there': E. Dalberg, case notes, Surrey; 'tottering around the
          tarmac': ICOS, p. 38; 'a small, stark card', 'Hello again': II Box 14,
          folder 'Peter', Sheffield.

pp. 38–40 'act from his soul alone': D. H. Lawrence, Kangaroo (1923), Cambridge,
          Cambridge University Press, 1994, p. 222; 'the resemblance to school':
          PS, personal communication; 'Brian Sewell': Hickman, pp. 31–32, 38,
          48; 'prayers', 'magic formulas': E. Dalberg, case notes, Surrey.

pp. 40–1 'a minor nervous breakdown': GJR to G. P. McCullagh, 4 April 1950;
          'McCullagh replied': G. P. McCullagh to GPR, 12 April 1950; 'seemed to
          take it philosophically': GJR to F. S. McNalty, 17 April 1950; 'Major J. R.
          Hawkins': undated notes in GJR's hand: II Box 14, folder 'Peter', Sheffield;
          'straight psychoanalysis': notes by GJR, 7 May 1950: II Box 14, folder
          'Peter', Sheffield.

pp. 41–2 'a rather unusual perversion', 'a possible Oedipus situation': G. F. Spaul
          to E. Cunningham Dax, 16 June 1950, Surrey; 'sub-health, maladjust-
          ment and emotional problems': T. M. Ling, 'Roffey Park Rehabilitation
          Centre and its Relation to British Industrial Medicine', Occupational
          Medicine 2.3 (1951), p. 118; 'delivering results by improving': http://
          www.roffeypark.com/index.php (accessed 7 August 2007); 'Ling would
          be visiting Portsmouth': GJR to G. F. Spaul, 22 May 1950.

pp. 42–3 'Ling thought his condition was grave': note by GJR 'Ling 6 June 1950',
          II Box 14, folder 'Peter', Sheffield; 'will probably agree': note of phone
          conversation with T. M. Ling, 8 June 1950, Surrey; 'Spaul wrote to
          Dax', 'expressed a wish': G. F. Spaul to E. Cunningham Dax, 16 June
          1950, Surrey; 'a medical board . . . insisted': ICOS p. 38; 'civil employ-
          ment': 'Record of Service', Army Personnel Centre.

pp. 43–4 'exonerated', 'accredited madman': PR to GJR 9 July 1973, II Box 14,
          folder 'Jim', Sheffield; 'ideas of reference': Lisa J. Phillips, Patrick D.
          McGorry, Alison R. Yung, Thomas H. McGlashan, Barbara Cornblatt

and Joachim Klostercötter, 'Prepsychotic phase of schizophrenia and related disorders: recent progress and future opportunities', *British Journal of Psychiatry* 187, 2005, s. 33–s. 44; *http://bjp.rcpsych.org/cgi/content/abstract/187/48/s33* (accessed 9 August 2007).

p. 44–5 'no work by him in the collection': I am grateful to Alice Jackson, curator of the Adamson Collection, for checking this for me; 'Deep Insulin Coma Therapy': Kingsley Jones, 'Insulin coma therapy in schizophrenia', *Journal of the Royal Society of Medicine*, vol. 92, March 2000, pp. 147–49.

p. 45–6 'on a suspicion': H. Bourne, 'The Insulin Myth', *Lancet* 1957, i, pp. 607–11; 'You're schizophrenic': PS, interview with NR, 26 August 2007; 'as if she had been in the camps': F76, 3 September 1991, Sheffield; 'increasingly obsessional', 'excellent contact', 'throwing his weight about', 'Public School Boy role': E. Dalberg, case notes, Surrey.

p. 46 'insulin helps to coalesce', 'concepts tend', 'favours the abstruse', 'weakened conceptual thinking', 'disordered judgement': clinical psychologist's note on tests conducted 14 July 1950, Surrey.

pp. 46–7 'important diagnostic evidence': Francis Reitman, *Psychotic Art*, London, Routledge, 1950, p. 42; 'The shock treatment was sensuous': *ICOS* pp. 38–9.

p. 48 'a barbarous violence on the body': *CR* p. 154; 'on the whole a happy home', 'powerful, strong personality', 'does not give in', 'he has no understanding', 'though far from brilliant', 'the disintegration appears': E. Dalberg, case notes, Surrey; 'Nan gave him money': Journal, 23 September 2000, PS.

p. 49 'dreamy', 'never be suited', 'discourage introspection', 'still only a boy: notes by GJR 23 August 1950, II Box 14, folder 'Peter', Sheffield; 'In one he was dead': *ICOS* p. 39; 'During these practice "deaths"': *CR* p. 154.

p. 51 'Sometimes I was a Wild man': *IS* p. 251.

Chapter 4: Love and Poetry 1950–54

pp. 53–4 'the chances of a relapse': notes by GJR on conversation with E. Dalberg, 23 August 1950; 'bad turn': GJR to T. M. Ling, 3 November 1950 (unsent); 'Siegfried Heinrich Foulkes': S. H. Foulkes to PR, 11 November 1950, and notes by GJR on conversation with S. H. Foulkes, 15 November 1950, II Box 14, folder 'Peter', Sheffield; 'opened up a new world to a very conventionally-educated boy', 'concerned to maintain the status quo': 48.04, n.d. (late 1982?), PR to Valerie Sinason, Sheffield; 'McNulty was anxious': Frank McNulty to GJR, 25 February 1950, II Box 14, folder 'Peter', Sheffield.

p. 54 'stunning': Kate (Redgrove) Tomkinson to NR, June 2007; 'John Sherlock': Hilary Semmel, interview with NR, 10 July 2007, and email to NR, 4 October 2008; 'being an artist means you never have to be bored': N36A January 1970, p. 57, Sheffield. This is a 'diary-letter' that Peter wrote to Barbara shortly after they separated; 'He wanted to be like her': N44B, 17 January 1972, Sheffield.

p. 55   'a great peace', 'a silence', 'a call to vocation', 'a coming together': *CR* pp. 70, 142; 'Caught in a fold of the living hills he failed': Redgrove Works A–C, HRC pp. 3–4.

p. 56   'knowledge about me', 'Netherne': 44B 29 January 1972.

p. 57   'Hormones ceased to interest me': 'Peter Redgrove Writes . . .', *Poetry Book Society Bulletin* 31, December 1961.

p. 58   'The science departments which I had joined': *CR* p. 17; 'draping his lanky figure': *IS* p. 235.

p. 58   'collaborative community': F. R. Leavis, *English Literature in Our Time and the University*, London, Chatto and Windus, 1969, p. 8; 'a man speaking solely': PR to GJR, 10 February 1952; 'I thank you from the bottom of my heart': PR to GJR, 25 February 1952; 'Old Tauntonians': PR to GJR, 20 January 1952, II Box 14, folder 'Peter', Sheffield.

pp. 59–60   'Eliot was the first poet': PR to NR, 7 February 1996, NR; 'Rain whose drops': 'Churchyard', Redgrove Works I–M, HRC.

pp. 60–1   'hair stood on end': *CR* p. 17; 'elegy for the Cornish tin-mining industry': 'Elegy for Wheal Jane', part of the 'Broken Ground' project, April 2001; 'tribal values': *CR* p. 68; 'Barbara came to live in Cambridge': PR interview with Elaine Feinstein, September 1999, II Box 2, Sheffield; 'at her father's insistence': interview with Hilary Semmel, 10 July 2007.

pp. 61–2   'an entertaining and stimulating friend': interview with Harry Guest, 22 August 2007; 'exotics': Daniel Huws, *Memories of Ted Hughes 1952–63*, Nottingham, Richard Hollis, 2010, p. 16; 'the sort of home': PR to GJR, 25 February 1952, II Box 14, folder 'Peter', Sheffield; 'Venusberg': Redgrove Works R–Z, HRC.

pp. 62–3   'When mists come whirling': 'An Employer's Intention to an Advertised Companion', Redgrove Works D–G, HRC; 'Lethe': Redgrove Works I–M, HRC; To His Mistress's Bladder': Redgrove Works I–M, HRC; 'The Anatomy Lecture': Redgrove Works A–C, HRC; 'The Laboratory': Redgrove Works I–M, HRC.

p. 63   'Imagination's other place': James Kirkup, *A Correct Compassion*, London, Oxford University Press, 1952, p. 80; 'deeply moved', 'particularly evocative': PR to James Kirkup, 15 October 1952; 'to send a poem', 'I hope I may one day': PR to James Kirkup, 22 October 1952, Sheffield Mss 255; 'Undergraduates interested': *Varsity*, 8 November 1952.

p. 63   'elocutionary golden voice': Philip Hobsbaum in 'Hobsbaum's Choice', BBC Radio 3, 30 January 2000; biographical information about Philip Hobsbaum: 'Philip Hobsbaum in Conversation', *The Dark Horse*, Summer 2002, p. 30.

p. 64   'a bearded man', 'All the Cambridge people': *IS* p. 231.

p. 64   Hobsbaum's recollections of Redgrove: Philip Hobsbaum, 'The Redgrove Momentum: 1952–2003', *The Dark Horse*, Summer 2003, p. 24, Philip Hobsbaum, 'The Group: An Experiment in Criticism', *The Yearbook of English Studies*, vol. 17, 1987, p. 76, and 'Hobsbaum's Choice'.

pp. 65–6   'that genius as a teacher': *CR* p. 19; 'He could see that people spoke':

IS p. 231; 'his influence was evil': interview with Harry Guest, 22 August 2007; 'one of the two greatest men he had met': 'Philip Hobsbaum in Conversation', p. 31; 'We recognised': F. R. Leavis, '*Scrutiny*: A Retrospect', *Valuation in Criticism and Other Essays*, Cambridge, Cambridge University Press, 1986, p. 223; 'It's all a matter of taste': PR to PH, 2 March 1961, Hobsbaum papers, HRC; 'scientific moles': *CR* pp. 16–17.

pp. 66–7   'Realisation attained by unconscious recognition': Redgrove Works N–P, HRC; 'important unconscious component': *CR* p. 58; 'was trying to steer one', 'wrote as scientists write': PR to NR, 16–25 February 1991, NR; 'not "*realized*"': Lee M. Jenkins, '*X/Self*: Kamau Brathwaite at the Crossroads', L.Collins and S. Matterson, eds. *Aberrations in Modern British and American Poetry*, McFarlane, 2011; 'separated the spirit': Ted Hughes, *Letters of Ted Hughes*, ed. Christopher Reid, London, Faber, 2007, p. 423; 'who felt that if you couldn't write *King Lear*': 'Philip Hobsbaum in Conversation' with Nicolas Tredell, *PN Review* 119, p. 22; 'scruffy wee man': Philip Hobsbaum, 'The Redgrove Momentum', p. 25.

p. 67   'ugly puffy fatso', 'This memory from my student days': PR, 'Last Thoughts', PS; 'verse-speaking lessons': interview with PS, 17 February 2007; 'almost ludicrously posh': interview with Peter Porter, 5 July 2007.

p. 68   Harry Guest's reminiscences: Harry Guest, interview with NR, 22 August 2007.

p. 69   'great style and . . . immediate clarity of thought': PR, interview with Peter Ryan, May 1977, Outstanding Box 22, Sheffield; 'Now it seems the artist': PR to GJR, 4 March 1953, II Box 14, folder 'Peter', Sheffield.

p. 69   'in his Disraeli period': Rodney Banister, 'Let's Start a Magazine', *The Spectator*, 5 June 1953, p. 726; 'dialogue between Elizabeth I and II': Emory Mss 854, Ff 38, undated.

p. 70-1   Redgrove on Gunn: PR to Blake Morrison, 6 September 1979, 239.80, Sheffield; 'a huge disappointment': Philip Hobsbaum, 'The Redgrove Momentum', p26, and 'Ted Hughes at Cambridge', *The Dark Horse*, Autumn 1999, p. 6; 'metropolitan centre', 'unpretentious provincial values': Daniel Huws, *Memories of Ted Hughes 1952–63*, p. 15; 'Peter was to recall': F67, 26 December 1990, Sheffield; 'Nation Language': Edward Kamau Brathwaite, *History of the Voice: The Development of Nation Language in Anglophone Caribbean Poetry*, London, New Beacon Books, 1984.

p. 71   'culturally marooned', 'pain & separation', 'suicide note': Kamau Brathwaite, *Barbajan Poems*, New York and Kingston: Savacou North, 1994, pp. 53–4, and *Other Exiles*, London, Oxford University Press, 1975, p. 7, both quoted in Lee M. Jenkins, '*X/Self*: Kamau Brathwaite at the Crossroads'.

pp. 71-2   'one original': Kamau Brathwaite, *Golokwati*, New York and Kingston, Savacou North, unpaginated; quoted in Lee M. Jenkins, '*X/Self*: Kamau Brathwaite at the Crossroads'; 'visited Redgrove': PR to Lee M. Jenkins,

23 August 2002, Lee Jenkins; 'dedication to Redgrove': the 1987 OUP edition of *X/Self* omitted the dedication of 'Letter from Roma' to Redgrove, against the author's wishes. It is restored in *Ancestors*, New York, New Directions, 2001, p. 383. Redgrove remained unaware of this dedication till the scholar Lee Jenkins drew it to his attention shortly before his death; 'diminished his enthusiasm and aptitude': GJR to G. P. McCullagh, 25 April 1953; 'assured Jim': G. P. McCullagh to GJR, 24 April 1953; 'Jim wrote to Dr Dalberg': GJR to Dr E. Dalberg, 26 April 1953, II Box 14, folder 'Peter', Sheffield; 'Dalberg thought': Netherne case file, Surrey; 'but must be told of illness': notes in GJR's hand, 4 May 1953, II Box 14, folder 'Peter', Sheffield.

pp. 72–3   'academically an extremely promising young man': G. P. McCullagh to E. Dalberg, 30 April 1953, Surrey; 'McCullagh told Jim': G. P. McCullagh to GJR, 16 June 1953, II Box 14, folder 'Peter', Sheffield; 'insufferable': Redgrove Works D–G, HRC; 'very crypto-erotic': PR to NR, 16 July 1985, NR.

p. 73   'Notturno': *Times Literary Supplement*, 16 October 1953, p. 655.

p. 74   'I am Lazarus, come from the dead': T. S. Eliot, 'The Love Song of J. Alfred Prufrock', *Collected Poems*; 'while only some of the verse': *Times Literary Supplement*, 18 December 1953, p. 814.

p. 74   'somewhat vague and unrealistic': E. Dalberg to G. P. McCullagh, 26 October 1953, Surrey.

p. 75   'the strength of the sentence': *CR* p. 82.

p. 76   'Tales of Hoffmann': John Ryland, email to NR, 23 March 2009.

pp. 77–8   'The Good Listener' (poem): Redgrove Works I–M, HRC; 'The Dance', 'For a Sculptor's Birthday': Redgrove Works D–G, HRC.

p. 79   'lent his poetry': Harry Guest, review of *Sheen*, *Tremblestone*, 5 July 2006, p. 86.

pp. 79–80   'He told Hughes's biographer': PR interview with Elaine Feinstein, September 1999, II Box 2, Sheffield; 'torturing destructive effect': Ted Hughes to Leonard Scigaj, 28 July 1989, Emory Mss 644, Box 53, ff. 3; 'total confusion': Drue Heinz, 'Ted Hughes: The Art of Poetry LXXI', *Paris Review* 134, Spring 1995, p. 85; 'Stop this – you are destroying us': Ted Hughes, *Winter Pollen*, London, Faber, 1994, pp. 8–9; 'Someone said there was this marvellous poet': PR interview with Elaine Feinstein, September 1999, II Box 2, Sheffield; 'a strange yowling', 'the whole of the music': PR, 'Gnat-Psalm' in Nick Gammage, ed., *The Epic Poise: A Celebration of Ted Hughes*, London, Faber, 1999, pp. 49–50; 'the apparently discordant beginnings': *CR* p. 100.

pp. 80–1   'a kind of knowledge': PR, 'Gnat-Psalm', pp. 49–50; 'The one man in the room': Sylvia Plath, *The Journals of Sylvia Plath*, ed. Karen V. Kukil, London, Faber, 2000, p. 212; 'whose "person" was dear to him': PR to NR, 2 October 1979, NR; 'this love was not reciprocated': interview with Peter Porter, 5 July 2007; 'so virile a man obsessed with manliness': PR to NR, 26 November 1990, NR; 'quite brotherly to me in the past': PR to NR, 24 November 1998, NR.

p. 81   'smelly old corduroys', 'wore suits and ties': Philip Hobsbaum, 'Ted

Hughes at Cambridge', *The Dark Horse*, Autumn 1999, pp. 6, 9.

pp. 81–2   'always the same black sweater': Sylvia Plath, *Letters Home, Correspondence 1950–63*, London, Faber, 1975, pp. 243–4; 'very much as a senior poet', 'already acquired a large reputation': Elaine Feinstein, *Ted Hughes: the Life of a Poet*, London, Weidenfeld and Nicolson, 2001, p. 31; Daniel Huws's reminiscences: Daniel Huws, *Memories of Ted Hughes 1952–63*, pp. 19–20.

p. 83   'how important you've been to me': TH to PR, n.d., Emory Mss 867, ff. 7; 'he had known two geniuses': Roger Garfitt, email to NR, 24 March 2010; PH's reminiscences of TH: Philip Hobsbaum, 'Ted Hughes at Cambridge', *The Dark Horse*, Autumn 1999, pp. 6–7.

pp. 83–4   'a working sense': PR to NR, 2 October 1979, NR; 'Five years in which I tried': TH to Keith Sagar, 25 March 1983, BL Add, 78757; 'Elaine Feinstein compliments': Feinstein, *Ted Hughes: The Life of a Poet*, p. 32; 'high on Merrydown': Peter Porter, interview with NR, 5 July 2007; 'writing limericks': Harry Guest interview with NR, 22 August 2007; 'a student lying in bed': N46A, 10 January 1973, Sheffield.

pp. 84–6   'that when you break the news to Peter': G. P. McCullagh to GJR, 22 June 1954; 'some form of degree': GJR to G. P. McCullagh, 8 November 1954; 'I did what I could': G. P. McCullagh to GJR, 18 January 1955, II Box 14, folder 'Peter', Sheffiel; 'two firsts': N56C, 12 August 1975, Sheffield; 'high spirits, elation almost': Daniel Huws to NR, 25 November 2007.

Chapter 5: *Marriage and the Group 1954–61*

pp. 87–8   'to get away from our families': N44B, 28 March 1972, Sheffield; 'dropped monthly egg': Hobsbaum Papers, 'London Group Master File', Glasgow; 'what a poet he could be': F151, 30 August 1997, Sheffield; 'hectic and happy': Hannah Hobsbaum-Kelly, interview with NR, 13 January 2009; Hilary Semmel's reminiscences: Hilary Semmel, interview with NR, 10 July 2007.

pp. 88–9   Odham's Press: II Box 14, folder 'Peter', Sheffield; 'ludicrously', 'contamination', 'Precious being!': Redgrove Works P–Z, HRC; PH on setting up London Group: 'Philip Hobsbaum in Conversation', Philip Hobsbaum, 'The Group: An Experiment in Criticism', *Yearbook of English Studies*, vol. 17, British Poetry Since 1945 Special Number, 1977, p. 76, Philip Hobsbaum, 'The Redgrove Momentum: 1952–2003', *The Dark Horse*, Summer 2003, p. 27, and Philip Hobsbaum, *The Group: An Exhibition of Poetry*, University of Reading Library, 17 June–10 December 1974, Catalogue.

pp. 89–90   'a poem that almost wrote itself': Redgrove Works, Notebook 26C, HRC; PP joining the Group: Peter Porter, interview with NR, 5 July 2007; ELS joining the Group: Edward Lucie-Smith, *The Burnt Child*, London, Gollancz, 1975, p. 163.

p. 90   Meeting of PR and MB: Martin Bell, 'Curriculum Vitae/Apologia/ Prognosis', Sheffield Mss 255.

pp. 90–1   MB's background: Martin Bell, 'IX Behaviours', Martin Bell correspondence [restricted] Sheffield; 'cauterised': Peter Porter, 'Introduction, Memoir and Critical Note', Martin Bell, *Complete Poems*, Newcastle upon Tyne, Bloodaxe, 1988, p. 15; 'languishing': PP, interview with NR, 5 July 2007; contributors to the Group: Hobsbaum Papers, Glasgow. There is also a large collection of 'songsheets' in the Group Archive at the University of Reading. There is considerable overlap, but there are also many sheets at Reading that are absent from Glasgow, including several by Redgrove.

p. 92   'Leavisite fierceness', 'send people away absolutely glowing': AB, interview with NR, 13 November 2007; 'a man he'd discovered': PP, interview with NR, 5 July 2007; 'fond of argument': Edward Lucie-Smith, *The Burnt Child* p. 165; 'Bell was respected': PP, interview with NR, 5 July 2007, and Alan Brownjohn, interview with NR, 13 November 2007; 'see into the poems': F73, 13 June 1991, Sheffield; 'Peter Redgrove is the only poet': Peter Porter, 'Peter Redgrove, a Brief Memoir', *Poetry Review* vol. 71 no. 2–3, Peter Redgrove Special Issue, 1981, p. 9; 'dominated the whole show': Philip Hobsbaum, 'The Redgrove Momentum: 1952–2003', p. 27.

p. 92   'At the very first meeting': Peter Porter, 'Peter Redgrove, a Brief Memoir', p. 9.

pp. 93–5   Group discussion: Philip Hobsbaum, 'The Group: An Experiment in Criticism', pp. 86–8.

p. 95   'Mr Hobsbaum's Monday Evening Meeting': Martin Bell, *Complete Poems*, ed. Peter Porter, Newcastle upon Tyne, Bloodaxe, 1988, p. 117; 'like many women writers of those days': Philip Hobsbaum, 'The Group: An Experiment in Criticism', p. 86.

pp. 95–6   'an intelligent clown at a seminary', 'always impeccably turned out': Philip Hobsbaum, 'The Group: An Experiment in Criticism', pp. 77, 79; 'When he wanted to wind Redgrove up': F132, 3 February 1996, Sheffield; 'cool, confident dogmatism': ELS to PH, 22 November 1959, Hobsbaum Papers, HRC; Hannah Hobsbaum: Hannah Hobsbaum-Kelly, interview with NR, 13 January 2009; 'Hobsbaum's Choice', Radio 3, 30 January 2000; 'at odds with William Empson': John Haffenden, *William Empson Vol. II: Against the Christians*, Oxford, Oxford University Press, 2006, pp. 469–83.

pp. 96–7   'psychic pressures': Edward Lucie-Smith, *The Burnt Child* p. 171; 'severe mental trouble': PR to Ian Fletcher, 28 March 1974, Group Papers, Reading; '*Lasciate ogni speranza*': PP, interview with NR, 5 July 2007; 'It Was a Violent Time': Martin Bell, *Complete Poems*, ed. Peter Porter, Newcastle upon Tyne, Bloodaxe, 1988, p. 119; 'that he would tear off my head', 'succeeded in throwing his opponent': PR to MB, 21 April 1976, Sheffield Mss 255.

pp. 98–9   'were asleep': AB, interview with NR, 13 November 2007; 'the two Peters did a reading tour together': PP, interview with NR, 5 July 2007; ELS on PR: ELS to PH, 20 May 1960, n.d., 21 February 1960, Hobsbaum Papers, HRC; PR on ELS: PR to PH, 19 May 1965, HRC Letters; 'sui generis', 'figures in a pantheon': PP, interview with NR, 5 July 2007; 'the only art he can take entirely seriously': Peter Porter, 'Peter Redgrove: A Brief Memoir', p. 9.

p. 99   Reflections by ELS: emails to NR, 6–11 January 2008.

pp. 99–100   'Unfriendly Flowers': Sheffield Mss 255; 'the tone and movement': PR, testimonial to Arts Council for MB, Sheffield Mss 255; 'intonation': PP, interview with NR, 5 July 2007; 'speaking out': Edward Lucie-Smith, *The Burnt Child* p. 169.

p. 100–1   Ginsberg and Corso: AB, interview with NR, 13 November 2007, *IS* p. 271, Sheffield; ELS on PR: ELS to PH, 1960? and n.d., Hobsbaum Papers, HRC; 'manipulative and worldly': PP, interview with NR, 5 July 2007; 'obsequious . . . then asks for a favour': TH to Olwyn Hughes, May 1956, Emory Mss 980 ff. 4; 'nobbling literary editors': PP, interview with NR, 5 July 2007.

pp. 101–2   'acknowledged Peter's generosity': TH to Lucas Myers, 16 November 1956, Emory Mss 865 Box 1 ff. 2; 'Peter adored Ted': PP, interview with NR, 5 July 2007; 'big and famous poet': N42J, Sheffield; 'Mr Eliot's inability', 'which arguably has more vitality': 'Comment', 14 June 1956, BBC Written Archives.

p. 102   George Fraser's group: AB, interview with NR, 13 November 2007, and Lucie-Smith, *The Burnt Child* pp. 172–3.

p. 103   'living on his wits', 'treaties and arrangements with the world': PR to Susan Fromberg Schaeffer, 31 May 1979, 24.14, Sheffield; 'With Ted I think we are': PR to PH, 2 January 1957, Hobsbaum Papers, HRC.

p. 104   PP on Dobrée: PP, interview with NR, 5 July 2007; 'not . . . a very nutritious transplantation': PR to PH, 2 January 1957, Hobsbaum Papers, HRC; 'met people there': PR to George Fraser, 21 September 1979, 29.47, Sheffield; 'trochaic inversions': Bonamy Dobrée, *Histriophone: A Dialogue on Dramatic Diction*, London, Hogarth Press, 1925, p. 8; 'did well enough at Odhams': PR to GJR, 8 October 1957, Sheffield; notes on Spanish preparations: Redgrove Works 'Unidentified', HRC.

p. 104–5   'crippled girl who never left her bed': PR to PH, 9 July 1957, Hobsbaum Papers, HRC; 'it would be an excellent thing': PR to Nan Redgrove, 9 July 1957, Sheffield; 'out-dazzled', 'believed profoundly': PP interview with NR, 5 July 2007; 'nice, sweet-natured': ELS email to NR, 8 January 2008; 'strong-minded': AB interview with NR, 13 November 2007; 'refused an invitation': Hannah Hobsbaum-Kelly, interview with NR, 13 January 2009; 'What have you got to fear?': N6, p. 11 (1958), Lilly.

pp. 106–7   'I do hope this Building Society': PR to Nan Redgrove, 9 July 1957, Sheffield; 'so you can see the mosquitoes', 'quite a lot of electric light', 'rather exercises in sympathy': PR to Nan Redgrove, 2 May 1957, Sheffield; 'a rather frivolous English colony': PR to Rupert Sheldrake, 17 May 1997, F147, Sheffield; Gamel Woolsey: PR to Donald Carne-Ross, 12 April, 26 May, 16 October 1957, BBC Written Archives; 'bound all these up': copy in Christine McCausland's possession.

p. 107   'feeling should be the guide': Redgrove Works, Notebook 4, HRC; 'At Malaga Cathedral': F 78, 9, 9 November 1991, Sheffield; 'Mrs X of fourty-four and over', 'To pace about one's room all night': Redgrove Works, Notebook 4, HRC; 'Spain is wearing a very different complexion': PR to PH, 6 August 1957, Hobsbaum Papers, HRC.

p. 108   'Barbara had had a bad time': Hilary Semmel, interview with NR, 10 July 2007; 'You won't explore': 'Dialogue', 'Poems – February to September 1957', CM; 'You saw right down': Ted Hughes, 'You Hated Spain', *Birthday Letters*, London, Faber, 1998, p. 39; 'Lucie-Smith observed': ELS to PH, 1 May [no year], Hobsbaum Papers, HRC.

p. 109   'Your eldest and most difficult son': PR to GJR, 8 October 1957, Sheffield; 'Hilary thought he throve in the army': Hilary Semmel, interview with NR, 10 July 2007; 'His friend Chris Harding thought': Chris Harding, telephone conversation, 30 January 2009.

p. 110   'this severe emblem relenting in death': PR to NR, 1 August 1987, NR; 'Queen's Guard', 'I have an inarticulate kind of feeling': GJR to PR, 15 January 1958, PR Letters, HRC.

p. 111   'somebody might', 'When I write of you': Redgrove Works, Notebook 5, HRC.

p. 111   'To comb this despair': N6, Lilly.

p. 113   'rather a beastly poem': PR to PH, n.d., Hobsbaum Papers, HRC; 'Seeing Barbara in labour': Redgrove Works, Notebook 7, HRC.

pp. 114–5 Gregory Fellowship: Bonamy Dobrée to A. N. Jeffares, 19 February 1962, Dobrée archive, Leeds; 'required him to be away from home': PR to Bonamy Dobrée, 22 April 1959, Dobrée archive, Leeds; 'Edward Lucie-Smith suggested': *CR* p. 21; 'treat me as a sort of consultant': PR to PH, 29 June 1958, Hobsbaum Papers, HRC; 'tribal values': *CR* p. 68; 'deregulate [his] senses': *CR* p. 177; 'Redgrove's Entry': PP, interview with NR, 5 July 2007; 'I often left a pair': PR, 'Last Thoughts', PS; 'rough passage': PR to PH, 1 September 1959, Hobsbaum Papers, HRC.

pp. 115–6 'less exigent': PR to PH, 22 October 1959, Hobsbaum Papers, HRC; 'a bit hard to swallow', 'would offend no one', 'thought the title rather weak': PR to Bonamy Dobrée, 22 April 1959, Dobrée archive, Leeds; 'Here and there, your subjects': GWR to PR, 21 January 1960, II Box 13, folder 'Peter', Sheffield.

p. 116   Larkin: *Guardian*, 5 February 1960, p. 6; Hall: *New Statesman*, 27 February 1960, p. 302; Wain: *Spectator*, 4 March 1960, p. 328.

pp. 116–7 A. Alvarez: *Observer*, 27 March 1960, p. 22.

p. 118   'Peter immediately drafted a riposte': PR to PH, 27 March, 28 March, 5 April 1960, Hobsbaum Papers, HRC; 'full of hatred of life': A. Alvarez to PH, 22 April [1960], Hobsbaum Papers, HRC.

p. 118   'very philosophical': TH to William and Edith Hughes (April 1960), Emory Mss 980, Box 1, Ff 19.

pp. 118–9 'he wished he had dwelt': PR to PH, n.d. (April–June 1960), Hobsbaum Papers, HRC; 'he chose ten poems': A. Alvarez, ed., *The New Poetry*, Harmondsworth, Penguin, 1962; 'Ted's personal excellence', 'fawning', 'poisoned': PR to PH, n.d. (April–June 1960), Hobsbaum Papers, HRC.

p. 120   'venal': PR to PH, 8 June 1960, Hobsbaum Papers, HRC; 'TH said he was coming and is not': N44B, 6 February 1972, Sheffield; 'Peter was nostalgic': PR to TH, 9 February 1988, II Box 5, Sheffield; 'a whole day drinking': TH to Lucas Myers, n.d. (late summer 1960), Mss 865, ff. 2, Emory; 'sub-Amis', 'four collections': 'Philip Hobsbaum in Conversation', p. 23; 'some of us let him down': PR to Ian Fletcher, 28 March 1974, Group Papers, Reading.

p. 121 Thalidomide: *CR* pp. 21–2; ELS on PR at Notley's: ELS to PH, n.d. (1960/1961), Hobsbaum Papers, HRC, and ELS to NR, emails, 6–7 January 2008; 'turquoise flesh': F163, 30 September 1998, Sheffield.

p. 122 'BA (Prelim)': PR to PH, 21 March 1961, Hobsbaum papers, HRC.

Chapter 6: The Gregory Fellowship 1961–66

pp. 123–4 'The houses reminded him': Redgrove Works, Notebook 17, HRC; 'a gigantic': ELS to PH, November 1961, Hobsbaum Papers, HRC; 'bright but passive': PR to PH, 6 November 1961, Hobsbaum Papers, HRC; 'the extraction by main force': PR to PH, 20 August 1961, Redgrove Letters, HRC; 'more at home in a university job': PR to Bonamy Dobrée, 3 October 1961, Dobrée Papers, Leeds.

pp. 124–5 'decadent' etc.: PR to PH, 27 December 1961, Hobsbaum Papers, HRC; 'not what you'd call a very *good* American university': PR to PH, 9 April 1962; 'a considerable disappointment': PR to PH, 20 May 1962, Hobsbaum Papers, HRC; 'terrific (in Blake's sense)': PR to Bonamy Dobrée, 22 March 1963, Leeds; 'horizontal snow': interview with Bill and Sue Redgrove, 20 May 2007; Reviews: Robin Skelton, *Critical Quarterly* 4.1, Spring 1962, pp. 91–2; P. N. Furbank, *Listener*, 8 February 1962 p. 265; George MacBeth, *London Magazine* NS vol. 2 no. 1, April 1962, p 85; Charles Tomlinson, *Poetry*, May 1962, pp. 109–10; John Press, *Sunday Times*, 28 January 1962; *TLS*, 16 February 1962; Donald Davie, *New Statesman*, 2 January 1962, p. 21.

p. 125–6 Alvarez review: *Observer*, 17 December 1961; 'television freshness': Arthur Calder-Marshall, *Listener*, 18 January 1962, p. 144.

p. 126–7 'discriminating patron of the arts': Herbert Read, 'Eric Craven Gregory' (obituary), *Burlington Magazine*, vol. 101, no. 673, April 1959, p. 149; 'regarded as rather strange fish': Bonamy Dobrée, Notes on the Gregory Fellowships (28 February 1956), 'Scholarships and Awards', Box 5, Leeds; 'hothouses of creativity': interview with Dennis Creffield, 1 May 2009; 'a tangible sense of committed debate': Jon Glover, 'Writing at Leeds in the 60s' (August 1984), Leeds University Library, Brotherton Collection MS 20c Silkin/8/GLO-3.

pp. 127–8 'nobody may write': PR to MB, n.d., Tulsa; 'the sense that poetry should be': Jon Glover, interview with NR, 21 February 2009; 'he is turned inwards': Jon Silkin and Anthony Thwaite, 'No Politics, No Poetry?', *Stand* 6.3, p. 19; 'an urbanity grown into showiness': Ken Smith, 'Late Reviews', *Stand* 6.4, pp. 67–71.

p. 129 'ludicrously posh': PP, interview with NR, 5 July 2007.

p. 130 'mesmeric and brilliant': Jeffrey Wainwright, interview with NR, 26

May 2009; 'a continuous process', 'the idea that whatever you do': Jon Glover, interview with NR, 21 February 2009.

pp. 131–2 'believe poetry should serve the state': PR to PH, 19 May 1965, Redgrove Letters, HRC; 'Actually I hate Geoffrey Hill': PR to MB, n.d. [1973?], CM; 'Our views on the reading and writing': N73, p. 169, 19 June 1983, Sheffield; 'by his own account': Carl Phillips, 'The Art of Poetry LXXX: Geoffrey Hill', *Paris Review*, vol. 42 no. 154, Spring 2000, p. 288; 'science fiction poetry': D. M. Thomas, interview with NR, 7 May 2009; 'It's a *beautiful* book': PR to MB, 16 February 1965/66, Tulsa.

pp. 132–3 'He recommended': report by A. N. Jeffares, 24 March 1965, Leeds; 'A prose statement': PR to MB, n.d., Tulsa; 'I started to write poetry': PR to NR, 26 November 1990, NR; 'this tiny little delicate mouth', 'almost as good to talk': PR to MB, n.d., Tulsa.

pp. 133–4 'bad influence': Dennis Creffield, interview with NR, 1 May 2009; Note on 'The Old White Man': Redgrove Works, Notebook 23, HRC; 'Barbara behaved particularly well': PR to MB, undated, Tulsa.

pp. 134–5 'Page of troubles', 'Do children draw as heavily on one's life': Redgrove Works, Notebook 24, HRC; 'Not until passion': Soren Kierkegaard, *Either/Or: A Fragment of Life*; 'Thus in three persones': William Langland, *The Vision of William concerning Piers the Plowman*, Passus XVI, II. 220–1, Oxford, Oxford University Press, 1869. (c. 1360–87)

pp. 135–6 'to have the ecstasies', 'EVERYTHING POSSIBLE TO BE BELIEVED', 'my own secret', 'that auto-erotic thing': Redgrove Works, Notebook 26, HRC; 'notes one makes in one's cups', 'I'm so miserable & stiff sober': Notebook 24, HRC; 'Evidently I can hear': Notebook 28, HRC; 'enlivening', 'Joy is a terror': Redgrove Works, Notebook 24, HRC; 'Dennis Creffield once saw him', 'Everything was transposed into magic', 'He taught me how to drink': Dennis Creffield, interview with NR, 1 May 2009.

p. 137 'private resource': PR to Dennis Creffield, n.d., Sheffield Mss 392, 2. 4; 'student photographer/ journalist from Oxford': Barbara H. Kellett, 'The Leeds Poets', *Isis*, 13 October 1965; 'Don't go in there': Jon Glover, interview with NR, 21 February 2009; 'He took me out': *IS* 239, II Box 16, Sheffield.

p. 138 'a touch of Cider with Rosie', 'pretty ways': Christine McCausland, interview with NR, 23 April 2009; 'heavy stuff': Dennis Creffield, interview with NR, 1 May 2009; 'Dilly said you're not fat': N44B, 27 January 1971.

pp. 139–40 'about the blessed lascivious humour': annotation to 'The Youthful Scientist Remembers' in a copy of *WP*, Mss 392, Sheffield; 'hesistance, lack of commitment, alienation, and frigidity': PR, interview with Peter Ryan, May 1977, Outstanding Box 22, Sheffield; 'For a certain kind of writer': PR, response to questionnaire from Alan Brownjohn, 1979, Leeds.

p. 140 Introduction to 'The God-Trap': *CR* pp. 63–5.

p. 141 'Drafts of these case notes': Redgrove Works, Notebook 27, HRC;

'wandering through a store': 'Bentalls Aubade', *WBMS* pp. 33–4.

p. 142   'a prose draft': Redgrove Works, Notebook 27, HRC.

pp. 143–4   'He himself was dead': Marie Peel, 'Introduction' to Peter Redgrove, *SS* (unpaginated); 'Indeed it was like this': PR to Marie Peel, 13 May 1974, Sheffield 61.02; reviews: John Fuller, *London Magazine*, March 1967, pp. 97–8; Michael Baldwin, *Books and Bookmen*, March 1967, p. 59; Howard Sergeant, *Poetry Review*, Spring 1967, p. 49; 'the best & biggest': TH to PR, n.d., Emory Mss 867, ff. 7.

p. 144   'they seem to come': TH to PR, Redgrove Works, Notebook 31, HRC; 'stands with Ted Hughes': M. L. Rosenthal, *The New Poets: American and British Poetry Since World War II*, London, Oxford University Press, 1967, p. 211; 'he read *Modern Man in Search of a Soul*': PR to Valerie Sinason, n.d. [1982?], 48.04, Sheffield; 'To confront a person': Jung 10.462, quoted Redgrove Works, Notebook 26, HRC.

pp. 145–6   'Right action': PR to Martin Dodsworth, 3 September 1979, Outstanding Box 6, Sheffield; 'very unstable', 'sensation and thinking': Redgrove Works, Notebook 29, HRC; 'O God, I am like my poor brother David': Redgrove Works, Notebook 24, HRC; 'automatic [or as he preferred to call it "sealed"] writing': Redgrove Works, Notebook 26, HRC; 'gives you schemes': Redgrove Works, Notebook 24, HRC; 'moved disparate elements': Seamus Heaney, 'The Group', *Honest Ulsterman*, 1978.

pp. 146–7   'of the guilt': Dennis Creffield, interview with NR, 1 May 2009; 'feel dishonoured by the profession': PH to PR, 4 January 1965, Sheffield Mss 255; 'having given in front of Barbara': PR to MB, n.d., Tulsa; 'I told him his poems were excellent': PR to Susan Fromberg Schaeffer, 31 May 1979, 24.15, Sheffield; 'I hope the emotions': PR to PH, 12 January 1966, Sheffield Mss 255.

pp. 147–8   'only in passing': George MacBeth to PR, 31 January 1966, BBC; 'very strong conceptions': PR to MB, 15 May 1966, Tulsa.

pp. 148–9   'I feel that my particular qualifications': PR, 7 April 1966, cited in correspondence with John Steers, 1982, Sheffield; 'I have been having': PR to BR, 19 November 1965, KT; 'otherwise we could not be proper lovers': *IS* p. 248.

Chapter 7: Crisis 1966–70

pp. 150–1   'Cornwall is largely supported': PR, 'One Man's Cornwall', BBC Radio, broadcast 7 December 1969, BBC Written Archives; 'Peter associated the broken rings', 'renewal': PR to John Layard (unsent), Redgrove Works, Notebook 32, HRC; 'She pointed out to him': Redgrove Works, Notebook 30, HRC.

p. 151   'The Resolve': Redgrove Works, Notebook 30, HRC; 'All I seem to be doing': PR to BR, n.d. [autumn 1966], KT.

p. 152   'as if something black and very very tall': PR, 'One Man's Cornwall'; 'on a journey out of Cornwall': Redgrove Works, Notebook 32B, HRC; 'big name': Francis Hewlett, interview with NR, 5 May 2007.

p. 153   'He reminded one of his students', 'teachers were at the same level as students': Dennis Lowe, email, 17 March 2009; 'extravaganza': Francis Hewlett, interview with NR, 5 May 2007; 'a measurer' etc.: Andrzej Jackowski, interview with Timothy Hyman, December 1988, *Resurgence* 142, pp. 31–4; 'There weren't enough chairs': Dennis Lowe, email, 16 March 2009.

p. 154   'he could bring his powerful intellect': Ray Hopley, email to NR, 8 July 2010; 'contrived image of the poet': Malcolm Ritchie, interview with NR, 12 August 2010.

p. 155   'for as you can see': BR to Dilly Creffield, 7 January 1967, Sheffield Mss 392; 'I want you to be happy', 'a constant, continuing relationship', 'the bond of mutual possession', 'an oppression had lifted': PR to Dilly Creffield, n.d., Sheffield Mss 392.

p. 156   'Dilly, aware in the weather': Copy of *Work in Progress* annotated for Dilly Creffield, Sheffield Mss 392.

pp. 156–7   'Dilly Creffield at her most glamorous and provoking': Copy of *Work in Progress* annotated for Dilly Creffield, Sheffield Mss 392; 'He would have enjoyed Dilly': Dennis Creffield, interview with NR, 1 May 2009; 'One of the beautiful good pounces': Redgrove Works, Notebook 33, HRC; 'I must change my life somehow': PR to Dilly Creffield, Sheffield Mss 392; 'Drink was the only tranquilliser': PR to P. J. Kavanagh, n.d. [1969], P. J. Kavanagh papers, BL.

p. 158   'Did D[illy] have orgasms': F131, 23–4 January 1996, Sheffield; 'Hopeless!': Dennis Creffield, interview with NR, 1 May 2009; 'making love with Peter was like masturbation': Malcolm Ritchie, interview with NR, 12 August 2010; 'did the Odalisque': F90, 24 October 1992, Sheffield; 'He also insisted': Kate Tomkinson, email to NR, June 2007; 'felt pushed out all the time': Francis Hewlett, interview with NR, 5 May 2007; 'her children testify': Bill Redgrove, interview with NR, 20 May 2007; Kate Tomkinson, email to NR, June 2007.

pp. 158–9   'I could do nothing': N45D, p. 105, Sheffield; 'I'm not a good father': N47B, 25 December 1973, Sheffield; 'extremely strong': Bill Redgrove, email to NR, 19 May 2010; 'a muddy creek': Bill Redgrove, interview with NR, 20 May 2007; PR to Dilly Creffield, n.d., Sheffield Mss 392; 'There was a wide expanse of mud': Ray Hopley, email to NR, 8 July 2010.

p. 160   'association with W. H. Auden and Christopher Isherwood': Charles Osborne, *W. H. Auden: The Life of a Poet*, London, Faber, 1980, pp. 59–62; Christopher Isherwood, *Lions and Shadows: An Education in the Twenties* (1938), London, Methuen, 1953; John Layard, 'Auden', II Box 3, Sheffield.

pp. 160–1   Layard and Jung: 'Jung', II Box 3, Sheffield.

pp. 161–2   'the paraphernalia of defence': John Layard, *The Lady of the Hare, A Study of the Healing Power of Dreams* (1944), Boston and Shaftesbury, Shambhala, 1988, p. 22; 'the Secret . . . of the clitoris': PR to NR, 9 March 1996, NR; 'social creep': Francis Hewlett, interview with NR, 5 May 2007.

p. 162   'that which has hitherto been most feared': John Layard, *The Lady of* the Hare, p. 18; 'evil was necessary': p. 46; 'It is as fatal': p. 69; 'God feeds on our sins': notes on Layard lecture, Redgrove Works, Notebook 31, HRC; 'the serpent telling Mary': draft letter to John Layard, 30 May 1967, Notebook 32, HRC; 'Peter took an overnight sleeper': PR to Cliff Ashcroft, 19 October 1989, F51, Sheffield.

pp. 163–4   'I sometimes think': PR to JL, 30 May 1967, Box 94, folder 7, San Diego; 'arouses in me feelings': John Layard to PR, Redgrove Works, Notebook 32, HRC; 'if the Jungian analysis': CR p. 126; Francis Hewlett and Layard: Francis Hewlett, interview with NR, 5 May 2007.

pp. 164–5   'The cathedral is the body of your mother': DMT, interview with NR, 7 May 2007; 'represent the personal parents': The Lady of the Hare, p. 21; 'opened up avenues': PR to NR, 16–25 February 1991, NR; 'dispensed with fees': Erika Duncan, 'Peter Redgrove and Penelope Shuttle – The Joys and Perils of Collaboration', Book Forum, vol. VII no.4, 1986, p. 18.

pp. 165–6   'Who is that with Peter?': Francis Hewlett, interview with NR, 5 May 2007; 'John made many mistakes': PR to James Greene, 18 January 1982, 50.01, Sheffield; 'such a fool': PR to Nan Redgrove, March 1969, II Box 14, folder 'Personal December 1992'; 'homosexual shadow': Malcolm Ritchie, interview with NR, 12 August 2010; 'I felt his little soft penis': IS p. 47; 'I can't seem to keep my temper': PR to JL, 13 June 1969, Box 94, folder 7, San Diego; 'You are hung up': N44A p. 57, 18 January 1972; 'Depression is withheld knowledge': CR p. 178.

pp. 166–7   'Two miraculous cures': IS p. 97, II Box 16, Sheffield; 'My poor friend': Redgrove Works, Notebook 32B, HRC; 'That's your mother': F73, 8 June 1991, Sheffield; 'You'll never get rid of that': F157, 4 February 1998, Sheffield.

pp. 167–8   'plasm', 'two demons', 'the Christ child', 'I love you', 'A little girl': Malcolm Ritchie, interview with NR, 12 August 2010.

p. 169   'birth of a deeply knowledgeable anima': John Layard to PR, 19 May 1970, 44B, Sheffield; 'couldn't be homosexual', 'a strongman': N47B, 14 December 1973; 'I must indeed sleep': 20 January 1972, 44B, Sheffield; 'too drunk to drive': Kate Tomkinson to NR, June 2007; 'nagged by his wife and relations': PR to GJR, 9 July 1968, II Box 14, folder 'Peter', Sheffield; 'wanted very earnestly': GJR to PR (draft) undated, folder 'Peter'.

p. 170   'to keep away from Cornwall for a bit': note by GJR, 25 July 1968, folder 'Peter'; 'Your health & welfare': GJR to PR, 3 December 1968, folder 'Peter'; 'Jim knew about Dilly', 'sticky wicket': notes by GJR, 25 July 1968, folder 'Peter'; 'Jim sent Barbara a cheque': BR to GJR, August 1968, folder 'Peter'; 'Barbara was no longer jealous': PR to Dilly Creffield, 1 August [1968?], Mss 392, Sheffield; 'I'm not here': Christine McCausland, interview with NR, 23 April 2009; 'fine, in bed': PR to Nan Redgrove, 31 March 1969, II Box 14, folder 'Personal 20 December 92', Sheffield; 'I was better with Barbara': PR to Nan Redgrove, 25 March 1969, folder 'Personal 20 December 1992'; 'The witch-figure': D. M. Thomas, introduction to Work in Progress, London, Poet and Printer,

1968, pv; 'the copy that Peter sent to Dilly': Mss 392, Sheffield.

p. 171   'the breaking of an allegiance': Redgrove Works, Notebook 33, HRC; 'Either Quasimodo is revealing': PR to JL, 13 June 1969, Box 94, folder 7, San Diego.

p. 172   'Quasimodo's Many Beds II': N36, p. 5, N44B, 31 January 1972, Sheffield.

p. 173   'as Redgrove': TH to PR, 5 August 1966, Redgrove Works, Notebook 30A, HRC; 'Redgrove later regretted': PR to Cliff Ashcroft, October 1987, 85.53, Sheffield; 'improve his feminine self-image': F124, 19 June 1995, Sheffield; 'professional man': IS p. 248; 'it wouldn't do': PR to JL, 2 April 1969, Box 94, folder 7, San Diego.

pp. 173–4   'a series of sexual affairs': PR to Karen Rood, 45.01, 14 June 1986, Sheffield; 'Perilla Wymark': CR p. 259, N42B, 31 January 1972; 'everything comes from you': PR to Nan Redgrove, 30 March 1969, II Box 14, folder 'Personal 20 Dec 92', Sheffield; 'the name of a certain friend': PR to Nan Redgrove, 25 March 1969; 'the quality of response in some other women': PR to Nan Redgrove, April 1969; 'do my odd things', PR to Nan Redgrove, 30 March 1969; 'You are a funny boy': F124, 14–16 June 1995; 'You'll never be sylph-like': N44B, 27 January 1971; 'Look at me': F73, 13 June 1991, Sheffield.

p. 175   'Jim's response was to make an investment': correspondence between PR and GJR, May 1969, II Box 23, folder 'PWR', Sheffield.

p. 175   Holiday in Dorset: PR to JL, 2 April 1969, San Diego.

pp. 175–6   'in some way anchored': Bill Redgrove, email to NR, 22 May 2010; Dilly's final exams: PR to Dilly Creffield, n.d. [May 1969], Mss 392.2.18, 2.19, 2.20, Sheffield; 'litany of despair': Christine McCausland, email to NR, 6 October 2009.

p. 177   'crying, crying, crying': Christine McCausland, interview with NR, 23 April 2009; 'she asked her rival': PS, private communication; 'I fear for [Barbara] if she knew': PR to Dilly Creffield, n.d. [May 1969], Mss 392.2.20, Sheffield; 'My child, you are made for love': Christine McCausland, interview with NR, 23 April 2009; 'only good for looking after alcoholics': Christine McCausland, email to NR, 15 October 2009.

pp. 177–8   'I am fond of Dilly, and so is Barbara': Dennis Creffield to PR (unsent draft), n.d. [July 1969], Dennis Creffield; 'If your lover and your wife are enemies': PR to Nan Redgrove, 17? July 1969, II Box 14, folder 'Personal 20 Dec 92', Sheffield; 'the marriage cracked': N44B, 17 January 1972, Sheffield.

p. 179   'My dear Peter': Dilly Creffield to PR, 9 September 1969, Dennis Creffield.

p. 180   'such intense concentration': PR, 'How We Met', Independent on Sunday, 16 August 1992, p. 61; 'astonished that it was not by a Continental writer': PS to NR, 20 July 1988, NR; 'simmering fever': PS to PR, 2 July 1969, PS; 'I was immediately attracted': PR to PS, n.d. [7 July 1969?], PS.

p. 181   'outrageous guesses about your life': PR to PS, n.d. [12 July 1969?], PS.

p. 181 'stout-wounded about the eyes', 'epically ingesting air', 'awkward, withdrawn man', 'the way he smokes': P. J. Kavanagh, 'Account of a Trip to the West of Ireland', unpublished, BL, P. J. Kavanagh papers.

p. 182 'turds resembled', 'kind lady': *CR* p. 32; 'the absorbed person of the first encounter': PR and PS, 'How We Met', *Independent on Sunday*, 16 August 1992, p. 61; 'I'm different inside': PR and PS, 'How We Met'; 'you made me feel very happy': PR to PS, August 1969, PS; 'dangerously indecisive': PR to PS, n.d. [autumn 1969], PS.

p. 183 'He could hear shouting and thumping': Bill Redgrove, interview with NR, 20 May 2007; 'sexually inadequate': N36A, p. 50, January 1970, Sheffield; 'fled to the Hewletts': Liz Hewlett, interview with NR, 5 May 2007; 'dragging Barbara by her hair': Hilary Semmel, interview with NR, July 2007; 'his violence was an act of love': Kate Tomkinson, email to NR, June 2007; 'Bill recalls walking home': Bill Redgrove, email to NR, 19 May 2010; 'Though it turned out': F100, 31 July 1993, Sheffield.

pp. 183–4 'That was terrible': F124, 19 June 1995, Sheffield; 'She had precipitated': J44B, 31 January 1972; 'Dearest', 'very touchy': PR to BR, 12 December 1969, KT; 'knows he is a stinker', 'vegetable', 'the village idiot': Nan Redgrove to BR, n.d. [late 1969/early 1970], KT; 'I can see this going': N36, 21–22 January 1970, Sheffield.

Chapter 8: A New Life 1970–75

pp. 186–7 'we are two ill people': N44B, 15 February 1972, Sheffield; 'Is it better without me?': 37A, 27 March 1970, Sheffield; 'There's Layard': PS, interview with NR, 17 February 2007; 'ran away': Malcolm Ritchie, interview with NR, 11 August 2010; 'Tomas the poor old man': 44B, 29 January 1972.

pp. 187–8 'tried to take out an injunction': Kate Tomkinson, email to NR, June 2007; 'In March he wrote': PR to BR [26 March 1970?], KT.

pp. 188–9 'It's certainly not going to be useful': BR to PR, 30 March 1970, KT; 'Peter Redgrove had studied': *WW*, p. 14.

pp. 189–90 'What could sound more patriarchal': Holly Laird, *Women Coauthors*, Urbana and Chicago, University of Illinois Press, 2000, p. 154; 'the beginnings of menstrual imagery': PR to Paul Matthews, 23 February 1984, 72.01, Sheffield; 'like & yet not like a game': 49G, August 1974, Leeds.

pp. 190–1 'In the first seven years': PR, 'How We Met', p. 61; 'sobbed in her pillow': PR, 44B, 5 February 1971, Sheffield.

pp. 191–2 'happier than he had been for years': PR to PS, 24 December 1970, PS; Conversation with mother: PR, Journal 40, 31 December 1970, Sheffield; 'regression into the former situation': PR, N40, 7 January 1971; 'walk across the water': PR, N39A, 23 November 1970, Sheffield; 'stirred up': N44B, 2 February 1972, Sheffield; '365 Stories About Her': N42B, Sheffield.

pp. 192–4 'Rimbaud's *Illuminations*' etc: 'read off into your own reveries', N43C, 16 January 1972, Sheffield; 'schizoid father', 'the person who observed':

PR, N44B, 7 February 197; information about early FPG: Derek Power, interview with NR, November 2008.

p. 194   'frightened', 'swimmingly grateful': N44B, 7 March 1972, Sheffield; 'an image & an object', 'been to the underworld': N44B, 11 March 1972; 'sudden connections': PJK to PR, pasted in 44B, 13 January 1972; 'de haut en bas': 44B, 22 January 1972; 'Hi Bish', PR to PJK, January 1972, P. J. Kavanagh Papers, BL.

p. 194–5   'claims he is driven', 'Mother's a nymphomaniac': P. J. Kavanagh, *A Happy Man*, London, Chatto and Windus, 1972, pp. 14, 16; 'seemed well-proportioned': PR, 8 February 1972, 44B; 'a super-simple': Ekbert Faas, *Ted Hughes: the Unaccommodated Universe*, Santa Barbara, Black Sparrow Press, 1980, p. 208; 'With *Crow*, Hughes joins': A. Alvarez, *Observer*, 11 October 1970.

p. 195–6   'cosy, unperplexing wallow': [Ian Hamilton], *Times Literary Supplement*, 8 January 1971, p. 30; 'violent, mistaken': PR to NR, 8 October 1978, NR; 'thin and panic-stricken': PR to NR, 14 April 1979, NR; 'the dark side of a personal sexuality': PR to NR, 26 October 1979, NR; 'the thought that TH is a sadist': N50/54, 30 May 1975, Sheffield; 'incarnating': PR to PJK, 27 May 1974, 184.06, Sheffield; 'a bit of magic': DMT, interview with NR, 7 May 2007; 'all stately and brittle', 'booming and vibrating': PR to PS, 19 October 1971, PS.

p. 197   'We agreed to a division of labour': PR to NR in conversation; 'playing the liberated guy'; 'obsessed': DMT, interview with NR, 7 May 2007; 'I long to open a suitcase': PR to PS, 23 October 1971, PS; 'enormous sexual energy', 'Watch it, Don': DMT, interview with NR, 7 May 2007.

p. 198   'watch my step', 'a *visual* arts college', 'I'm sick of your bloody poets': PR to Hilda Trench, 1 August 1973, 234.01, Sheffield; 'a clash of values', 'propositions were made': Hilda Trench to PR, 2 August 1973, 234.01, Sheffield; 'At one board meeting': Francis Hewlett, interview with NR, 5 May 2007.

p. 199   'our first poem together': PR, F168, 21 March 1999, Sheffield.

pp. 200–1   'an account of Penelope's orgasm': PR to NR; 'battered', 'directionless and unfocussed': Alan Brownjohn, *New Statesman*, 21 July 1972, p. 97; 'pretentious bombast': Clive Wilmer, *Spectator*, 7 October 1972, p. 545; 'the most exciting body': Peter Porter, *Guardian*, 14 September 1972; 'There's never less than pleasure': AB to PR, 5 September 1972, 176.28, Sheffield.

pp. 201–1   'for me, the best British collection': DMT to PR, 4 August 1972, 176.26, Sheffield; 'sit in a trance': CR, p. 87.

pp. 203–4   'the other "Entropy"': BR to PR, 4 December 1975, folder 'Barbara', Sheffield; 'I thought it was 2 altogether at this stage': PR to Bruce Berlind, 21 November 1973 (note added later), folder 'America 1974–5', Sheffield.

pp. 204–5   'fascinated by the QE2': PS, introduction to *The Glass Cottage*, Devoran, Stride Publications, 2006, p. 8; 'Colgate has a very handsome campus': 10 September 1974, PR to Norman Franklin, 33.08, Sheffield; 'The American young': PR to Lionel Miskin, 29 October 1974, 60.20, Sheffield; 'Good

God, I had no idea': William Arrowsmith to PR, 19 November 1974, 60.10, Sheffield.

pp. 205–6 'ultimatum': PR to William Arrowsmith, 21 November 1974, 60.10, Sheffield; 'upperclassmen': R. L. Blackmore to PR, 4 December 1974, Sheffield; 'the amount of linen': John S. Morris to PR, 10 December 1974, Sheffield; 'it is best not to put': PR to unknown correspondent [R. L. Blackmore?], n.d. [December 1974], Sheffield.

pp. 206–7 'one of those private colleges': PP to PR, 5 October 1970, 176.07, Sheffield; 'Ivy League': PR to Michael Finn, 5 November 1973, 234.04, Sheffield; 'felt like an invisible person': PR, *Colgate Maroon*, 25 February 1975; 'Ted Hughes told Bruce': Bruce Berlind to NR, email, 24 May 2007; 'Jannice had died from an overdose': PP to PR, 3 January 1975, 184.18, Sheffield; 'without telling anybody': PR to Ian Fletcher, 29 April 1975, Reading.

pp. 207–8 'a life of extraordinary intensity': Marguerite Feitlowitz, email to NR, 9 September 2009; 'A great injustice': Alan Sherman, *Colgate Maroon*, 4 March 1975; 'less haunted and overbearing': PR to Ian Fletcher, 14 October 1974, 107.06, Sheffield.

Chapter 9: The Wise Wound 1975–79

p. 209 'he could not help doing so unconsciously': PS, interview with NR, 10 October 2009.

p. 210 'infected our age': PR, 'The Wet Dream of Albert Einstein', *Meridian* p. 13, 1977, p. 3.

pp. 211–2 'Dewan's work': WW p. 156; 'values of ovulation': WW p. 71; 'mental children': WW p. 21; 'It was more about Nan than about me': PS, interview with NR, 10 October 2009; 'A child may resemble': WW p. 24; 'Western Protestant Capitalist culture': WW p. 66.

pp. 212–3 'real magic': WW p. 215; 'evolutionary mistake': Ted Hughes, 'Baboons and Neanderthals: a Rereading of *The Inheritors*', John Carey, ed., *William Golding: the Man and his Books*, London, Faber, 1986, pp. 161–88; 'a life-raft': PS to NR, 10 October 2009; 'a system of thought': W. B. Yeats, *A Vision*, quoted Notebook 26, HRC; 'A less broken & confused intelligence': Notebook 27, HRC.

pp. 213–4 'despair': Norman Franklin to Giles Gordon, 3 December 1975, 232.21, Sheffield; 'hormonal robots': correspondence with *Contemporary Review*, 13 September 1978 to 20 January 1979, 84.23, Sheffield; 'far & away the most convincing': TH to PR [undated 1978], *Letters of Ted Hughes*, pp. 391–2.

pp. 214–5 'real Hughes': PR to TH, 7 October 1978, 84.04, Sheffield; 'the start of one love': 'The Pregnant Father', C; 'his anger at the thought': N44B, 15 February 1972, Sheffield; 'dreams of Penny throwing crockery': N45C, 14 February 1973, Sheffield; 'Penny became upset': N56C, 22 July 1975, Sheffield; 'Yes, we should have a child': PS, interview with NR, 10 October 2009.

pp. 215–6 'like being in a road accident': PS, *Independent*, Section 2, 30 September 1996, p. 5; 'Them – something there as I kneeled accepted':

N58A, Sheffield; 'I instigated having the baby': PS and PR, interview with Sally Vincent, *Observer*, 3 December 1978, p. 37; 'Daddy upstairs and Daddy writing': PS, interview with Sally Vincent; 'benevolent, amused presence', 'in the middle of that creative relationship': Zoe Redgrove, interview with NR, 26 August 2007.

p. 217   'tumours of galloping dry rot': PR to Graham Bradshaw, 24 December 1984, 83.01, Sheffield; 'I want to ask you'; 'I'm afraid I'll not be here', 'I would certainly like a sight of you': PR to BR, 3–6 August 1976, folder 'Barbara', Sheffield.

p. 218   'cannot contemplate', 'an apparent family reconciliation': PR to GJR, 23 July 1978, folder 'Barbara', Sheffield; 'wasn't bothered': Bill Redgrove, interview with NR, 20 May 2007.

pp. 218–9   'felt somehow responsible', 'thought it was unlucky': Claire Fox, interview with NR, 10 July 2007; 'walked away', 'far too interested', 'had a lot of difficulty forgiving': Bill Redgrove, interview with NR, 20 May 2007.

p. 221   'Hughes has a genuine respect': Craig Raine, 'Different Animals', *London Magazine*, November 1977, pp. 75–9. See also PR's letter, April 1978, pp. 79–82, and Raine's reply, July 1978, pp. 81–3.

p. 221   'cracker': Craig Raine to PR, 14 February 1983, Outstanding Box 4, Sheffield; 'Hughes was complaining': TH to PR, 14 October 1979, Outstanding Box 10, Sheffield.

pp. 221–2   'Your cry goes to my heart': PR to TH, n.d.; 'God bless you': TH to PR, n.d., Outstanding Box 10, Sheffield.

pp. 222–3   'erratic genius', 'a commanding leadership quality', 'a sort of prophet–disciple relationship', 'a relationship of the ether': Brian Miller, interview with NR, 14 November 2008; 'Your enthusiasm for my work': PR to Brian Miller, 2 October 1975, 185.11, Sheffield; 'ignored and deritualised': WW, p. 235.

pp. 223–4   'it's not for nothing': Ian McIntyre to John Tydeman, 13 August 1979, BBC Written Archives; 'too many emotional similarities': PR to Susan Fromberg Schaeffer, 11 May 1979, 24.15, Sheffield; 'reminiscences': TH to Keith Sagar, 30 May 1977, BL Add. Mss. 78757, f.l.

pp. 224–5   'this particular poetic "tone of voice"': Charles Monteith to Giles Gordon, 27 March 1977, Outstanding Box 4, Sheffield; 'feeling all the time': Giles Gordon to PR, 2 February 1978; 'You are . . . the only': Giles Gordon to PR, 15 February 1978, 232.95, Sheffield; 'Without doubt': Robert Nye to PR, 18 July 1979, 24.05, Sheffield.

pp. 225–6   'I wish you could get it straight': PR to Robert Nye, 16 August 1979, 24.05, Sheffield; 'all manner of visceral incantatory stuff: Robert Nye, review of WNP, *The Times*, 17 January 1980; 'very hurt': PR to Martin Booth, 14 May 1982, Outstanding Box 5, Sheffield; 'At best, Redgrove seems more *inspired*': proof of Nye's review, Outstanding Box 5, Sheffield; 'My marriage broke up': PR to John Milne (unsent), February 1972, Outstanding Box 1, Sheffield.

pp. 226–7   'intervened disastrously', PR to Ian Fletcher, 14 October 1974, 107.06,

Sheffield; 'Penelope will not countenance': PR to MB, June 1976, restricted correspondence, Sheffield.

pp. 227–8   'despondency and madness' (Wordsworth, 'Resolution and Independence'): MB to PR, 24 May 1976, restricted correspondence, Sheffield; 'I shall call upon': MB to Christine McCausland, 2 April 1977, McCausland; 'blood-brother': MB to PR, 3–6 September 1976; 'Magus', 'guru': MB to PR, 2 June 1976, restricted correspondence, Sheffield.

pp. 228–9   'analyst, confessor': MB to PR, 12 September 1977, Sheffield restricted; 'Did you know that Martin Bell has died?': PR to TH, 16 February 1978, 84.04, Sheffield; PH on PR: PH, *Tradition and Experiment in English Poetry*, London and Basingstoke, Macmillan, 1979, pp. 310–17; 'killed me and buried me': PR to PH, 6 March 1979, not sent, 184.01, Sheffield.

p. 229   'exceedingly generous', 'I am sure': PR to PH, 12 March 1979; 'overwhelmed with pleasure': PR to PH, 13 October 1979, 84.01, Sheffield.

Chapter 10: Breaking Connections 1980–85

p. 231   'the goddess-priestess of the old religion': N44, 4 February 1972, Sheffield.

pp. 232–3   'He's a monster': 9 June 1983, N73, Sheffield; 'conjuring tricks': CR pp. 24–5; 'The tricks are tuning devices': PR to Graham Bradshaw, 17 July 1982, 235a.37, Sheffield; 'I think I know some secrets': PR to Stewart and Janet Farrar, 9 February 1984, 59.02, Sheffield.

pp. 233–4   'Society for Creative Occultism': PR to Cliff Ashcroft, 25 February 1987, CA; 'I am not, and have never been': PR to Robert Nye, 16 August 1979, 24.05, Sheffield; 'It's possible though': PR to Cliff Ashcroft, 11 February 1987, CA.

p. 234   'form a link on the inner': PR to Kathleen Raine, 21 July 1982; 'I have been working out of Geburah': PR to Kathleen Raine, 22 June 1982, Outstanding Box 8, Sheffield.

pp. 235–6   'The Jewish Kabbalist saw': David Bakan, *Sigmund Freud and the Jewish Mystical Tradition*, 1958, London, Free Association Books, 1990, p. 272; 'Insight is *Daath*': Bakan, p. 281; 'a sacrifice of the sexual energies': Kathleen Raine to PR, n.d.; 'dream in which they were swimming together': Kathleen Raine to PR, 18 October 1982, Outstanding Box 8, Sheffield; 'at stressful times': PR and PS to Frater Damon, 21 September 1978; 'special rite of KPR': PR to Richard White, 24 August 1982, Outstanding Box 9, Sheffield.

pp. 236–7   'noticed things about traditional procedure': PR to Kathleen Raine, 27 November 1982; *Quest* assignments and correspondence, Outstanding Box 8, Sheffield; 'objects which are present in both worlds': CR, p. 106; 'English is my magick mirror': PR to Richard White, 12 July 1982, Outstanding Box 9, Sheffield.

pp. 237–8   'When the senses open for me': PR to Stewart and Janet Farrar, 17 February 1984, 59.02, Sheffield; 'I was . . . the pupil of a great adept': PR to Ithell Colquhoun, 10 July 1984 [not sent], Outstanding Box 8,

Sheffield; 'Layard was his real basis': PR to Stewart and Janet Farrar, 4 March 1984, 59.02, Sheffield.

pp. 238-9   PR on the Obby Oss: *CR* pp. 245-8; 'he was a stranger': Kate (Redgrove) Tomkinson to NR, May 2010.

p. 240   'tendency to Whitmannerism': PR to Charles Tomlinson, 1 November 1983, Outstanding Box 5, Sheffield; 'a book which makes all the difference': Charles Tomlinson to PR, 19 November 1983, 69.05, Sheffield.

p. 240   Muriel Bradbrook, review of *AB*: *Temenos* 4.

pp. 241-2   'germs', 'incubation': PR, 'Work and Incubation', *CR* pp. 58-62.

p. 242   Trickey: Keith and Carolyn Trickey, interview with NR, 26 August 2007.

p. 243-4   'It is not the bad book': PR to PJK, 11 December 1981, Outstanding Box 10, Sheffield; 'Thomas had congratulated him': DMT to PR, 22 May 1975, 238.2, Sheffield; 'But why Falmouth, Don?': PR to DMT, 12 September 1982, Outstanding Box 13, Sheffield; *extremely strong opposition*': Patrick Heron to W. V. Watton, 22 May 1978, folder 'Retirement', Sheffield; 'major snub': Derek Toyne, interview with NR, 5 May 2007.

p. 244   'This must never happen again': PR to John Steers, 29 April 1982, folder 'Retirement'; 'Peter had invited Charles Causley': PR to David Cottington, 18 May 1982, folder 'Retirement'; 'personal reasons': Tom Cross, phone conversation with NR, 11 August 2007; 'mixed up in the occult': PR to John Steers, 21 May 1982, folder 'Retirement'; 'sarcastic parody': PR to David Cottington, 28 May 1982, folder 'Retirement'; 'imitate Peter Redgrove department': Derek Toyne, interview with NR, 5 May 2007.

p. 245   'proudly displayed' and 'no mention': as of February 2010; 'in all the years I spent': Martina Edwards to Derek Toyne, March 1983, folder 'Retirement Letters', Sheffield; 'the Oscar of broadcasting': Brian Miller, interview with NR, 14 November 2008.

p. 246   'I should need to disassemble': PR to Peter Bayley, 10 October 1982, 235a.39, Sheffield.

p. 247-8   Correspondence with Frances Horowitz, 17 May – 12 June 1983, Outstanding Box 8, Sheffield.

p. 248   'the interpretation of the dream': Bakan, *Sigmund Freud and Jewish Mysticism*, pp. 261-2.

p. 249   PR and Renée Gregorio: Renée Gregorio to NR, November 2009.

p. 251-2   'your ordinary semi-unknown Faber author': PR to Norman Franklin, 14 September 1985, folder 'Seckers', Sheffield; 'bleat of complaint': Norman Franklin to PR, 7 November 1985, folder 'Seckers'.

p. 253   'I cannot express': J. H. Barclay to PR, 27 September 1981, Outstanding Box 10, Sheffield; 'spoke directly': PR to PH, 30 April 1985, Hobsbaum Papers, Glasgow.

Chapter 11: The Death of the Father 1986–89

pp. 254-5   'took him away as a person': Claire Fox, interview with NR, 10 July 2007; 'standing up to the doctors': PR to Pete Redgrove, 11 November

1986, 83.09, Sheffield; 'get himself back together': Claire Fox to NR; 'coming as it does': *www.surreyhealers.org.uk/absent_healing.htm*, accessed 13 May 2010; 'the family is estranged': PR to Michael Ash, 17 March 1986, 83.09, Sheffield.

pp. 255–6   'so far hardly more than a word of hope': *BG* p. 159; 'a kind of war-poem': PR to Ian Fletcher, 10 October 1974, 107.6, Sheffield; Ritter, Schelling, Novalis: *BG* p. 1; 'The feeling-in-the-air': *BG* pp. 111–12.

p. 257   'remains of a primitive culture': C. G. Jung, *Memories, Dreams, Reflections*, London, Fontana, 1967, p. 184.

p. 257   'somatic unconscious': *BG* p. 67.

pp. 257–8   Jung and Oedipus: Jung, *Collected Works* vol. 5, *Symbols of Transformation*, p. 182, vol. 10, *Civilisation in Transition*, p. 378, and vol. 17, *The Development of Personality*, p. 75, and *BG* pp. x, xxvi, 103.

p. 258   'questing, visualising modern scientific intelligence': *BG* p. xx; 'I have a close friend': PR to Nicholas Culpepper, 19 June 1986, II Box 3, Sheffield.

p. 259   'that there was some particular operation': PR to Francis X. King, 18 November 1988, Outstanding Box 4, Sheffield; 'enquiring about Crowley's whereabouts': PR to W. F. Ryan, 1 March 1990, II Box 3, folder: 'Frater Damon Cave of Saturn etc', Sheffield; 'always putting me down': N77, 2 June 1987, Sheffield; 'smells & electricity': N77, 9 June 1987.

p. 260   'a lovely warm man': Cliff Ashcroft, interview with NR, 27 February 2010; 'Public School homosexual bully': F50, 14 September 1989, Sheffield; 'an imaginary figure', 'my own obsession', 'wanted to place his affection', 'the destructive rejection': N77, 29 October 1988, Sheffield; 'I would have been completely split': page from journal in notes and correspondence, II Box 8, Sheffield.

pp. 261–2   'positive father': F44, March 1989, Sheffield; 'I said how he was too much for me': N77, 16 August 1987, Sheffield; 'My mother's at the helm': F66, 30 November 1990, Sheffield.

p. 262   'capacity to handle business affairs': PR to GJR, 2 March 1989, II Box 14, folder 'Jim', Sheffield; 'I would have done it badly': page from journal in notes and correspondence, II Box 8, Sheffield; 'Woke realising must cancel': F43, March 1989, Sheffield; 'death-poem': F45, 14 May 1989, Sheffield; 'Don't be afraid': F45, 28 April 1989, Sheffield.

pp. 263–4   'Your father tortured you': F45, 14 May 1989, Sheffield; 'retained throughout his life': Revd Chris Garrett, II Box 14, folder 'Jim', Sheffield; Gerard Woodward, Sylvia Kantaris and FPG: Gerard Woodward, interview with NR, 15 November 2008; Sylvia Kantaris to PR, 16 February and 27 March 1988, PR to DMT, 4 March 1988, II Box 13, Sheffield.

p. 264   'I like 23 enough': RR to PR, 13 March 1986, folder 'Secker's', Sheffield; 'feeling of whole-hearted enthusiasm': PR to RR, n.d. [early 1986], folder 'Secker's'; 'baggy and under-edited': RR to NR, 25 January 2005, NR.

p. 265   'a rather mad': Angela Carter, 'Mechanical Magic', *Evening Standard*, 13 April 1989.

Chapter 12: Decade of Mourning 1990–98

p. 268   'Supposing someone takes offence': F92, 21 December 1992; 'I have fear about the Sheffield Agreement': F94 p. 97, 25 February 1993.

p. 269   'After deep immersion': Robin Robertson to PR, 9 May 1991, II Box 20, Sheffield.

pp. 269–70 'I would be very happy': PR to Robin Robertson, 17 May 1991; 'I feel a few more pages': PR to Robin Robertson, 14 June 1991; 'a Gaia book': PR to Robin Robertson, 1 July 1991, II Box 20, Sheffield; 'something lyrical': Robin Robertson to NR, 25 January 2005, NR.

p. 270   'allowed the reader': Rupert Loydell to NR, 29 July 2004, NR; 'alternative stream': PR to Rupert Loydell, 16 October 1989, 36.01, Sheffield.

pp. 272–3 'purify': F107 p. 54, 20 February 1994; 'still had power': F107, p. 52, 25 February 1994, Sheffield; 'B making me look bad': 31 August 1994, 'Spares', Sheffield; 'like a wake': Hilary Semmel, interview with NR, 10 July 2007; 'She told Kate', Kate (Redgrove) Tomkinson to NR, June 2007.

pp. 273–4 'And flights of angels': Journal, 23 December 1994, 'Spares', Sheffield; 'command performance': Kate (Redgrove) Tomkinson, email to NR, 10 May 2010; 'made part of the world': Journal, 20 December 1994, 'Spares', Sheffield; 'to make B live again': Journal, 24 December 1994, 'Spares', Sheffield; 'Sex not good since B's death': F122 p. 36, 8 May 1995.

pp. 274–5 'Barbara's passing': PR to PP, 17 February 1996, F132 p. 37; 'Robin Robertson later reflected': Robin Robertson to NR, 25 January 2005, NR; 'genuine, sincere and a great admirer of your work': Jacqueline Korn to PR, 14 June 1995, II Box 7, Sheffield; 'Oedipal rivalry': PR to Jacqueline Korn, 10 November 1995, II Box 21, Sheffield.

p. 276   'Republican (or other) reservations': TH to PR, 16 June 1996; 'are close to your own': PR to TH, 28 June 1996, II Box 4, Sheffield; 'felt a great sense of betrayal': PR to M. L. Rosenthal, 9 July 1985, 4.1, Sheffield.

pp. 276–7 'quite like old times': PR to TH, 16 September 1996, II Box 4, Sheffield; 'for everything': PR, notes for an (abortive) obituary, II Box 8, Sheffield; Biff cartoon: *Guardian Weekend*, 17 October 1998, p. 85; draft outline of *IS*: F148, 21 June 1997, Sheffield; 'an autobiography to convey ideas': F147, 25 April 1997, Sheffield.

pp. 277–8 'I use events in my life': *IS*, II Box 16, Sheffield; 'the memoir of a poet': Jacqueline Korn, interview with NR, 13 November 2007; 'He spent a lot of time', 'I don't feel like I'm divorced', 'I saw him born': Claire Fox, interview with NR, 10 July 2007; 'Ben Jonson his best piece of poetry': F163, 16 October 1998, Sheffield; 'issues that weren't already gone': Bill Redgrove, interview with NR, 20 May 2007; 'Look after Dad': PS, interview with NR, 14 December 2007.

p. 279   'DEATH OF TED HUGHES ANNOUNCED': F163, 28 October 1998; 'alighting from the little train': F164, 28 November 1998, Sheffield.

Chapter 13: The Final Years 1999–2003

pp. 280–1   'horrors' etc.: F170, 5 May 1999, Sheffield; 'bulging and aged brown leather briefcase': Caroline Carver, 'Memories of Peter Redgrove', *Acumen* 47, September 2003, p. 84; 'I see myself': F170, 7 May 1999, Sheffield.

pp. 281–2   'One could sense the whole page': PR to Peter Abbs, n.d. [May 2001?], PS; 'vibrant': Victoria Field, interview with NR, 27 August 2007.

p. 282   'lost so much': F171, 17 May 1999, Sheffield; 'Gunwalloe feelings': Journal, 7 August 2000, PS.

p. 282   'give him a good kicking': Michael Bayley, interview with NR, 21 June 2010.

pp. 283–4   'being shut up with senile people', 'violation', 'dreadful', 'I need a holiday too', 'unbelievably patient and gentle': CC journal; 'What about the books?': Jacqueline Korn, interview with NR, 13 November 2007.

pp. 284–5   'heartbreaking': Michael Bayley, interview with NR, 10 September 2007; 'addictive happy pill': PS, interview with NR, 14 December 2007.

pp. 285–6   'the kindest and most dutiful of women': Eleanor Maxted, interview with NR, 27 November 2010; 'These are no discrete pieces': PH, 'Peter Redgrove' in *British Writing* vol. 6, Scribner, 2001; 'She had made the journey to Sheffield': Kate (Redgrove) Tomkinson to NR, May 2010; 'She always felt': Kate Tomkinson to NR, June 2007.

pp. 286–7   'working day and night', 'They seemed to be drifting', '*Shining* moments': Michael Bayley, interview with NR, 21 June 2010.

p. 287   Meditation group: Eleanor Maxted, interview with NR, 27 November 2010.

p. 288   'Her face looked black with anger', 'living with a madwoman': CC journal; 'like a little child', 'But I don't know any men': Michael Bayley, interview with NR, 21 June 2010; 'I love him so much': CC journal.

p. 289   'blokey': Victoria Field, interview with NR, 27 August 2007; 'fill the house with flowers': Michael Bayley, interview with NR, 21 June 2010.

p. 290   'He recorded the conversation': F132, 3 March 1996, Sheffield.

pp. 290–1   'wearing only one shoe': PS, interview with NR, 10 October 2009; 'wrap up against the cold': CC journal; 'one of the side-effects', 'too far gone': Michael Bayley, interview with NR, 21 June 2010; 'weeping and wailing': Keith Trickey, interview with NR, 25 August 2008.

p. 291   'tutor', 'Take it, take it': Michael Bayley, interview with NR, 21 June 2010.

pp. 291–3   'an absolute delight': Jacqueline Korn, interview with NR, 13 November 2007; 'I'm sorry, but I really don't know', 'No, you read it': Michael Bayley, interview with NR, 21 June 2010; 'Thank you, Michael, for letting me know': Michael Bayley, interview with NR, 21 June 2010.

p. 293   'Dorothy . . . had phoned': DC diary; 'cry for help': PS, interview with NR, 10 October 2009.

pp. 294–5   'The paramedics', 'combative', 'Sometimes he responded': PS, 'The Whole World's Water', David Kennedy, ed., *Necessary Steps*, Exeter,

Shearsman Books, 2007, p. 146, p. 10; 'Get me out of here': Eleanor Maxted, interview with NR, 27 November 2010.

pp. 295–6   'the most ecstatic smile': Michael Bayley, interview with NR, 21 June 2010; 'in an amazing way': Zoe Redgrove, interview with NR, 26 August 2007; 'incredibly peaceful': Victoria Field, interview with NR, 27 August 2007.

Epilogue

p. 297   'the greatest poet of his time': Philip Hobsbaum, Obituary of Peter Redgrove, *Independent*, 17 June 2003; 'a sustained and heroic commitment': Obituary of Peter Redgrove, *The Times*, 17 June 2003; 'It is like part of one's universe': PH to PS, 20 June 2003, PS.

p. 298   'intensified into inchoate misery', 'The cowed spirit in me': PS, 'The Whole World's Water', David Kennedy, ed., *Necessary Steps*, Exeter, Shearsman Books, 2007, p. 149.

p. 298   'She was seeing a Jungian counsellor' etc.: PS, interview with NR, 14 December 2007.

p. 299   'It was a sunny windy April afternoon', 'brought poetry back into my life', 'so much of Peter's personality': 'The Whole World's Water', pp. 150–52.

p. 300   'Zoe and I waded': PS, 'The Whole World's Water', p. 163.

Index